ADVANCES IN NEUROLOGY

Volume 77

Advances in Neurology

INTERNATIONAL ADVISORY BOARD

Advances in Neurology
Volume 77

Consciousness
At the Frontiers of Neuroscience

Editors

Herbert H. Jasper, M.D., Ph.D.
Emeritus Professor
Department of Physiology
Université de Montréal
Pavillon Paul-G.-Desmarais
Montreal, Quebec H3T 1J4, Canada

Laurent Descarries, M.D.
Professor
Departments of Physiology and of Pathology and Cellular Biology
Université de Montréal
Pavillon Principal
Montreal, Quebec H3C 3J7, Canada

Vincent F. Castellucci, Ph.D.
Professor and Head
Department of Physiology
Université de Montréal
Pavillon Paul-G.-Desmarais
Montreal, Quebec H3T 1J4, Canada

Serge Rossignol, M.D., Ph.D.
Professor
Department of Physiology
Director, Centre de Recherche en Sciences Neurologiques
Université de Montréal
Pavillon Paul-G.-Desmarais
Montreal, Quebec H3T 1J4, Canada

Lippincott - Raven
PUBLISHERS
Philadelphia • New York

Acquisitions Editor: Mark Placito
Manufacturing Manager: Kevin Watt
Supervising Editor: Kimberly Swan
Production Service: Colophon
Indexer: Indexing Research
Compositor: Lippincott–Raven Electronic Production
Printer: Maple Press

Printed in the United States of America

9 8 7 6 5 4 3 2 1

Library of Congress Cataloging-in-Publication Data
Consciousness: at the frontiers of neuroscience / editors, Herbert H. Jasper...[et al.].
    p.   cm. — (Advances in neurology, ISSN 0091-3952 ; v. 77)
  Includes bibiographical references and index.
  ISBN 0-7817-1504-0
  1. Consciousness—Congresses.   2. Cognitive neuroscience—Congresses.
  3. Jasper, Herbert H. (Herbert Henri), 1906– Congresses.   I. Jasper, Herbert H. (Herbert Henri), 1906–   . II. Université de Montrél. Centre de recherche en sciences neurologiques. International Symposium (19th : 1997 : Montréal, Québec) III. Series.
    [DNLM: 1. Consciousness congresses. 2. Brain—physiology congresses. 3. Neuropsychology congresses. W1 AD684H v. 77 1998/ WL 705 C755 1998]
  RC321.A276 vol. 77
  [QP411]
  616.8 s—dc21
  [612.8′2]
  DNLM/DLC
for Library of Congress   98-5989
                                                                  CIP

To Dr. Herbert H. Jasper, O.C., M.D.C.M.,
on the occasion of the symposium in his honor

Brain

Anatomist,
Do thou this brain behold,
See how the glistening membrane sits
Astride each rounded fold
And each fissure fits.
This smooth surface deceives
For underneath there daily raged
Electric impulses fires
Of thought and word
And ill conceived desires,
And strains of music faintly heard.
The kind the mind remembers,
The ever flowing impulse stream
Saw dawn and sunset
And all that came between.
At night the glowing embers
Would fitful blaze in dreams
Illuminating the hidden places
In black bedrock seams,
And cold nightwatchmens' faces
Pausing beside secret doors
In dark caverns where
Were kept the memory stores.
Anatomist,
Treat this brain with care
For all I ever was is here.

Jack Somerville
May 1997

Advances in Neurology Series

Contents

Contributing Authors

David J. Chalmers, B.Sc., Ph.D. *Professor of Philosophy, Department of Philosophy, University of California, Santa Cruz, Santa Cruz, California 95064*

Patricia S. Churchland, B.Phil. *Professor of Philosophy, Department of Philosophy, University of California at San Diego, Salk Institute, La Jolla, California 92093*

Gerald M. Edelman, M.D., Ph.D. *Director, The Neurosciences Institute, Chairman, Department of Neurobiology, 10640 John Jay Hopkins Drive, San Diego, California 92121*

Michael S. Gazzaniga, A.B., Ph.D. *David T. McLaughlin Distinguished Professor, Center for Cognitive Neuroscience, Dartmouth College, 6162 Silsby Hall, Hanover, New Hampshire 03755-3547*

Jeffrey A. Gray, Ph.D. *Professor of Psychology, Department of Psychology, Institute of Psychiatry, De Crespigny Park, Denmark Hill, London, England SE5 8AF, United Kingdom*

David H. Hubel, M.D. *John Franklin Enders University Professor of Neurobiology, Department of Neurobiology, Harvard Medical School, 220 Longwood Avenue, Boston, Massachusetts 02115*

Herbert H. Jasper, M.D., Ph.D. *Emeritus Professor, Department of Physiology, Université de Montréal, Pavillon Paul-G.-Desmarais, 2960, chemin de la Tour, Montreal, Quebec H3T 1J4, Canada*

Barbara E. Jones, Ph.D. *Department of Neurology and Neurosurgery, McGill University, Montreal Neurological Institute and Hospital, 3801 University Street, Montreal, Quebec H3A 2B4, Canada*

Edward G. Jones, M.D., Ph.D. *Professor of Anatomy and Neurobiology, California College of Medicine, University of California, Irvine, California 92717-1275*

Christof Koch, Ph.D. *Professor of Computation and Neural Systems, Division of Biology, California Institute of Technology, 1200 East California Boulevard, Pasadena, California 91125*

André Roch Lecours, M.D. *Professor, Institute universitaire de geriatrie de Montréal, Department of Medicine, Université de Montréal, 4565, chemin Queen Mary, Montreal, Quebec H3W 1W5, Canada*

Benjamin Libet, S.B., Ph.D. *Emeritus Professor, Department of Physiology, University of California, San Francisco, 513 Parnassus Avenue, San Francisco, California 94143-0444*

Rodolfo R. Llinás, M.D., Ph.D. *Professor and Chairman, Department of Physiology and Neuroscience, New York University School of Medicine, 550 First Avenue, New York, New York 10016*

Alan J. McComas, B.Sc., M.B., B.S. *Emeritus Professor of Biomedical Sciences, Department of Biomedical Sciences, McMaster University Medical Centre, 1200 Main Street West, Hamilton, Ontario L8N 3Z5, Canada*

Urs Ribary, Ph.D. *Research Associate Professor, Department of Physiology and Neuroscience, New York University School of Medicine, 550 First Avenue, New York, New York 10016*

Mircea Steriade, M.D., Ph.D. *Professor and Head of the Laboratory of Neurophysiology, Faculty of Medicine, Université Laval, Ste-Foy, Quebec G1K 7P4, Canada*

Giulio Tononi, M.D., Ph.D. *Senior Fellow in Experimental and Theoretical Neurobiology, The Neurosciences Institute, 10640 John Jay Hopkins Drive, San Diego, California 92121*

Philip D. Zelazo, Ph.D. *Associate Professor of Psychology, Department of Psychology, University of Toronto, St. George Campus, Toronto, Ontario M5S 1A1, Canada*

Philip R. Zelazo, Ph.D., D.Sc. *Professor of Psychology and Associate Professor of Pediatrics, Department of Psychology, McGill University at The Montreal Children's Hospital, 2300 Tupper Street, Montreal, Quebec H3H 1P3, Canada*

Preface

What? Where? When? How? Why?

Science sans conscience n'est que ruine de l'âme.
Rabelais
(Lettre de Gargantua à Pantagruel, Pantagruel, 1532)

Near the end of a century which is seeing the life sciences extend their reach from molecular engineering to the modeling of cognitive processes, it is perhaps not surprising to witness a surge of interest for empirical and theoretical studies of "consciousness." Humans seem to be seizing this opportunity to reintegrate in their universe a part of themselves that had largely escaped them through dualism since the beginnings of history. Consciousness has become the subject of best-sellers, specialized journals, and scientific meetings. Such debunking is no doubt imputable to its crucial interest for every human being, but even more to the rapid advances in all disciplines that contribute to its understanding, from philosophy to psychology, morphology to physiology, neurology to psychiatry.

The meeting at the origin of this book was meant to illustrate current neuroscientific points of view on consciousness, from the variety of experimental and conceptual approaches that now converge in the growing knowledge of the neural bases of conscious experience. In doing so, two extremes had to be avoided: the sterile, dogmatic, top-down discourse, and the bluntly reductionistic, chaotic, bottom-up elaboration.

A simple plan was followed. As a start-up, there was the need for a definition (or definitions), to be able to state the goals, the "What is it that we would like to understand?" For this, one usually turns to philosophy, the art and practice of definitions, through which it communicates thinking. Since Aristotle, philosophical definitions are taken from the kind and the specific difference. The kind expects to grasp the nature of a being, whereas the specific difference excludes everything else from consideration. Otherwise, there would be little to talk or even to think about. Inevitably, however, this brings up the problem of the edges. Where or when does a predefined entity begin and end?

The scientific approach is different in many ways. Rather than attempting to isolate consciousness per se as the study object, scientists prefer, or are content to try, to understand conscious processes, conscious experiences, consciousness as a property, as a function or functions, or even as a product (or products). They see little merit in debating about consciousness itself unless they know which of its particular aspects is being envisaged. Furthermore, they tackle only aspects of consciousness in which regularities may be observed, leaving aside, or to others, unpredictable (and untestable) manifestations of its uniqueness in different individuals. Once equipped with operational definitions, scientists ask about the processes or "organizations" that give rise, subtend, or attend to conscious events, even if they are acutely aware that, having isolated some parts, they might have lost the whole.

As soon as they grasp a little of the "what," the next questions for neuroscientists are the "where" and the "when." By considering consciousness as a property, function, or product, whether normal or abnormal, they find meaning to the following questions: "Where and when does consciousness begin and end in any brain function?"; "Where and when through evolution, through individual life?" First and foremost, they also ask the question of "how."

Depending on their methodology and the corresponding point of view, they elaborate different types of mechanisms and computations, at various "analytical" levels that depend on the phenomenon to be accounted for. They seek causal links, but only within or between adjacent analytical levels, knowing that validity is often lost when the distance (and hence the jump) between such levels is too great. Irrespective of the level considered, they accept the lingering of the "hard problem": "How does subjective consciousness, for instance, emerge from any conscious experience?" Indeed, the links at the lowest levels may even be misleading. What "emerges" at those levels has probably little to do with consciousness per se (e.g., the sound or sign becoming symbol), because the very concept of emergence is a product or content of consciousness at its highest levels of manifestation. Again, in order to know the "where," the "when," and the "how," the "what" remains to be defined.

Without working hypotheses, neuroscientists will hardly be satisfied. In broad terms, they may consider consciousness as a property or function of the brain, some sort of an open loop phenomenon, with entries and outlets, in constant mutation, including or not including specific systems for vigilance, selective attention, memory, metarepresentation, and so on. To speak neuronal, they may associate conscious experience to dedicated networks in the brain, "reentry maps," "reverberant" or "autoreferential loops," "efferent or reafferent copies," "correlative discharges," "comparators," "attentional supervisors," and so on. Together with self-organization (complexity), they will generally view the activity of a multitude of neuronal units as one of the primary neurobiologic requirements for consciousness. "Binding" of the various ongoing activities into a gestalt will be explained by some synchrony of neuronal firing or other modes of detection of coincidences.

The question of the "why" is perhaps the most arduous because it necessarily calls for a top-down answer, and the conceptual gap is huge between the phenomenon to be explained and the cognitive levels at which the knowledge is solid (instructive, verifiable, perfectible). On this point, perplexity is probably the most appropriate attitude nowadays, certainly preferable to dogma.

In the particular context of the present meeting, however, one should add a very important reason, and a genuine one in its very simplicity: "Because of Herbert H. Jasper." Because Herbert Jasper, in his 91st year of life, is willing to share with us his immense experience, curiosity, and enthusiasm. Because more than 40 years have already elapsed since he coedited a book entitled *Brain Mechanisms and Consciousness,* at a time when most of us had not yet engaged in their scientific destiny. Because for many of these years, as individuals, we had the good fortune to work with him, and to enjoy and profit from his reflections, his consciousness, and the unique friendship of a person who has lived through all the major developments of modern neuroscience. This meeting was a marvelous occasion to honor him and pay tribute to his pioneering contributions, knowing that he would have never accepted a mere homage nor a passive attendance. Consequently, Herbert Jasper is now coediting this book, having coorganized, contributed to, and participated most actively in the symposium.

The eighteen chapters of this book do not strictly follow the order of the presentations at the meeting, but their regrouping in six unequal sections reflects its original structure. In the second section, "Consciousness as a Study Object," David J. Chalmers and Patricia S. Churchland describe modern philosophical perspectives and current expectations from theories on consciousness. In the third section, "Consciousness as a Function," a series of reports by Herbert H. Jasper, Edward G. Jones, Barbara E. Jones, Rodolfo R. Llinás and Urs Ribary, and Mircea Steriade deal with various anatomical, electrophysiological, and neurochemical properties of neuronal systems implicated in the processing of sensory information related to conscious experience, the sleep-waking cycle, the synchronization of corticoneuronal activity, and thalamo-corticothalamic interactions. The fourth section, "Contents of Consciousness," presents aspects of neuropathology (Alan J. McComas), the psychology of child development (Philip R. Zelazo and Philip D. Zelazo), neurolinguistics (A. Roch Lecours), cognitive neuropsychology (Michael S. Gazzaniga), and modern neuropsychiatry (Jeffrey A. Gray), which need to be accounted for in any explanatory description of conscious experience. In the fifth section, "Models of Conscious Experience," Benjamin Libet proposes a testable model of conscious brain function as a lead into studies of the visual system. These have been kept for the end, as one of the best illustrations of the successes of combined approaches in providing insights into a conscious function, through modern neuroanatomy and electrophysiology (David H. Hubel and Christof Koch) and through large-scale neural simulations and theoretical analyses (Giulio Tononi and Gerald E. Edelman). The meeting concluded with a General Discussion led by the four chairs of the sessions (Laurent Descarries, Edward G. Jones, Alan McComas, and Benjamin Libet). The discussions following the conferences and the final discussion were recorded and edited. They are published here *in extenso* for the benefit of all readers, as they provided remarkable leads into future directions for research.

We hope that *Consciousness: At the Frontiers of Neuroscience* will leave you with the sentiment that scientific knowledge of consciousness, as of any other subject, is a progressive elaboration; that it is opening new frontiers by the use of a multilevel and multifaceted scientific approach; and that it is beginning to provide some explanation(s) for a reality that will most probably, and interestingly, turn out to be quite different from that originally put in question.

Laurent Descarries
Vincent F. Castellucci
Serge Rossignol

Acknowledgments

This monograph is the 19th in a series of reports based on the proceedings of an annual international symposium organized by the Centre de Recherche en Sciences Neurologiques of the Université de Montréal. The cost of this annual meeting is mainly defrayed by an operating grant of the University to the Centre. Complementary financial support received from the Savoy Foundation, the Medical Research Council of Canada, the Faculty of Medicine, and Novartis is also gratefully acknowledged. We also want to thank several persons who helped with the organization of the symposium, mainly Daniel Cyr, Jeanne Faubert, France Lebel, Chantal Nault, Louise Piché, Janyne Provencher, and Ginette Simard, and especially Paul Cizek and Lauren Sergio for their faithful transcriptions of all discussion recordings.

ADVANCES IN NEUROLOGY

Volume 77

Consciousness: At the Frontiers of Neuroscience,
Advances in Neurology, Vol. 77,
edited by H.H. Jasper, L. Descarries,
V.F. Castellucci, and S. Rossignol.
Lippincott–Raven Publishers, Philadelphia © 1998.

1

Historical Perspective

Herbert H. Jasper

Department of Physiology, Université de Montréal,
Montreal, Quebec, H3T 1J4, Canada

I would like to set the present symposium on consciousness in historical perspective, beginning with the first symposium held near Montreal in 1954, with several succeeding conferences I have attended, until the international symposium organized by Dr. Jean-Pierre Cordeau in 1970.

The first international scientific meeting on consciousness was held near Montreal, at the Alpine Inn at St. Marguerite in the Laurentian Mountains, in 1954, over 40 years ago. It was known as "The Laurentian Conference on Brain Mechanisms and Consciousness." It was organized in 1952, at the United Nations Educational, Scientific, and Cultural Organization (UNESCO) House in Paris, with the help of Jean F. Delafresnaye, executive director of the Council for International Organization of Medical Sciences, under the joint auspices of UNESCO and the World Health Organization. The principal organizers were Edgar D. Adrian (United Kingdom), Frederic Bremer (Belgium), and Herbert H. Jasper (Canada), who was chairman of the symposium (Fig. 1).

This Laurentian Conference was a satellite to two international congresses: The Third International Congress of Electroencephalography and Clinical Neurophysiology, held in Boston, and the Nineteenth International Congress of Physiological Sciences, held in Montreal. It was motivated largely by recent research upon what was then called the ascending brain stem reticular activating sys-

tem, described by Moruzzi and Magoun (1), the thalamic recruiting system, described by Morison and Dempsey (2), and which we later called the thalamic reticular system (3,4), and the centrencephalic integrating system, postulated by Dr. Wilder Penfield, which were all believed to play important roles in determining states of consciousness and the integration of voluntary movements (5–8).

The main participants in the Laurentian conference on Brain Mechanisms of Consciousness were as follows:

Edgar D. Adrian, Trinity College, Cambridge (United Kingdom)

Mary A.B. Brazier, Massachusetts General Hospital, Boston (United States)

Frederic Bremer, Université de Bruxelles (Belgium)

Alfred Fessard, Collège de France, Paris (France)

Henri Gastaut, Université de Marseille (France)

Donald O. Hebb, McGill University, Montreal (Canada)

Rudolph Hess, Jr., University of Zurich (Switzerland)

Herbert H. Jasper, McGill University, Montreal (Canada)

Richard Jung, University of Freiburg (Germany)

Lawrence S. Kubie, Yale University, New Haven, Connecticut (United States)

FIG. 1. Participants in the Laurentian Conference on Brain Mechanisms and Consciousness, The Alpine Inn, St. Marguerite, Quebec, Canada, 1954. Front row: Lashley, Penfield, Adrian, Brazier, Jasper, Bremer, Magoun, Greene. Second row: Gastaut, Rioch, Fessard, Morison, Hess, Olszewski, Grey Walter, Mahut, Jung, Li, Hebb, Kubie. Third row: Ajmone-Marsan, Whitlock, Moruzzi, Nauta, Courtois, Ingvar, Buser.

Karl S. Lashley, Harvard University, Cambridge, Massachusetts (United States)

Horace W. Magoun, University of California, Los Angeles (United States)

Robert S. Morison, Harvard University, Cambridge, Massachusetts (United States)

Guiseppi Moruzzi, University of Pisa (Italy)

Walter J. Nauta, Walter Reed Center, Washington, DC (United States)

Jerzy Olszewski, McGill University, Montreal (Canada)

Wilder Penfield, McGill University, Montreal (Canada)

David M. Rioch, Walter Reed Center, Washington, DC (United States)

W. Grey Walter, University of Bristol, Bristol (United Kingdom)

David. G. Whitlock, Walter Reed Center, Washington, DC (United States)

In addition to the above 20 principal contributors, there were a number of postdoctoral students, who assisted with the recording and transcription of all discussions with the help of experienced secretaries working day and night, so that it could be edited by the participants themselves before the end of the meeting and included in the final publication (9). The book was published simultaneously in the United States by Charles C. Thomas (Spingfield, IL) and in Canada by Ryerson Press (Toronto). It was soon to become a classic in the neuroscience literature of the time.

This first international symposium on consciousness laid the ground for much of the work I performed with my colleagues at the Neurological Institute of McGill University and at the Université de Montréal for over 40 years, up to the present.

Another landmark international symposium was held 10 years later, in 1964, at the Pontifical Academy of Sciences in Rome. It was called a "Study Week on the Brain and Conscious Experience," organized largely by Sir John Eccles, under the auspices of the Pontificia Academia Scientiarium in Vatican City and with the cooperation of Pope Paul VI, with whom we had an audience.

The study week was led off by Dr. Marc L. Colonnier, a distinguished neuroanatomist from the Université de Montréal, who had been recruited by Jean-Pierre Cordeau as a founding member of our initial group of neuroscientists. Marc Colonnier's lecture on "The Structural Design of the Neocortex" proved to be an excellent introduction to the whole meeting. It was followed by the talk on "Cerebral Synaptic Mechanisms" given by John Eccles, who also edited the general discussion and the entire book for publication (10).

Other important contributors to this Pontifical Academy meeting on the Brain and Conscious Experience were as follows:

P.O. Anderson, Structure and Function of Archicortex

V.B. Mountcastle, Neural Replication of Somatic Sensory Events

R. Granit, Sensory Mechanisms in Perception

O. Creutzfeldt et al., Information Transmission in the Visual System

B. Libet, Brain Stimulation and Conscious Experience

H.L. Teuber, Perception after Brain Injury

W. Penfield, Speech Perception and the Cortex

E.D. Adrian, Consciousness

H.H. Jasper, Brain Mechanisms and States of Consciousness

F. Bremer, Neurophysiological Correlates of Mental Unity

R.W. Sperry, Brain Bisection and Consciousness

J.C. Eccles, Conscious Experience and Memory

G. Moruzzi, Functional Significance of Sleep for Brain Mechanisms

C.G. Phillips, Precentral Motor Area

D.M. MacKay, Conscious Control of Action

A.O. Gomes, Brain Consciousness Problem

W.H. Thorpe, Ethology and Consciousness

C. Heymans and A. Schaepdryver, Dopamine and Central Transmission

H. Schaefer, Psychosomatic Problems

I can assure you that this study week at the Vatican Academy of Science, including the audience with the Pope, was a most memorable experience for us all. The Pope gave us a warm welcome but made it quite clear that there were aspects of the study of consciousness, such as the soul and spiritual life, that were more pertinent to the church than to scientific discussion.

Six years later, in 1970, another conference, this time organized by Jean-Pierre Cordeau (Fig. 2), took place at Mont Tremblant Lodge,

FIG. 2. Professor Jean-Pierre Cordeau first Director (1964–1971) of the newly formed Centre de Recherche en Sciences Neurologiques of the Université de Montréal, and organizer of the International Symposium in Neurosciences in Honor of Herbert H. Jasper, held at the Mont Tremblant Lodge, in the Laurentian Mountains, north of Montreal.

in the Laurentian Mountains near Montreal. This Mont Tremblant symposium proved to be the first in our series of international meetings in neurologic sciences to be held under the auspices of the Université de Montréal. It was entitled "Recent Contributions to Neurophysiology: International Symposium in Neurosciences." It took place just a few years after I had left McGill University to join Jean-Pierre Cordeau and his colleagues to form the Research Laboratories in Neurological Sciences, the forerunner of our present center.

I would like to quote briefly from the publication of the proceedings of the Mont Tremblant meeting (11):

> Foreword. In the early autumn of 1970, . . . more than two hundred former students, coworkers and friends of Dr. Jasper congregated at Mont Tremblant, in the Laurentian Mountains north of Montreal, to pay tribute to the man who had inspired their work and to whom they owe much of their own dedication to the study of brain sciences. The hardwood forest of the Laurentian Shield had put on for the occasion its glorious autumn finery in a riotous outburst of colors.
>
> Neuroscientists came from many parts of the world. Some bearing gifts in the form of scientific papers which were presented during these three memorable days. Many more came to listen and, by their presence, to pay homage to a beloved fellow scientist, teacher and friend.

The published volume of the Mont Tremblant symposium contains the papers and discussions that followed, a wide spectrum ranging from basic fundamental biophysics through sophisticated microneurophysiology, all the way to electroencephalography and clinical neurology. It also contains, in lieu of a preface, two very personal contributions. They are the texts of two after-dinner speeches, one presented by Lord Adrian, and the other by Wilder Penfield. Both pay hommage to Herbert Jasper, the man and the scientist. They reflect the personal warmth and affection toward him that found so vivid and tangible an expression during these 3 memorable days.

Lord Adrian entitled his contribution "Forty Years of Progress in Neurophysiology." It ended with the following paragraph:

At all events, our labour, wherever it leads, has been greatly assisted by Herbert Jasper. He is one of the pioneers who has helped us to clear a pathway through the forest as well as a chief organiser of the whole operation. If it ends by leading us out into open country, we shall certainly need new maps of the natural world, new ways of thinking about it, and what we are doing inside it. It will be a triumph for neurophysiology, but I am not altogether convinced that we shall be the happier as well as the wiser for what we shall learn. I shall close with a quotation from Louis Stevenson: "To travel hopefully is a better thing than to arrive, and the true success is to labour." Herbert Jasper has played an indispensable part in our labour and we have met tonight to show him how grateful we are.

Wilder Penfield described how we came to be working closely together, as close friends and colleagues, for over 27 years at the Montreal Neurological Institute. We shared our dedication to seeking an understanding of the human brain either through basic research, or from detailed studies of the function of the brain during various forms of epileptic seizure.

Our work together in the operating room on the exposed brains of epileptic patients was most important, as was our sailing and skiing together on weekends. Penfield also emphasized my work on the international scene with the International Brain Research Organization, and our work together for the publication of the book *Epilepsy and the Functional Anatomy of the Human Brain* (8).

These two opening addresses were just the beginning of a most exciting program of papers, including contributions from the following colleagues and friends (Fig. 3):

Robert Naquet, Marseille, France
Dan Pollen, Boston, Massachusetts
Donald Tower, Bethesda (NIH), Maryland
Cosimo Ajmone-Marsan, Bethesda (NIH), Maryland
Arthur Ward, Jr., Seattle, Washington
Robert Schwab, Boston, Massachusetts
Reginald Bickford, San Diego, California
Vernon Brooks, New York, New York
Arthur O. Bishop, Durham, North Carolina
William P. Wilson, Clemson, South Carolina

FIG. 3. Over 200 participants from the International Symposium in Neurosciences in Honor of Herbert H. Jasper, organized by Professor Jean-Pierre Cordeau, held at Mont Tremblant, Quebec, Canada, September 24–26, 1970.

John Knott, Iowa City, Iowa
Ali Monnier, Paris, France
Otto Creutzfeldt, Gottingen-Nikolausberg, West Germany
David Hubel, Boston, Massachusetts
Patrick Wall, London, England
Carl Pfaffman, New York, New York

I was particularly happy to have such a successful international symposium organized by Jean-Pierre Cordeau. Unfortunately, this was the last symposium that he was to attend, for he died suddenly of a heart attack while it was being prepared for publication. We were all devastated by his loss, just as we were beginning to succeed in creating the Centre de Recherche en Sciences Neurologiques. Jean-Pierre Cordeau had given us a good start with lots of inspiration for the future, which is still with us.

I am particularly pleased with the subject and scope of the present scientific meeting held in the year following my 90th birthday. The ancient brain–mind problem has been radically transformed by the revolutionary advances in the neurosciences that have taken place in recent years. I am quite sure that this will become apparent with this symposium.

REFERENCES

1. Moruzzi G, Magoun HW. Brain stem reticular formation and activation of the EEG. *Electroencephalogr Clin Neurophysiol* 1949;1:455–473.
2. Morison RS, Dempsey EW. A study of thalamocortical relations. *Am J Physiol* 1942;135:281–292.
3. Jasper HH. Diffuse projection systems: the integrative action of the thalamic reticular system. *Electroencephalogr Clin Neurophysiol* 1949;1:405–420.
4. Jasper HH. Functional properties of the thalamic reticular system. In: Adrian ED, Bremer F, Jasper HH, eds.

Brain mechanisms and consciousness. Oxford, England: Blackwell Scientific, 1954;374–401.

5. Penfield WG. The cerebal cortex in man. I. The cerebral cortex and consciousness (Harvey Lecture, 1936). *Arch Neurol Psychiatry* 1938;40:417–442.

6. Penfield WG. Epileptic automatism and the centrencephalic integrating system. *Assoc Res Nerv Ment Dis Proc* 1952;30;513–528.

7. Penfield WG. Studies of the cerebral cortex of man: a review and interpretation. In: Adrian ED, Bremer F, Jasper HH, eds. *Brain mechanisms and consciousness.* Oxford, England: Blackwell Scientific, 1954:284–309.

8. Penfield WG, Jasper HH. *Epilepsy and the functional anatomy of the human brain.* Boston: Little, Brown, 1954.

9. Adrian ED, Bremer F, Jasper HH, Delafresnaye JF, eds. *Brain mechanisms and consciousness.* Oxford, England: Blackwell Scientific, 1954.

10. Eccles JC, ed. *Brain and conscious experience.* New York: Springer-Verlag, 1966.

11. Cordeau J-P, Gloor P. Recent contributions to neurophysiology; International Symposium in Neurosciences in Honour of Herbert Jasper. *Electroencephalogr Clin Neurophysiol Suppl* 1972;31:1–208.

Consciousness: At the Frontiers of Neuroscience,
Advances in Neurology, Vol. 77,
edited by H.H. Jasper, L. Descarries,
V.F. Castellucci, and S. Rossignol.
Lippincott–Raven Publishers, Philadelphia © 1998.

2

The Problems of Consciousness

David J. Chalmers

Department of Philosophy, University of California, Santa Cruz, California 95064

TYPE I AND TYPE II PHENOMENA

Our chair introduced this session by distinguishing "top-down" and "bottom-up" approaches to consciousness. The work of Herbert Jasper illustrates the value of a bottom-up approach, but I suppose that I will be presenting a top-down view here. This sort of approach has its limits, but it is useful at least at the start of this sort of discussion. That way we can see just what the problems are and what the lay of the land is, before we get into the bottom-up approach—the correlated discharges and the afferent and efferent connections—to make the detailed progress that comes later. So I will start by presenting an overview of the problems of consciousness from the lofty perspective of the philosopher. I will also concentrate on the question of how we might be able to construct a stable, self-sustaining science of consciousness.

I was asked to speak on the topic of definitions and explanations because philosophers are supposed to be very good at definitions. Sadly, one thing you find out if you do some philosophy is that philosophers are not much better at definitions than anybody else. In fact, the history of philosophy shows that defining anything is a bit of a hopeless task. Definitions are the kind of things which come at the end of the game, not at the beginning of the game. The more important something is, the harder it is to define. So instead of defining a concept like consciousness, it may be more interesting to point at the various phenomena that are at play in the vicinity. After all, any word in English is ambiguous, and the word "consciousness" is no exception. When different people talk about consciousness, they are typically talking about very different things. So if someone asks, "How do you explain consciousness?", there is no single answer, because "consciousness" does not refer to just one phenomenon. Once we start to separate out specific phenomena, we might be able to give more unified answers to those questions.

So, what are some of the phenomena people talk about when they are talking about consciousness? To start with, in a liberal use of the term, a central phenomenon of consciousness is sensory discrimination. Speaking very loosely, one might say that an organism is conscious of an object in its environments when it can discriminate information about that object in its environment and do something with it. So in this sense, you will have consciousness in a sea slug. On the other hand, some of the more interesting phenomena of consciousness come in when one proceeds further into the cognitive system. For example, consider the integration of information inside a nervous system. How does all that information from different modalities and different areas get integrated inside a brain? This is frequently thought of as one of the central problems of consciousness. Another central phenomenon is the accessibility of information to a subject. How is it that a cognitive system can have access to information about the world and about itself and use that information in the control of behavior? This leads directly into another crucial phenomenon, which is that of verbal report. How do we have access to information such that we can report on that information and talk about it? This yields perhaps the most popular operational definition for consciousness in the sciences, perhaps because it is so easy to pin down: a human being is said to be conscious of some information precisely when that information is verbally reportable. There are also phenomena of self-monitoring. For example, how can a cognitive system monitor its own states, by some kind of a feedback loop? Finally, there are problems in the voluntary control of behavior. When I consciously move my arm, this is under my control. How is this kind of control of behavior managed?

Now these phenomena are all somehow related to each other; they are all in some sense problems of consciousness. On the other hand, there is a sense in which none of these are the core phenomenon of consciousness. When people say that consciousness is the great scientific challenge of our time, or the last ill-understood phenomenon, the phenomenon at issue is not usually integration and discrimination, or access and verbal report, but subjective experience. We, as conscious beings, have subjective experience of our minds and of the world. It feels like something to be a conscious being. States of subjective experience are states that feel like something. When I look out at the audience, I perceive the audience visually. I have visual sensations, visual experiences of colors, of shapes, of objects, of individual people, and this feels like something from the first-person point of view. When I listen, I consciously experience a little hum, a few coughs, some sounds in the background, and something similar goes on in all the sensory modalities. I have experiences of certain mental images, the feeling of certain kinds of emotions, and the stream of conscious thought. These are what we might call paradigmatical first-person phenomena, and in some ways these are the phenomena that are at the core of consciousness.

Some people argue that we should reserve the word "consciousness" for these phenomena of subjective experience. Personally, I think that there is not much point in getting into arguments about a word. One can use the word "consciousness" for all these phenomena, as long as one makes some sort of distinction between them. What is interesting are the different kinds of problems these phenomena pose. I do not want to prejudice anybody about these problems, but sometimes it is useful to divide them up into different categories. So I will call them, relatively neutrally, the type I phenomena and the type II phenomena. The type I phenomena are the phenomena of discrimination, integration, report, and the like, and the type II phenomena are those of subjective experience.

THE EXPLANATORY CHALLENGE

The problems in these two categories pose different kinds of challenges. The type I phenomena all have something in common. They are all defined in terms of cognitive and behavioral functions. To explain these phenomena, all we need to do is explain how some system in the brain performs some functional role in the control of cognition and behavior. With reportability, for example, we need to explain the function of producing verbal reports. So if someone says, "Explain consciousness," in the sense of "Explain reportability," what you need to do is explain how that function is performed. And when it comes to explaining the performance of functions, we have a nice, well-developed methodology. What you do is specify a mechanism, a mechanism that can perform the function. Within neuroscience one will typically look at a neural mechanism; within cognitive science and artificial intelligence one will look at some kind of computational mechanism. Frequently one will try to do both, giving a neural and a computational story. So, for example, to explain sensory discrimination or aspects of integration, one will give a neural and/or a computational mechanism that can perform those functions. And in these cases, for the type I phenomena, once you have explained how the functions are performed, you have explained everything. You have explained what is at issue.

Indeed, if you look at reductive explanations throughout science, you see this pattern again and again. By reductive explanation, I mean the kind of explanation where one explains a high-level phenomenon wholly in terms of certain lower level phenomena. The kinds of problems to which reductive explanation is applied are very typically problems about the performance of functions.

Take the problem of life. When it comes to explaining life, what do we need to explain? We need to explain phenomena such as reproduction, adaptation, and metabolism; these are all functional phenomena. One gives a story about mechanisms that perform the functions, and this explains them. Something similar goes for genetics, where one explains the transmission of hereditary information; for learning, where one explains the adaptation of behavior in response to certain kinds of environmental stimulation; and maybe even for phenomena such as light and heat, where one explains things such as the transmission of visual information, the expansion of metals in response to certain kinds of stimulations, the flow of heat, and so on. In every case what needs explaining are functions.

To explain the performance of a function, what does one do? One gives a mechanism. Take the problem of genetics. This is really the problem of explaining the function of transmission of hereditary characteristics from one generation to the next. How did this problem get solved? Watson and Crick came along and specified a mechanism—DNA replication—that can perform this function. One can tell a plausible story about how this mechanism performs the function of transmitting information from one generation to the next. Once this story is appropriately elaborated and confirmed, one has solved the central problem of genetics. Things work something like this for most phenomena in science, and certainly those that fall into the type I or functional category.

What makes the type II phenomena different? I have spoken so far as if there is just one type II phenomenon, subjective experience. This may be misleading. There are many different type II phenomena, as there are many different phenomena of subjective experiences: visual experience, auditory experience, emotional experience, imagistic experience, and so on. And we do not have any certainty at the start that all these different phenomena will be amenable to the same kind of explanation. Nevertheless, one can group them at the start into the category of type II or subjective phenomena. What is unusual about these phenomena is that they do not seem to be defined, on the face of it, in terms of the performance of functions. When it comes to explaining experience—the subjective experience of vision or of hearing, or the fact that we are conscious at all—we are not trying to explain how we respond or move, or how any function is performed. It is a different kind of problem, one for which functional explanation is not so obviously appropriate.

One way to put this distinction is that for the type I phenomena, explaining certain functions—how the brain performs a role—suffices to explain the phenomena. But for the type II phenomena, there is a further question in the vicinity. Even once one has explained all the functions in the vicinity—discrimination, integration, access, report, and so on—there remains, potentially, something else to explain. We still need to explain how the performance of these functions should be conscious, or accompanied by subjective experience. This is a further question to which an answer to the first question does not guarantee us an answer. Now it may happen that in the course of answering the first question we are led to the crucial insights that will lead us to answering the second question. That cannot be ruled out. But the distinction between type I and type II phenomena is that for type I phenomena we know that explaining the functions suffices: we were concerned with only the functions in the first place. For type II phenomena, we do not know that. Therefore, if there is a link, it will be a more indirect link. The kind of functional explanation that worked so well elsewhere does not apply so directly here.

The basic problem of subjective experience can be put this way. The standard methods, which have been very successful in neuroscience and cognitive science, largely have been developed to explain structure and to explain function. We specify the fine-grained structure and dynamics of a neural or computational process, and this enables us to explain some sort of higher level structure and function, whether it be gross behavior or some more complex internal process such as discrimination, integration, and memory. The structure and function of neurons gives you a story about the structure and dynamics of perception, for example. This works terrifically well for most problems in neuroscience and cognitive science: the type I problems. But the problem of experience is not just a problem of explaining structure and function, so the standard reductive methods as they stand are incomplete.

A little bit of structure and dynamics can get you a long way in science: it gets you to a lot more structure and a lot more dynamics. But that is all it gets you to. For most problems, where all we need to explain is structure and function, that is enough. But when we have something that needs to be explained that is not initially characterized in terms of function, then there is a potential gap. It is what some philosophers have called an explanatory gap in theories of subjective experience.

Take your favorite neural or computational theory of the processes underlying consciousness. A hackneyed example is one of the theories involving synchronized oscillations in the cortex, which come to bind certain kinds of information together. What does this potentially explain? Potentially, such a theory might explain all kinds of interesting aspects of binding, of integration, of storage of information in working memory, maybe even of how this gets used in the control of behavior. These are important structural and functional questions. But when it comes to the question of why it is that this should somehow support subjective experience, the theory is silent. There is an explanatory gap between the story you tell about the oscillations and the manifest fact that this somehow results in subjective experience. On the face of it, the structural and functional theory is logically compatible with the absence of experience; therefore, nothing in the theory alone tells you how you get to subjective experience. That is the basic problem of consciousness, and there are many different responses.

CONSTRUCTING A SCIENCE OF CONSCIOUSNESS

Rather than attack that problem head-on right now, I am going to step back a little and ask, "How is it that we can construct a science of consciousness?" That is, what will be the shape of a field that simultaneously is a science and takes consciousness seriously? I think that this is a particularly pressing question now, with consciousness subject to such waxing and waning of interest. It was a very popular subject in the late 19th century, then interest in consciousness waned for many decades. It has undergone periodic resurgences. It is in the middle of such a resurgence now. The question is, is it going to be possible to have a stable and self-sustaining science of consciousness that is not subject to these vicissitudes in the ways that we have seen in the past? It is hard to say, but I hope so. At the very least, we can look at the shape a science of consciousness might take, and we might look at what some of its projects might be. Of course there will be more than one project: a science of consciousness will have many different paths. But we can ask what the various components will be. Again, I will look at these projects always while keeping one eye on the central, or core, phenomena of subjective experience.

Project 1: Explain the Functions

The first project is that of explaining type I phenomena, the functions I discussed at the beginning: discrimination, integration, access, self-monitoring, report, and so on. In a way this is the most straightforward project. We have seen that these are clearly amenable to the relatively standard methods of reductive explanation. You give a neural or computational story about how these functions are performed, and that explains the phenomena at issue. I expect that most of the work in a meeting like this one is going to be in this paradigm. There are all kinds of examples of this sort of work around the place. There are the various synchronized oscillation models, for example, of the integration of information in the brain. At the cognitive level there is something like Baars's global work-space model of information integration and dissemination. There are various reentrant circuit models of perception, memory, integration, and self-monitoring.

As with all approaches to consciousness, this approach has strengths and limitations. The strengths are that here, we are dealing with phenomena that are wholly intersubjective. In studying discrimination, integration, access, and report, things are straightforwardly objective and measurable, and none of the difficult epistemological problems of subjectivity come into play. As functional phenomena, they are amenable to the same kind of reductive methods that seem to work elsewhere in science. Because of this, I expect that these phenomena will go on to be the "meat and potatoes" of the field. This is a good thing, because it is here that there is the most straightforward possibility of progress.

The limitation, of course, is that this approach does not directly address the problems of subjective experience. It is addressing a different set of phenomena. This is not to say that one cannot make a bridge to subjective experience, but to make that bridge one has to do something else over and above explaining the functions. Therefore, in dealing with the meat and potatoes, it will be important to keep an eye open in the background on how we might build that bridge. That is, we need to consider how our work on these type I phenomena is relevant to the type II phenomena of experience. I am not saying the work is irrelevant, but it is a question that has to be addressed directly rather than ignored.

Project 2: Isolate the Neural Correlates of Consciousness

The second project I will look at is that of isolating the neural basis of consciousness, or what is sometimes called the *neural correlate of consciousness*. In this project, we aim to isolate the neural and cognitive systems such that information is represented in those systems when and only when it is represented in consciousness. One can at least hypothesize that there is some neural locus such that for information to make it into consciousness, it has to be represented somehow in that neural locus. Of course, it may not work out this way. It may be that for information to make it into consciousness it needs just to make it into one of many different areas, perhaps not even functionally localizable. There may well be many different neural correlates of consciousness in different modalities, at different levels of description. But in any case this provides an initial question to shape one's approach.

A large number of such proposals have been made already. I have made a list of a number of them in another paper (1). I called this the "neural correlate zoo," analogous to what particle physicists sometimes call the "particle zoo," where they have 237 elementary particles, or thereabouts. It can sometimes seem that 237 different neural correlates of consciousness have been put forward, ever since Descartes got the whole thing started with his talk about the pineal gland as the seat of the mind. The *locus classicus* in the contemporary discussion of these ideas is probably the suggestion by Wilder Penfield and Herbert Jasper that the intralaminar nucleus in the thalamus is the basis of consciousness (2). More recently, Crick and Koch proposed that 40-Hz oscillations in the cortex are crucial (3); Milner and Goodale have suggested that the ventral pathways in the inferior temporal cortex are the basis of visual consciousness (4); and Bogen has revived Penfield's and Jasper's ideas about the intralaminar nucleus (5). There has even been speculation about the role of quantum effects in microtubules, from Hameroff and Penrose (6).

It may be that many of the proposals are compatible. They may be dealing with neural correlates of different aspects of consciousness, or at different points in the processing pathway, or at different levels of description. On the other hand, it is likely that many of these proposals are simply wrong. Indeed, it may well be that at this stage of inquiry all of them are wrong. But we have some interesting ideas to go forward with.

This work is useful in sneaking up on the problem of subjective experience. We are starting from the structural component that we understand well and trying to build a bridge, and the first element in that bridge is isolating the most relevant physical systems. Many or most people doing this work are indeed concerned with the neural correlates of subjective experience itself. In Logothetis's work on binocular rivalry in monkeys, for example, one finds certain neurons, in visual area V5 and in inferior temporal cortex, that correlate with what the monkey seems to be experiencing (7). Different stimuli are presented to each eye. The monkey responds as if it sees just one of them, and presumably it experiences just one of them. Then certain neural systems are found to correlate strongly with the stimulus that the monkey perceives, rather than the stimuli that are presented. So this is helpful in providing the first part of a bridge to consciousness.

Of course there are certain limitations here. First, this kind of work always depends on certain preexperimental assumptions to get off the ground. When picking out a certain kind of neural process as a correlate of consciousness, one needs some kind of criterion for ascribing consciousness to a system in the first place. This will be a functional criterion: report, behavior, and so on. And those assumptions are substantial and preexperimental. Some of them are very straightforward. For example, where there is verbal report, there is consciousness. When someone says they are conscious, they are conscious. Now that is an assumption. It is not guaranteed to be true, but as assumptions go in science, it is a fairly safe one. Once you move away from language-using systems, it gets much more difficult, of course. Much of this work takes place in monkeys, who cannot use verbal report, so you have to use more indirect criteria, such as criteria of deliberate and controlled behavior in a number of different modalities. When you can say that information is being used in deliberate and controlled behavior, we will say that subjective experience is underlying it. Perhaps this is not obvious; in any case, all I want to point out here is that some assumptions—a little philosophy—is needed to get this kind of work off the ground. This introduces an element of danger into the process, but it seems to be an element that people can live with.

The other limitation, of course, is that working on the neural basis of consciousness gives you something more akin to correlation rather than explanation, at least at the start. We find that when there is such and such a neural process, there is subjective experience, and one can maybe have a detailed system of correlations but nothing here gives you a full explanatory story on its own. The central question in the background is, of course, how and why it is that this neural process should yeild subjective experience. Just giving a correlational story is not going to answer that question. This is not to denigrate this important work; it is simply to point to the existence of a further crucial question in the background that we eventually need to answer.

Project 3: Explain the Structure of Consciousness

A third important component of a science of consciousness is that of accounting for the structural features of consciousness. Consciousness has many different aspects, and it has a very complex structure. My visual field has a geometry: there are relationships between all sorts of experiences in my visual field. Color space has a complex three-dimensional structure, and so on. These structural features of experience are particularly amenable to neuroscientific explanations. Relationships between subjective experiences, similarities and differences, relative intensities and durations, and so on, are all objectively represented. In fact, this sort of information is straightforwardly reportable, so it must be represented within the cognitive system. This leads us to the possibility of at least an indirect account of the structural features of consciousness, by giving an account of corresponding structural features in the information that is made available for access and report inside the brain. So one can tell a reductive story about the three-dimensional structure of neurally encoded color space, which provides an indirect explanation of the three-dimensional structure of experienced color space. The same goes for the geometry of the phenomenal visual field. Indeed, I think if one looked at much of what goes on in the field of psychophysics, it has precisely this form: trying to account for structural features of conscious experience indirectly in terms of structural properties of stimuli and of underlying processing.

This project allows one to account for many specific structural features of consciousness, at least once we grant that consciousness exists in the first place. It also gives a more systematic link between consciousness and underlying processes. However, it has certain limitations. First, it does not get us immediately to the nonstructural features of consciousness, the quality, for example, of redness as opposed to the quality of blueness. It will tell us about their similarities and differences, but it will not tell us why one is one way rather than the other way, or why they have their specific intrinsic natures. Second, it does not explain why consciousness exists in the first place. This kind of work takes it for granted that consciousness exists and goes on to explain some of its features. But this kind of work relies on a kind of high-level bridging principle to get off the ground. We make a postulate: similarities and differences in conscious experience correspond to similarities and differences in underlying information processing. Using that postulate that takes consciousness for granted, then, the work gets off the ground. Therefore, one should not overread this kind of work as providing a complete explanation of consciousness in terms of brain processes. Nevertheless, it is very useful.

Project 4: Bridge the Gap

Finally, let me say a word about the fourth and final project, which is my favorite. This project focuses on the how and why of subjective experience itself. It is the project of explaining the connection between physical processes in the brain and subjective experience: how is it that these processes yield consciousness at all? What are the basic principles that explain why the connection holds, and that account for experiences' specific nature? This may be the most difficult question when it comes to consciousness. You may say, "Well, this is one that we want to put off a little bit. It is not something that everybody needs to be working on right now, and it may take us 50, 100, 150 years." Nevertheless, I think one can look at the problem now and at least make certain inferences about the kind of work that is going to be required to get at this problem.

One thing that we know right now is that certain standard methods, in and of themselves, do not provide a solution. Standard reductive explanation, in terms of structure and function, will explain more structure and function, but at the end of the day we are going to be left with the question of how this functioning supports subjective experience. At the very least, one will have to either transfigure the problem of consciousness into a different problem, to make it addressable, or expand the explanatory methods. I will look at the option that involves expanding the explanatory methods.

Some people suggest that to get subjective experience into the picture, one needs some extra physical ingredient: maybe more physics, quantum mechanics, chaos theory. I think all these methods ultimately suffer from some very similar problems. They are well suited toward explaining structure and function, but they still only get you to more complex structure and dynamics. We are still in the type I domain, whether it comes to a quantum mechanical explanation of decision making or a chaotic explanation of complex behavior. It seems that more physics and more processing is not enough to bridge the gap.

Instead, I think we need to supplement a structural/functional account with what we might call bridging principles to cross the gap to conscious experience. First, one tells a story about processing. Nothing in that story on its own entails the existence of conscious experience, but we supplement this story about processing with some bridging principles. These bridging principles tell us that where we have certain kinds of processing, or certain kinds of physical properties, one will have certain kinds of conscious experience. One will then have a theory: an account of processing plus bridging principles, which will jointly entail and explain the existence of consciousness. The processing part is the part we all know about and are familiar with already. The crucial question is the nature of the bridge.

If what I have said so far about structure and function is right, these bridging principles will not be entailed by the story about underlying processing. Nothing in the story about structure and function will tell you why these bridging principles are true. Therefore, we will have to take some element of this bridge

as basic elements in our theory, not to be further explained. And in that sense, those principles will be analogous to basic laws in physics. We are used to the idea that in science one needs to take something for granted, a starting point on which everything else can be built. But one wants to make what one takes for granted as simple as possible. If structure and function do not explain experience on its own, we want to add the minimal component to our theories that will bring subjective experience in.

This may sound fine in theory, but what is the methodology for discovering these principles? How can we arrive at our final and fundamental theory of consciousness? Obviously it will not happen any time soon, but I think there is a methodology here. We need to study and systematize the regularities between processing and phenomenology. We will try to build up systematic connections between objective and subjective properties, and then we will try to explain these regularities by a set of underlying principles.

These principles will start out quite complex. At the very beginning we will have initial principles connecting reportability and consciousness, for example, or complex behavior and consciousness, as a kind of guide leading us to something more specific. We can then move to specific empirical principles connecting specific neural systems with conscious experience. We will have some sort of nonreductive principle saying that when you have certain kinds of activity, for example, in the intralaminar nuclei, you have certain kinds of conscious experience. These principles will be useful, but they will still be complex. One would not want to invoke a connection between the intralaminar nuclei and consciousness as a primitive element in one's scientific theory: one wants to explain why this connection holds in terms of simpler and more universal principles, plus some details of boundary conditions and local conditions and the like. This reflects a methodology found throughout science, where we explain the complex in terms of the simple.

Therefore, we want to explain the emergence of complex consciousness from complex systems in a brain in terms of certain simpler bridging principles. Also, we want to make the primitive component in our theory, the component that goes unexplained, as small as possible. If what I have said is right, one cannot reduce that primitive component to zero. To reduce that component to zero would be to say that the story about experience could be logically deduced from the structural and functional story about the brain, and that is a pipedream. Nevertheless, one wants to add the minimal component that is going to cross the bridge.

There are a couple of ways in which a theory of consciousness will be different from theories in other domains. The first is that in other domains, no primitive bridging principles are usually required. For example, in explaining life, an account of interactions between the various functional components of a living system is enough to eventually explain reproduction, metabolism, and all the phenomena of life. One does not need any further primitive bridges to explain why these functions yield life. But for consciousness, we need primitive vertical bridges in the theoretical structure. Philosophers can argue back and forth about the nature of these bridges. Some philosophers say, "We will call them fundamental laws." Other philosophers say, "We will call them identities" (so that a certain brain process is "identical" to a certain kind of experience). That is a philosophical argument that does not matter much here. The important point is that these principles are going to be explanatorily primitive at some point, in order to get the theory off the ground.

A second important point is that a science of consciousness will be in a deep sense a first-person science. In this domain, you cannot get away from first-person phenomenology. If you throw away first-person phenomenology about subjective experience, you have thrown away the data. The initial data for postulating subjective experience come from the first-person point of view. Without the first-person data, one has a science of consciousness without consciousness. So some sort of phenomenological study is crucial to a theory of subjective experience, if only to get a theory off the ground. This sometimes works by a simple bootstrapping process. One does enough phenomenology to know that when I am conscious of something I can report it and I can talk about it. One then uses that simple principle to bootstrap oneself to other cases. Other people are talking about consciousness; we say, "They are making the reports, so they are conscious," and we bootstrap to data about their consciousness in that way. Other times, phenomenology may play a more detailed role, as in careful introspective studies of one's experience and how it correlates with underlying processes. Either way, the role of phenomenology in a theory of consciousness is ineliminable. One cannot have a science of subjectivity without bringing in the subject.

You might worry that this leads to an uncomfortable loss of intersubjectivity. There is something to this: the privacy of subjective experience data means that the data are not as easily and universally accessible as in other domains. But this is not to say that the theory will be ungrounded. A theory of subjective experience will remain grounded both in the third-person data and in first-person phenomenological data. You need both sorts of data to get a theory of subjective experience off the ground. We all have access to this sort of data, and our theories will be evaluated according to how well they fit the data. Once we have the simplest set of principles that predicts the data about experience from facts about processing, then I think we will have good reasons to accept those principles as true.

For now, this is a long way off. People can speculate on what these principles might be, but it may be 5 or 50 or 500 years until we have a really good theory. So it is not something I am recommending that everybody concentrate on now. I have speculated elsewhere (8) about the shape of a theory, but at this point it is only speculation. For a detailed bridge we need more detailed research. Not everyone will be working on this bridge directly while they are working on the meat-and-potatoes questions. But while they are working on those questions, they can at least keep an eye on the phenomena of experience and note any systematic connections between processing and experience. In the end, this sort of thing—careful experiment, phenomenology, connection, systematization, and simplification—may lead us to the universal principles in virtue of which processing supports experience, and thus to the core of a theory of consciousness.

REFERENCES

1. Chalmers DJ. On the search for the neural correlate of consciousness. In: Hameroff S, Kaszniak A, Scott A, eds. *Toward a science of consciousness II.* Cambridge, MA: MIT Press, 1998.
2. Penfield W, Jasper HH. *Epilepsy and the functional anatomy of the human brain.* Boston: Little, Brown, 1954.
3. Crick F, Koch C. Toward a neurobiological theory of consciousness. *Seminars in the Neurosciences* 1990;2: 263–275.
4. Milner AD, Goodale MA. *The visual brain in action.* Oxford, England: Oxford University Press, 1995.
5. Bogen JE. On the neurophysiology of consciousness, part I. *Consciousness and Cognition* 1995;4:52–62.
6. Hameroff SR, Penrose R. Conscious events as orchestrated space-time selections. *J Consciousness Studies* 1996;3:36–53. [Reprinted in Shear J, ed. *Explaining consciousness: the hard problem.* Cambridge, MA: MIT Press, 1997.]
7. Sheinberg DL, Logothetis NK. The role of temporal cortical areas in perceptual organization. *Proceedings of the National Academy of Sciences USA* 1997;94: 3408–3413.
8. Chalmers DJ. *The conscious mind: in search of a fundamental theory.* New York: Oxford University Press, 1996.

DISCUSSION

Moderated by Laurent Descarries

Christof Koch: David, I can understand how from a phenomenological point of view it makes sense to distinguish type I and type II phenomena; but I would submit that, from an empirical point of view, this distinction might be misleading because you never seem to get in a human the second without the former. In blindsight, you do not have a lot of visual function left. The degree of visual function that is left in blindsight is very primitive. Thus, I do not think you can have this zombie, somebody totally lacking in consciousness but without lack of function. A zombie is a logical possibility, sure, just like a Centaur, but that does not make it any more relevant to investigating consciousness. Empirically, you will never lose one class of phenomena without the other, so your distinction might not make a lot of sense in the real world.

David Chalmers: I agree that the two go together. Consciousness goes hand in hand with certain sorts of complex function, and there are no zombies in the real world. That is precisely what one would expect in the framework I have been developing, in which there are bridging principles saying that wherever there are certain sorts of processing, there are certain sorts of experience. But one still needs to make a distinction between the two, because one needs to separate out the various phenomena that need explaining, no matter how well they are correlated. Explaining the functions is one thing and explaining the experience is another. We can know that the two go together, but we still need to know why they go together. If one does not make the distinction at the start, one will not be able to properly raise this sort of crucial question.

Benjamin Libet: I would argue just the opposite from Christof Koch and partly from David Chalmers. The functions in the first category can virtually all be accomplished unconsciously. It is not necessary to have consciousness for those functions. And it is in fact subjective experience or awareness that is the central feature of consciousness, not the unconscious processes. There was a big review of this by Max Velmans a few years ago, bringing together the evidence for the idea that even in human beings, all of these other cognitive functions and so on can be accomplished unconsciously (1).

David Chalmers: I think this is right at least for phenomena which are specified in a coarse-grained way, such as perception, memory, and learning. We know that all those things can be done unconsciously. But, as Christof says, there are functional differences between the conscious and the unconscious forms. Often the conscious form has a greater complexity of processing, for example. So, consciousness may still correlate with certain complex functions. This comes up particularly clearly in the case of verbal report. Verbal report is itself a function that is very closely correlated with consciousness, as witnessed by the fact that most experimental work uses it as the main criterion for consciousness. So, I do not think that there is a complete dissociation between experience and function, though there may be some dissociation.

Allan Smith: One of the first people to really associate consciousness with the nervous system was René Descartes, who postulated in a series of brilliant insights that a stimulus, such as a painful burn of the skin, could be conducted by the nerves up through to the brain, to a region of the brain he called the sensorium, to give rise to conscious experience. This he succinctly put in the often quoted phrase, "I think, therefore I exist." What many people do not realize is that this eventually led to René's demise. It seems that one night he was in a Paris bistro and it was getting near closing time, and the bartender said, "Last call! Will you have another round René?" To which René answered, "I think not," and disappeared.

I tell that only partly as a joke. The serious side is that thought is an integral and important part of consciousness, at least to the extent that if we stop thinking, we are not conscious. An extension of that idea is that animals are conscious, but it requires a certain critical mass of nervous system in order to sustain consciousness. All animals are not conscious; those that have nervous systems based on strings of loosely associated ganglia are probably not capable of consciousness. They may be capable of complex sensory discrimination, as you have described, but I do not think they can sustain consciousness.

David Chalmers: I think that is one of the questions for which we still do not have an answer. But I can see no good reason to deny consciousness in animals, even fairly simple animals. They may lack certain complex forms of consciousness, such as self-consciousness, but they still have consciousness of the world. This probably goes down to mice and perhaps even to flies. But it is not something we know for sure, as we do not have a consciousness meter to wave at the animals. So we do not want to start a theory by making a presumption here. Once we develop a theory based on the human case, though, it may tell us something about animals. We work toward the simplest connecting principles in our own case, connecting processing and consciousness, and then extend them to cases further from home. It might turn out, for example, that the central regularities of consciousness involve certain sorts of perceptual discrimination and availability, while complex capacities such as language and self-monitoring are inessential. If that emerges from our theory of human consciousness, we can apply it to draw conclusions about animal consciousness. But one has to start with the core cases.

Peter Carlen: Based on your lecture I have come to the conclusion that type I can all be modeled and that we are going to get to the answers for most of the type I phenomena. Type II might be just how we feel about type I phenomenon, which we may never be able to model. Although, maybe someday we might be able to model computers to give out feelings. This is a naive thought, but I would like your opinion on that.

David Chalmers: Yes, the type I phenomena are certainly open to modeling, and our current methods of modeling have been developed precisely to explain type I phenomena. That goes for both computational and neural models. But we also want to capture the type II phenomena. I suppose that one aspect of these is how we feel about the type I phenomena, but more generally there is the issue of how we feel about the world and how the world feels to us. I do not think that standard models on their own capture type II phenomena. But maybe one could build a model that we can supplement by some very simple bridges to get a theory of the type II phenomena. That might be a way to model consciousness indirectly.

Peter Carlen: But highly complex intellectual functioning, which we would ascribe to consciousness, such as beating the world masters at chess, can already be done by a machine. So, what we are left with then is mainly how we feel about that.

David Chalmers: That is one part of what we are left with. We are left also with more general aspects of consciousness, such as what we subjectively experience when we are playing chess. Presumably chess computers do not feel and experience much at all, compared with our rich experience. Of course, their functioning is also very simple, compared with our complex functioning. Chess turns out to be one of the easy things to do. So, at least at the moment, computers and humans differ in both type I and type II phenomena.

Rodolfo R. Llinás: Well, this is going to be very short. I thought such a theory was called dualism, and the problem that people have with dualism is that it makes bridges into nothing. For instance, in looking at force and at how one moves, let us remember that for a long time people did not understand muscle contraction, and now we do. However, from a philosophical point of view, some may argue that we really do not know how we move, because we do not know what force really is. Well, no one suffers about that problem. Similarly, it seems to me that as in the case of force, the type II problem is going to get smaller and smaller and will ultimately disappear as we understand more about type I issues.

David Chalmers: If by a bridge into nothing you mean that there will be nothing to explain, I think that this is very implausible. The phenomena of subjective experience are data—to deny subjective experience is to deny the data. So what really matters is how we are going to explain these data. The fact is that if we concentrate only on explaining the type I phenomena, the functions, we will never even come to grips with the data. To explain discrimination, integration, and so on is just to explain something else. You are dealing with an incomplete catalog of the data. Of course, there might be a way of getting from an explanation of those things to an explanation of subjective experience. But in order to do that, one has to build a bridge.

Incidentally, there is an important difference between the case of consciousness and the cases you mention of muscles in biology and so on. For the biological problems of life, the data that needed to be explained were the functions of reproduction, adaptation, movement, and so on. This has not changed over the years; all that has changed is people's hypotheses about how to explain the functions. So, the data were always type I data here. When it comes to consciousness, the data that need to be explained are the various type I functions, but also subjective experience. I do not think any of these problems are going to go away. It does not matter whether one is a dualist or a materialist. When it comes to subjective experience, the only choices are to deny the data or to build a bridge. Without the bridge, you are just looking the other way.

Discussion Reference

1. Velmans M. Is human information processing conscious? *Behav Brain Sci* 1991;14:304–312.

Consciousness: At the Frontiers of Neuroscience,
Advances in Neurology, Vol. 77,
edited by H.H. Jasper, L. Descarries,
V.F. Castellucci, and S. Rossignol.
Lippincott–Raven Publishers, Philadelphia © 1998.

3

What Should We Expect from a Theory of Consciousness?

Patricia S. Churchland

Department of Philosophy, University of California at San Diego,
Salk Institute, La Jolla, California 92093

Within the domain of philosophy, it is not unusual to hear the claim that most questions about the nature of consciousness are essentially and absolutely beyond the scope of science, no matter how science may develop in the 21st century. Some things, it is pointed out, we shall never ever understand, and consciousness is one of them (1–5). One line of reasoning assumes that consciousness is the manifestation of a distinctly nonphysical thing, and hence has no physical properties that might be explored by techniques suitable to physical things. Dualism, as this view is known, is still to be found among those within the tradition of Kant and Hegel, as well as among some with religious convictions.

Surprisingly, however, strenuous foot dragging is evident even among philosophers of a materialist conviction. Indeed, one might say that it is the philosophical fashion of the 1990s to pronounce consciousness unexplainable and to find the explanatory aspirations of neurobiology to be faintly comic if not rather pitiful.[1] The very word "reductionism" has come to be used more or less synonymously with "benighted scientism run amok," where scientism apparently means "applying scientific techniques to domains where they are inapplicable." McGinn, perhaps the most unblushing of the naysayers,

insists that we cannot expect even to make any headway on the problem (3). Ironically, perhaps, here we are at a conference in honor of Dr. Herbert Jasper who was a great pioneer in moving neuroscience forward on this problem, and where results will be presented allegedly showing additional progress on the problem.

Because I am quite optimistic about future scientific progress on the nature of consciousness, my aim here, as a philosopher, is to address the most popular and influential of the skeptical arguments and to explain why I find them unconvincing. Thus, the overall form of the paper is negative, in the sense that I want to show why a set of naysaying arguments fails. The positive aspect of the story derives from the actual progress being made on the topic, but I shall leave it to my neuroscience colleagues to present the data and details on that. Section 1 will focus on skeptical arguments raised essentially in protest to reductionist programs, and section 2 will examine a range of skeptical arguments arising from consideration of what we do not yet know.

REDUCTIONISM: SHOULD WE EXPECT AN EXPLANATION AT ALL?

As a framework for my discussion, I shall first characterize the notion of scientific reduction, as we understand it from examples in

---

[1]There are of course well-known exceptions (6–9).

the history of science. In its starkest description, a reduction is an explanation of some macrolevel phenomenon in terms of the organization and constituents of some lower level microphenomenon. That is, the macroproperties are discovered to be the outcome of the nature of the elements at the microlevel, together with their dynamics and interactions. In the classic examples, this means that the causal powers of the macrophenomenon are explained as a function of the dynamics and causal powers of the microphenomenon. Is the function a simple function—such as that the "whole is nothing but the sum of the parts"? Virtually never. Summation is a supremely simple function, and macroproperties such as temperature in a gas or reflection of light or being a visible spark or inheriting red hair are anything but simple functions of their causally potent underlying structures.

What does the history of science show about reductive explanations that might be helpful in understanding the issue before us? Let me try to answer this by briefly discussing three cases. The first concerns the discovery that we could identify temperature in a gas as the mean kinetic energy of its constituent molecules. This then permitted coherent, unified explanation of temperature phenomena such as conduction, of why temperature and pressure are related in the way they are, of why heated things expand. The first success with gases allowed the extension of the explanatory framework to embrace liquids and solids, and eventually plasmas and even empty space. As a theory, it was far more successful than the caloric theory, which postulated a subtly compressible fluid as increasing in volume when a thing's temperature increases. Substances differ in the rate at which caloric fluid can flow through them, and at which they can acquire or lose caloric fluid.

The explanation of the nature of light can be seen as another successful example of scientific reductionism. In this instance, the macrotheory (optics) came to be seen as explainable in terms of microtheory (theory of electromagnetic radiation [EMR]); visible light turned out to be EMR, along with x-rays, utlraviolet rays, radio waves, and so forth. Note also that here, as elsewhere, further questions remain to be answered; hence, there is a sense in which the reduction is typically incomplete. If the overarching mysteries are resolved, however, that is usually sufficient for scientists to consider an explanation—and hence a reduction—to be essentially in place.

Reductions can be very messy, in the sense that the mapping of properties from micro to macro can be "one:many" or even "many:many," rather than the ideal "one:one." Although the case of light reducing to EMR is relatively clean, the case of phenotypic traits and genes is far less clean. Genes, as we now know, cannot be counted on to be single stretches of DNA, but may involve distinct segments of DNA. Additionally, a given gene may participate in different macroproperties as a function of prior conditions (10). Nevertheless, many molecular biologists see their explanatory framework as essentially reductive in character, mainly because a causal route from base pair sequences to traits such as Huntington's disease can be traced or at the very least, sketched in outline. The details can be expected to be filled out as experimental results come in. On the other hand, the lack of a clean line has prompted some philosophers, for example, Philip Kitcher, to propose that perhaps these messy cases are best thought of as not genuinely reductive. I view that as essentially a semantic recommendation, which promises some clarity in understanding, but which also has the drawback that in fact most scientists view molecular biology as an impressive instance of reductive explanation—incompleteness, messiness, and complexity notwithstanding. I am inclined to stick with the word "reduction," despite the complications in the biologic domain, because there is really nothing suitable to take its place, and because linguistic inertia is usually a sign that current usage is in fact useful.

Given this general characterization of reduction and reductionism, I shall now address five skeptical problems.

Should We Expect Consciousness to "Go Away"?

One difficulty, according to the skeptics, is that if consciousness is reduced to neuronal activities, then we are landed in the absurd position of saying that my pains, tastes, and so forth are not real (11). This worry is, in my view, based on misinformation concerning what reductions in science do and do not entail.

Therefore, the short answer to the topic question is, "No, pains will not cease to be real just because we understand the neurobiology of pain." That is, a reductive explanation of a macrophenomenon in terms of the dynamics of its microstructural features does not mean that the macrophenomenon is not real or is scientifically disreputable or somehow explanatorily unworthy or redundant. Even after we achieved an explanation of light in terms of EMR, the theory of optics continues to be useful to discover new things. Nobody thinks light is not real, as a result of Maxwell's equations. Rather, we think we understand more about the real nature of light than we did before 1873. Light is real, no doubt about it. But we now see visible light as but one segment of a wider spectrum that includes x-rays, ultraviolet, and radio waves. We can now explain a whole lot at the macrolevel that we were unable to explain before, such as why a beam of light passed through a narrow slit shows a two-smudge interference pattern.

Somewhat similar comments can be made concerning the aftermath of the reductive achievement of statistical mechanics. Temperature is taken to be a real property, and the study of the macrolevel itself remains in good standing. Thermodynamics continues to be capable of revealing new and interesting scientific truths, despite the existence of statistical mechanics, and indeed it is well aided by its undergirding.

Sometimes, however, hitherto respectable properties and substances do turn out to be unreal. The caloric theory of heat, for example, did not survive the rigors of science, and caloric fluid turned out not to be real. The theory was explanatorily problematic, especially when it had to address this problem: if heat from rubbing is to be explained by release of caloric in the spaces between the atoms, it should run out after a while. But, oddly for the theory, rubbing can be continued indefinitely and the heat does not stop being produced. If anything, rubbed things get hotter the longer they are rubbed. The molecules-in-motion approach could explain this quite simply: macromotion is translated into micromotion. Caloric theory also stumbled in its energy calculations for steam engines. On the caloric accounting, some caloric had to have disappeared by the end of a period of steam engine activity, but the data proved otherwise. The molecules-in-motion theory got the accounting correct, because it claimed that the micromotions (heat) were transformed into macromotions: movement of the engine wheel. In the end, caloric fluid was no match for molecular motion as an approach to thermal phenomena.

Theories range themselves on a spectrum of how little or how much of the macrotheory comes to be modified as a result of increasing explanatory reach of the microtheory. Revision of hypotheses is a major hallmark of science and how it makes progress, so it is no surprise to see revision as reductive macromicro progress is made. The degree of revision required will obviously vary from case to case and will depend on how the facts fall out. What will be the fate of our current conception of consciousness as we discover more about the nature of the brain will depend on the facts of the matter and the long-term integrity of current macrolevel concepts (12).

Some revisions to the concept of consciousness, as it stood circa 1950, are already in evidence, owing to the impact of data on core beliefs about consciousness. The discovery by Sperry and his colleagues concerning the effects of commissurotomy did, I think, make it evident that unity in conscious experience has a lot to do with the connections in brain wiring, and hence was not a kind of transcendental necessity. Research on sleep and dreaming revealed that there was far more dreaming going on than introspection was led to believe, and that even in matters of dream content, considerations of learning and "neural housekeeping" probably play at least as important a role as conflict resolution or wish fulfillment. In addition, the regularity in nightly cycles of behavioral state and their control over brain stem mechanisms such as the locus ceruleus and the giant neurons of the pons strongly implicate a neurobiologic, rather than a psychological, explanation. The discoveries concerning the biologic parameters of dreaming have been critical in shifting our understanding away from a Freudian or Jungian conception of the nature and significance of dreaming to a more biologically based conception (13).

Blindsight constitutes another phenomenon where research showed something very disruptive to our a priori assumptions: conscious, deliberate behavior could be based on visual signals of which the subject had no visual experience (14,15). Initially, many philosophers found this so counterintuitive as to be a violation of rationality itself, although it has now become accepted as a puzzling phenomenon whose empirical basis can be studied. Of comparable significance is the discovery that even in perception, introspective data can mislead us concerning the nature of the psychological processes involved. There are many examples here, but perhaps an especially dramatic one is the finding that in visual perception, only a tiny area (about 2 degrees) of the visual field is foveated and hence perceived in crisp detail at any given moment. Saccades, made about every 300 milliseconds, and neuronal integration of signals across saccadic movement, contribute to the illusion of full-field detail. Additionally, a whole range of data from neurology—from anosognosia to the amnesias to Balint's syndrome—show that conscious belief structures are not organized strictly according to the canons of logic.

The possibility that conscious experience may well be an assortment of various capacities flying in loose formation is now uncontroversial, but a mere 20 years ago it seemed outrageous. By the 1990s, it had been generally acknowledged that quite different phenomena, such as (a) perceptual awareness, (b) something like metacognition (knowing that you do not know how many second cousins you have), and (c) knowing that you want to convert your bonds to stocks, may be subserved by rather different neurobiologic mechanisms.

In sum, the short answer to the lead question, "Should we expect consciousness to go away?" is this: "No." The various phenomena we group together as conscious phenomena will not, of course, go away. Nevertheless, we may come to conceptualize them in somewhat different—and perhaps even very different—ways.

Should We Expect Consciousness to Be Emergent?

As a prelude to warning neuroscience off the topic, we are often told that consciousness is an emergent property. But what does it mean to call a property emergent? On one version, it means that there can be no explanation of that property in microterms. Consequently, if it is then claimed that consciousness cannot be explained because it is emergent, that simply comes to this obviously circular hypothesis: consciousness cannot be explained because it cannot be explained.

To avoid the circularity, some investigators (16,17) have suggested a more careful meaning of the word "emergent": if a property is emergent, then it cannot be predicted from knowledge of the microproperties. For example, it is alleged that even if you did know all the microproperties of water, you could not predict that it would be wet. If the macroproperty cannot be predicted from knowledge of the microproperties, the story goes, then science will never be able to explain it as the outcome of microproperties. This view tends to see prediction and explanation as two sides of the same coin. Philosophers have objected to this on the grounds that prediction and explanation are not in fact complementary, as the metaphor implies. It is generally considered that physics does have an explanation for the wetness of water, whether anyone could have predicted it from the microproperties.

Additionally, there is a logical reason why predictability does not work very well as a criterion for eventual explainability: the very same ideas that support the hunch that something cannot be explained are invoked to support the premise that no one could predict the macroproperty, even if they knew the microstructure. Thus, there is a circularity here as well. Broad thought it would help if you took the predictor to be an archangel, and others have suggested that an omnipotent god might serve in that role. Thought experiments that depend on agreeing what a very smart archangel might or might not be able to predict tend to lack credibility and certainly lack consensus, and I confess I do not find them very helpful as an index of anything.

Perhaps the most sophisticated argument on this approach is owed to the Australian philosopher Frank Jackson (18). In sum, Jackson's idea was that there could exist someone, call her Mary, who knew everything there was to know about how the brain works but still did not know what it was to see the color green (suppose she lacked "green cones and wiring," to put it crudely). This possibility Jackson took to show that qualia (the visual experience itself) are therefore not explainable by science. That is, if qualia were just patterns of neural activity, then if Mary knows what neural activity allegedly constitutes having a visual experience of green, then she should know what green qualia are like.

There are various weaknesses in this argument, but the main problem with the argument is that to experience green (have green qualia), certain wiring has to be in place in Mary's brain, and certain patterns of activity have to obtain. Because by Jackson's own hypothesis she does not have that wiring, then presumably the relevant activity patterns in visual cortex are not caused and she does not experience green. Her knowing all of the relevant neurobiology (not unlike Broad's imag-

ined archangel) presumably involves propositional knowledge, and probably the learning is widely distributed in the brain.

Who would expect her visual cortex—V4, let us suppose—would be activated in the green qualia pattern just by virtue of her propositional (linguistic) knowledge about activity patterns in V4? Not me, anyhow. Jackson's argument has to assume that either knowing the neurobiology of green qualia somehow will bring about experiencing green qualia or that qualia are not scientifically approachable. But both alternatives are probably false. I suppose that knowing the neurobiology of green qualia could somehow bring about experiencing green qualia, but I see no reason to expect that it should. Via channels bypassing the color circuits, Mary can have propositional knowledge, including the knowledge of what her own brain lacks in terms of "green qualia wiring." As Teller (19) put it, the subjectivity of the experience is just the having of the experience, not some ineffable kind of knowledge. Nothing whatever follows about whether science can or cannot explain qualia.

Within neuroscience, there is a useful and nonmystical notion of emergence: a property is emergent if it is a network property, if it is the outcome of the intrinsic properties of the neurons, together with the way they interact. In this less metaphysical sense, the rhythmicity of the stomatogastric ganglion of the lobster is an emergent property (20). One reason to prefer this more neutral meaning of "emergent" is that it leaves open the question of whether a property is emergent because it is an explainable network property, or because it is an unexplainable nonphysical property (21).

Should We Expect that I Could Know What You Experience?

This question is most pointedly raised in the context of the inverted spectrum problem, and I shall address it in that form. To illustrate, consider the possibility that your color experiences (color qualia) might be systematically inverted relative to mine; e.g., where you see red, I see green, and so on. Noting that there could be systematic behavioral compensation that would cover experiential differences, skeptics have urged that even looking inside would be unavailing. Allegedly, no conceivable test could ever show similarity or inversion in our color experiences. The lesson we are invited to draw is that consciousness is intractable scientifically because intersubjective comparisons are impossible. Some philosophers think that this is not merely a problem about what we can and cannot know, but evidence that consciousness is a metaphysically different kind of thing from brain activity.

In addressing this issue, I shall make one assumption: that conscious experiences are in some systematic causal connection to neuronal activity. That is, they are not utterly independent of the causal events in the brain. To deny the assumption is to slide into a version of dualism known as psychophysical parallelism, meaning that mental events and physical events are completely independent of each other causally and just happen, amazingly enough, to run in parallel "streams."

Normal human color vision is known to depend on three cone types, each of which is tuned to respond to light of particular wavelengths. Cone inputs are coded by color-opponent cells in the retina and lateral geniculate nucleus, and project to double-opponent cells in the parvocellular blob pathways of the cortex. Cells in cortical area V4 appear to code for color regardless of wavelength composition of the light from the stimulus and appear to subserve the perceptual phenomenon known as color constancy. Lesions to the cortical area known as V4 result in achromatopsia (loss of all color perception) in humans and monkeys. Also relevant to behavioral determinations of differences in experience is the fact that the relationships between hue, chroma (saturation), and value (lightness) define an asymmetric solid (Munsell color quality space). This implies that radical differences in perception should be detectable behaviorally, given suitable tests. That is, "A

is more similar to B than to C" relationships between colors are defined over the Munsell quality space, and if there is red/green inversion, the similarity relationships to yellow, orange, pink, etc. will not remain the same.

Given the progress to date, it seems likely that the basic neurobiologic story for color processing can be unraveled. For similar reasons, it looks likely that the basic story for touch discrimination and its mechanisms in the somatosensory thalamus and cortex also can be unraveled. For example, it seems evident that if someone lacks "green" cones, or lacks "red/green" opponent cells, or lacks a V4, they will not experience the visual perception of green. Comparable circuitry and comparable behavioral discriminations seem to be presumptive of comparable experiences; that is, comparable qualia (22). The skeptic, however, insists that no data—not behavior, not anatomy, not physiology—could ever show qualia inversion. Incidentally, what is at issue here is not that minor differences in such things as hue or brightness might go undetected, but that even huge differences, such as red/green inversions or brightness/dullness inversion, might be in principle absolutely undetectable.

To approach this matter somewhat indirectly, let us first consider a vivid example where it is evident that a perceptual inversion is likely detectable, namely, inverted "shape" qualia. Could Alphie have "straight qualia" whenever Betty has "curved qualia" (and vice versa) and the difference be absolutely undetectable? In this example, because two modalities—vision and touch—can access the external property, it seems easier to agree that together, behavioral data and wiring data permit us to make a reasonable determination of similarity and differences. That is, the problem is not essentially less tractable than determining whether two people digest food in the same way or whether two cats in free fall right themselves in the same way.

Much the same is usually conceded for pleasure/pain inversion, and within vision, of near/far inversion in stereopsis. Random dot stereograms are already a reliable determinant of (a) whether a subject has stereopsis at all, and (b) whether there is an inversion between two subjects. If we factor in data from "near/far" cells in V1, then insisting on absolute undetectability begins to look unreasonable. It seems a bit like insisting that it is absolutely undetectable whether the universe was created 5 minutes ago, complete with all its geologic records, its fossil records, history books, and my memories, etc. Skepticism carried to that extreme just ceases to be scientifically interesting and becomes philosophical in the pejorative sense of the term.

In the case of shape inversion, the skeptic can remain a skeptic by going one of two ways, neither of which helps his sweeping antireductionist defense:

1. No qualia—not shape, not temperature, not pain—can be compared across subjects, even to a degree of probability. They are one and all absolutely incomparable. For all I know, you might experience the color red when I experience pain.
2. The neurobiology of shape qualia (rough/ smooth, etc.) can be compared, and perhaps even the neurobiology of stereopsis, but color vision is different.

The first appears to depend only on an antireductionist resolve, without any independent argument. In that case, we really are looking at a circular argument. The only escape from the circle is to fall into the embrace of dualism, and worse, of the deeply implausible psychophysical parallelism rendition of that already implausible doctrine.

The second makes a major concession so far as qualia in general are concerned. Having conceded that some qualia are scientifically approachable, the skeptic no longer shields subjectivity as such, but only subjectivity for certain classes of experience, namely color vision. This looks far less powerful than the original position, and it starts the skeptic down a slippery slope. For having made this concession, it now becomes easier for the reductionist to push hard on the point that comparisons in receptor properties, wiring proper-

ties, connectivity to motor control, and so forth, will augment (as it already does) behavioral data, and allow us to compare capacities across individuals. Similar arguments can be made for other single-modality experiences: stereopsis, sound, pain, temperature, feeling nauseous, feeling dizzy, etc. That is, as long as awareness of color has a causal structure in the brain, and as long as it is not a property of soul-stuff utterly detached from all causal interaction with the brain, data from psychology (e.g., the color-hue relationships) and neuroscience (tuning curves for the three cone types in the retina, wiring from the retina to cortex and intracortically) predict that big differences in color perception will correlate with big differences in wiring and in neuronal activity. In the context of a more detailed knowledge of the brain in general, rough comparisons between individuals ought to be achievable, subject to the usual qualifications unavoidable in any science (22).

Should We Expect Explanations of What Is Going on in Someone's Mind, Moment by Moment?

The question of how detailed a theory has to be in order to count as yielding an explanation is not straightforward and varies with the motivations for wanting an explanation. The desire to control a phenomenon, or to predict exactly what will happen next, may require more detail than the desire to grasp the general go of it. Thus, we basically understand the weather, but because it is a complex dynamic system with many variables, we cannot predict exactly where a tornado will form or where within inches or even kilometers it will move once formed. On the other hand, sometimes good intervention in a phenomenon can be achieved with minimal understanding, as when lithium salts were found to bring manic depression under control but almost nothing was understood about how this was achieved.

The complexity of the human nervous system makes detailed, moment-to-moment prediction highly unlikely. Additionally, intervention in the system to obtain the data on the relevant parameters, perhaps neuron by neuron, would change the basic conditions and frustrate the prediction. Certainly at this stage we have no noninvasive technology at the neuronal level of resolution to achieve that end. However, the same is true of predicting exactly where Tony Gwynn will hit a baseball. Measurements to obtain the data will change the data, and there are too many variables to compute. As a practical matter, therefore, thought-by-thought monitoring looks unlikely.

Consequently, I suspect that determining from a person's neuronal profile whether someone will choose a Ford Bronco or a Chevy Yukon is not a reasonable goal for the near future, although advances in technology may improve predictions. As with predicting the weather, data do narrow the range of possible outcomes, and together certain general assumptions, reasonably close predictions are possible. Predicting such matters as attentional shifts or coming to a decision may well be possible, just as one can make a very good guess where Gwynn will hit if you know Gwynn's batting history, the strengths and weaknesses of the team in the field, the pitcher's repertoire and his history in this game, and who is on base.

Should We Expect a Reduction from the Behavioral Level Directly to the Neuronal Level?

Nervous systems appear to have many levels of organization, ranging in spatial scale from molecules such as serotonin, to dendritic spines, neurons, small networks, large networks, areas, and systems. Although it remains to be determined empirically what exactly are the functionally significant levels, it is unlikely that explanations of macroeffects such as perceiving motion will be explained directly in terms of the most microlevel. More likely, high-level network effects will be the outcome of smaller networks, and those effects in turn of the participating neurons and their interconnections, and those in turn of the properties of protein channels, neuromodulators, and neurotransmitters, and so forth. One misconception about the reductionist strategy

dubs it as seeking a direct explanatory bridge between highest level and lowest levels. This idea of "explanation in a single bound" does stretch credulity, but neuroscientists are not remotely tempted by it. In contrast, the view I am advocating here prefers to predict that reductive explanations will proceed stepwise from highest to lowest, always agreeing of course that the research should proceed at all levels simultaneously (23).

USING IGNORANCE AS A PREMISE[2]

Perhaps the most common argument of those skeptical of neurobiologic progress consists of stressing what we do not know and using this as a basis for arguing about what we cannot know. McGinn, for example, repeatedly insists that the problem of how the brain could generate consciousness is "miraculous, eerie, even faintly comic" (3). Finding the problem difficult, he concludes, "This is the kind of causal nexus we are precluded from ever understanding, given the way we have to form our concepts and develop our theories" (3). McGinn is by no means alone here. Fodor, too, thinks he can already tell that the question is unanswerable—not just now, not just given what we know so far, from unanswerable ever (24). Vendler mocks the ambitions of neuroscience by saying that it is obvious, from the nature of sensation, that our conscious selves "are in principle beyond what science can explain" (1). That we are trying to unravel the mystery is, in Vendler's view, a consequence of the overweening assumption that there are no questions science cannot answer.

In general, what substantive conclusions can be drawn when science has not advanced very far on a problem? Not many. One of the basic skills we teach logic students is how to recognize and diagnose the range of nonformal fallacies that can undermine an ostensibly appealing argument: what it is to beg the question, what a non sequitur is, and so on. A prominent item in the fallacy roster is *argu-*

---

[2]Portions of this section are drawn from my article, "The Hornswoggle Problem." *J Consciousness Studies* 1996;402–8.

mentum ad ignorantiam: argument from ignorance. The canonical version of this fallacy uses ignorance as the key premise from which a substantive conclusion is drawn. For example, we really do not understand much about a phenomenon P. (Science is largely ignorant about the nature of P.) Therefore, we do know that (a) P can never be explained, or (b) nothing science could ever discover would deepen our understanding of the phenomenon P, or (c) P can never be explained in terms of properties of kind S.

In its canonical version, the argument is obviously a fallacy: none of the tendered conclusions follow, not even a little. Surrounded with rhetorical flourish, much brow furrowing, and hand-wringing, however, versions of this argument can hornswoggle the unwary (25).

From the fact that we do not know something, nothing very interesting follows: we just do not know. Nevertheless, the temptation to suspect that our ignorance is telling us something positive, something deep, something metaphysical or even radical, is ever present. Perhaps we like to put our ignorance in a positive light, supposing that but for the profundity of the phenomenon, we would have knowledge. But there are many reasons for not knowing, and the specialness of the phenomenon is, quite regularly, not the real reason. I am currently ignorant of what caused an unusual rapping noise in the woods last night. Can I conclude it must be something special, something unimaginable, something . . . alien . . . otherworldly? Evidently not. For all I can tell now, it might merely have been a raccoon gnawing on the compost bin. Lack of evidence for something is just that: lack of evidence. It is not positive evidence for something else, let alone something of a humdingerish sort. That conclusion is not very glamorous perhaps, but when ignorance is a premise, that is about all you can grind out of it.

Now if neuroscience had progressed as far on the problems of brain function as molecular biology has progressed on transmission of hereditary traits, then of course we would be in a different position. But it has not. The only thing you can conclude from the fact that at-

tention is mysterious, or sensorimotor integration is mysterious, or that consciousness is mysterious is that we do not understand the mechanisms.

Moreover, the mysteriousness of a problem is not a fact about the problem, it is not a metaphysical feature of the universe; it is an epistemologic fact about us. It is about where we are in current science, it is about what we can and cannot understand, it is about what, given the rest of our understanding, we can and cannot imagine. It is not a property of the problem itself.

It is sometimes assumed that there can be a valid transition from "we cannot now explain" to "we can never explain," so long as we have the help of a subsidiary premise, namely, "I cannot imagine how we could ever explain . . ." But it does not help, and this transition remains a straight-up application of argument from ignorance. Adding "I cannot imagine explaining P" merely adds a psychological fact about the speaker, from which again, nothing significant follows about the nature of the phenomenon in question. Whether we can or cannot imagine a phenomenon being explained in a certain way is a psychological fact about us, not an objective fact about the nature of the phenomenon itself. To repeat, it is an epistemologic fact about what, given our current knowledge, we can and cannot understand. It is not a metaphysical fact about the nature of the reality of the universe.

Typical of vitalists generally, my high school biology teacher argued for vitalism thus: I cannot imagine how you could get living things out of dead molecules. Out of bits of proteins, fats, sugars— how could life itself emerge? He thought it was obvious from the sheer mysteriousness of the matter that it could have no solution in biology or chemistry. Typical of lone survivors, a passenger of a crashed plane will say: I cannot imagine how I alone could have survived the crash, when all other passengers died instantly. Therefore, God must have plucked me from the jaws of death.

Given that neuroscience is still very much in its early stages, it is actually not a very interesting fact that someone or other cannot imagine a certain kind of explanation of some brain phenomenon. Aristotle could not imagine how a complex organism could come from a fertilized egg. That, of course, was a fact about Aristotle, not a fact about embryogenesis. Given the early days of science (500 BC), it is no surprise that he could not imagine what it took many scientists hundreds of years to discover. I cannot imagine how ravens can solve a multistep problem in one trial, or how temporal integration is achieved, or how thermoregulation is managed. But this is a (not very interesting) psychological fact about me. One could, of course, use various rhetorical devices to make it seem like an interesting fact about me, perhaps by emphasizing that it is a really, really hard problem, but if we are going to be sensible about this, it is clear that my inability to imagine how thermoregulation works is pretty boring.

The "I-cannot-imagine" gambit suffers in another way. Being able to imagine an explanation for P is a highly open-ended and underspecified business. Given the poverty of delimiting conditions of the operation, you can pretty much rig the conclusion to go whichever way your heart desires. Logically, however, that flexibility is the kiss of death.

Suppose someone claims that she can imagine the mechanisms for sensorimotor integration in the human brain but cannot imagine the mechanisms for consciousness. What exactly does this difference amount to? Can she imagine the former in detail? No, because the details are not known. What is it, precisely, that she can imagine? Suppose she answers that in a very general way she imagines that sensory neurons interact with interneurons that interact with motor neurons, and via these interactions, sensorimotor integration is achieved. Now if that is all "being able to imagine" takes, one might as well say one can imagine the mechanisms underlying consciousness. Thus, "the interneurons do it." The point is this: if you want to contrast being able to imagine brain mechanisms for attention, short-term memory, planning, etc. with being unable to imagine mechanisms for con-

sciousness, you have to do more than say you can imagine neurons doing one but cannot imagine neurons doing the other. Otherwise, one simply begs the question.

To fill out the point, consider several telling examples from the history of science. Before the turn of the 20th century, people thought that the problem of the precession of the perihelion of Mercury was essentially trivial. It was annoying, but ultimately, it would sort itself out as more data came in. With the advantage of hindsight, we can see that assessing this as an easy problem was quite wrong: it took the Einsteinian revolution in physics to solve the problem of the precession of the perihelion of Mercury. By contrast, a really hard problem was thought to be the composition of the stars. How could a sample ever be obtained? With the advent of spectral analysis, that turned out to be a readily solvable problem. When heated, the elements turn out to have a kind of fingerprint, easily seen when light emitted from a source is passed through a prism.

Consider now a biologic example. Before 1953, many people believed, on rather good grounds actually, that in order to address the copying problem (transmission of traits from parents to offspring), you would first have to solve the problem of how proteins fold. The former was deemed a much harder problem than the latter, and many scientists believed it was foolhardy to attack the copying problem directly. As we all know now, the basic answer to the copying problem lay in the base pairing of DNA, and it was solved first. It is humbling to realize that the problem of protein folding (secondary and tertiary) is still not solved. That, given the lot we now know, does seem to be a hard problem.

What is the point of these stories? They reinforce the message of the fallacy of the argument from ignorance: from the vantage point of ignorance, it is often very difficult to tell which problem is harder, which will fall first, what problem will turn out to be more tractable than some other. Consequently our judgments about relative difficulty or ultimate tractability should be appropriately qualified and tentative. Guesswork has a useful place, of course, but let us distinguish between blind guesswork and educated guesswork, and between guesswork and confirmed fact. The philosophical lesson I learned from my biology teacher is this: when not much is known about a topic, do not take terribly seriously someone else's heartfelt conviction about what problems are scientifically tractable. Learn the science, do the science, and see what happens.

When McGinn says we have been working on the problem of consciousness for a long time, he seems surprisingly innocent of what it takes to even begin to study the brain basis for the phenomenon. Whereas groundbreaking discoveries in astronomy could be made with a crude telescope, as when Galileo discovered the moons of Jupiter, figuring out how neurons do what they do requires high-level technology. And that, needless to say, depends on immense infrastructural science: on cell biology, advanced physics, and 20th century chemistry. It requires sophisticated modern notions such as molecules and proteins, as well as modern tools such as the light microscope and electron microscope.

Most importantly, making progress in how brains work depended on understanding electricity. This is because what makes brain cells special is their capacity to signal one another by causing microchanges in each others' electrical state. Living as we do in an electrical world, it is sobering to recall that as late as 1800, electricity was typically considered deeply mysterious and quite possibly occult. Only after discoveries by Ampere and Faraday at the dawn of the 19th century was electricity clearly understood to be a physical phenomenon, behaving according to well-defined laws, and capable of being harnessed for practical purposes.

Finally, consider Vendler's admonition: we cannot expect to solve all problems, answer all questions. Let us agree with him: some questions may never be answered. What follows from this as concerns the problem of the neurobiology of consciousness? Absolutely nothing. Suppose this problem is really very hard. What follows from that? Nothing. We cannot tell, from the vantage point of ignorance, that a given problem cannot be solved. Problems do not come with the information "I am unsolvable" pinned to their shirts.

CONCLUSIONS

Given the current state of cognitive science and neuroscience, it is reasonable to expect we shall understand more about the nature of consciousness as more is revealed about how in general the brain works (26). In particular, with increased understanding of the nature of sensory systems, attentional mechanisms, short-term memory, working memory, dreaming, imagery, planning, and so forth, probably the neurobiology of consciousness will come into focus (12,27,28). Clearly, we need to understand in detail the role of back projections (reentrant signaling) in such phenomena as filling in and complex pattern recognition (29). We need to understand the meaning of the physiologic data on binocular rivalry (30), as well as the significance of neuropsychological phenomena such as illusions of body image and confabulation (31,32). Undoubtedly there will be many surprises along the way, and some discoveries may cause us to reconceptualize the very problem itself. Although each of the skeptical arguments considered here command powerful intuitive appealing and for that reason alone must be taken seriously, none commands significant credence once examined and analyzed. That they are flawed does not, of course, show that neuroscience will in fact be successful in expanding our understanding of consciousness, only that the skeptics' conclusions regarding the mere possibility are unconvincing.

REFERENCES

1. Vendler Z. The ineffable soul. In: Warner R, Szubka T, eds. *The mind-body problem: a guide to the current debate.* Oxford, England: Blackwells, 1994:317–328.
2. Swinburne R. Body and soul. In: Warner R, Szubka T, eds. *The mind-body problem: a guide to the current debate.* Oxford, England: Blackwells, 1994:311–316.
3. McGinn C. Can we solve the mind-body problem? *Mind* 1989;98:349–366. [Reprinted in Warner R,

Szubka T, eds. *The mind-body problem: a guide to the current debate.* Oxford: Blackwells, 1994:99–120.]

4. Nagel T. Consciousness and objective reality. In: Warner R, Szubka T, eds. *The mind-body problem: a guide to the current debate.* Oxford: Blackwells, 1994:63–68.

5. Warner R. In defense of a dualism. In: Warner R, Szubka T, eds. *The mind-body problem: a guide to the current debate.* Oxford, England: Blackwells, 1994:343–354.

6. Churchland PM. *Matter and consciousness,* 2d ed. Cambridge, MA: MIT Press, 1987.

7. Dennett DC. *Consciousness explained.* New York: Little, Brown, 1991.

8. Flanagan O. *Consciousness reconsidered.* Cambridge, MA: MIT Press, 1992.

9. Flohr H. Qualia and brain processes. In: Beckermann A, Flohr H, Kim J, eds. *Emergence or reduction.* New York: Gruyter, 1992:220–240.

10. Kitcher P. 1953 and all that. A tale of two sciences. *Philos Rev* 1984;43:335–374.

11. Searle J. *The rediscovery of the mind.* Cambridge, MA: MIT Press, 1992.

12. Churchland PM. *The engine of reason, the seat of the soul.* Cambridge, MA: MIT Press, 1994.

13. Hobson A. *The dreaming brain.* New York: Basic Books, 1988.

14. Weiskrantz L. *Blindsight: a case study and implications.* Oxford, England: Oxford University Press, 1986.

15. Weiskrantz L. *Consciousness lost and found.* Oxford: Oxford University Press, 1997.

16. Broad CD. *The mind and its place in nature.* London: Routledge & Kegan Paul, 1951.

17. Popper K. *The self and its brain: part I.* New York: Springer-Verlag, 1978.

18. Jackson F. Epiphenomenal qualia. *Philos Q* 1982;32: 27–136.

19. Teller P. Subjectivity and knowing what it's like. In: Beckermann A, Flohr H, Kim J, eds. *Emergence or reduction.* New York: Gruyter, 1992:180–200.

20. Selverston AI, Moulins M. *The crustacean stomatogastric system: a model for the study of central nervous systems.* Berlin: Springer-Verlag, 1987.

21. Bechtel W, Richardson R. *Discovering complexity: decomposition and localization as strategies in scientific research.* Princeton, NJ: Princeton University Press, 1993.

22. Clark A. *Sensory qualities.* Oxford: Clarendon, 1993.

23. Churchland PS, Sejnowski TJ. *The computational brain.* Cambridge, MA: MIT Press, 1992.

24. Fodor J. West coast fuzzy. *Times Literary Supplement* 1995, Aug. 25:5–6.

25. Churchland PS. The hornswoggle problem. *J Consciousness Studies* 1996:402–408.

26. Llinás RR, Paré D. The brain as a closed system modulated by the senses. In: Llinás RR, Churchland PS, eds. *The mind-brain continuum.* Cambridge, MA: MIT Press, 1996:1–18.

27. Crick F. *The astonishing hypothesis.* New York: Scribner's, 1994.

28. Churchland PM. The rediscovery of light. *J Philosophy* 1996;93:211–228.

29. Edelman G. *Bright air, brilliant fire.* New York: Basic, 1992.

30. Leopold DA, Logothetis N. Activity changes in early visual cortex reflect monkeys' percepts during binocular rivalry. *Nature* 1996;379:549–553.

31. Gazzaniga MS, LeDoux JE. *The integrated brain.* New York: Plenum, 1978.

32. Ramachandran VS, Levi L, Stone L, et al. Illusions of body-image: what they reveal about human nature. In: Llinás RR, Churchland PS. *The mind-brain continuum.* Cambridge, MA: MIT Press, 1996:29–60.

33. Churchland PM, Churchland PS. Recent work on consciousness: philosophical, theoretical and empirical. *Semin Neurosci* 1997;17:101–108.

34. Van Gulick R. What would count as explaining consciousness? In: Metzinger T, ed. *Conscious experience.* Lawrence, KS: Allen Press, 1995:61–80.

DISCUSSION

Moderated by Laurent Descarries

John C. Fentress: My question is for both previous speakers perhaps. I am wondering to what extent it is useful to ask the superficially simple question, What types of operations or functions would be possible with the addition of subjective experience that would be impossible without the addition of subjective experience? The reason I ask is that potentially, if this question could be answered, it could provide some type of a bridge. If it cannot be answered, then it seems to me, as an outsider, that the bridge becomes more difficult to discover.

Patricia S. Churchland: One of the difficulties with the question is that the word "possible" is so unconstrained that it supports any hypothesis from the truly silly to the quite reasonable. Consequently, I prefer to ask what functions in fact brains use consciousness for. Other philosophers will say, "Ah yes, but I am interested in what *in principle* a brain could do without consciousness." Could there be brains on Mars that can do absolutely everything I do—including giving a talk—without consciousness? Now I am sort of a flat-footed pragmatist when you get right down to it, and my problem is that I do not have the slightest idea how to answer the question about the Martians. Not the slightest. What, other than data, can constrain our reasoning here? What I do think we can answer, and hence, because I am interested in progress, I think we should try to answer, is what functions in fact we need consciousness for. Here, I think the work that Ben Libet, for example, has done concerning planning and decision making and its prior activity is very interesting. But I am really very wary of asking the "possible" question if it means what *in principle* is possible, because that is one of those things that philosophers call thought experiments. The trouble with philosophers' thought experiments is that there is typically too much thought and not enough experiment.

Stuart R. Hameroff: Since, thus far at least, consciousness only exists in living systems, your comments about life are very interesting. Are you implying that the problem of the nature of life was solved with the genetic code in 1953?

Patricia S. Churchland: I was not actually implying exactly that, but I think people should have thought by 1953 that they might want to rethink vitalism as a theory of the nature of life.

Stuart R. Hameroff: The point is that even if you know the primary amino-acid sequence of a protein, you have not solved the folding problem, the conformational states, and so forth. This is a very good example of a reductionist approach which fails. We cannot understand how proteins work. We do not really know what life is. For example, how do we know that life does not involve a quantal process?

Patricia S. Churchland: It is true that we do not have complete reductions. In my reduction slide I made that very point. Everywhere in science there are residual questions. My concern is this: should we take the residual questions as being a sign that we have to postulate a whole new universe of entities like souls or experience? Or should we keep working? Now it is probably a good idea in science to have people working on different sides of the problem and pushing different theories as hard as they can. Scientifically, however, it has been very difficult to be a vitalist since the advent of molecular biology. I think it is actually becoming extremely difficult to be a dualist as well. But I am sure you could manage it if you really tried.

Stuart R. Hameroff: Vitalism implies that life involves some laws which do not follow the laws of science or different laws. Even then, and the same applies to consciousness, there may be underlying science that has not been discovered yet.

Patricia S. Churchland: Yes, there could be. I am just betting on the brain as the basis for consciousness at this point.

Jeffrey A. Gray: I just wanted to come back to the question raised a little while ago: If we could only know what it is that you can do with and without conscious experience, we would be a long way forward. Of course that is correct, but I do not think we actually know the answer to that question. I am not talking about philosophical thought experiments, I am just talking about the experimental facts. Benjamin Libet has already mentioned Max Velmans's very important review in about 1991 in *Behavioral and Brain Sciences,* where he went through the experimental evidence from a large number of different psychological (mainly) paradigms, and showed one after the other

that all of the things that we have the illusion of doing—using conscious experience as an essential component of achieving something—all of those things are done without conscious experience necessarily intervening in the doing. The conscious experience always comes afterwards, too late. And the truth of the answer to that question is that we do not know at present, as a matter of flat-footed pragmatism, Patricia, what it is that conscious experience brings to the party.

Patricia S. Churchland: I absolutely agree, which is why I said in answer to John Fentress's question that I think experimental work is where we can actually make progress. Experimental as opposed to this other sort of "dreamy-what-if" stuff which I am not very interested in.

Lofti B. Merabet: You talked about this vantage point of ignorance that should not be used as an excuse not to attack the problem of consciousness. I think that is right. Nonetheless, why is it that even today some people we call the mysterians, like McGinn and so on, do believe that we cannot understand consciousness much in the same way that rats cannot understand calculus.

Patricia S. Churchland: Yes, that is the Colin McGinn argument. You can work on the little rat and really try to get him up to speed, but he is just not going to understand calculus. Now, how does McGinn know that we are like the rat vis-à-vis the problem of consciousness? I mean, maybe he is right, but what precisely is the evidence? How could you know, especially at this early stage? Now, one of the points McGinn makes is, "Gee, you know, we have been working on this problem a long time and we have not made progress, so that should count as evidence that we are like the rats vis-à-vis the question of consciousness." In fact, we have not actually been scientifically working on it all that long. Bear in mind that it was easy for really revolutionary discoveries to be made in astronomy with quite simple tools. Galileo did it with a very crude telescope. It was quite easy to make progress in basic chemistry using very simple tools. To make significant progress in neuroscience, you had to have very sophisticated technology, meaning you already had to have a very sophisticated science. You cannot figure out what neurons are and how neurons work unless you at least know what electricity is, and that did not come about until about the 1850s. In the early part of the 1800s, people really did not understand what electricity was—many of them thought that it was a kind of occult force. Nobody had the slightest idea that electricity was probably the critical thing to understand in order to understand the nature of the brain. It is really only in the very recent past that we have come to have significant tools and techniques, such as microelectrodes, staining, imaging, to really begin to address the problem. We are still lacking certain crucial techniques. We need to be able to do something like multi-electrode single-cell recording in humans in a safe way that does not violate our ethical principles. We currently have no technique for getting that kind of information. In sum, I think it is obvious that there is not one shred of evidence in support of McGinn's hypothesis. He is using what we do not know as a basis for claiming what we cannot know. That is a logical fallacy.

*Consciousness: At the Frontiers of Neuroscience,
Advances in Neurology,* Vol. 77,
edited by H.H. Jasper, L. Descarries,
V.F. Castellucci, and S. Rossignol.
Lippincott–Raven Publishers, Philadelphia © 1998.

4

Sensory Information and Conscious Experience

Herbert H. Jasper

*Department of Physiology, Université de Montréal,
Montreal, Quebec, H3T 1J4, Canada*

By way of introduction, I would like to recount how Edward G. Jones and I happen to be associated in the same part of this symposium on consciousness. Dr. Ted Jones has been a close friend and colleague for many years, dating from before he moved from Washington University in St. Louis by a devious route to his present position as Professor of Neuroanatomy and Neurobiology at the University of California in Irvine.

We were drawn together by his outstanding work on the cerebral cortex and thalamocortical relationships and his kindness in citing my electrophysiologic studies on the thalamic reticular system in his book on the cerebral cortex and in special sessions of the Society for Neuroscience, which he organized in my honor over the years. He participated in international meetings held in Montreal when he was a guest in our home, and became a personal friend of my wife, Mary Lou, as well.

More recently, Ted and I were associated with a Neuroscience Research Program (NRP) Colloquium held in 1980 at the Marine Biological Laboratories in the Woods Hole Marine Biological Laboratories in Woods Hole, Massachusetts. I had been working with Francis O. Schmidt on several NRP events over the years, especially for the symposium held in honor of his 70th birthday at the Kresge auditorium of the Massachusetts Institute of Technology in October 1973 (1).

Frank Schmidt had subsequently asked me, together with Floyd Bloom, Maxwell Cowan, Gerald Edelman, Ann Graybiel, Brenda Milner, and Pasko Rakic, to take part in a penultimate session of the Program on the higher functions of the cerebral cortex to be entitled The Organization of the Cerebral Cortex (2). This was in 1979, a time when I was also actively engaged in the series of Annual International Symposia organized by our Centre de Recherche en Sciences Neurologiques at the University of Montreal.

At the NRP Colloquium, published by MIT Press in 1981, Dr. Jones gave a fascinating lecture entitled "Anatomy of Cerebral Cortex: Columnar Input-Output Organization," in the section Organization and Connections of the Neocortex (3). In this report, he described observations on thalamic afferents from the intralaminar nuclei of the thalamus to various cortical areas, visualized by the method of retrograde axonal tracing with horseradish peroxidase. He had thus found a direct cortical projection from cells in intralaminar thalamic nuclei. The cells of origin for this projection were distributed just as we had described them by electrophysiologic techniques in our previous work on the thalamic reticular system. This won me an apology from a well-known neuroanatomist, who had doubted our findings in the past. It gave me even more confidence in the existence and importance of the thalamic reticular system as an entity separate from the cortical afferents arising from specific thalamic nuclei. It was little wonder, therefore, that Ted Jones and I became associated in this symposium on brain mechanisms of consciousness.

THE THALAMIC RECRUITING SYSTEM

We had begun immediately after the second world war, in 1946, a series of studies with refined stereotaxic methods, aiming to confirm and extend the work of Morison and Dempsey on the recruiting system of the thalamus, and that of Moruzzi and Magoun on the reticular activating system of the brain stem. We were fortunate in having a flood of excellent research fellows joining us, including Jan Droogleever-Fortuyn from The Netherlands, Cosimo Ajmone-Marsan from Italy, John Hunter from Australia, and Gus Stoll and John Hanbery from the United States, among others.

We were soon able to confirm and extend the excellent work of Morison and Dempsey by demonstrating conclusively that there was a separate neuronal system in the intralaminar nuclei of the thalamus that could control the spontaneous electrical activity of the entire cerebral cortex and made important connections with the basal ganglia. With Jan Doogleever-Fortuyn, an accomplished neuroanatomist from The Netherlands, we mapped this recruiting system in the thalamus and its organized distribution to various areas of the cerebral cortex.

In collaboration with a neurosurgical fellow, Dr. John Hanbery, we also showed that the projection of thalamocortical fibers responsible for recruiting responses from intralaminar regions was independent of the specific thalamic nuclei, because these responses persisted after the total electrocoagulation of these nuclei in the cat (4). Cortical evoked potentials after discrete local stimulation within the intralaminar thalamus were produced after long latencies of about 20 milliseconds, compared with only 1- to 2-mil-

lisecond latencies for cortical responses after stimulation of the specific thalamic nuclei. Obviously, the system of thalamocortical afferents mediating the recruiting response was distinct from that mediating specific sensory signals (Figs. 1 and 2).

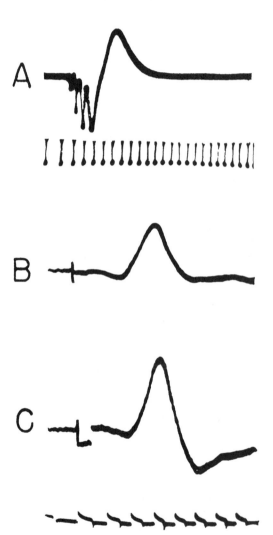

FIG. 1. A: Oscilloscope records of a typical specific primary evoked potential complex in visual cortex in the cat after about 1 millisecond latency after a single brief shock to the lateral geniculate nucleus in the thalamus. B and C: Responses from the same site in the visual cortex with much longer latency (about 20 milliseconds) after stimulation of the intralaminar nuclei of the thalamus, nucleus ventralis lateralis (B), and nucleus centralis lateralis (C).

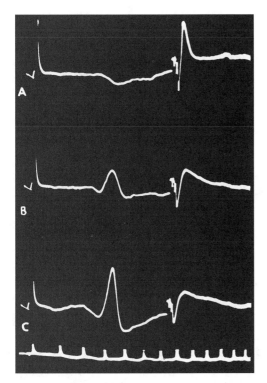

FIG. 2. Oscilloscope records of interaction of recruiting and specific visual sensory responses to lateral geniculate stimulation in the cat. **A:** A small recruiting response in the visual cortex after intralaminar thalamic stimulation followed by a large specific response to lateral geniculate stimulation. **B:** Beginning of recruiting response with over 20 milliseconds latency followed 40 milliseconds later by diminished specific sensory visual cortex response. **C:** A larger surface negative recruiting response followed by a further decrease in the specific response in the visual cortex. Time line, 10 milliseconds.

The schematic diagram in Fig. 3 depicted the areas in the cat thalamus from which recruiting responses were obtained. For these experiments, we had used especially constructed stereotaxic stimulating electrodes with closely spaced bipolar fine insulated wires sealed into a hypodermic steel needle electrode, which was grounded to reduce the spread of current. The steel needle was inserted along stereotaxic coordinates by means of a calibrated stereotaxic frame carrying a micromanipulator for accurate placement of the stimulation. It proved very accurate indeed, because a change from a specific short-latency response to a longer latency recruiting response would occur by moving the electrode by only about 100 μm. Note that this diagram was drawn before it was shown by the Scheibels that the rim of reticular nucleus surrounding the thalamus contained cells that send their axons back into the thalamus and not to the cortex, as do the many thalamocortical projection fibers within which they are enmeshed. Nowadays, these cells are known to be uniformly GABAergic (see Chapter 8).

I would like to point out that there were several regions adjacent to specific nuclei but outside the histologic boundaries of the intralaminar nuclei that also gave good recruiting responses, namely the suprageniculate nucleus, the paramedial nucleus adjacent to the nucleus medialis dorsalis and so on (Fig. 3). These additional areas evoking recruiting responses may possibly correspond to the additional thalamic areas that are now being described by Ted Jones after calbindin immunostaining (see Chapter 5) and which project rather diffusely to layers I and II of cerebral cortex. It is obvious that the recruiting response zone is not confined to the classical intralaminar nuclei of the thalamus and, from my experience, that the more posterior parts of the reticular nucleus should not be included in the recruiting system.

States of Reactivity of Specific Systems Controlled by Stimulation of the Recruiting System

My own contribution to the Woods Hole Symposium in 1979 was entitled "Problems of Relating Cellular and Modular Specificity to Cognitive Functions: Importance of State-Dependent Reactions" (5). We then reported that the state of reactivity of the cortex could be controlled by the nonspecific afferents from the thalamus. For example, upon stimulation of the motor cortex with subthreshold currents with no motor response, the same currents produced large responses after simultaneous stimulation of the intralaminar

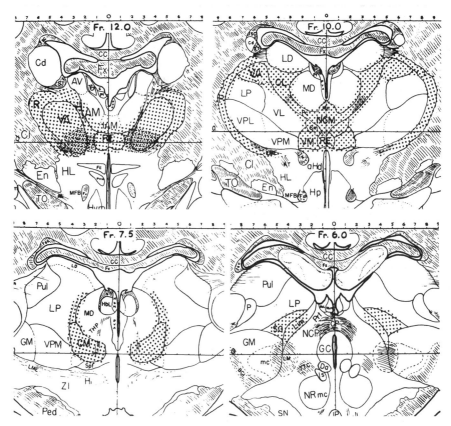

FIG. 3. Schematic diagrams of four frontal planes of the cat thalamus: Fr-12, Fr-10, Fr-7.5, and Fr-6.0. Stippled areas represent locations of sites where recruiting responses were obtained summarizing many carefully calibrated points verified by histologic studies. The lateral extension of the reticular nucleus in Fr-10 did not produce generalized recruiting responses and should not have been stippled. Double stippling in the VA thalamic nucleus was an area in which anteriorly conducting pathways were most dense. Note that some areas were not within intralaminar nuclei, but adjacent to specific nuclei such as the nucleus suprageniculatus (SG) in Fr-6.0. Cd, caudate; Cl, centralis lateralis; CM, centrum medianum; HL, hypothalamus; LD, lateralis dorsalis; LP, lateralis posterior; MD, medialis dorsalis; NCM, centralis medialis; Pul, pulvinar; R, reticularis; RE, reuniens; SG, suprageniculate; VA, ventralis anterior; VL, ventralis lateralis; VM, ventralis medialis; VPL, ventralis posterolateralis; VPM, ventralis posteromedialis.

thalamus, indicating a remarkable increase in reactivity of the motor cortex (Fig. 4).

I quoted experiments by Evarts and Tanji, in which they had conditioned monkeys to respond in an opposite manner, push or pull, for a food reward to the same stimulus (a slight flexion of the paw), while recording pyramidal cell discharge in the motor cortex. A red or green light was flashed 2 to 4 seconds before the flexor stimulus. After the red light, reward was given following a "pull" response, whereas after the green light, reward followed the "push" response. The pyramidal cells that fired during the pull response after the red light were inhibited in response to the same stimulus after the green light. This was a beautiful example of a state-dependent response in opposite direction to the direct response to the same stimulus.

I also cited experiments of Serge Rossignol on spinal cats treated with clonidine, in which electromyograms were taken from flexor and

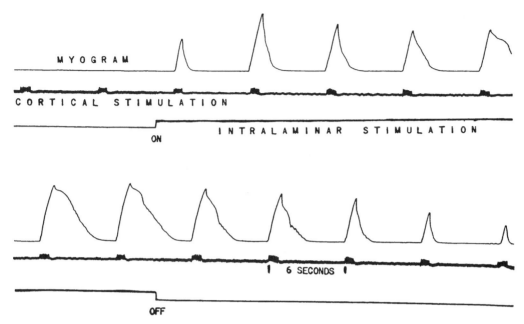

FIG. 4. Facilitation of motor cortical reponses to subliminal electrical stimulation by simultaneous stimulation of the intralaminar thalamus to produce recruiting response in motor cortex. Motor responses were recorded from muscles contracting in response to the motor cortex and intralaminar stimulation. Note that the facilitation outlasted the intralaminar stimulation by about 40 seconds.

extensor muscles of both legs while the animal was walking on a treadmill. Flexor responses were obtained to a light pressure on the paw when the leg was in the flexion phase, but the same stimulus produced an extensor response if the leg was in the extension phase of the walking cycle. The reactive state of the spinal cord during walking thus produced a complete reversal in the reflex response to the same stimulus.

In electrophysiologic experiments with Costa Stefanis in our laboratories at the Montreal Neurological Institute, we had obtained intracellular recordings from pyramidal tract neurons during stereotaxic stimulation of the intralaminar thalamus. Sustained depolarization was produced in the pyramidal cells by intralaminar stimulation, as well as spike discharges coincident with the recruiting waves of the surface cortical recruiting response (6). Using a similar technique, Dan Pollen in our laboratories was able to show that the slow wave of the spike-and-wave response to three-per-second stimulation of the intralaminar thala-

mus was associated with a prolonged hyperpolarizing inhibitory potential in pyramidal cells, sufficient to completely block their response to incoming sensory stimuli (7). This generalized inhibition of cortical cells, as in epileptic petit mal seizures in humans, had profound effects on the state of consciousness of the animal.

With Cosimo Ajmone-Marsan and other colleagues, we could then demonstrate in complementary studies that the cerebral cortex itself projects back to those areas of the intralaminar thalamus and brain stem that are part of this widely distributed system of neurons involved in setting the reactive states of the brain related to states of consciousness (8).

Recruiting Responses in Sensory Cortical Areas

During the summer after the Laurentian Symposium of 1954 on Brain Mechanisms and Conscious Experience, Dr. Magoun invited us to his laboratories in California to attempt to resolve a problem raised regarding

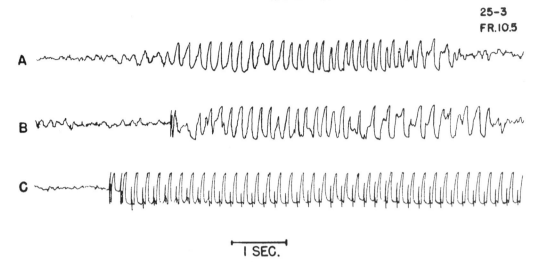

FIG. 5. Recruiting responses during single and repetitive stimuli to the intralaminar thalamus in the lightly anesthetized cat. Recording electrical activity with implanted bipolar electrodes over the pericruciate cortex at rest (**A**), after a single 1-millisecond electrical pulse to the intralaminar thalamus (**B**), and during five-per-second stimulation of the intralaminar thalamus (**C**).

the lack of recruiting responses in sensory receiving areas of the cortex. I was joined by Robert Naquet, whom I had known in Henri Gastaut's laboratories in Marseille and with Elizabeth King from Magoun's laboratory.

We were able to find good recruiting responses in cortical sensory receiving areas, providing the animals were given small doses of phenobarbital to decrease their alertness during the experiment (Fig. 5). The recruiting responses were apparently blocked by alerting responses in cats, just as the alpha waves are blocked in the human electroencephalogram (EEG) (9).

NEUROCHEMICAL STUDIES

Numerous transmitter-defined systems are likely to be engaged in mediating the so-called "unspecific" effects of subcortical regions on cortical activity. For many years, I was fortunate in being closely associated with an outstanding neurochemist by the name of K.A.C. Elliott, director of the Donner Neurochemical Laboratories of the Montreal Neurological Institute of McGill University. I was then able to collaborate with him and several

of his students and colleagues in order to combine our electrophysiologic studies with measures of the neurochemical substances liberated at the same time as we recorded gross and microphysiologic activity from the same cortical tissue. We used a superfusion technique for the collection of extracellular fluid liberated from cortical tissues being studied. Subsequently, we also used microiontophoretic techniques to study the effect of the injection of small amounts of neurochemical substances in the vicinity of the recording microelectrodes. I can give only a brief summary of some of the results of these studies at this time. We began with studies of acetylcholine and then proceeded with studies of the amino acids and the monoamines. Principal colleagues in these studies were K.A.C. Elliott, Leon Wolfe, Gastone Celesia, and Nico Van Gelder. I was then joined at the University of Montreal by Ikuko Koyama from Japan and by Tomás Reader from Argentina.

Acetylcholine

There was consistently a marked (severalfold) increase in the concentration of acetylcholine in extracellular cortical fluid during arousal from sleep produced by sensory stimulation or electrical stimulation of the brain stem reticular system (10–12).

Amino Acids

Arousal produced a consistent increase in excitatory amino acids, glutamate and aspartate, and in some instances a decrease in the inhibitory amino acid, gamma amino butyric acid, GABA (13,14).

Monoamines

Arousal was associated with a decrease in the liberation of noradrenaline, serotonin and dopamine, simultaneously with the increase in acetylcholine (15–17).

These results provided convincing evidence that neurochemical substances played an important role in controlling the state of consciousness and arousal in experimental animals. They were obviously only preliminary, but a comprehensive summary of neurochemical controls in cerebral cortex was to be the subject of a symposium held in Montreal, in honor of my 80th birthday, in July 1986.

This international symposium, organized by Massimo Avoli, Tomás Reader, Robert Dykes, and Pierre Gloor, was entitled Neurotransmitters and Cortical Function, From Molecules to Mind (18). It brought together leading workers in many fields of neuroscience, most of whom were friends and colleagues I had known well over the years. There were 75 outstanding contributors, and the publication comprised 38 chapters in all, including a final report entitled "Molecular Controls and Communication in Cerebral Cortex," in which I was able to join my colleagues to give my impressions of the whole symposium, a most pleasant task (19).

Neuropeptides

During this symposium, several presentations addressed the anatomy and physiology of the neuropeptides. These many substances have taken increasing importance in the regulation of the excitatory states of the brain, as modulators of the classical, more rapid neurotransmitter actions. Neuropeptides are often found combined with classical neurotransmitters in the same axonal terminals. They produce longer lasting actions, in part because there is no uptake mechanism once they are released in the synaptic cleft. Their actions may be complex, including intracellular effects on nerve metabolism and growth, often through second messengers such as adenylyl cyclase.

As cotransmitters, the peptides usually enhance primary transmitter actions, but they also can have distinctive behavioral effects of their own, such as effects on thirst (angiotensin), feeding behavior (neuropeptide Y and galanin), and pain perception (the enkephalins). They also may have important actions on general arousal, attention, and motivation. Peptides also may be implicated in learning and memory storage (20).

EEG PATTERNS AND STATES OF CONSCIOUSNESS

Habituation of the Arousal Response in Cats

Investigation of the electrical activity of the brain during the arousal response to sleep in cats was made possible by a study carried out with Seth Sharpless, then a postdoctoral student in Donald Hebb's Department of Psychology at McGill University (21). Under phenobarbital anesthesia, we implanted insulated wired recording electrodes throughout the brain in cortical and subcortical regions, including the auditory cortex. The electrical activity was recorded from all of these regions simultaneously, several days later. We found that they all showed large slow waves when the cats were asleep. All regions showed the arousal EEG pattern with no slow waves when the animals were awakened. The cats were aroused by a well-controlled auditory stimulus delivered from a tape recorder so that it could be repeated in identical form time after time in a sound-insulated laboratory. These experiments were conducted after midnight so as not to be disturbed by accidental sounds.

Repetition of a given tone, e.g., at 500 Hz, 20 or 30 times caused complete habituation and disappearance of the electrical arousal response to this tone. Then any change in the tone, e.g., to a 100-Hz tone, would immediately awaken the animal with an arousal response in the EEG from all brain regions. Also, after habituation to one tone, the cat could be awakened by a slight puff of air on the face. Habituation was remarkably specific to one stimulus. This showed that the brain was perceiving the nature of the sensory stimuli accurately even when it was deeply asleep (Fig. 6).

We then used a series of clicks to which the animals could also become habituated by repetition, with arousal disappearing in 20 to 30 trials. In this way, we could record the evoked potentials from the auditory cortex during the habituation process. We found that auditory cortical evoked potentials continued as large as before, even increased slightly, although the arousal response was completely absent (Fig. 7). This showed that the arousal response was controlled by systems of neurons throughout the brain that were independent of specific sensory cortical systems, which continued to function adequately even during deep sleep. The cats would awaken immediately, however, with a slight change in the stimulus frequency, or the substitution of a puff of air for the sound.

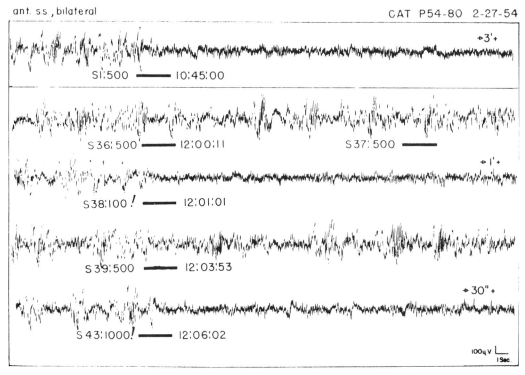

FIG. 6. Cortical electrograms from implanted electrodes in the cat during habituation of the arousal response to auditory tones of different frequencies administered during sleep. The first tracing shows the arousal response in suprasylvian gyrus to the first presentation of a 500-Hz tone. The second tracing shows habituation with no arousal response to the same tone after 37 presentations, S37:500. The third tracing shows an arousal response to a novel tone, S38:100. In the fourth tracing, the 500-Hz tone is repeated: S39:500 shows persistence of habituation to this tone. The fourth tracing is a subsequent arousal response to a novel tone, S43:1000.

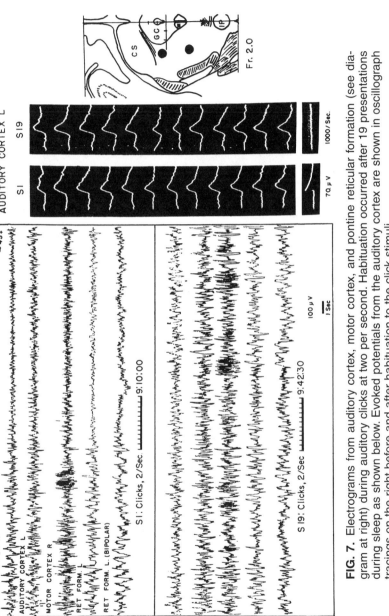

FIG. 7. Electrograms from auditory cortex, motor cortex, and pontine reticular formation (see diagram at right) during auditory clicks at two per second. Habituation occurred after 19 presentations during sleep as shown below. Evoked potentials from the auditory cortex are shown in oscillograph tracings on the right before and after habituation to the click stimuli.

We concluded that there had to be a separate neuronal system in control of the arousal response, apparently independent of the specific sensory systems mediating responses of sensory cortex. Habituation of the arousal response could be abolished only by changing the stimulus or by discrete lesions in the pontine reticular formation bilaterally. Removal of the entire auditory cortex bilaterally did not abolish the habituation to repeated auditory stimuli.

These experiments, although quite laborious to perform, did demonstrate that states of sleep and arousal were controlled mostly by the pontine reticular formation, not by primary sensory pathways to cerebral cortex, except when fine frequency discriminations were required, necessitating cortical sensory receiving areas as well. Habituation of the arousal response did not significantly alter cortical sensory evoked potentials arriving in the primary auditory cortex.

Electrophysiologic Studies in Humans

In human subjects, as well as in cats and in primates, the electrical activity of the brain could be recorded with gross and single-unit microelectrodes in response to sensory stimulation during states of conscious alertness or unconsciousness, which were assessed by judging the behavioral activity as normal or abnormal. The EEG pattern had been found to be a reliable objective indicator of the general state of consciousness as well as of states of local activation. Rapid eye movement (REM) sleep and alpha coma were special exceptions, indicating special forms of sleep and coma. Local sensory evoked potentials were recorded from specific cortical sensory receiving areas in response to detailed qualities of the stimulus pattern, even when administered during barbiturate anesthesia which precluded conscious experience. Millions of synaptic events thus occurred in the brain without conscious awareness of them, although they conveyed unconscious information of importance to the maintenance of bodily functions and homeostasis.

During sleep, even in the presence of loud noises to which one may be accustomed, sleep may not be disturbed except by certain stimuli that one has learned to be of special importance, such as the cry of a baby for his mother or hearing one's own name unexpectedly. A novel stimulus in a noisy environment or even a decrease in the noise to which one is accustomed may cause awakening. On the other hand, a stimulus that has been linked to some important emotional or painful experience may cause awakening from deep sleep, indicating that the brain can understand the meaning of some sensory information even during deep sleep.

Microelectrode Stereotaxic Studies of the Firing of Single Cells in the Human Thalamus of Awake Patients During Surgical Operations for Dyskinesia

In collaboration with Dr. Gilles Bertrand, at the Montreal Neurological Institute, we were able to study the firing of single neurons in the human thalamus. The recordings were obtained in awake patients, during operations for the treatment of dyskinesias such as Parkinson's disease. We were able to see, to hear, and to record the firing of single thalamic cells while exploring many areas throughout the thalamus using a tungsten microelectrode and a special stereotaxic technique (Fig. 8). We could then discover areas where the cell would be firing in synchrony with the tremor as well as with voluntary movements and in response to sensory stimulation. The patient would be able to respond verbally to his or her conscious experiences throughout the operation. The technique and results of these studies have been published in a series of papers with Dr. Bertrand (22–25).

Dr. Bertrand was able to learn the firing patterns of cells and fibers in different regions of the human thalamus as a guide to the location of the microelectrode. Light touch would produce responses in cells in the sensory nuclei, ventralis posterior and anterior. From the intralaminar nuclei, discharges would be

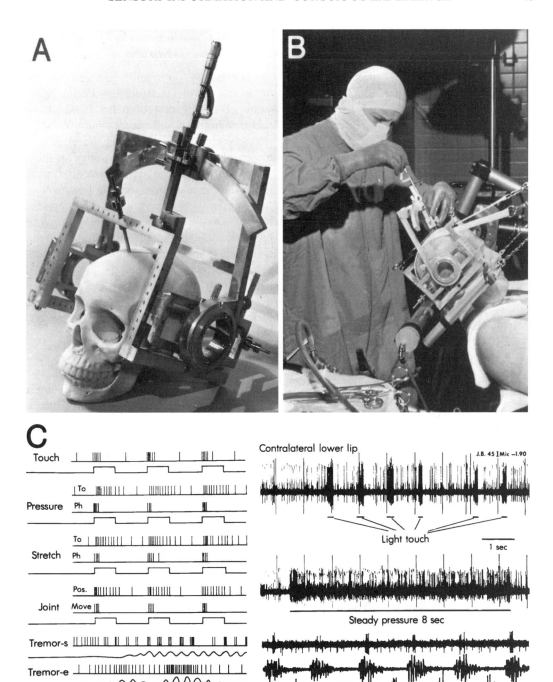

FIG. 8. Microelectrode stereotaxic studies of the firing of single cells in the human thalamus in waking patients during operations for dyskinesia with Dr. Gilles Bertrand. **A:** The stereotaxic instrument attached to a skull. **B:** Dr. Bertrand adjusting the microelectrode with apparatus attached to a human patient. **C:** Diagramatic illustration of various forms of unit responses to sensory stimulation, spontaneous tremor, and voluntary movement (*left*). Oscilloscope records of sensory responses (light touch and steady pressure) and during spontaneous tremor as related to electromyograms of tremor movements (*right*), and the movements themselves (*below*).

recorded from light stimulation of the hand at first, but would disappear on repetition and could not be confirmed, as though habituated to repeated stimulation. We called these cells "novelty detectors," probably related to the habituation of the arousal reaction observed with Seth Sharpless. This was in marked contrast to the cells in the sensory nuclei, which would respond to even a very light touch that the patient might not even feel if he or she was being distracted at the time. These studies gave a most dramatic view of the functional properties of various parts of the human thalamus in relation to conscious experience and voluntary movement.

STUDIES OF EPILEPTIC BRAIN

Reproduction of the Three-per-Second Bilateral Spike-and-Wave Pattern of Petit Mal Epilepsy

In addition to the confirmation in more detail of the recruiting responses of Morison and Dempsey by stimulation of the intralaminar thalamus and some additional zones, Jan Doogleever-Fortuyn and I were able to reproduce with a 3-Hz stimulus, to our surprise, the three-per-second spike and wave very similar to that seen in petit mal or "absence" epileptic seizures, which are characterized by a sudden loss of consciousness (Fig. 9)[1]. With the help of John Hunter, we also were able to produce behavioral absence or "arrest" attacks in unanesthetized monkeys by stimulation of the intralaminar thalamus at three per second during recording from the cortex bilaterally with implanted electrodes (28). These attacks were similar to those seen in epileptic patients during petit mal seizures.

---

[1]These results were presented at the meeting of the Association for Research in Nervous and Mental Diseases in New York, in 1946 (26). Morison was present at this meeting, together with many other notable neurologists and neuroscientists. Penfield also was there to present our views on "Highest Level Seizures" (27). It was at the meeting of this same organization, in 1952, that Penfield presented the hypothesis of the centrencephalic integrating system and centrencephalic seizures.

Loss of Consciousness in Epileptiform Seizures

I also had the opportunity to investigate the apparent loss of consciousness during many years of observation of many hundreds of seizures during electroencephalographic studies or during experiments on the effects of electrical stimulation and recording from exposed human cortex. These records were taken during operations for the treatment of focal epilepsy by Dr. Penfield. The apparent loss of consciousness during many forms of epileptic seizure supports important conclusions regarding brain mechanisms of consciousness, although it may be misleading if the nature of the apparent loss of consciousness is not carefully analyzed in the various forms of seizure. There seem to be several mechanisms involved (29).

Inhibitory Seizures

The classical absence or petit mal seizure is characterized by only an apparent loss of consciousness for a brief period of time (10 to 20 seconds). It may last longer in some patients, and in some it progresses to a generalized convulsive seizure. The patient suddenly stops moving, which we have called the arrest reaction, when reproduced in animals. He or she no longer speaks or responds to questions and stares into space with slight clonic twitches of his eye lids and sometimes of the face bilaterally. The EEG shows the classical bilaterally synchronous, three-per-second spike-and-wave pattern.

Our microelectrode studies have shown that the brief spike is excitatory and the long slow wave is associated with a profound hyperpolarization and inhibition of cortical nerve cells. When patients are tested during an attack, there may be an upgoing plantar reflex with inability to move the legs on command. In some cases, after an attack, we have asked patients why they did not reply. They would say they heard us but could not speak. After the termination of the spike-and-wave in the EEG, they would quickly return to normal in most cases. Their plantar reflexes were normal, with upgoing

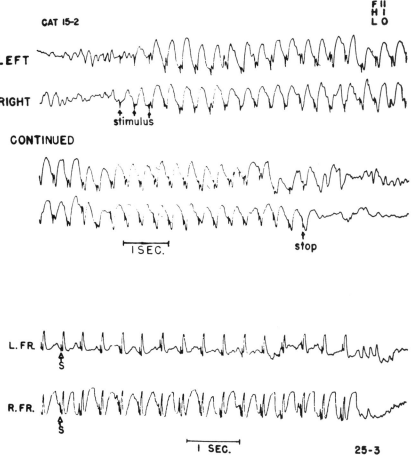

FIG. 9. Reproduction of the three-per-second spike-and-wave pattern of petit mal (absence) epileptic seizures by intralaminar thalamic stimulation (n. centrum medianum) at a frequency of 3 Hz. The two tracings below were taken from gyrus proreus in response to 3-Hz stimulation of nucleus centralis lateralis, showing some assymetry in the form of the spike-and-wave complex in the left and right frontal cortices in the cat.

toes, and they could stand and walk. It seemed that this was not a complete loss of consciousness but mostly a profound inhibition and arrest of speech with some preservation of memory. In other cases, there was an apparently complete loss of consciousness and amnesia for the period of the attack.

Amnesia and Disruption of Normal Integrative Functions

Amnesia forms an important part of temporal lobe seizures. At the beginning of their attacks, the subjects may be able to respond to questions with only a little confusion in replies. As the attack progresses, they cease to respond normally and may have complete amnesia with the major attack. However, in some cases after brief attacks, the patients may remember the questions they were asked during the confusion or aura at the beginning of the attack, during which time they were apparently still conscious. The combination of psychical disturbances with automatic movements gave rise to the description of such seizures as "psychomotor."

The epileptic discharge may disrupt the normal functions of a given cortical area causing aphasia or other defects simulating a loss of consciousness. Epileptiform discharge or electrical stimulation within Broca's speech area causes aphasia, never speech, but without a true loss of consciousness. Penfield and I have described many such cases in our book *Epilepsy and the Functional Anatomy of the Human Brain* (29).

Centrencephalic and Corticoreticular Seizures

Penfield's view of a centrencephalic integrating system and centrencephalic seizures has received much criticism from many sources. This system had never been given any precise anatomic identity except hypothetically. After much reconsideration, Penfield thought there might be several centrencephalic systems, and a separate one for voluntary movements. He also thought that the limbic system might be involved, as suggested by Walle Nauta (30).

David Prince and David Farrel (1969) had found that the spike-and-wave pattern, similar to that which characterized petit mal epilepsy, could be produced by the injection of large amounts of penicillin into experimental animals (31). This was taken up by Peter Gloor at the Montreal Neurological Institute, who performed many studies attempting to prove that such penicillin-generalized seizures were of cortical, not subcortical, origin. He introduced the term "corticoreticular seizures." He attempted to prove over many years that this term was more accurate than Penfield's term "centrencephalic seizures." (32).

Finally, in 1983, Massimo Avoli, George Kostopoulus, and Jean Gotman, postdoctoral fellows in Peter Gloor's EEG Department, conducted an excellent study of penicillin seizures with multiple microelectrodes simultaneously recording from cortical and thalamic regions in cats. They were able to show that such seizures involved groups of single neurons in the thalamus as well as in the cortex (33). The onset could be either in the thalamus or cortex. There was obviously a close interrelationship between the two possible origins that was quite consistent with Penfield's view of "centrencephalic seizures."

I was then asked by my former student, Gastone Celesia, then editor of the *EEG Journal,* to provide a guest editorial on the subject of a "Current Evaluation of the Concepts of Centrencephalic and Corticoreticular Seizures" (34). In this article, I gave a complete account of Penfield's views, which he had modified over the years to reply to much criticism. I expressed doubts that penicillin seizures could be considered a good model for petit mal epilepsy in humans because there was no evidence of a convulsant drug, such as penicillin, in patients with petit mal epilepsy. Also, there was much recent evidence that such seizures could be more accurately reproduced in animals by stereotaxic stimulation of the thalamus and brain stem, as shown by several of my postdoctoral fellows at the Institute. Two were neurosurgeons, Phanor Perot and Bryce Weir, and two were neurophysiologists, Dan Pollen and Ken Reid. They did not need penicillin to regularly reproduce an exact duplicate of the petit mal spike-and-wave bilateral cortical discharge together with petit mal–like epileptiform attacks by stereotaxically accurate placement of stimulating electrodes in the intralaminar thalamus and simultaneously in the pontine reticular formation. They found that paired stimulation of the pons with a series of repeated conditioning shocks preceding each in a series of single shocks to the intralaminar thalamus regularly reproduced the bilateral spike-and-wave of petit mal epilepsy. These studies (35–38) were reviewed in my guest editorial.

I concluded this review as follows:

Reflecting upon these conclusions, while writing this review for my old friend and student, Gastone Celesia, I am not sure we should continue using the concept of "centrencephalic seizures," but I am sure that there is no good reason for exchanging it for corticoreticular seizures. There are many centrencephalic systems involved in the highest level integrations underlying conscious mental life and the control of goal-directed behavior. Many widely distributed cell assemblies and neurochemical mechanisms are involved in centrencephalic integration as proposed by Penfield. It is perhaps better to describe the attacks objectively as "primarily generalized" (with initial loss of consciousness) rather than to use terms with anatomical connotations which are as yet unknown or uncertain.

THE BRAIN–MIND PROBLEM

In his last publication, *The Mystery of the Mind,* Penfield reached the conclusion that the brain–mind problem could not be solved because he had spent his entire life trying to do so without success (39). He allowed that conscious experience might be a separate form of reality. He suggested that I might be wasting my time seeking answers in electrophysiologic or neurochemical functions of the brain, even though there were obviously close relationships.

I am not prepared to agree with Penfield that there may be no solutions to the brain–mind problem, although I do agree that we have not yet found that illusive link between the special brain mechanisms involved in conscious awareness and mental activity. I do believe that there is some neuronal organization specialized for this purpose, widely distributed throughout the brain and varying with the behavioral activities at each moment in the stream of consciousness, many centrencephalic mechanisms if you will, but they are too vague at present to be used to describe different forms of epileptic attack in the present state of our knowledge. However, the search is becoming more and more exciting and worth the effort despite its bewildering complexity.

I have become convinced during the writing of this manuscript that there are distributed systems of neurons in the brain stem, diencephalon, and cerebral cortex that are of particular importance in the control of states of consciousness and perceptual awareness. Physiologic studies of these systems show that they operate much slower than the specific sensory and motor systems. This would lend support to the work of Benjamin Libet showing that conscious experience requires a longer time than that required for the arrival of specific sensory impulses to cerebral cortex.

ACKNOWLEDGMENT

Support for many years of the early work represented in the above manuscript was provided by the Rockefeller Foundation. I owe to my father, a minister and religious scholar, the inspiration and impetus at a very early age, to dedicate my life to brain research and brain–mind–behavior relationships. I also would like to express great appreciation to the University of Montreal and to the Medical Research Council of Canada for their generous support in helping to establish the Centre de Recherches en Sciences Neurologiques, which enabled us to bring together so many outstanding and enjoyable colleagues over the years in 19 consecutive annual international symposia such as the present one. Finally, I would like to express my most sincere appreciation and gratitude for the collaboration of numerous outstanding postdoctoral research fellows in neuroanatomy and in neurochemistry, who deserve much of the credit for the success of most of the research upon which this chapter is based, and without whom it would have been impossible.

REFERENCES

1. Jasper HH. Philosophy or physics-mind or molecules. In: Worden FG, Swazey JP, Adelman G, eds. *The neurosciences: paths of discovery*. Cambridge, MA: MIT Press, 1975:401–422.
2. Schmidt FO, Worden F, Adelman G, Dennis S, eds. *The organization of the cerebral cortex*. Cambridge, MA: MIT Press, 1981.
3. Jones EG. Anatomy of cerebral cortex: columnar input-output organization. In: Schmidt FO, Worden F, Adelman G, Dennis S, eds. *The organization of the cerebral cortex*. Cambridge, MA: MIT Press, 1981:199–235.
4. Hanbery J, Jasper HH. Independence of the diffuse thalamo-cortical projection system shown by specific nuclear destruction. *J Neurophysiol* 1953;16:252–271.
5. Jasper HH. Problems of relating cellular or modular specificity to cognitive functions: importance of state dependent reactions. In: Schmidt FO, Worden F, Adelman G, Dennis S, eds. *The organization of the cerebral cortex*. Cambridge, MA: MIT Press, 1981:375–393.
6. Jasper HH, Stefanis C. Intracellular oscillatory rhythms in pyramidal tract neurones in the cat. *Electroencephalogr Clin Neurophysiol* 1965;18:541–553.
7. Pollen DA. Intracellular studies of cortical neurones

during thalamic induced wave and spike. *Electroen-cephalogr Clin Neurophysiol* 1964;17:398–404.

8. Jasper HH, Ajmone-Marsan C, Stoll J. Corticofugal projections to the brain stem. *Arch Neurol Psychiatry* 1952:67:155–166.

9. Jasper HH, Naquet R, King EE. Thalamo-cortical recruiting responses in sensory receiving areas in the cat. *Electroencephalogr Clin Neurophysiol* 1955;7:99–114.

10. Shute CCD, Lewis PR. The ascending cholinergic reticular system, olfactory and sub cortical projections. *Brain* 1967;90:497–520.

11. Sie G, Jasper HH, Wolfe L. Rate of ACH release from cortical surface in "encéphale" and "cerveau isolé" cat preparations in relation to arousal and epileptic activation of the ECoGram. *Electroencephalogr Clin Neurophysiol* 1965;18:206.

12. Celesia G, Jasper HH. Acetylcholine released from the cerebral cortex in relation to state of activation. *Neurology* 1966;16:1053–1064.

13. Jasper HH, Kahn RT, Elliott KAC. Amino acids released from cerebral cortex in relation to its state of activation. *Science* 1965;147:1448–1449.

14. Jasper HH, Koyama I. Rate of release of amino acids from cerebral cortex in the cat as affected by brain stem and thalamic stimulation. *Can J Physiol Pharmacol* 1969;47:889–905.

15. Descarries L, Reader TA, Jasper HH, eds. *Monoamine innervation of cerebral cortex*. New York: Alan R Liss, 1984.

16. Reader TA, Jasper HH. Interactions between monoamines and other transmitters in cerebral cortex. In: Descarries L, Reader TA, Jasper HH, eds. *Monoamine innervation of cerebral cortex*. New York: Alan R Liss, 1984:195–225.

17. Reader TA, Ferron A, Descarries L, Jasper HH. Modulatory role of biogenic amines in the cerebral cortex; micro-iontophoretic studies. *Brain Res* 1979;160:217–229.

18. Reader TA, Dykes RW, Gloor P, eds. *Neurotransmitters and cortical function, from molecules to mind*. New York: Plenum, 1986.

19. Jasper HH, Reader T, Avoli M, Dykes RW, Gloor P. Molecular controls and communication in cerebral cortex. In: Reader TA, Dykes RW, Gloor P, eds. *Neurotransmitters and cortical function, from molecules to mind*. New York: Plenum, 1986:593–605.

20. Jasper HH. Philosophy or physics—mind or molecules. In: Worden FG, Swazey JP, Adelman G, eds. *The neurosciences: paths of discovery*. Cambridge, MA: MIT Press, 1975:401–422.

21. Sharpless S, Jasper HH. Habituation of the arousal reaction. *Brain* 1956;79:655–680.

22. Jasper HH, Bertrand G. Stereotaxic microelectrode studies of single thalamic cells and fibres in patients with dyskinesia. *Trans Am Neurol Assoc* 1964;79–82.

23. Jasper HH, Bertrand G. Recording from microelectrodes in stereotaxic surgery for Parkinson's disease. *J Neurosurg* 1966;24:219–221.

24. Jasper HH, Bertrand G. Thalamic units involved in somatic sensation and in voluntary and involuntary movements in man. In: Purpura DP, Yahr MD, eds. *The thalamus*. New York: Columbia University Press, 1966: 365–390.

25. Bertrand G, Jasper HH, Wong A, Matthews G. Microelectrode recording during stereotaxic surgery. *Clin Neurosurg* 1969;16:328–355.

26. Jasper HH, Droogleever-Fortuyn J. Experimental studies of the functional anatomy of petit mal epilepsy. *Assoc Res Nerv Ment Dis Proc* 1947;26:272–298.

27. Penfield WG, Jasper HH. Highest level seizures. *Assoc Res Nerv Ment Dis Proc* 1946;26:252–271.

28. Hunter J, Jasper HH. Effects of thalamic stimulation in unanesthetized animals. *Electroencephalogr Clin Neurophysiol* 1949;1:305–324.

29. Penfield WG, Jasper HH. *Epilepsy and the functional anatomy of the human brain*. Boston: Little, Brown, 1954.

30. Penfield WG. Epilepsy, neurophysiology and some brain mechanisms related to consciousness. In: Jasper HH, Ward A Jr, Pope A, eds. *Basic mechanisms of the epilepsies*. Boston: Little, Brown, 1969:791–814.

31. Prince DA, Farrel D. Centrencephalic spike-wave discharges following parenteral penicillin injections in the cat. *Neurology* 1969:19:309–310.

32. Gloor P. Generalized cortico-reticular epilepsies. Some considerations on the pathophysiology of generalized bilateral synchrony. *Epilepsia* 1968;9:249–263.

33. Avoli M, Gloor P, Kostopoulos G, Gotman J. An analysis of penicillin-induced generalized spike and wave discharges using simultaneous recordings of cortical and thalamic single neurones. *J Neurophysiol* 1983;50: 819–837.

34. Jasper HH. Guest editorial: current evaluation of the concepts of centrencephalic and cortico-reticular seizures. *Electroencephalogr Clin Neurophysiol* 1991; 78:2–11.

35. Perot P. *Mesencephalic-thalamic mechanisms in wave and spike seizures*. PhD thesis, McGill University, Montreal, 1963.

36. Pollen P, Reid KH, Perot P. Microelectrode studies of experimental 3/sec wave and spike in the cat. *Electroencephalogr Clin Neurophysiol* 1964;17:57–67.

37. Weir B. Spike-wave from stimulation of the reticular core. *Arch Neurol* 1964;11:209–218.

38. Weir B, Sie BG. Extracellular unit activity in cat cortex during the spike and wave complex. *Epilepsia* 1966;7: 30–43.

39. Penfield WG. *The mystery of the mind*. Princeton: Princeton University Press, 1975.

Consciousness: At the Frontiers of Neuroscience,
Advances in Neurology, Vol. 77,
edited by H.H. Jasper, L. Descarries,
V.F. Castellucci, and S. Rossignol.
Lippincott–Raven Publishers, Philadelphia © 1998.

5

A New View of Specific and Nonspecific Thalamocortical Connections

Edward G. Jones

Department of Anatomy and Neurobiology, University of California,
Irvine, California 92717-1275

The thalamus, because of its widespread, reciprocal connections with the cerebral cortex, is one of the fundamental elements in the neural circuitry that underlies the phenomenon of consciousness. Whatever the totality of the neural structures generating consciousness, it is essential that they have the capacity to achieve widespread and essentially simultaneous dissemination of the relevant neural activity across the forebrain. The precise, topographically organized, and area-specific projections of the sensory and motor relay nuclei of the thalamus make them unlikely candidates for the dispersal of thalamic activity across the cortex, although their fine-grain organization is obviously an important component of the pathways leading to the act of perception. Nevertheless, alterations in the behavior of large ensembles of thalamocortical relay cells in the sensory, motor, and other thalamic nuclei are accompaniments of changes in the conscious state, as reflected in the electroencephalogram, and the electroencephalographic waves recorded from the surface of the cortex clearly serve as indices of consciousness (1,2).

Historically, it has been recognized that the precise thalamocortical connections of the principal sensory relay nuclei of the thalamus make these connections unlikely candidates for the relay of the more general aspects of thalamic neuronal behavior to the cortex. Consequently, there has been a repeated search for a more diffuse or generalized system of thalamocortical connections, less closely linked to the periphery than the principal sensory relay nuclei, that would provide diffuse connections between the thalamus and cortex to be used as a basis for switching between states of consciousness. The intralaminar and perhaps associated (so-called paralaminar) nuclei often have figured prominently in experimental studies as the likely origins of a diffuse projection system (3–5). The function of this diffuse projection, on rather insecure anatomical grounds believed to be to superficial cortical layers (6), was considered to be manifest in the recruiting response, that long-latency, high-voltage, slow, surface-negative potential that spreads across the cerebral cortex, waxing and waning as it does so, after low frequency electrical stimulation of the intralaminar nuclei (3–5). The recruiting response was thought to be a good candidate for regulating the spontaneous electrical rhythms of the cerebral cortex that accompany changes in behavioral state. The recruiting response, from its wave form, could be expected to depend on the presence, close to the cortical surface, of the terminations of a unique set of thalamocortical fibers (5), but the belief that these arose in the intralaminar

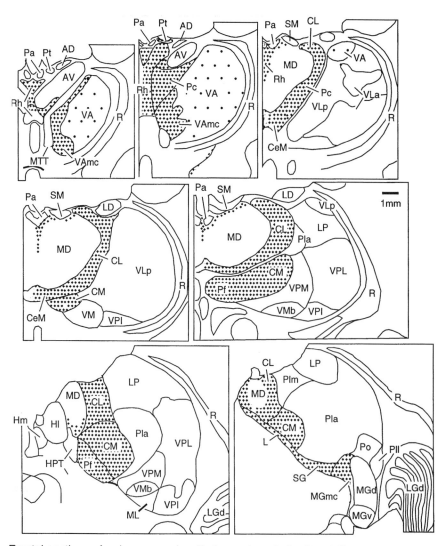

FIG. 1. Frontal sections of a rhesus monkey thalamus in anterior (*top left*) to posterior order, showing the distribution of retrogradely labeled cells in experiments in which retrograde tracers were injected into the ipsilateral striatum. AD, anterodorsal nucleus; AV, anteroventral nucleus; CL, central lateral nucleus; CeM, central medial nucleus; CM, centre médian nucleus; Hl, lateral habenular nucleus; Hm, medial habenular nucleus; HPT, habenulo peduncular tract; L, limitans nucleus; LD, lateral dorsal nucleus; LGd, dorsal lateral geniculate nucleus; LP, lateral posterior nucleus; MGmc, magnocellular medial geniculate nucleus; MD, medial dorsal nucleus; MGd, dorsal medial geniculate nuclei; MGv, ventral medial geniculate nucleus; ML, medial lemniscus; Pa, paraventricular nuclei; Pf, parafascicular nucleus; Pla, anterior pulvinar nucleus; Pli, inferior pulvinar nucleus; Pll, lateral pulvinar nucleus; Plm, medial pulvinar nucleus; Po, posterior nucleus; Pt, parataenial nucleus; R, reticular nucleus; Rh, rhomboid nucleus; SG, suprageniculate nucleus; SM, stria medullaris; VA, ventral anterior nucleus; VAmc, magnocellular ventral anterior nucleus; VLa, ventral lateral anterior nucleus; VLp, ventral lateral posterior nucleus; VMb, basal ventral medial nucleus; VPI, ventral posterior inferior nucleus; VPL, ventral posterior lateral nucleus; VPM, ventral posterior medial nucleus.

nuclei was based on very casual anatomical observations (6). With the demonstration of the substantial projection of the intralaminar nuclei to the striatum (caudate nucleus, putamen, and nucleus accumbens), the recruiting response and especially the idea of a diffuse, superficially projecting thalamic neuronal system fell into disrepute (7,8). Although anatomical work with new tracers in the 1970s confirmed that the major outflow of the intralaminar nuclei is to the striatum, it also has been demonstrated that substantial numbers of intralaminar cells project to the cerebral cortex (9), but not as diffusely as originally proposed (10,11). There are conflicting reports about their exact layer(s) of termination in the cortex (12–14).

Of particular interest to the subject of the present symposium is newer anatomical work indicating that the thalamic origin of a superficial cortical projection, although including the intralaminar nuclei, may not be confined to them (10,14,15). Figure 1 illustrates the nuclei that are now known to be the sources of thalamic projections to the striatum in monkeys. Based on the evidence of a striatal projection, the intralaminar nuclei in monkeys can now be considered to incorporate the magnocellular ventral anterior nucleus (VAmc) and parts of the principal ventral anterior nucleus, anteriorly, as well as the limitans-suprageniculate (Li-SG) and magnocellular medial geniculate (MGmc) nuclei, posteriorly (16,17). The inclusion of nuclei such as the magnocellular ventral anterior nucleus and the limitans, suprageniculate, and magnocellular medial geniculate nuclei extend the sources of the thalamostriatal projection outside the confines of the traditional intralaminar nuclei. The magnocellular ventral anterior nucleus forms one of the "paralaminar nuclei" described by other investigators. Other "paralaminar" nuclei include the densocellular division of the mediodorsal nucleus, which the present author includes in the central lateral nucleus. By extension, it might be inferred that the sources of diffuse thalamocortical projections would also conform to the

same set of nuclei as that which projects to the striatum. However, it is the purpose of this chapter to show that a diffusely projecting matrix is common to the whole thalamus, intralaminar and principal nuclei alike. Its cells of origin are unconstrained by nuclear borders in the thalamus, and its projections are similarly unconstrained by the borders between architectonic and functional fields in the cerebral cortex.

This chapter will show that anatomically there are two fundamentally different sets of thalamocortical relay cells, one type of which projects diffusely and the other, better known, in a specifically focused manner. There has been a trend in recent studies to view thalamic cells in all nuclei, apart from the intrinsic GABAergic interneurons, as physiologically essentially similar (18) and to see the various state-dependent thalamocortical rhythms as depending on the collective oscillation of large ensembles of identical thalamic relay neurons, independent of any differences in the extent or laminar terminations of their axons within the cortex (19,20). The new data presented here show that the diffusely projecting matrix provides a basis for the spread of rhythmicity across thalamic nuclei and cortical areas, so that the whole thalamus and cerebral cortex can be engaged during changes in behavioral state (1,2,21–23).

CHEMICAL IDENTITIES OF THALAMOCORTICAL RELAY NEURONS IN MONKEYS

Recent work on the chemical identities of thalamocortical relay neurons in monkeys are presented in the next section. The data show (Fig. 2) that a set of diffusely projecting thalamocortical neurons whose axons terminate in superficial layers of the cerebral cortex is distributed throughout the whole dorsal thalamus, unconstrained by nuclear borders or by differences between intralaminar and other nuclei. These cells form a background matrix to the whole thalamus. Upon this matrix, in certain nuclei, a core of middle layer–project-

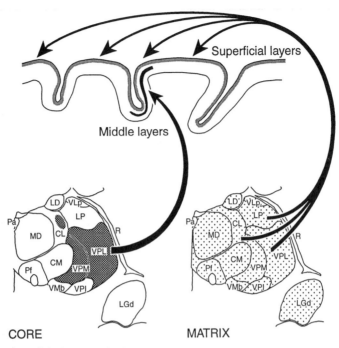

FIG. 2. The new view of thalamocortical connections outlined in the present account. Area-specific projections to middle layers of the cortex arise from a core of cells that are found in the sensory and certain other relay nuclei and in some of the intralaminar nuclei. Overall, projections to superficial layers arise from a matrix of cells extending through the whole thalamus and unconstrained by borders between nuclei or by the division of the thalamus into intralaminar and principal nuclei.

ing thalamocortical neurons is imposed. Their thalamic distribution is constrained by the classical nuclear borders of the thalamus, and they are particularly enriched in the sensory and motor relay nuclei. Every nucleus, intralaminar and principal, contains matrix cells, but only certain nuclei, including especially the sensory and motor relay nuclei, contain the core cells as well. In nuclei or parts of nuclei in which core cells are absent, there is an elaboration of the matrix, so that more matrix cells are present than in nuclei or parts of nuclei in which core and matrix cells are intermingled.

Core and matrix cells have different types of input–output connections. In nuclei in which a core is present (e.g., the principal sensory relay nuclei), the core cells receive subcortical inputs from ascending pathways that are highly ordered topographically, and whose axon terminations are confined within

the borders of the nucleus. The core cells and their inputs have well-defined receptive field properties and strong stimulus-response coupling. The core cells project with the same high degree of topographic order upon one or a few fields of the cerebral cortex, providing the basis for a representational map, and in some well-known instances segregation of functionally distinct components of a sensory pathway. In the cortex, the terminations of the core cells are constrained by the architectonic and functional boundaries between fields and are focused on middle layers of the cortex. In nuclei in which the matrix is enhanced, subcortical inputs are typically from more diffusely organized pathways, and their distribution is not restricted by the borders of individual nuclei. The diffuse input pathways considered here are those such as the spinothalamic tract and the indirect brain stem auditory pathways. A case is made for the existence of a comparable pathway in the retinogeniculate projection below. These diffuse inputs and the cells upon which they terminate retain some relationship to the periphery, but commonly lack easily definable receptive fields and have less precise stimulus-response coupling. The matrix cells upon which they appear preferentially to terminate project diffusely to more than one area of the cerebral cortex. Here, unlike the projections of the core cells, the projections are unconstrained by architectonic or functional boundaries, and the axons terminate in superficial layers of the cortex. The diffuse subcortical inputs to the thalamic matrix should not be confused with the nonspecific cholinergic and monoaminergic brain stem afferents to the thalamus from which they are distinct. However, the action of the nonspecific pathways upon thalamic cells represents one of the most powerful state-dependent drives acting on the thalamus (1,2).

THE TWO CLASSES OF THALAMIC RELAY CELL IN MONKEYS

Immunoreactivity for the calcium-binding proteins, parvalbumin and 28-kDa calbindin, has identified two fundamentally different classes of relay cells in the monkey thalamus (25–31). Cells stained for another calcium binding protein, calretinin, appear to form a subgroup of the calbindin cells. Other supporting data have been drawn from immunocytochemistry or in situ hybridization histochemistry for other neuron-specific proteins or messenger RNAs. Among these are the CAT301 antigen and type II calcium/calmodulin–dependent protein kinase (32–35). Most work has been performed on the three main sensory nuclear complexes: the ventral posterior nucleus and related nuclei, the medial geniculate complex, and the dorsal lateral geniculate nucleus. However, sufficient work has been performed on other nuclei, including those of the intralaminar group (27), to incorporate them into an overall scheme stating that calbindin cells form a superficially projecting matrix that extends through all thalamic nuclei, whereas middle-layer–projecting parvalbumin cells form a core only in certain nuclei or subnuclei. There is a high degree of complementarity so that when parvalbumin cells are absent, the calbindin cells are correspondingly increased.

Ventral Posterior Complex

The ventral posterior complex consists of the ventral posterior medial (VPM) and ventral posterior lateral (VPL) nuclei, which receive the terminations of the trigeminal and medial lemnisci, respectively, and together represent the principal thalamic relay to the primary somatosensory cortex of the postcentral gyrus. A number of other nuclei are associated with VPM and VPL. These include the basal ventral medial (VMb) nucleus (once called the parvocellular division of VPM) and the ventral posterior inferior (VPI) nucleus, which form the visceral and taste relay nuclei of the thalamus. Parvalbumin immunoreactive cells are present in large numbers in VPM and VPL but are absent from VMb and VPI (Figs. 3 and 4). In VPM, the parvalbumin cells are restricted to the aggregations of cells called rods that run anteroposteriorly through VPM and can be seen as periodic concentrations of cytochrome oxidase (CO) staining. The rods are the morphological correlates of the thalamic representation of the face and of peri- and intraoral structures (30,31). In VPL, the parvalbumin cells are aggregated in a manner that conforms to the lamella-like arrays of relay cells that form the representation of the contralateral side of the trunk and contralateral limbs (29). Unlike parvalbumin cells, calbindin-immunoreactive cells are distributed throughout all four nuclei of the ventral posterior complex. In VPL and VPM, their distribution coincides with the distribution of the parvalbumin cells, although their density is less. In VMb and VPI where parvalbumin cells are absent, only calbindin cells are present. In any thalamic nucleus, where parvalbumin cells are present, there is invariably dense histochemical staining for CO, but calbindin-rich nuclei or parts of nuclei invari-

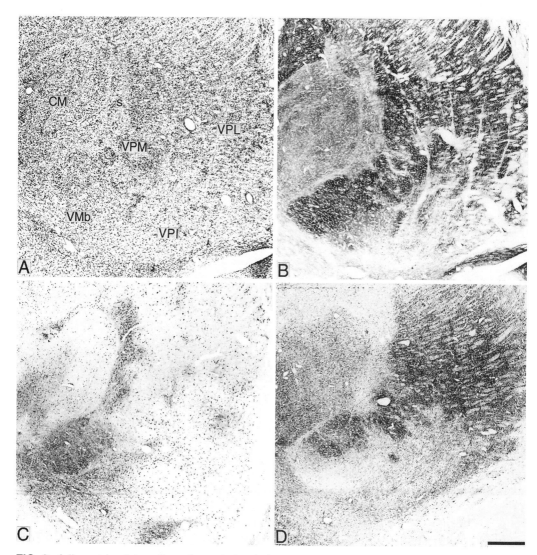

FIG. 3. Adjacent frontal sections through the thalamus of a macaque monkey, stained with thionin (**A**), for cytochrome oxidase (**B**), or immunocytochemically for calbindin (**C**) or parvalbumin (**D**). Parvalbumin cells in VPL and VPM are restricted to regions rich in CO activity. Calbindin cells extend throughout all nuclei of the ventral posterior complex and have increased numbers in the small-celled (s) region of VPM and in VPI and VMb. Bar 750 μm. From material illustrated in Rausell et al. (29).

ably show weak staining for CO. In VPM and VPL there are a number of zones of fairly constant location that show localized reductions of parvalbumin cells and of CO activity and are instead dominated by calbindin cells and weak CO staining. In VPM, calbindin-rich, CO-weak zones are insinuated between the parvalbumin-rich, CO-strong rods and form a rather large S region along the medial edge of VPM. These CO-weak, calbindin-rich zones are directly continuous with the CO-weak, calbindin-rich VMb and VPI. The calbindin cells of VPI also extend uninterruptedly into VPL and become continuous with calbindin-only, CO-weak zones that intervene between the lamellae of more numerous parvalbumin cells. As VPM and VPL narrow to their posterior poles, the calbindin-rich, CO-

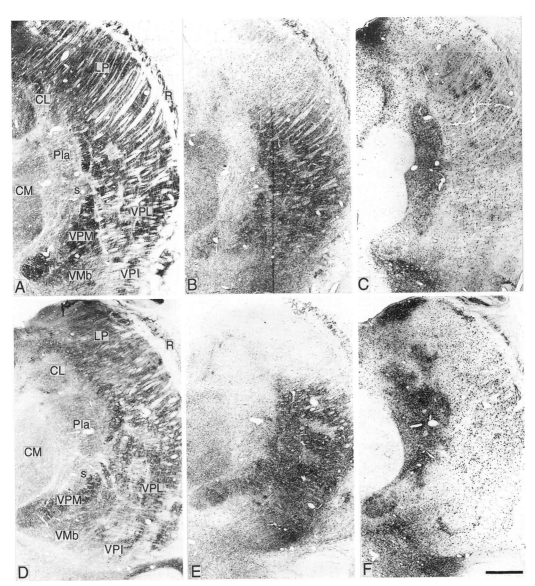

FIG. 4. Trios of adjacent frontal sections through the thalamus of a macaque monkey stained for CO (**A and D**) or immunocytochemically for parvalbumin (**B and E**) or calbindin (**C and F**) showing expansion of the CO-weak, calbindin-rich S region toward the posterior pole of VPM (**F**). Bar 1 mm. From material illustrated in Rausell et al. (29).

weak, parvalbumin-negative S region of VPM, VMb, and VPI expand to form a large, calbindin-only region coextensive with the posterior nucleus. The posterior nucleus is intercalated between the ventral posterior, medial geniculate, limitans-suprageniculate, and anterior pulvinar nuclei at the caudal pole of the thalamus and corresponds to the porta

thalami of Hassler (36) in humans. Through it runs the spinothalamic tract. Anteriorly, the CO-weak, calbindin-rich zones of VPM, VPL, VMb, and VPI extend uninterruptedly into the ventral lateral posterior (VLp) nucleus, which forms the cerebellar relay predominantly to the motor cortex (37–39). In this nucleus, parvalbumin cells are again imposed as a core on a background of calbindin cells. The calbindin cells can thus be seen as a continuous matrix, extending from the ventral lateral nucleus back to the posterior nucleus, with enhancements in VMb, VPI, and the posterior nucleus, as well as in parts of VPM and VPL, especially the S region of VPM.

Medial Geniculate Complex

The medial geniculate complex is composed of the ventral (MGv) nucleus, which forms the principal relay to the primary auditory cortex, the dorsal nucleus, which in monkeys is divided into the anterodorsal (MGad) and posterodorsal (MGpd) subnuclei and projects to areas around the primary auditory cortex, and the magnocellular (MGmc) nucleus, which projects widely upon auditory and more far-flung areas of the cortex (28,39). The distributions of parvalbumin and calbindin cells show many parallels with their distributions in the ventral posterior complex (Fig. 5). Parvalbumin cells form the majority of the cells in MGv, and calbindin cells are relatively few. In MGad, many parvalbumin cells are present but there is an increased number of calbindin cells. In MGpd, parvalbumin cells gradually disappear upon moving from anterior to posterior, and at the posterior pole of the medial geniculate complex, formed entirely by MGpd, only calbindin cells are found. The calbindin cells in this posterior part of MGpd resemble those of the S region of VPM in extending without interruption into adjacent nuclei. Here they extend across the dorsal border of MGpd into the adjacent inferior pulvinar (Pli) nucleus where they become continuous with the larger population of calbindin cells found in Pli. MGmc is characterized by the presence of intermittent islands of calbindin and parvalbumin cells. The large cells that give the nucleus its name are calbindin positive (28).

Dorsal Lateral Geniculate Nucleus

The dorsal lateral geniculate (LGd) nucleus of most old-world primates is characterized by the presence of six principal laminae of cells (layers 1–6), with intervening interlaminar plexuses of white matter. External to lamina 1 among the fibers of the entering optic tract is a group of smaller neurons, referred to as the S laminae. The S laminae are usually referred to in the plural because fibers from the ipsi- and contralateral retinae end in two alternating sheets within them. Cells identical to those of the S laminae are also found in smaller numbers among the fibers of the interlaminar plexuses and even to some extent around the perimeter of layer 6. The relay cells of the six principal laminae are virtually all parvalbumin immunoreactive (27). The S laminae and the cells located in the interlaminar plexuses between the principal laminae are virtually all calbindin immunoreactive (Fig. 6). The calbindin cells also show colocalization of the alpha isoform of the multifunctional protein kinase, alpha-type II calcium/calmodulin–dependent protein kinase (CAMKII-α), an enzyme expressed only in cells using excitatory amino acid transmitters in the primate forebrain (33–36) (Fig. 5). Although parvalbumin cells dominate the principal laminae, calbindin/CAMKII-α cells are not excluded from these laminae and permeate the whole nucleus, small numbers of them extending from the S laminae and interlaminar plexuses into the principal laminae among the parvalbumin cells. The calbindin/CAMKII-α cells also extend beyond the confines of the LGd nucleus into adjacent nuclei, just as in the ventral posterior and medial geniculate complexes. In the posterior part of the LGd nucleus, where it becomes enveloped in the anterior pole of the inferior pulvinar nucleus, the calbindin/CAMKII-α cells extend uninterruptedly across the intervening medullary lamina and, like those in the posterodorsal medial geniculate nucleus, become continuous with the larger population of calbindin cells in Pli (Fig. 6).

The calbindin cells in all nuclei are consistently smaller than the parvalbumin cells, although the calbindin cells are by no means

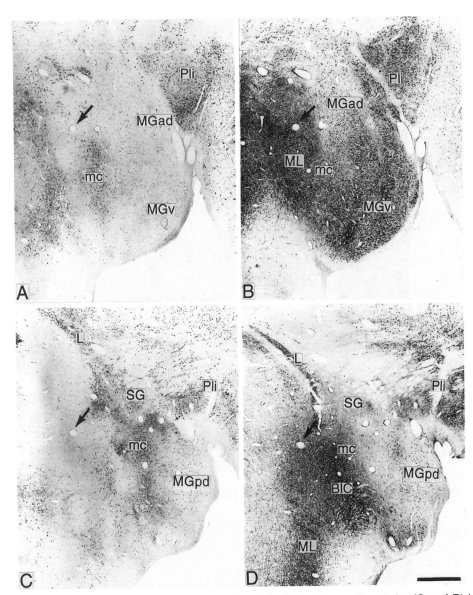

FIG. 5. Pairs of adjacent frontal sections through middle (**A and B**) and posterior (**C and D**) levels of the medial geniculate complex of a macaque monkey, showing the large number of parvalbumin cells in the ventral nucleus (MGv) and in parts of the magnocellular nucleus (mc), and the matrix of calbindin cells in these and in the anterodorsal (MGad) and posterodorsal (MGpd) nuclei. BIC, brachium of inferior colliculus; Pli, inferior pulvinar nucleus. Bar 500 mm. Arrows indicate the same blood vessel. From material illustrated in Molinari et al. (28).

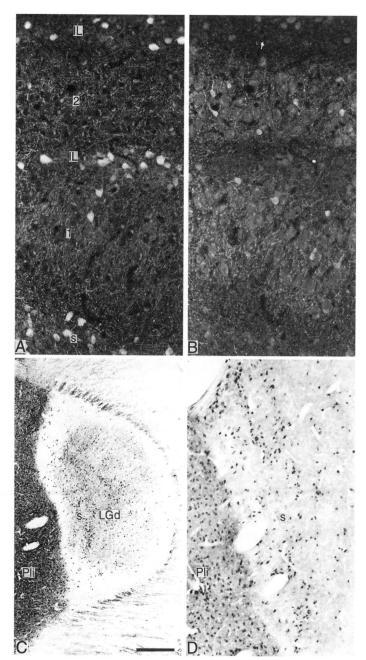

FIG. 6. A and B: Fluorescence photomicrographs of the same microscopic field, showing calbindin immunoreactive cells stained by rhodamine immunofluorescence restricted to the S laminae and interlaminar plexuses of the dorsal lateral geniculate nucleus, as well as parvalbumin-immunoreactive cells stained by fluorescein immunofluorescence in two of the principal laminae (A) (1,2). Jones and Hendry (27). **C and D:** Immunoperoxidase-stained sections showing the calbindin cells of the dorsal lateral geniculate nucleus, labeled by immunoreactivity for alpha-type II calcium/calmodulin-dependent protein kinase extending across the border into the adjacent inferior pulvinar nucleus (Pli). From material illustrated in Tighilet et al. (36). Bar 40 μm (**A and B**), 500 μm (**C**), 200 μm (**D**).

very small, as suggested by some reports on the LGd nucleus. In a series of different regions sampled from the ventral posterior complex, calbindin cells had somal areas of 180 to 200 μm^2 and parvalbumin cells had

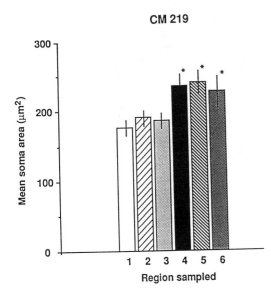

CM 219

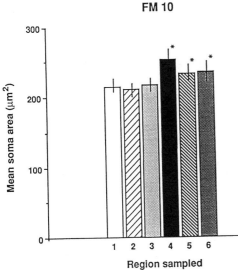

FM 10

FIG. 7. Sizes of somata of calbindin (1–3) and parvalbumin immunoreactive cell bodies (4–6) in the core (1 and 4), medial (2 and 5) and anterodorsal (3 and 6) parts of VPL in two monkeys. Asterisks indicate statistically significant ($p < 0.001$) size differences. Reprinted with permission from Rausell et al. (29).

somal areas of 200 to 250 μm^2 (29). Similar size differences were found in the medial geniculate complex and LGd (Fig. 7).

It is also important to note that in the dorsal thalamus of monkeys, calbindin- and parvalbumin-immunoreactive cells are all thalamocortical or thalamostriatal relay cells. With rare exceptions, neither of the two calcium-binding proteins is found in the intrinsic GABAergic interneurons (27). This contrasts with certain other species, such as the cat, in which intrinsic interneurons appear to be parvalbumin immunoreactive (42). Outside the dorsal thalamus of all species, including primates, parvalbumin is expressed in the second set of thalamic GABA cells, namely those of the reticular nucleus (2).

DIFFERENTIAL CORTICAL PROJECTIONS OF PARVALBUMIN AND CALBINDIN CELLS IN MONKEYS

The cortical projections of the calbindin and parvalbumin cells in the three thalamic nuclei described above have been studied experimentally in double-labeling paradigms. These studies show that, regardless of the nucleus in which they lie, parvalbumin cells invariably project to middle layers (III–IV) of the cerebral cortex, whereas calbindin cells project to superficial layers (I, II and probably upper III). Moreover, parvalbumin cells project in a topographically ordered fashion to single cortical fields, whereas calbindin cells project more widely, commonly spreading their axons across architectonic or functional boundaries in the cortex.

The two sets of cells can be more or less selectively labeled by retrograde transport of fluorescent dye tracers applied to the surface of the cortex, or injected via micropipettes into the middle layers (26,28,29,31,33). Applications of dyes to the surfaces of the somatosensory, auditory, or visual areas of the cerebral cortex affecting layers I–II and possibly upper layer III (Fig. 8A), invariably resulted in retrograde labeling only of calbindin-immunoreactive cells in the ventral

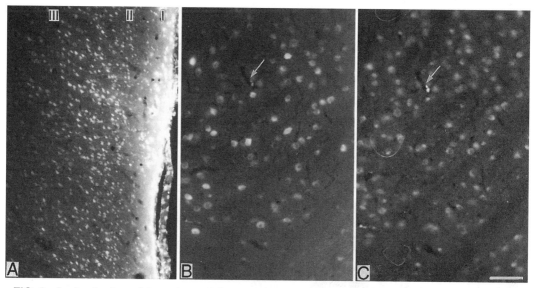

FIG. 8. A: Application of the retrogradely transported tracer, Fast Blue, to the surface of the cerebral cortex. The dye penetrates only into superficial layers and results in retrograde labeling of only calbindin-immunoreactive cells in the thalamus. B and C: Fluorescence micrographs from the same microscope field, showing neurons labeled by retrogradely transported Fast Blue (**B**) and immunoreactive for calbindin (**C**) after dye application of the type shown in **A**. From material illustrated in Rausell et al. (29) and Rausell and Jones (31). Bar 100 μm (**A**), 50 μm (**B and C**).

posterior, medial geniculate, or lateral geniculate nuclei (Fig. 8B and C). Deeper injections of dye resulted in retrograde labeling of a majority of parvalbumin-immunoreactive cells in the same nuclei, but with labeling of a few calbindin cells as well, probably because the injections involved axons of calbindin cells ascending to superficial layers. Even without double immunocytochemical labeling for parvalbumin or calbindin, the sizes of thalamic cells retrogradely labeled from superficial applications or middle-layer injections of dye in the somatosensory or auditory areas also reflect the differential labeling of the two classes of cells (29). Superficially projecting cells are invariably smaller than middle-layer projecting cells (Fig. 9). In the MGmc nucleus its groups of parvalbumin cells were labeled by deeper injections and its groups of calbindin cells by superficial applications. These differential projections also were confirmed by single-fiber tracing, combining PhaL labeling and immunocytochemical staining of the

fibers (39). In LGd, applications of retrograde tracer to the surface of the primary visual cortex retrogradely labels only calbindin cells in the S layers and interlaminar plexuses, whereas injections deeper into the visual cortex predominantly label parvalbumin cells in the principal laminae (33).

The retrograde tracing studies, combined with immunocytochemistry for parvalbumin and calbindin, show that, in addition to having layer-specific projections, the two sets of thalamic cells project in a widespread or more focused manner on the cortex. Calbindin cells project widely and diffusely on the cortex, whereas the projections of parvalbumin cells are much more specific. Applications of retrograde tracer to the surface of the somatosensory cortex, while predictably labeling calbindin cells in VPL and VPM, invariably label calbindin cells in the adjacent VPI, Po, anterior pulvinar (Pla), and VLp nuclei as well. These nuclei form the thalamic relays to other areas of the cortex,

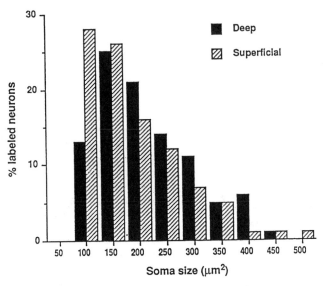

FIG. 9. Percentages of neurons with different somal areas taken from corresponding regions of the right and left VPL nucleus of a monkey in which horseradish peroxidase was injected into middle layers of the somatosensory cortex on one side (deep) and Fast Blue was applied to the surface of the same area of cortex on the other side (superficial). Cells labeled from the superficial dye placement are smaller than those labeled from the middle layer injection. Reprinted with permission from Rausell et al. (29).

including the anterior parietal, periinsular, and motor cortex. Injections into middle layers of the somatosensory cortex, by contrast, label parvalbumin cells only in the somatotopically related part of VPL or VPM. In the medial geniculate complex, comparable experiments show that calbindin cells in all the nuclei project widely to cortical areas surrounding the primary auditory cortex, whereas parvalbumin cells in MGv project topographically to the primary area only (28) (Fig. 10). In the LGd nucleus it has been known for many years that cells in the principal layers project only to area 17, whereas those of the S laminae and interlaminar zones project more widely to areas 17 and 18 and possibly to other fields of the extrastriate region (45,46). These experiments in the three principal sensory relay nuclei of the monkey thalamus show that the calbindin and parvalbumin cells, respectively, form diffuse and more specifically organized pathways to the cerebral cortex.

DIFFUSE AND FOCUSED SUBCORTICAL INPUTS TO CALBINDIN MATRIX AND PARVALBUMIN CORE

The subcortical inputs to the calbindin- and parvalbumin-specific sets of relay cells in the dorsal thalamus of monkeys also appear to have the same characteristics of diffuseness and focus exhibited by the cortical projections of the two sets of relay cells. The diffuse inputs clearly retain some of the features of the sensory pathway and its thalamic relay nuclei with which they are associated, but they are less closely coupled to the peripheral sense organs or retinal ganglion cells than the more precise input pathways. Afferent fiber tracing and/or immunocytochemical staining of the brain stem afferents to the ventral posterior and medial geniculate nuclei show that different fiber pathways are more or less specifically targeted on calbindin or parvalbumin rich regions or whole nuclei (Figs. 10 and 11).

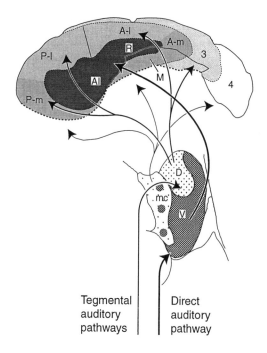

Tegmental | Direct
auditory | auditory
pathways | pathway

FIG. 10. Schematic view of the organization of the input–output connections of the medial geniculate complex. The ventral nucleus (V), which is rich in parvalbumin cells, receives the terminals of the most direct, oligosynaptic pathway from the contralateral ventral cochlear nucleus and projects to the parvalbumin-rich primary auditory cortical areas (AI and R). The dorsal nuclei (D), in which the calbindin matrix predominates, receive inputs predominantly from less direct auditory pathways located in the lateral mid-brain tegmentum and project to auditory cortical areas surrounding the primary areas (A-l, A-m, M, P-l, P-m). These areas display less strong parvalbumin immunostaining. Areas 3 and 4 beyond the surround display weak or absent parvalbumin immunostaining. The magnocellular nucleus (mc) receives inputs from a variety of sources, not all of them auditory. It contains a calbindin matrix with islands of parvalbumin cells and projects widely upon all auditory and adjacent fields. Based on data in Molinari et al. (28).

In the ventral posterior complex (29,31), the terminations of the medial and trigeminal lemnisci, the fibers of which are all parvalbumin positive, end only in the parvalbumin-rich VPL and VPM nuclei. Here the fibers end in the well-known somatotopic order. The spinothalamic and spinal trigeminothalamic pathways ending in the same nuclei terminate in widespread, dispersed bursts of terminals that extend well outside the confines of VPL and VPM into VMb and VPI, as well as adjacent nuclei such as VLp, Pla, Po, and CL. The bursts of terminals in VPL, VPM, CL, and VLp are concentrated in the calbindin-rich, CO-weak, parvalbumin-deficient zones of these nuclei; the Pla and Po nuclei overall are CO weak, deficient in parvalbumin cells, and rich in calbindin cells (Figs. 12 and 13). It is not yet clear if all the spinothalamic and spinal trigeminothalamic fibers are calbindin positive (29).

In the medial geniculate complex, it is known that the parvalbumin-rich MGv and MGad nuclei are the sole termini of tonotopi-

FIG. 11. (*Left*) Schematic view of the organization of input–output connections of the dorsal lateral geniculate nucleus in macaques. The principal laminae (1–6) are dominated by parvalbumin cells and receive inputs from wavelength-specific (P) or broad band (M) retinal ganglion cells. The parvalbumin cells project to subdivisions of layer IV of area 17 only. The calbindin-rich S layers and interlaminar plexuses are innervated by other ganglion cells and by the superior colliculus (not shown). These retinal inputs may extend into the adjacent inferior pulvinar nucleus. The calbindin cells project to superficial layers of both areas 17 and 18, including to the CO-rich blobs of area 17. (*Right*) Schematic view of the organization of input–output connections of the ventral posterior nuclear complex. Medial and trigeminal lemniscal fibers terminate in the parvalbumin rich cores of the VPL and VPM nuclei. The parvalbumin cells project to layers IIIB and IV of the somatosensory cortex. Spinothalamic and spinal trigeminothalamic fibers terminate more diffusely and are concentrated in regions in which the calbindin matrix is enriched, namely the S region of VPM, patches in VPL, and the VMb and VPI nuclei. The calbindin cells project to superficial layers of the somatosensory and adjacent areas of the cortex. Based on data from Rausell and Jones (30,31) and Rausell et al. (29).

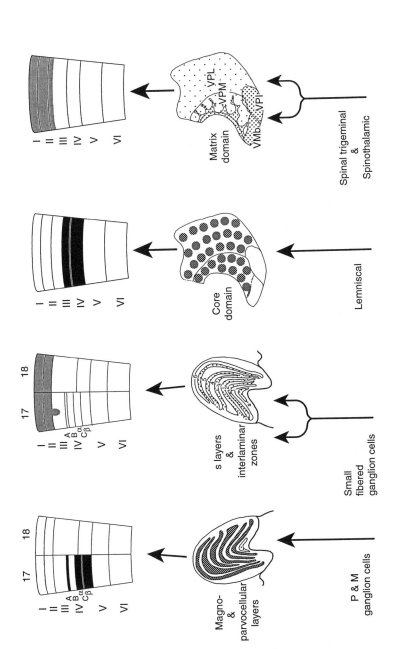

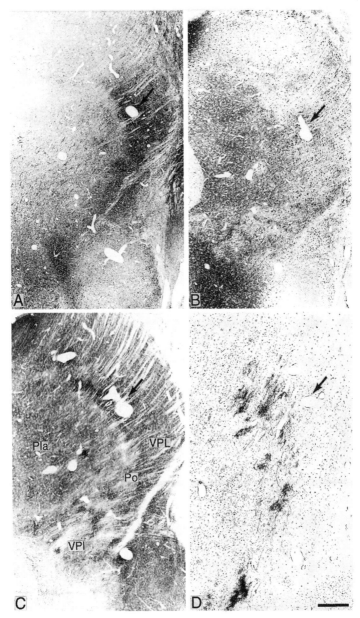

FIG. 12. Frontal sections toward the posterior pole of the VPL nucleus of a macaque monkey, stained for parvalbumin (**A**) or calbindin (**B**) immunoreactivity, for cytochrome oxidase (**C**) or for spinothalamic fiber terminations labeled with wheat germ agglutinin–conjugated horseradish peroxidase (**D**). The parvalbumin-weak, CO-weak but calbindin-rich matrix expands into the region of the posterior nucleus (Po), and there is a concentration of spinothalamic terminations in the matrix. From material illustrated in Rausell et al. (29). Bar 500 μm. Arrows indicate same blood vessel.

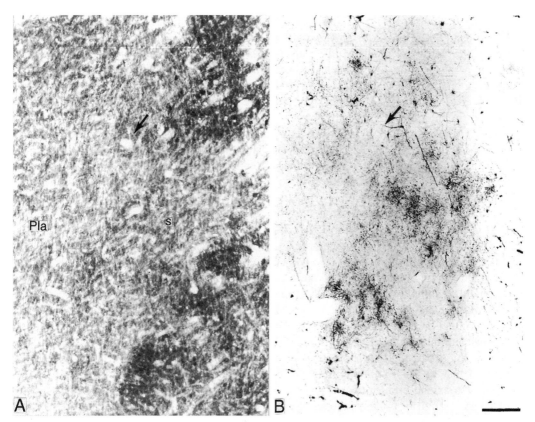

FIG. 13. Adjacent sections through the middle of the VPM nucleus, showing terminations of fibers arising from the caudal nucleus of the spinal trigeminal complex (**A**), anterogradely labeled with wheat germ agglutinin–conjugated horseradish peroxidase, ending in relation to the CO-weak, calbindin-rich S region of the nucleus. The terminations avoid the CO-stained patches in which parvalbumin cells are concentrated (**B**). From material illustrated in Rausell and Jones (31). Bar 100 μm.

cally ordered inputs from the central nucleus of the inferior colliculus. These inputs form the most direct ascending auditory pathway from the contralateral cochlea (Fig. 9). The afferent fibers in this pathway are all parvalbumin positive (28). The MGpd nucleus, which is calbindin rich and parvalbumin weak, is innervated by less direct auditory pathways that ascend in the lateral mid-brain tegmentum. These fibers are all calbindin positive and terminate in diffuse fashion throughout most of the dorsal nuclei, although the details are not fully known. The tegmental inputs retain some of the modality properties of the primary auditory pathway, but they have less precise characteristics than those of the more direct pathway to the ventral

and anterodorsal nuclei. Cells in the cat medial geniculate nuclei equivalent to the MGpd of the monkey, for example, show less sharp frequency tuning than cells in MGv, are driven, if at all, at longer latency by auditory stimuli, and fatigue more readily (44). MGmc is innervated by both parvalbumin and calbindin fibers that come from multiple sources, not all of them auditory. The responses of cells in this nucleus are mixed.

Retinal fibers to the LGd of monkeys include both parvalbumin- and calbindin-immunoreactive groups (27), but it is not yet known if they end selectively in relation to the calbindin and parvalbumin geniculate relay cells (Fig. 10). Physiologically, the parvalbumin-rich principal laminae receive retinotopically ordered inputs from the color-coded (P) or broad-band (M) groups of retinal ganglion cells (45,49), and these inputs can be considered comparable to the lemniscal and direct auditory inputs to the ventral posterior and ventral medial geniculate nuclei. Possibly, the retinal fibers ending in the principal laminae will prove to be all parvalbumin positive. Inputs to the S laminae and interlaminar zones come from both the retina (50) and the superficial layers of the superior colliculus (47,51). It is not known if the former inputs are made up specifically of calbindin-positive fibers. However, the tectal inputs resemble the diffuse spinothalamic and spinal trigeminothalamic inputs to the ventral posterior complex or diffuse auditory tegmental inputs to the medial geniculate complex in extending their terminations uninterruptedly from a series of patchy terminal foci in the Pli nucleus into the S laminae and interlaminar zones of the LGd nucleus. Some early experimental evidence suggested that retinal terminations in the S laminae also extend into Pli (48). There have been no physiological studies of the retinal inputs to the S laminae and interlaminar zones of monkeys, but they have been likened, by anatomical analogy, to the W-cell inputs to the LGd nucleus of the cat (33,52). If the inputs do resemble the W-cell system, they should display less fine topographic organization, less easily defined receptive fields, and sluggish or easily fatigued responses. Such properties would be clearly analogous to those of the spinothalamic and auditory tegmental inputs to the calbindin matrix of the ventral posterior and medial geniculate complexes.

PARVALBUMIN AND CALBINDIN CELLS IN THE INTRALAMINAR AND OTHER DORSAL THALAMIC NUCLEI

I have suggested in the preceding paragraphs that each of the three principal sensory relay nuclear complexes of the monkey thalamus is made up of a matrix of calbindin cells driven by less precise subcortical inputs that project diffusely to superficial layers of the cerebral cortex. This matrix is overlain by a

core of parvalbumin cells driven by precise, topographically ordered inputs, which project to middle layers of cortex in an area-specific manner. The organizational plan presented seems compelling for the ventral posterior, medial geniculate, and lateral geniculate nuclei. In the following paragraphs I shall attempt to draw evidence supporting the theory that this organizational pattern can be extended throughout the whole dorsal thalamus without preference for relay or intralaminar nuclei.

In the intralaminar nuclei, in the broadest sense, as defined by striatal outputs (Fig. 1), there are some regions in which calbindin cells and parvalbumin cells comingle exactly as in large parts of VPL and VPM; in others, they form more or less completely segregated clusters, resembling the S zone of VPM, and by analogy, the alternating principal and S laminae/interlaminar plexuses of the LGd nucleus. Segregated zones of this type are especially seen in posterior CL, MGmc, and Li-SG. In the centre médian and parafascicular nuclei, parvalbumin cells predominate, and calbindin cells are virtually excluded (Fig. 14). In other nuclei such as the anterior CL nucleus, calbindin cells instead predominate over parvalbumin cells (27). Whether both calbindin and parvalbumin cells project to the striatum is unknown. In terms of their cortical projections, however, to the extent that they have been studied, the calbindin cells in the intralaminar nuclei project to superficial layers of quite wide areas of the cerebral cortex and the parvalbumin cells project to middle layers of more restricted areas. There is both anatomical and physiological evidence for superficial and middle-layer projecting intralaminar cells in the cat (53,54). We also may anticipate from experimental evidence in the cat that the majority of cortically projecting intralaminar cells do not have collaterals to the striatum and vice versa (10,11,15). It appears then that the intralaminar complex contains some nuclei with mixed subpopulations of cells having middle-layer and superficial cortical projections and others with largely segregated sub-

Parvalbumin   Calbindin

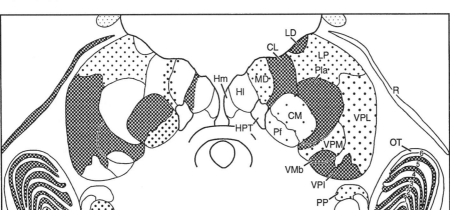

FIG. 14. Distribution of parvalbumin and calbindin immunoreactive cells in a frontal section through the middle of the macaque thalamus. In the intralaminar nuclei, parvalbumin cells dominate the centre médian and parafascicular nuclei but are uncommon in the central lateral nucleus. Calbindin cells dominate the central lateral nucleus but are uncommon in the centre médial and parafascicular nuclei. The anterior pulvinar nucleus (Pla) displays the opposite reciprocity. Redrawn from Jones and Hendry (27).

populations of the two cell types. The parallel with the three sensory relay nuclei seems striking. The striatally projecting cells would form a much larger subpopulation additional to the cortically projecting cells and are found in all intralaminar nuclei. It will be interesting to determine if they include both calbindin and parvalbumin cells and, if so, whether the two types have diffuse and focused projections to the striatum as they do to the cortex.

Outside the confines of the intralaminar nuclei or the principal sensory relay nuclei, calbindin- and parvalbumin-immunoreactive cells are distributed in a similar manner (27). The matrix of calbindin cells extends throughout all nuclei; in some, such as VLp, which receive the terminations of fibers arising in the deep cerebellar nuclei and project to the motor cortex, there is a preponderance of parvalbumin cells; in others, such as the anterior ventral lateral (VLa) nucleus, which receives the terminations of fibers arising in the internal segment of the globus pallidus and

projects predominantly to the premotor cortex, or the Pli nucleus, which receives the terminations of fibers arising in the superior colliculus and projects to the extrastriate cortex, there are approximately equal numbers of calbindin and parvalbumin cells; in others, such as the anterior pulvinar nucleus (Pla), whose inputs are ill defined but which projects to the anterior parietal cortex, there are essentially only calbindin cells (Fig. 14). In view of the evidence presented above, it can be inferred that the projections of thalamic nuclei that contain a majority of parvalbumin cells, regardless of their position within or outside the internal medullary lamina, will be predominantly to middle layers of circumscribed cortical areas; the projections of any nuclei that contain a majority of calbindin cells will be to superficial layers and will spread diffusely across a number of adjacent cortical areas. In nuclei in which parvalbumin and calbindin populations are more evenly mixed, the projections will be to both superficial and middle layers. The presence of diffusely projecting calbindin cells and more precisely focused parvalbumin cells in the same thalamic nucleus can make the interpretation of experiments based on retrograde anatomical labeling difficult if the investigator is constrained by traditional beliefs because one or more thalamic nuclei will contain retrogradely labeled cells depending on the extent of involvement of superficial cortical layers in an injection of tracer.

THE ROLE OF THE DIFFUSELY PROJECTING MATRIX CELLS IN THALAMIC FUNCTION

When the forebrain switches between activities associated with changes in conscious state, it is evident that the whole thalamus will be engaged, not simply its nuclei independently (1,2,19,21,22,24,55,56). In considering how large numbers of thalamic cells could be recruited into collective action, it is necessary to invoke some form of intrathalamic or recurrent thalamocorticothalamic connection that will carry neuronal activity across nuclear borders. During slow-wave sleep, low-frequency oscillations in the delta and spindle frequency ranges prevail in thalamic and cortical cells. These depend on recurrent burst firing of relay cells as they recover from reticular nucleus–imposed inhibition (18,57–61). Here, intranuclear connections between adjacent reticular nucleus cells (62,63) may be sufficient to ensure spread of the inhibitory influence across nuclei in the underlying dorsal thalamus (60), especially when the oscillations are synchronized by corticothalamic connections (19–21,55,56). During conscious attention and in rapid eye movement (REM) sleep, higher frequency oscillations in the 40-Hz range predominate. When these are propagated across thalamic nuclei and cortical areas, they may serve to bind together activities of all cortical areas essential to the act of perception. For this spread of activity to occur, it has been proposed that a cortical area, activated by a sensory stimulus, should engage, by corticothalamic connections, an intralami-

nar nucleus and, thence, via putative connections between intralaminar nuclei and the diffuse projections of these intralaminar nuclei, other areas of the cerebral cortex (23). The difficulty in this argument is that intrathalamic connections between intralaminar nuclei have never been convincingly demonstrated, although recent evidence indicates the presence of intranuclear collaterals of striatally projecting cells in the parafascicular nucleus of the rat (64). The evidence from the immunocytochemical studies of calbindin and parvalbumin cells, indicating the existence of diffusely projecting calbindin-positive relay cells in all nuclei, makes it unlikely that the intralaminar nuclei are the sole contributors to the recruitment of widespread cortical areas under these conditions. It also demonstrates that connections between nuclei within the dorsal thalamus are not necessary to provide a basis for spread of thalamocortical activity across multiple cortical areas. The new findings also help to resolve the paradox that the primary visual and auditory areas, unlike other areas of the cortex, do not project to the classical intralaminar nuclei. They obviously project to other diffusely projecting nuclei, such as nuclei of the pulvinar and the magnocellular medial geniculate nucleus that are organized along similar lines to the intralaminar nuclei.

Once a sensory area of the cerebral cortex is engaged by its specific thalamocortical projection, its corticothalamic feedback to calbindin cells of its thalamic relay nucleus will enable activity to be transferred to adjacent cortical areas via the diffuse projections of the calbindin cells. These areas, in feeding back via corticothalamic projections to their own thalamic relay nuclei, would engage the calbindin cells of these new relay nuclei, and so on; in this way, activity would be dispersed across the whole cortex. The process of recruiting thalamic nuclei via corticothalamic connections would be greatly enhanced by corticothalamic fibers that return to thalamic nuclei other than that from which their area of origin receives its principal thalamic input.

The majority of corticothalamic fibers arising in a particular area of the cortex return to the relay nucleus projecting to that area. Such fibers arise from cells in layer VI of the cortex. In area 17, for example, layer VI returns corticothalamic fibers to the LGd. In most, perhaps all, cortical areas, however, a second set of corticothalamic fibers arises from cells in layer V. These invariably project to thalamic nuclei other than that from which the principal thalamocortical projection to the area arises. Axons arising in layer V of the visual cortex, for example, reach parts of the pulvinar (65), those arising from layer V of the primary auditory cortex reach the dorsal and magnocellular medial geniculate nuclei (66,67), and those arising from layer V of the primary somatosensory area reach the intralaminar nuclei and the anterior pulvinar nucleus (68,69). In many of these cases, the nuclei receiving the layer V inputs, e.g., the anterior pulvinar nucleus and the anterior intralaminar nuclei, are especially enriched in superficially projecting, calbindin-immunoreactive cells. It is possible that nuclei of this type, with a predominance of superficial cortical projections, are particularly involved in the recruitment of cortex and thalamus into collective action.

SUMMARY

Past theories about the circuitry that promotes integration of the whole cerebral cortex and thalamus during forebrain activities that underlie different states of consciousness have relied on the intralaminar nuclei as the sources of diffuse thalamocortical projections that could facilitate spread of activity across many cortical areas. Evidence is presented to show the presence of a matrix of superficially projecting cells extending throughout the whole thalamus that could form a substrate for diffusion of activity across the cortex. The superficially projecting cells in monkeys are distinguished by immunoreactivity for the calcium-binding protein calbindin. They are found in all thalamic nuclei and are increased in some nuclei. They not only project to superficial layers of the cortex but do so over wide areas, unconstrained by boundaries between areas. They are innervated by subcortical inputs that lack the topographic order and physiological precision of the principal sensory pathways. Superimposed on the matrix, but only in certain nuclei, is a core of cells characterized by immunoreactivity for another calcium-binding protein, parvalbumin. These project to middle layers of the cortex in an area-specific and topographically ordered manner. They are innervated by subcortical inputs that are typically precise in having a high degree of topographic order and readily identifiable physiological properties. The parvalbumin cells provide the sensory and other inputs to the cortex that are to be used as a basis for perception. The diffusely projecting calbindin cells can form a basis for the engagement of multiple cortical areas and thalamic nuclei, especially when recruited by corticothalamic connections. Diffusion of activity across multiple areas and thalamic nuclei is essential for the binding of all aspects of sensory experience into a single framework of consciousness.

ACKNOWLEDGMENT

This work was supported by Grants NS21377 and NS22317 from the National Institutes of Health, United States Public Health Service. I thank Drs. D.L. Benson, M.E. Dell'Anna, T. Hashikawa, S.H.C. Hendry, G.W. Huntley, M.G. Leggio, M. Molinari, and E. Rausell for their contributions.

REFERENCES

1. Steriade M, Jones EG, Llinás RR. *Thalamic oscillations and signalling.* New York: Wiley, 1990.
2. Steriade M, Jones EG, McCormick DA. *Thalamus.* Oxford, United Kingdom: Pergamon, 1997.
3. Hanberry J, Jasper HH. Independence of diffuse thalamo-cortical projection system shown by specific nuclear destructions. *J Neurophysiol* 1953;16:252–271.
4. Jasper HH. Diffuse projection systems: the integrative activity of the thalamic reticular system. *Electroencephalogr Clin Neurophysiol* 1949;1:405–420.

5. Jasper HH. Unspecific thalamocortical relations. In: Field J, Magoun HW, Hall VE, eds. *Handbook of physiology.* Section 1, Neurophysiology, Volume 2. Washington, DC: American Physiological Society, 1960: 1307–1321.

6. Lorente de Nó R. Cerebral cortex: architectonics, intracortical connections. In: Fulton JR, ed. *Physiology of the nervous system.* New York: Oxford University Press, 1938:274–301.

7. Powell TPS, Cowan WM. A study of thalamo-striate relations in the monkey. *Brain* 1956;79:364–389.

8. Powell TPS, Cowan WM. The interpretation of the degenerative changes in the intralaminar nuclei of the thalamus. *J Neurol Neurosurg Psychiatry* 1967;30: 140–153.

9. Jones EG, Leavitt RY. Retrograde axonal transport and the demonstration of non-specific projections to the cerebral cortex and striatum from thalamic intralaminar nuclei in the rat, cat and monkey. *J Comp Neurol* 1974; 154:349–738.

10. Macchi G, Bentivoglio M, Molinari M, Minciacchi D. The thalamo-caudate versus thalamo-cortical projections as studied in the cat with fluorescent retrograde double labeling. *Exp Brain Res* 1984;54:225–229.

11. Macchi G, Bentivoglio M. The thalamic intralaminar nuclei and the cerebral cortex. In: Jones EG, Peters A, eds. *Cerebral cortex.* Vol. 5. Sensory-motor cortex and aspects of cortical connectivity. New York: Plenum, 1986:355–401.

12. Herkenham M. Laminar organization of thalamic projections to the rat neocortex. *Science* 1980;207:532–534.

13. Jones EG. Possible determinants of the degree of retrograde neuronal labeling with horseradish peroxidase. *Brain Res* 1975;85:249–253.

14. Glenn LL, Steriade M. Discharge rate and excitability of cortically projecting intralaminar thalamic neurons during working and sleep states. *Neuroscience* 1982;2: 1387–1404.

15. Steriade M, Glenn LL. Neocortical and caudate projections of intralaminar thalamic neurons and their synaptic excitation from midbrain reticular core. *J Neurophysiol* 1982;48:352–371.

16. Hunt CA, Jones EG. The exact distribution of striatally-projecting thalamic neurons in the monkey. *Neurosci Abstr* 1988;14:188.

17. Jones EG. Defining the thalamic intralaminar nuclei in primates. In: Gainotti G, Bentivoglio M, Bergonzi P, Ferro FM, eds. *Neurologia e scienze base. Scritti in onore di Giorgio Macchi.* Milan, Italy: Università Cattolica del Sacre Cuore, 1989:161–194.

18. Jahnsen H, Llinás R. Ionic basis for the electroresponsiveness and oscillatory properties of guinea-pig thalamic neurones in vitro. *J Physiol Lond* 1983;349: 227–248.

19. Contreras D, Destexhe A, Sejnowski T, Steriade M. Spatiotemporal patterns of spindle oscillations in cortex and thalamus. *J Neurosci* 1997;17:1179–1196.

20. Contreras D, Steriade M. State-dependent fluctuations of low-frequency rhythms in corticothalamic networks. *Neuroscience* 1996;76:25–38.

21. Contreras D, Steriade M. Cellular basis of EEG slow rhythms: a study of dynamic corticothalamic relationships. *J Neurosci* 1995;15:604–622.

22. Jahnsen H, Llinás R. Electrophysiological properties of

23. Llinás R, Ribary U. Coherent 40-Hz oscillation characterizes dream state in humans. *Proc Natl Acad Sci U S A* 1993;90:2078–2081.

24. Steriade M, Contreras D. Relations between cortical and thalamic cellular events during transition from sleep patterns to paroxysmal activity. *J Neurosci* 1995;15: 623–542.

25. Diamond IT, Fitzpatrick D, Schmechel D. Calcium binding proteins distinguish large and small cells of the ventral posterior and lateral geniculate nuclei of the prosimian Galago and the tree shrew (*Tupaia belangeri*). *Proc Natl Acad Sci U S A* 1993;90:1425–1429.

26. Hashikawa T, Rausell E, Molinari M, Jones EG. Parvalbumin- and calbindin-containing neurons in the monkey medial geniculate complex: differential distribution and cortical layer specific projections. *Brain Res* 1991;544: 335–341.

27. Jones EG, Hendry SHC. Differential calcium binding protein immunoreactivity distinguishes classes of relay neurons in monkey thalamic nuclei. *Eur J Neurosci* 1989;1:222–246.

28. Molinari M, Dell'Anna ME, Rausell E, Leggio MG, Hashikawa T, Jones EG. Auditory thalamocortical pathways defined in monkeys by calcium binding protein immunoreactivity. *J Comp Neurol* 1995;362:171–194.

29. Rausell E, Bae CS, Viñuela A, Huntley GW, Jones EG. Calbindin and parvalbumin cells in monkey VPL thalamic nucleus: distribution, laminar cortical projections, and relations to spinothalamic terminations. *J Neurosci* 1992;12:4088–4111.

30. Rausell E, Jones EG. Histochemical and immunocytochemical compartments of the thalamic VPM nucleus in monkeys and their relationship to the representational map. *J Neurosci* 1991;11:210–225.

31. Rausell E, Jones EG. Chemically distinct compartments of the thalamic VPM nucleus in monkeys relay principal and spinal trigeminal pathways to different layers of the somatosensory cortex. *J Neurosci* 1991;11: 226–327.

32. Benson DL, Isackson PJ, Hendry SHC. Jones EG. Differential gene expression for glutamic acid decarboxylase and type II calcium-calmodulin-dependent protein kinase in basal ganglia, thalamus and hypothalamus of the monkey. *J Neurosci* 1991;11:1540–1564.

33. Hendry SHC, Yoshioka TA. Neurochemically distinct third channel in the macaque dorsal lateral geniculate nucleus. *Science* 1994;264:575–577.

34. Jones EG. Modern views of cellular thalamic mechanisms. In: Bentivoglio M, Spreafico R, eds. *Cellular thalamic mechanisms.* Amsterdam, The Netherlands: Elsevier, 1989:1–22.

35. Tighilet B, Huntsman MM, Hashikawa T, Murray KD, Isackson PJ, Jones EG. Cell-specific expression of type II calcium/dependent protein kinase isoforms and glutamate receptors in normal and visually deprived lateral geniculate nucleus of monkeys. *J Comp Neurol* 1997; 390(2):278–296.

36. Hassler R. Anatomy of the thalamus. In: Schaltenbrand G, Bailey P, eds. *Introduction to stereotaxis with an atlas of the human brain.* Stuttgart, Germany: Thieme, 1959:230–290.

37. Asanuma C, Thach WT, Jones EG. Distribution of cere-

guinea-pig thalamic neurons: an in vitro study. *J Physiol Lond* 1983;349:205–226.

bellar terminations and their relation to other afferent terminations in the ventral lateral thalamic region of the monkey. *Brain Res Rev* 1983;5:237–265.

38. Rouiller EM, Liang F, Babalian A, Moret V, Wiesendanger M. Cerebellothalamocortical and pallidothalamocortical projections to the primary and supplementary motor cortical areas: a multiple tracing study in macaque monkeys. *J Comp Neurol* 1994;345: 185–213.

39. Hashikawa T, Rausell E, Molinari M, Jones EG. Patchy and laminar terminations of medial geniculate axons in monkey auditory cortex. *J Comp Neurol* 1995;362: 195–208.

40. Sakai ST, Inase M, Tanji J. Comparison of cerebellothalamic and pallidothalamic projections in the monkey (*Macaca fuscata*): a double anterograde labeling study. *J Comp Neurol* 1996;368:215–228.

41. Morison RS, Dempsey EW. A study of thalamo-cortical relations. *Am J Physiol* 1942;135:281–292.

42. Stichel CC, Singer W, Heizmann CW. Light and electron microscopic immunocytochemical localization of parvalbumin in the dorsal lateral geniculate nucleus of the cat: evidence of coexistence with GABA. *J Comp Neurol* 1988;268:29–37.

43. Weber JT, Huerta MF, Kaas JH, Harting JK. The projections of the lateral geniculate nucleus of the squirrel monkey: studies of the interlaminar zones and the S layers. *J Comp Neurol* 1983;213:135–145.

44. Calford MB. The parcellation of the medial geniculate body of the cat defined by the auditory response of single units. *J Neurosci* 1983;3:2350–2364.

45. Hubel DH, Livingstone MS. Color and contrast sensitivity in the lateral geniculate body and primary visual cortex of the macaque monkey. *J Neurosci* 1990;10: 2223–2237.

46. Yukie M, Iwai E. Direct projection from the dorsal lateral geniculate nucleus to the prestriate cortex in macaque monkeys. *J Comp Neurol* 1981;201:1–14.

47. Harting JK, Casagrande VA, Weber JT. The projection of the primate superior colliculus upon the dorsal lateral geniculate nucleus: autoradiographic demonstration of interlaminar distribution of tectogeniculate axons. *Brain Res* 1978;150:593–599.

48. Campos-Ortega JA, Hayhow WR, Clüver PF de. A note on the problem of retinal projections to the inferior pulvinar of primates. *Brain Res* 1972;22:126–130.

49. Schiller PH, Logothetis NK, Charles ER. Functions of the colour-opponent and broad-band channels of the visual system. *Nature* 1990;343:68–70.

50. Kaas JH, Huerta MF, Weber JT, Harting JK. Patterns of retinal terminations and laminar organization of the lateral geniculate nucleus of primates. *J Comp Neurol* 1978;182:517–554.

51. Harting JK, Huerta MF, Hashikawa T, Van Lieshout DP. Projection of the mammalian superior colliculus upon the dorsal lateral geniculate nucleus: organization of tectogeniculate pathways in nineteen species. *J Comp Neurol* 1991;304:275–306.

52. Fitzpatrick D, Itoh K, Diamond IT. The laminar organization of the lateral geniculate body and the striate cortex in the squirrel monkey (*Saimiri sciureus*). *J Neurosci* 1983;3:673–702.

53. Molinari M, Leggio MG, Dell'Anna ME, Giannetti S, Macchi G. Chemical compartmentation and relationships between calcium-binding protein immunoreactivity and layer-specific cortical and caudate-projecting cells in the anterior intralaminar nuclei of the cat. *Eur J Neurosci* 1994;6:299–312.

54. Rydenhag B, Olausson B, Shyu BC, Andersson S. Localized responses in the midsuprasylvian gyrus of the cat following stimulation of the central lateral nucleus in thalamus. *Exp Brain Res* 1986;62:11–24.

55. Contreras D, Destexhe A, Sejnowski T, Steriade M. Control of spatiotemporal coherence of a thalamic oscillation by corticothalamic feedback. *Science* 1996; 274:771–773.

56. Contreras D, Steriade M. Synchronization of low-frequency rhythms in cortico-thalamic networks. *Neuroscience* 1996;76:11–24.

57. Bal T, von Krosigk M, McCormick DA. Role of the ferret perigeniculate nucleus in the generation of synchronized oscillations in vitro. *J Physiol Lond* 1995;483: 665–685.

58. Huguenard JR, Prince DA. Intrathalamic rhythmicity studied in vitro: nominal T-current modulation causes robust antioscillatory effects. *J Neurosci* 1994;14: 5485–5502.

59. Kim U, Bal T, McCormick DA. Spindle waves are propagating synchronized oscillations in the ferret LGNd in vitro. *J Neurophysiol* 1995;74:1301–1323.

60. McCormick DA, Bal T. Sleep and arousal: thalamocortical mechanisms. *Ann Rev Neurosci* 1997;20: 185–216.

61. Warren RA, Agmon A, Jones EG. Oscillatory synaptic interactions between ventroposterior and reticular neurons in mouse thalamus in vitro. *J Neurophysiol* 1994; 72:1993–2003.

62. Deschênes M, Madariaga-Domich A, Steriade M. Dendrodendritic synapses in the cat reticularis thalami nucleus: a structural basis for thalamic spindle synchronization. *Brain Res* 1985;334:165–168.

63. Yen C-T, Conley M, Hendry SHC, Jones EG. The morphology of physiologically identified GABAergic neurons in the somatic sensory part of the thalamic reticular nucleus in the cat. *J Neurosci* 1985;5: 2254–2268.

64. Deschênes M, Bourassa J, Doan VD, Parent A. A single-cell study of the axonal projections arising from the posterior intralaminar thalamic nuclei in the rat. *Eur J Neurosci* 1996;8:329–343.

65. Rockland KS. Two types of corticopulvinar terminations: round (type 2) and elongate (type 1). *J Comp Neurol* 1996;368:57–87.

66. Ojima H. Terminal morphology and distribution of corticothalamic fibers originating from layers 5 and 6 of cat primary auditory cortex. *Cerebral Cortex* 1994;4: 646–663.

67. Ojima H, Murakami K, Kishi K. Dual termination modes of corticothalamic fibers originating from pyramids of layers 5 and 6 in cat visual cortical area 17. *Neurosci Lett* 1996;208:57–60.

68. Jones EG, Wise SP, Coulter JD. Differential thalamic relationships of sensory motor and parietal cortical fields in monkeys. *J Comp Neurol* 1979;183:833–882.

69. Pons TP, Kaas JH. Connections of area 2 of somatosensory cortex with the anterior pulvinar and subdivisions of the ventroposterior complex in macaque monkeys. *J Comp Neurol* 1985;240:16–36.

DISCUSSION

Moderated by Laurent Descarries

Laurent Descarries: May I use my privilege as chairman to ask for more information? In trying to account for conscious experience, many neuroscientists have insisted on the importance of reentry, i.e., feedback circuitry, in the thalamocortical system among others. In the context of this new view of the thalamocortical projections, do you have any data on the selectivity of the input from cortex to your core or matrix cells?

Edward G. Jones: Yes, in fact we have done a certain amount of work mainly in the auditory system on this, and my colleague Yuki Ojima has been the principal person involved. But there is work from other systems, although I have to confess primarily in rodents, which suggests that the corticothalamic axons arising from different layers of the cortex, layers V and VI, are differentially targeted. And it looks as though in the medial geniculate, at least, those more diffusely distributed axons of layer V cells are actually targeting the matrix region in a more diffuse manner, whereas the rather larger population of layer VI cells, perhaps the best characterized corticothalamic population of cells, these target only the principal ventral medial geniculate nucleus where they have this highly topographic, very focused organization. Obviously, if the diffuse system is to be recruited to spread activity which is emanating from a sensory-relay nucleus across a wider territory of cortex, then the layer V projection to the matrix would be a way to do it.

Rodolfo R. Llinás: Very beautiful work as always, Ted. Now, there is an intriguing issue which comes to mind. You have demonstrated in the past that there is topography to the inputs from intralaminar nuclei to the cortex. Now, is there topography also to the basal ganglia?

Edward G. Jones: Yes, of course.

Rodolfo R. Llinás: And is it corresponding also to the topography between the cortex and the basal ganglia?

Edward G. Jones: There is a certain amount of work on the cat, which suggests that that is indeed the case: those areas of the putamen which receive their input from the centre médian and more caudal part of central lateral nuclei are the targets of the corticostriatal projection from the sensorimotor areas. This is fairly well defined.

Rodolfo R. Llinás: Is it a two-way system? In other words, can the nonspecific nuclei reach the cortex two ways: directly, through the first layer, and somehow through the basal ganglia?

Edward G. Jones: No, because the basal ganglia do not project to the cortex.

Rodolfo R. Llinás: They do project to the thalamus, however.

Edward G. Jones: Right, but their output to the thalamus is much more highly focused. There is certainly an input to the intralaminar system, but the greater part, the greater number of their fibers are actually focused upon one of the components of the ventrolateral system and thus upon the premotor cortex. But in terms of topography, I want to extend my proposal beyond the intralaminar system because there is a topography in this diffuse system that I referred to. Those zones of the matrix which are closest to the lateral geniculate nucleus certainly send their axons diffusely, but to areas of the cortex which are visual in their connotations. Those parts of the matrix which are closest to the medial geniculate nucleus send their projections diffusely, but to territories of the cortex which have auditory connotations and so on.

Christof Koch: Ted, some people, such as Joe Bogen (1), argue that consciousness per se is generated in the intralaminar nuclei of the thalamus (ILN). There is a problem that has always bothered me with this proposal. We know that consciousness goes hand in hand with very specific sensory information. For instance, I can be conscious of a sideways-moving yellow tennis ball. If the ILN is the seat of consciousness, then how can it convey this specific sensory information? It is my understanding that, at least in the macaque monkey, there are very few connections from MT, IT, or even V1 back into the ILN.

Edward G. Jones: This is true, but what I am trying to do is extend it to help you out, because the matrix now is receiving from layer V of the visual areas, but it is not necessarily the matrix that is associated with the intralaminar nuclei.

Christof Koch: You suggest that the matrix is very diffuse and projects to a very large area, while the sensory content of consciousness can be highly specific. If ILN plays the crucial role in consciousness that its supporters have argued for, you require lots of very specific point-to-point projections from cortex to the ILN.

Edward G. Jones: Yes, but both systems are involved here. I mean in consciousness I cannot believe that one of these systems I have demonstrated is uniquely activated to the exclusion of the other. So, I think both of these systems are going to be engaged in the act of consciousness.

Jeffrey A. Gray: Is there any difference in the connections of the parvalbumin and calbindin type cells with the nucleus reticularis thalami, either way, connecting to or receiving from?

Edward G. Jones: This is a very good question. And you may have noticed the reticularis cells are parvalbumin immunoreactive. So, when I say that GABA cells were not immunoreactive for parvalbumin or calbindin, it is only the intrinsic cells; the reticular nucleus cells are immunoreactive for parvalbumin. But in terms of your question, I really have no firm information, but it looks to us as though both types of cells do have collaterals in the reticular nucleus. Whether one is more diffusely distributed in the reticular nucleus and the other more focused I do not know, but that of course would be of great interest.

David H. Hubel: Can you say just a bit more about how these two systems in the visual system relate, in 17, to the blobs versus nonblob regions, which certainly have something to do with the intralaminar versus laminar zones in the geniculate? And V2, or 18, where you have the three types of stripes, only two of which stain strikingly with cytochrome oxidase.

Edward G. Jones: I do not have anything on area 18 in relation to the stripes, David. In terms of the inputs to the superficial layers of area 17, I am confident that the S and intralaminar zones are projecting to layers I and II, and I think these also target the blobs as well. But there has been to my knowledge no really clean experiment yet which shows definitively that the S layers are targeted, say, specifically on the blobs, to the exclusion, say, of parvalbumin cells in the principal layers which might go there as well. I just do not think that this is resolved as yet. I am sure there are people who are quite capable of doing that.

Stuart R. Hameroff: Your matrix of cells, do you happen to know: are they or could they be connected by gap junctions?

Edward G. Jones: They are not connected by gap junctions. I have never seen a gap junction in the thalamus. If they are there, they must be extremely rare. And I think that would be the experience of virtually every other electron microscopist who has looked in the thalamus. There are some unusual sorts of desmosomal type junctions in many thalamic nuclei, but these are not, I think, in the nature of gap junctions; they are more typical of adhesive type junctions which hold the glomeruli together. Gap junctions might be present in the developing thalamus, however.

Discussion Reference

1. Bogen JE. On the neurophysiology of consciousness: I. An overview. *Consciousness Cognition* 1995;4:52–62.

Consciousness: At the Frontiers of Neuroscience,
Advances in Neurology, Vol. 77,
edited by H.H. Jasper, L. Descarries,
V.F. Castellucci, and S. Rossignol.
Lippincott–Raven Publishers, Philadelphia © 1998.

6

The Neural Basis of Consciousness Across the Sleep–Waking Cycle

Barbara E. Jones

*Department of Neurology and Neurosurgery, McGill University, Montreal Neurological Institute
and Hospital, Montreal, Quebec, H3A 2B4, Canada*

Estimated as originating in Indo-Aryan oral tradition dating as far back as 2000 B.C., the Upanishads described three distinct mental states during the human lifetime. According to translations of the original Sanskrit texts and later Hindu interpretations, these three states are waking, dreaming, and dreamless sleep (1). In waking, the physical world is experienced by the self, using the sense organs as its instruments, yet the perceptions of waking originate within the self, the infinite consciousness. In dreaming, the self creates objects—"pleasures, joys, and delights"—or even "frightful things" (1). Afterwards, the self drifts into a state of deep sleep, characterized by complete rest and peace, due to the absence of the objects, desires, or fears of dreams. In that dreamless sleep, the "self has no consciousness of objects and yet is not unconscious" (1).

NEUROPHYSIOLOGIC CORRELATES OF THREE MENTAL STATES

The wisdom of these early Hindu scriptures has been largely borne out in our contemporary study of the neural basis of sleep–wake states during this century. First, in the discovery and examination of the neurophysiologic changes that accompany behaviorally defined sleep–wake states, it became evident that three distinct states occur across the sleep–waking cycle in mammals: waking, slow-wave sleep, and paradoxical or rapid eye movement (REM) sleep (Fig. 1).

1. Waking is characterized by a responsive and often active state of the organism during which awareness or full consciousness is readily demonstrable in humans. The electroencephalographic (EEG) activity recorded from the cerebral cortex is characterized by low-voltage fast activity; eye movements are present; and muscle tonus is tonically as well as phasically high.

2. Slow-wave sleep is characterized as a behaviorally quiet state, when responsiveness to sensory stimuli is greatly reduced, and movements, except for positional shifts, are minimal. The EEG is characterized by high-voltage slow activity, including sleep spindles (12–14 Hz) and delta waves (1–4 Hz); eye movements are absent; and muscle tonus is tonically reduced but still present. During slow-wave sleep, the progressive change in EEG activity from the appearance of spindles to the prevalence of delta activity has been divided into stages (1–2 in cats; 1–4 in humans). Across these stages of slow-wave sleep in humans, responsiveness to sensory

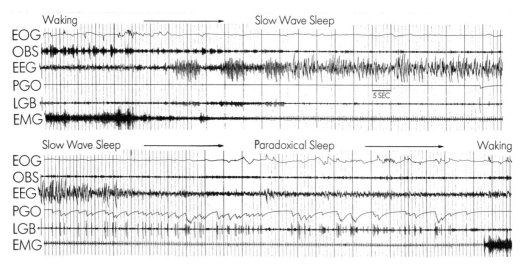

FIG. 1. Polygraphic recording from a cat showing transition from waking to slow-wave sleep and from slow-wave sleep to paradoxical sleep (or REM sleep). Decrease in eye movements (EOG) and muscle tone (EMG) along with decrease in sensory processing through olfactory bulbs (OBS) is evident in the transition from waking into slow-wave sleep (*upper panel*), when the EEG activity changes from one of low voltage fast to spindles (12–14 Hz) and then high voltage slow waves (delta, 1–4 Hz). In the transition into paradoxical sleep (*lower panel*), rapid eye movements (EOG) appear while muscle tonus (EMG) disappears, and sensory processing through olfactory bulbs (OBS) remains dampened. The EEG activity resembles that of waking as low voltage fast. Intense barrages of activity are evident within the visual system as spikes that are recorded in the lateral geniculate (LGB) yet originate in the pons and travel through the geniculate to the occipital cortex (as pontogeniculooccipital spikes). EOG, electrooculogram; OBS, olfactory bulb spindles (field potential recording filtered for 40 Hz); EEG, electroencephalogram (bipolar frontooccipital recording); PGO, pontogeniculooccipital (spike detector); LGB, lateral geniculate body (field potential recording for PGO spikes); EMG, electromyogram (recorded from muscles of the neck). Reprinted with permission from Friedman and Jones (88).

stimuli decreases progressively (2), but nonetheless persists because a response or awakening can always be elicited by increasing the intensity of sensory stimuli.

3. Paradoxical or REM sleep is characterized as a behaviorally active state because, as originally noted in human infants, rapid eye movements occur, as do frequent small movements or twitches of the extremities (3). During this paradoxical sleep, as it was called in the cat (4), the EEG is similar to that during waking, characterized by low-voltage fast activity. A barrage of activity is evident within the visual system as spikes in the lateral geniculate and the visual cortex. However, this activity originates within the brain stem, not the external environment, because the eyes are closed and the potentials are generated in the pons and transmitted from there to the geniculate and occipital cortex (as pontogeniculooccipital [PGO] spikes). The responsiveness to external (somato-) sensory stimuli is even further reduced during REM sleep than during slow-wave sleep (2). Moreover, tonus in the postural muscles is not only reduced but actually absent, marking the muscle atonia that characterizes this state. It is during this REM or paradoxical sleep state that dreaming was first documented to occur when human subjects were awakened from different stages and states of sleep (5).

NEURAL IMAGING AND RECORDING DURING SLEEP–WAKE STATES

In recent years, it has become possible to examine regional changes in cerebral activity during sleep–wake states in humans by use of neural imaging techniques that measure metabolism or blood flow that change as a function of neural activity (6). At the Montreal Neurological Institute, we have recently examined the changes in regional cerebral blood flow (rCBF) that occur in the transition from relaxed waking through stages 1 through 4 of slow-wave sleep in humans using the $H_2^{15}O$ bolus injection technique with positron emission tomography (PET) (7). In these studies, we were able to examine rCBF as a function of delta and spindle EEG activity using linear regression analysis. Delta and spindle activity were most dramatically negatively correlated with rCBF in the thalamus (Fig. 2). A negative correlation also was found in the rostral pontomesencephalic tegmentum of the brain stem.

These results in humans reflect the physiologic changes that have been documented to occur in animals in the passage from waking into slow-wave sleep (Fig. 3). Thus, neurons in the brain stem reticular formation, particularly those located in the rostral pontomesencephalic tegmentum, decrease their rate of firing before the onset of sleep (8). These neurons of the brain stem reticular activating system project rostrally in a dorsal trajectory into the midline, medial, and intralaminar thalamic nuclei, which comprise the nonspecific thalamocortical projection system that provides a widespread activating influence to the cerebral cortex (9–13). With the decrease in afferent input from the brain stem reticular neurons, the cortically projecting neurons within the thalamus undergo disfacilitation. This disfacilitation results in a slight hyperpolarization of the thalamic relay neurons, which can be sufficient to produce a change in their mode of firing from a tonic mode during waking to a phasic, bursting mode during sleep (14,15). Moreover, GABAergic neurons of the thalamic nucleus reticularis, which sur-

round the thalamus, are similarly disfacilitated and begin to burst when minimally hyperpolarized. They actively hyperpolarize the thalamic relay neurons, entraining them first in a spindle, then in a delta frequency bursting discharge, subtended by rebound low-threshold spikes. We believe that it is this active inhibition, in addition to the disfacilitation, of thalamic relay neurons that is reflected in the decrease in rCBF in the human thalamus in association with delta and spindle EEG activity. The focused decrease in the midline–medial thalamus in association with sleep spindles may reflect the initial inhibition of the widespread thalamocortical projection system in the early stages of sleep that may be responsible for the loss of conscious awareness.

Physiologic studies in animals have shown that the cortical neuronal response to peripheral somatosensory stimulation is progressively reduced during slow wave sleep to 80% during light sleep (stages 1–2) and to 65% during deep sleep (stages 3–4) as compared with waking (16). This reduction is due to a decrease in the transfer of afferent input through the thalamus (ratio of excitatory input to output) that is reduced by as much as 50% during slow-wave sleep (17). The decrease in transmission would explain the increasing threshold for the response to sensory stimuli during slow-wave sleep. But the additional inhibition of the nonspecific thalamocortical projection system would moreover explain the loss of conscious awareness that depends on widespread activation of the cerebral cortex and not simply local activation of a specific sensory cortical region. Indeed, it is known from cases of human and animal lesions that in the absence of the nonspecific thalamocortical projection system and/or the ascending reticular activating system (18–21) (Fig. 3), conscious awareness and the waking state are absent and impossible to evoke by any intensity of sensory stimulation. In such cases of coma, consciousness is truly lacking, in contrast to natural slow-wave sleep, in which it is always accessible.

In our human studies, we also found regional decreases in CBF in the cerebral cortex

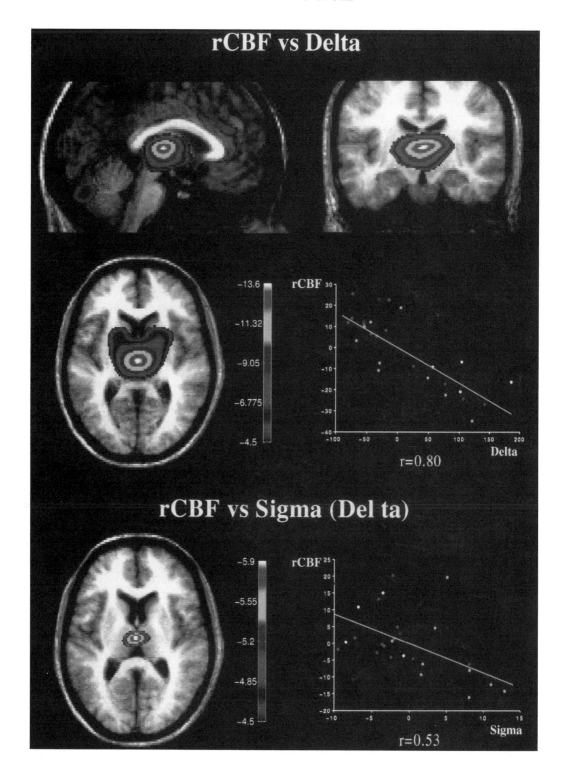

COLORPLATE 1. Positron emission tomography (PET) images superimposed on magnetic resonance images (MRI) showing decreases in normalized rCBF as a function of delta (*top*) and sigma (spindle, *below*) EEG activity in the passage from waking through slow-wave sleep in humans. Maximal significant negative covariation with delta is localized over the thalamus, shown in sagittal, coronal, and horizontal planes (*above*, with t values scaled by color). As seen in the scatterplot (*right*), rCBF decreased in the thalamus with increasing amplitude of delta activity across sleep stages (waking = blue; drowsy = cyan; stage 1 = green; stage 2 = yellow; stage 3 = red; stage 4 = white). After removing the effect of delta, significant negative covariation of rCBF with sigma activity was localized in a more restricted region, centered over the midline-medial thalamus, as shown in a horizontal section (*below*). rCBF, regional cerebral blood flow. Reprinted with permission from Hofle et al. (7).

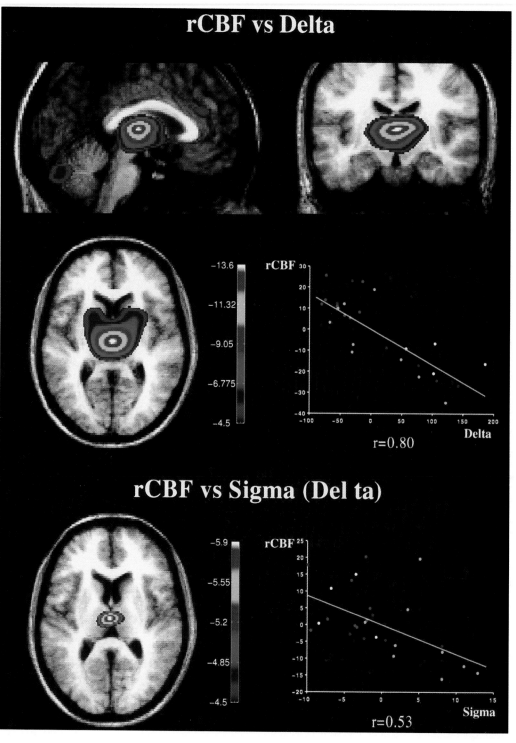

rCBF vs Delta

rCBF vs Sigma (Del ta)

r=0.80

r=0.53

(See reverse for caption.)

as a function of delta activity, as would be expected given the decrease in thalamic activity. However, these decreases were localized in prefrontal and cingulate regions of the cortex, those regions receiving the predominant projections from the midline, medial, and intralaminar nuclei and known to be important in cortical arousal (22). In contrast and to our surprise, despite the closing of the thalamic afferent gateway to the cerebral cortex, regional increases in CBF were evident in sensory regions, most particularly in the visual cortex and in the secondary auditory cortex. In view of reports of non-REM dreaming, we considered it possible that these activations could reflect visual and auditory–phonologic imagery occurring during slow-wave sleep (7). In fact, after the first early report claiming that almost all dreaming occurred during REM sleep (5), subsequent studies found that thought processes also could be evoked upon awakening from slow-wave sleep, when subjects were asked "if anything were going through their minds" (23). It was found that as in REM sleep, visual imagery was present in the majority of reports from slow-wave sleep; however, the imagery and reports were less vivid and characterized by less organismic involvement in motor and affective dimensions than reports from REM sleep. The relatively frequent reports of "thinking" as compared with "dreaming" in slow-wave sleep have led to the notion of sleep "mentation" occurring during slow-wave sleep. However, one point is clear from these studies: mental activity is always present in the sleeping brain (23), even if this activity is not easily accessible to waking consciousness.

In a recent study using PET imaging of rCBF changes during sleep in humans, investigators reported distinctive regional changes in brain activity during REM sleep (24). In this state, from which dream reports also were obtained during the experiment, the upper brain stem and thalamus were activated, as were regions of the limbic forebrain, including notably the amygdala, entorhinal cortex, and cingulate cortex. This pattern indicates that REM sleep and dream reports are associated with activation of (a) the brain stem reticular activating system and the thalamic specific and nonspecific cortical projection systems, and (b) limbic structures involved in emotional processes, memory, and cortical arousal. At the same time, the prefrontal cortex was relatively inactive, suggesting an attenuation of processes important in episodic and working memory (24) and perhaps explaining why unless awakened from a dream, the sleeping person has no memory of the dream. Once awakened, the individual may encode and organize the images and story as a dream and remember them as a dream episode, distinct from waking conscious episodes and reality. Given the widespread activation of brain stem and thalamocortical systems during REM sleep, the images and stories are more easily seized by waking consciousness, and are more memorable as events, than those of slow-wave sleep.

The distinctive pattern of activation shown by PET images during REM sleep and dreaming in humans reflects in part what has been derived from the neurophysiologic study of REM or paradoxical sleep in animals (25). First, the state of REM sleep is generated by

◄

FIG. 2. Positron emission tomography (PET) images superimposed on magnetic resonance images (MRI) showing decreases in normalized rCBF as a function of delta (*top*) and sigma (spindle, *below*) EEG activity in the passage from waking through slow-wave sleep in humans. Maximal significant negative covariation with delta is localized over the thalamus, shown in sagittal, coronal, and horizontal planes (*above*, with t values scaled by color). As seen in the scatterplot (*right*), rCBF decreased in the thalamus with increasing amplitude of delta activity across sleep stages (waking = blue; drowsy = cyan; stage 1 = green; stage 2 = yellow; stage 3 = red; stage 4 = white). (See colorplate 1.) After removing the effect of delta, significant negative covariation of rCBF with sigma activity was localized in a more restricted region, centered over the midline-medial thalamus, as shown in a horizontal section (*below*). rCBF, regional cerebral blood flow. Reprinted with permission from Hofle et al. (7).

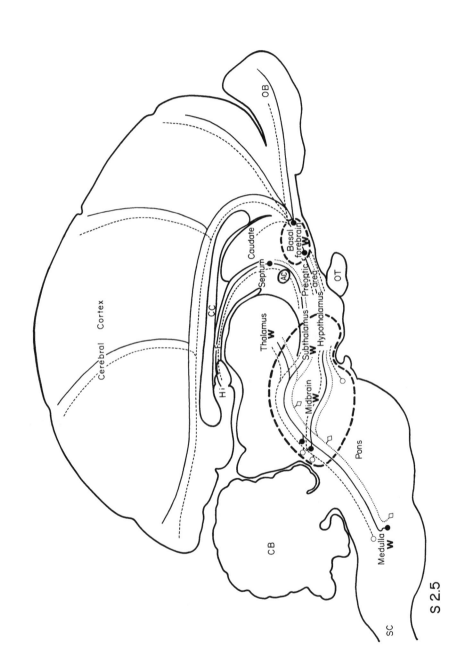

S 2.5

neurons within the brain stem because the principal components of that state are evident within the rhombencephalon after removal of the forebrain, and the state is eliminated by lesions of the pontine tegmentum (26,27) (Fig. 4). Neurons within the pontomesencephalic tegmentum increase their firing rate before and during REM sleep (8). As during waking, this increased discharge is transmitted to the thalamic specific and nonspecific projection systems, resulting in thalamocortical activation. The thalamic inhibition present during slow-wave sleep is thus lifted during this state (28), yet the arousal threshold to sensory stimulation is higher during REM sleep than during slow-wave sleep. Indeed, the attenuation of somatosensory transmission to the cortex is greater than 90% during REM sleep (16). But this attenuation is due to inhibition at the level of the first- and second-order sensory as well as interneurons in the spinal cord and brain stem (29–31). The suppression of somatosensory transmission parallels the inhibition of motor neurons in the spinal cord and brain stem that occurs during REM sleep and is initiated in the pontine tegmentum (30,32) (Fig. 4). Thus, during a state when the brain stem activating system reaches maximal levels of discharge and transmits this discharge to the forebrain through thalamocortical systems, peripheral sensory input is inhibited and motor output is blocked. It is during this state, lacking sensory–motor contact with the external world and thus reality, that the forebrain attains levels of activity equal to the maximal levels of arousal, and as evident from human PET studies, accompanied by maximal activation within the limbic system.

THEORIES REGARDING THE FUNCTION OF DREAM SLEEP

In consideration of the dream process and its possible function, investigators have attempted to relate dreaming to the physiology of REM sleep. Given the apparent random pattern of discharge by the pontine reticular neurons that drive the forebrain, it was proposed by Hobson and McCarley (33) that dreams are the result of this random activation reaching the cortex and stimulating a synthesis of the random processes by the cortex, resulting in formulation of the dream. This activation–synthesis hypothesis was proposed as a neurobiologic basis for dreaming to counter Freud's psychoanalytic theory of dreaming. Freud believed that the psyche controlled the dream process, generating symbols through defense mechanisms to disguise the subconscious desires and fears of the mind. Such extreme order presumably generated by the cortex would be in contrast to the chaos presumably generated by the brain stem, which these two theories propose and contrast. Yet, even if the activity in the brain stem were completely random, it would subsequently be modulated by the cortex, through corticobulbar feedback. Neurophysiologic evidence from Jouvet's lab-

---

FIG. 3. Sagittal drawing of the cat brain showing the regions of the brain that are most critically involved in generating and maintaining cortical activation and the waking state. Indicated by large W's (for waking) are areas of the brain from which electrical stimulation elicits, and where cells are maximally active during, waking and/or cortical activation. These areas include the ascending reticular activating system of the brain stem, the midline-medial and intralaminar nonspecific thalamocortical projection system, and the basal forebrain. Encircled by dashed lines are regions where lesions result in the most dramatic and permanent loss of cortical activation and a clinical state of coma. Within these regions are glutamatergic neurons of the reticular formation (diamonds), which project to the nonspecific thalamocortical projection system, noradrenergic neurons of the locus ceruleus (as well as other catecholaminergic neurons, *open circles*), which project in a diffuse manner to subcortical relays and directly to the cerebral cortex, and cholinergic neurons (*filled circles*), which project from the pontomesencephalic tegmentum to subcortical relays and from the basal forebrain to the cerebral cortex in a widespread manner. AC, anterior commissure; CB, cerebellum; CC, corpus callosum; Hi, hippocampus; OB, olfactory bulb; OT, optic tract; S, sagittal; SC, spinal cord. Reprinted with permission from Jones (21).

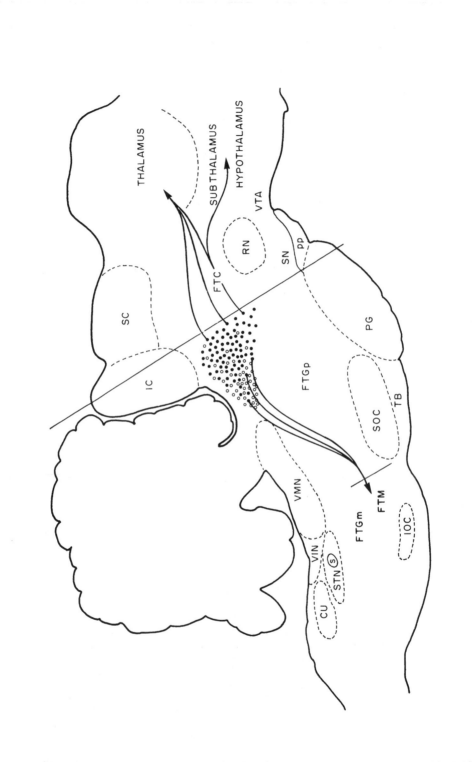

oratory has shown that the phasic activity, which arises in the pons and is transmitted to the geniculate and then to the occipital cortex in the form of PGO spikes (Fig. 1), contains a high degree of information when submitted to analysis according to entropy theory (34). The complex pattern of PGO spiking is determined in part by corticobulbar feedback because decortication results in an impoverishment of its pattern (35). Indeed, perhaps the complexity of activity in REM sleep arises as in other systems on the border of order and chaos or on the "edge of chaos" (36). The high frequency of bizarre associations and scene shifts during dreaming may be the result of sudden barrages of activity from the brain stem reticular formation. Surely such intense activation evoking old memories yet stimulating new associations with old or recent information must serve an important function in learning and memory.

Indeed, many investigators have posited an important function of dreaming in the early programming and practice of species-specific behaviors (34,37) and in the continued learning and incorporation of important new behaviors and information into memory (38). Although it has not been shown that sleep is essential for learning or memory, evidence has indicated that both slow-wave and REM sleep, particularly REM sleep, may maximize these processes and be important for memory of particularly complex tasks (39). REM sleep is increased in amount during a particular period after learning of a new task, and if effected during this paradoxical sleep window, deprivation of the state will result in memory deficits. Most interestingly, it was discovered by Winson several years ago (40) that within the hippocampus, which is integral to the limbic memory circuits, neurons that have discharged during waking because of association with a particular place fire at a higher rate (than neurons lacking the place-associated discharge) during the following episode of sleep. The increased discharge occurs in both slow-wave sleep and REM sleep, suggesting that consolidation of memory circuits could occur during both states of sleep. Buzsaki (41) proposed that such consolidation could occur during slow-wave sleep, when sharp waves in the hippocampus transmit high-frequency impulses out to neocortical targets via the entorhinal cortex. Evidence for hippocampal replay has indicated an increased tendency for ensembles of neurons to fire and, moreover, to fire in particular sequences during slow-wave sleep, reflecting the order in which the cells fired during spatial exploration and learning of the previous waking episode (42,43). The mechanism by which memory consolidation is thought to occur is through long-term potentiation (LTP) of synapses and neural circuits. LTP is maximal when stimuli are delivered to the hippocampus with a theta

FIG. 4. Sagittal drawing of the cat brain stem showing the region and neurons critically involved in the generation of paradoxical or REM sleep. The line rostral to the pontine tegmentum represents the most caudal transection of the brain, which still permits paradoxical sleep signs in the brain stem and periphery. Rostral to such a transection, no signs of paradoxical sleep are evident in the forebrain, which also can be removed without eliminating this state. The short line caudal to the pontine tegmentum indicates a small transection, which results in the loss of the descending muscle atonia of the state. Within the pontomesencephalic tegmentum are represented the cholinergic neurons (*filled circles*), which discharge during and are critically involved in the generation of paradoxical sleep and project both rostrally into the forebrain and caudally and locally into the brain stem tegmentum. Concentrated caudal to, although partially intermingled with, the cholinergic cells, are noradrenergic neurons of the locus ceruleus, which cease firing during paradoxical sleep. CU, cuneate nucleus; FTC, central tegmental field; FTGm and p, medullary and pontine gigantocellular tegmental fields; FTM, magnocellular tegmental field; IC, inferior colliculus; IOC, inferior olivary complex; RN, red nucleus; PG, pontine gray; pp, pes pedunculi; SC, superior colliculus; SN, substantia nigra; SOC, superior olivary complex; s and STN, solitary tract and nucleus; TB, trapezoid body; VIN and VMN, inferior and medial vestibular nuclei; VTA, ventral tegmental area. Reprinted with permission from Jones (25).

rhythmicity (4–10 Hz) and minimal when delivered at a slower frequency, within a delta range (1–3 Hz) (44,45). Across a natural sleep–waking cycle, LTP is readily induced during an alert waking state and REM sleep but rarely produced during slow-wave sleep (46). It would thus appear more likely that potentiation of circuits and consolidation of memory would occur maximally during REM sleep, when theta activity is prominent, than during slow-wave sleep, when delta activity is prominent. On the other hand, across the sleep cycle, REM sleep could be important for the working of a process-based memory and

slow-wave sleep could be important for the subsequent development of a structural-based memory (47), particularly in view of the evidence that increased protein synthesis, which would underlie structural changes, occurs during slow-wave sleep (48).

MECHANISMS OF GLOBAL CORTICAL ACTIVATION DURING WAKING AND REM SLEEP

In reexamining the cortical EEG activity associated with sleep–wake states by spectral analysis, it has recently become apparent that

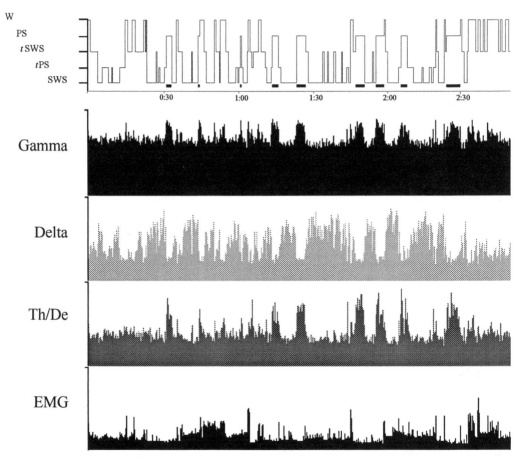

FIG. 5. Sleep hypnogram showing variation of high-frequency gamma (30–60 Hz), delta (1.5–4 Hz), theta (4.5–8.5 Hz, expressed as theta/delta ratio), and EMG across sleep–wake states in the rat. High-frequency gamma and theta are maximal in amplitude during paradoxical sleep (PS) and active periods of waking (W) and vary reciprocally with delta activity, which is maximal during slow-wave sleep (SWS). EEG activity expressed as arbitrary amplitude units were scaled to maximum using spectral analysis. tSWS and tPS indicate transitional states. Data from Maloney et al. (50).

the low-voltage fast pattern originally described during waking and REM sleep contains a high-frequency oscillation in the gamma range (40–60 Hz) in humans (49) and animals and, moreover, that this gamma oscillation occurs together with a slower frequency oscillation in a theta range (4–10 Hz) in rats (50) (Fig. 5). The parallel occurrence of a high-frequency gamma and low-frequency thetalike oscillation on the cortex during REM sleep had been noticed in earlier studies in cats and humans (51,52). Gamma activity occurs in amplitudes, like theta, that are as high in REM sleep as during the most aroused waking states (50). Moreover, the coherence in gamma activity between distant cortical areas is as high in REM sleep as during the most aroused waking states (Fig. 6). Such coherence suggests the possibility for integrated activity across widely distributed cortical regions. Indeed, coherent firing at a gamma frequency (around 40 Hz) has been posited to underlie the temporal and spatial binding of distributed sensory-motor and/or cognitive processes (53–55). Gamma activity in the neocortex may ride on a slower oscillation with a theta rhythmicity, as was originally shown to be the case in the hippocampus (56,57). In the rat, the coherence in theta activity across cortical regions is higher than that of gamma, and as for gamma, it is equally high during aroused waking as during REM sleep and higher than the coherence for delta activity during slow-wave sleep (50) (Fig. 6). These results suggest that REM sleep, like the alert waking state, is characterized by maximal and coherent gamma and theta activity in the neocortex, as in the hippocampus, and that the high coherence of these activities during these states may provide for binding and integration of spatially distributed processes, as would be involved in conscious processing on the one hand during waking and subconscious replay and consolidation on the other hand, that could occur during REM sleep.

In considering the potential subcortical mechanisms for the modulation of cortical gamma activity, the nonspecific thalamocortical system is of course important both as the rostral relay for the ascending reticular activating system and as the thalamocortical activating system that must act in coordination with the specific thalamocortical systems (49,54,58). However, other widespread or diffuse projection systems may modulate gamma activity in a state-dependent manner. From the brain stem, it was originally proposed that noradrenergic neurons of the locus ceruleus nucleus, which provide a diffuse innervation to the entire central nervous system, could be responsible for state modulation associated with cortical activation (59,60). Subsequent studies indicated that noradrenergic locus ceruleus neurons may normally enhance or prolong cortical activation but are not necessary for cortical activation of waking and moreover are not involved in the cortical activation that occurs during REM sleep (61). In fact, by single-unit recording studies, it was subsequently shown that noradrenergic neurons are off during REM sleep and that the cessation of firing of these neurons is a prerequisite for the appearance of REM sleep (62). Cholinergic neurons of the pontomesencephalic tegmentum and basal forebrain have long been proposed to represent an integral component of the ascending reticular activating system (63). Early pharmacologic studies showed an important role for acetylcholine in both waking and REM sleep (64) and indicated that REM sleep could be triggered by an enhancement of acetylcholine levels after the depletion of monoamines (65). Moreover, Jasper showed that acetylcholine release measured from the cerebral cortex was at its highest levels in association with cortical activation and during waking and REM sleep (66,67). Lesion evidence shows that cholinergic neurons within the pontomesencephalic tegmentum are critical for the generation of REM sleep (68). Through both long ascending forebrain projections and local projections into the brain stem reticular formation (69,70), these cholinergic neurons may be important for state changes in descending and ascending systems (Fig. 4), including the generation of theta activity that occurs during waking and REM sleep (71). Cholinergic neurons in the septum

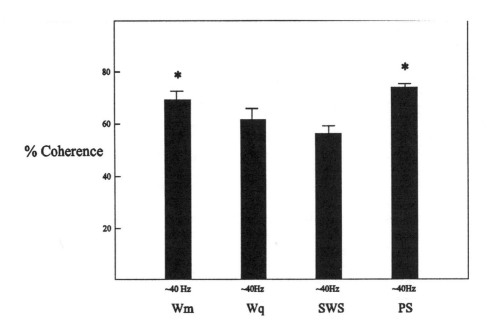

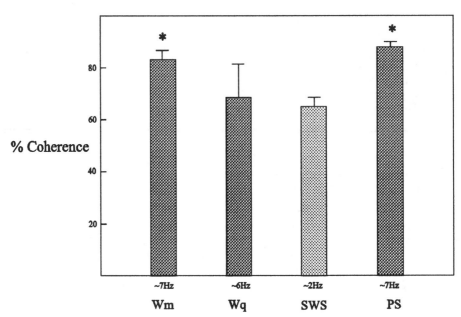

FIG. 6. Coherence in prevalent peak high-frequency (*top*) and low-frequency (*bottom*) EEG activity as a function of state. High-frequency gamma activity (at 40 Hz) shows high coherence between cortical areas (cingulate and occipital) during waking moving (Wm) and paradoxical sleep (PS) that is significantly higher than that during waking quiet (Wq) and slow-wave sleep (SWS) (*$p < 0.05$, repeated measures ANOVA and post hoc tests). In parallel, peak low-frequency activity is of significantly higher coherence during these active waking (Wm) and PS states than during quiet waking and SWS. The peak low frequency is in the theta range during active states. Data from Maloney et al. (50).

that project to the hippocampus are known to be important if not critical for the generation of theta in the hippocampus (72). Colocalized GABAergic neurons in the septum, which also project to the hippocampus (73), are also important for theta activity (72).

ROLE OF CHOLINERGIC/ GABAERGIC BASALOCORTICAL PROJECTION SYSTEM IN GLOBAL, COHERENT CORTICAL ACTIVATION

Based on several lines of evidence, we propose that cholinergic and codistributed GABAergic neurons located in the basal forebrain, yet coextensive with those in the septum, project in parallel to the neocortex and provide a rhythmic modulatory influence to the neocortex that stimulates gamma and theta activity across large cortical expanses in a coherent manner during the states of aroused waking and REM sleep. Such integral activity could provide the basis for coherent processes underlying consciousness during waking and subconscious replay and consolidation during REM sleep.

The first line of evidence for a role of cholinergic and GABAergic basal forebrain neurons in limbic and isocortical modulation is neuroanatomic. We recently found that as was shown to be the case for the septohippocampal projection, magnocellular GABAergic neurons project together with cholinergic basal forebrain neurons in similar proportions to both limbic and isocortical regions (74). Thus, in retrograde transport from the orbitofrontal or parietal cortex, we found relatively large, retrogradely labeled GABAergic (glutamic acid decarboxylase–immunoreactive) neurons intermingled with similarly large, retrogradely labeled cholinergic (choline acetyltransferase–immunoreactive) neurons in the medial septum-diagonal band, magnocellular preoptic nucleus, and substantia innominata (Fig. 7). Another surprising finding in this study was that the retrogradely labeled cells were distributed across all these nuclei from both cortical target areas, indicating a widespread distribution of cortical projections. By different densi-

ties of retrograde labeling within the cells, however, it also was found that a greater density of terminals must be focused within a more limited cortical target area, thus showing the previously documented topographic organization of primary targets of the basalocortical neurons (75). In addition, however, the cholinergic and GABAergic neurons would both appear to have collaterals to more widespread regions of the cortex such that overlapping projections would encompass the hippocampus, limbic cortex, and isocortex. Accordingly, the basalocortical projection could provide a synchronous modulatory input to multiple cortical regions, as might be important for integral, coherent functioning of spatially distributed cortical neurons.

The second line of evidence for a role of cholinergic and GABAergic basal forebrain neurons in modulating cortical activity comes from electrophysiologic evidence, which at this time has been obtained in vitro (76,77) and awaits confirmation in vivo. With the realization that elucidation of the respective roles of cholinergic and GABAergic neurons in the modulation of cortical activity will depend on electrophysiologic recording of immunohistochemically identified cells, I initiated with my colleagues, Alonso and Muhlethaler, a series of studies in guinea pig brain slices to characterize these cells. First, it was found that the biocytin-filled neurons, which were subsequently dual stained for choline acetyltransferase and were thus cholinergic, burst at a low frequency in the slice (Fig. 8A and C). The bursts were subtended by low-threshold calcium spikes, which may thus provide the cholinergic cells with intrinsic properties for rhythmic bursting in vivo. In addition to this slow bursting mode, the cholinergic cells also fire tonically, yet also at a relatively low frequency (>15 Hz), which may be related to the relatively prolonged action of acetylcholine through muscarinic receptors on cortical pyramidal cells (78). Second, noncholinergic neurons in the basal forebrain (77) and similarly those in the septum (79) also display rhythmic discharge properties;

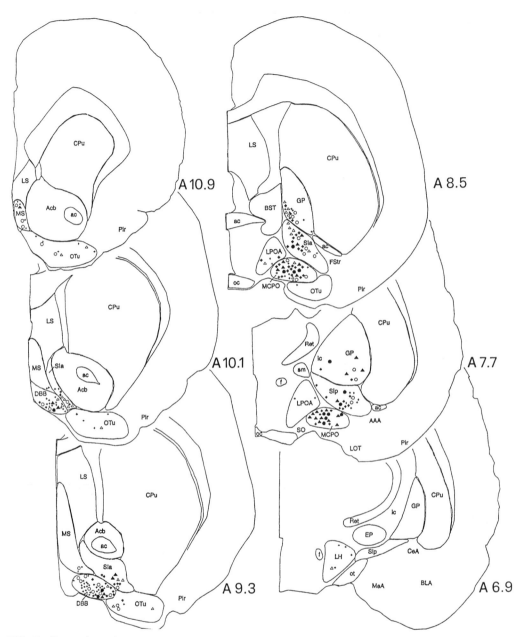

FIG. 7. Coronal sections through the rat forebrain showing the distribution of cortically projecting cholinergic and GABAergic neurons in the basal forebrain. After injections of cholera toxin (CT) into the prefrontal (orbitofrontal) cortex, retrogradely labeled cells were plotted in material dual-immunostained for CT and choline acetyltransferase (ChAT) or CT and glutamic acid decarboxylase (GAD) in adjacent sections. Retrogradely labeled GABAergic cells (CT+/GAD+, *triangles*) are intermingled with retrogradely labeled cholinergic cells (CT+/ChAT+, *circles*), together with other singly retrogradely labeled cells (CT+/ChAT-, *pluses*). Whereas lightly retrogradely labeled cells (*open symbols, thin pluses*) were widely distributed through the basal forebrain, darkly retrogradely labeled cells (*filled symbols, bold pluses*) were clustered in the magnocellular preoptic nucleus (MCPO) and substantia innominata (SI). These patterns most likely reflect widespread collaterals of the basal forebrain cell population, whose cortical projections are otherwise topographically organized according to a higher density of focalized arborization. Reprinted with permission from Gritti et al. (74).

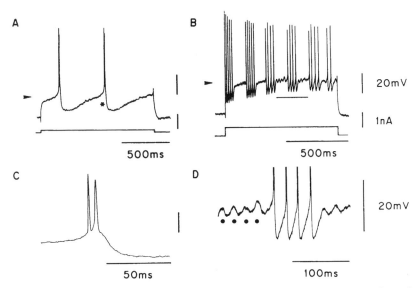

FIG. 8. Electrophysiologic traces showing intrinsic rhythmic properties of cholinergic and noncholinergic neurons in the basal forebrain. Cholinergic cells (*left*, **A**) display low-threshold calcium spikes (*, enlarged in **C**) when depolarized from a hyperpolarized level. Noncholinergic cells (*right*, **B**) display clustered spikes interspersed with subthreshold oscillations (— , enlarged in **D**, ⊙) both at a high, gamma range frequency (here 40 Hz) and recurring at a low, theta range frequency (here 6 Hz). In vitro intracellular recordings in the guinea pig basal forebrain slice. (Arrowheads indicate levels of resting membrane potential.) Data from Alonso et al. (77) and Muhlethaler et al. (89).

however, in this case the rhythm and mechanism are very different from those of the cholinergic cells. Noncholinergic cells are fast spiking cells (>20 Hz) and often fire in a gamma range of frequencies in the slice (40–60 Hz) (Fig. 8B and D). In addition, depending on the level of the membrane, these cells tend to fire in clusters of spikes, between which subthreshold membrane potential oscillations are present at approximately the same gamma frequency. The clusters occur with a slow rhythmicity (2–10 Hz) that is often within a theta range. These results in vitro suggest that cholinergic and GABAergic neurons could fire in a coordinated manner in vivo to modulate cortical activity according to a slow theta rhythm on which the faster gamma rhythm rides.

Before confirmation of the activity profiles of cholinergic and GABAergic neurons in vivo, we recently examined the potential influence of the cholinergic and GABAergic cortically projecting neurons on cortical EEG activity and state through pharmacologic manipulation of these neurons by local microinjections into the basal forebrain in continuously recorded, naturally sleeping–waking rats (80). First, it was found that inactivation of the basal forebrain cell complex with procaine led to a loss of cortical activation, including the attenuation of both gamma and theta, and a prevalence of slow, irregular delta activity (Fig. 9). From previous in vitro pharmacologic results, it was known that NMDA can produce a robust rhythmic burst discharge in the cholinergic basalis cells (81). We thus subsequently examined the effect of microinjections of NMDA in the region of the nucleus basalis (82). NMDA produced prolonged cortical activation and behavioral arousal associated with an increase in high-frequency gamma activity and rhythmic theta activity (Fig. 9). These results suggest that rhythmic bursting by basal forebrain neurons produces an enhancement of gamma activity together with rhythmic theta modulation in the cortex.

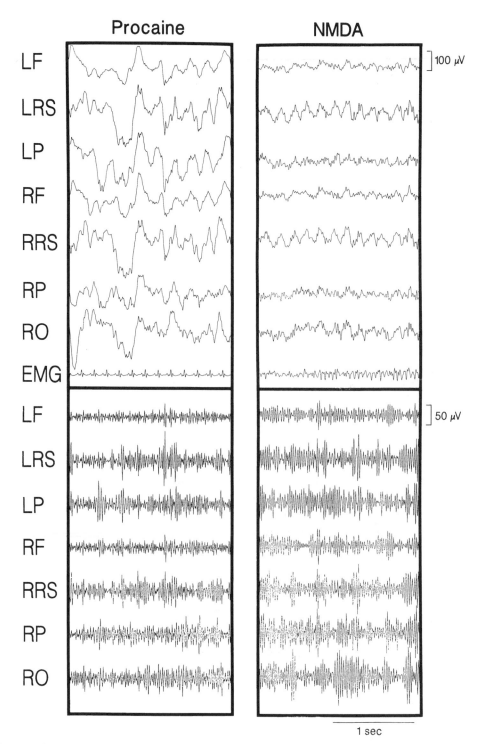

FIG. 9. EEG activity after microinjections of procaine (*left*) and NMDA (*right*) into the basal forebrain cholinergic cell area of the rat. Procaine resulted in continuous slow, irregular activity in a delta range (here 2 Hz, unfiltered EEG in upper set of traces) and relatively low-amplitude gamma (filtered for 30.5–58 Hz, lower set of traces). NMDA produced rhythmic low-frequency thetalike EEG activity (here 6 Hz) accompanied by relatively high amplitude gamma activity. Data from Cape and Jones (80,82).

As has been shown to be the case in the hippocampus (83,84), cholinergic and GABAergic basalocortical neurons may innervate the interneurons in the cerebral cortex (85,86), which in turn could pace the pyramidal neurons by inhibitory postsynaptic potentials (IPSPs). Temporal coherence in spatially distributed pyramidal cell discharge would thus be provided by the synchronous envelopes between IPSPs occurring at gamma and theta frequencies and thus allowing coherence of firing among functionally integrated populations of pyramidal cells.

In summary, consciousness depends on global, coherent activation of thalamocortical systems that is provided during waking by activation of the brain stem reticular activating system, including glutamatergic, as well as noradrenergic and cholinergic neurons (87). In addition, cholinergic neurons of the basal forebrain, together with codistributed GABAergic neurons, which project in a parallel, widespread manner to hippocampus and neocortex, provide a state-dependent rhythmic input that activates the cortex and promotes activity within gamma and theta frequencies, thus providing a temporal organization for coherent discharge in spatially distributed yet functionally linked cortical neurons. Whereas glutamatergic and cholinergic neurons are active during both waking and REM sleep, noradrenergic neurons are off during REM sleep. Sensory transmission and motor output are blocked, and prefrontal cortical regions appear relatively inactive, allowing for activation of sensory–motor, association and memory circuits within thalamocortical and limbic systems without input or output that would establish the reality of the waking world and without episodic or working memory that would otherwise catalog the events outside that reality. The dream sensory–motor and affective images thus remain in the subconscious unless waking intrudes to bring them to waking consciousness and accordingly commit them to waking memory as dream events and episodes distinct from waking reality. The global activation during dreaming provides a replay of waking material from recent and long-term memory stores and accordingly provides a process for formation and consolidation of old and new associations. The consolidation is potentiated by theta modulation transmitted to the archi- and neocortex by the basalocortical system. During slow-wave sleep, the brain is not inactive or totally unresponsive; however, given the attenuation of both the brain stem reticular activating system and the thalamus, imagery and thought processes occur by activation in limited primary and secondary sensory regions of the cerebral cortex. These processes of sleep mentation are less organized, less vivid, and have less emotional content than the dreams of REM sleep, and they are more difficult to bring to waking consciousness, for which they must be seized by the global activating processes, including the basalocortical system, that are largely disabled during slow-wave sleep. By these differential processes, slow-wave sleep is often perceived as a quiet, restful state upon awakening, whereas REM sleep is more often perceived as the dream state, in which vivid, sometimes bizarre images involving coherent yet dynamically changing themes occur, sometimes pleasureful, sometimes frightful, and often emotionally toned. Thus, our current understanding of the neural basis of consciousness across the sleep–waking cycle reveals three distinctly different configurations of neural activity underlying three distinctly different mental states that the Hindu scholars had described so long ago.

ACKNOWLEDGMENT

I thank Karen Maloney and Edmund Cape, graduate students, who contributed to the preparation of this chapter. Research was supported by the Medical Research Council of Canada (Grants 6464 to B.E.J. and SP-30 to Neuroimaging at the Montreal Neurological Institute).

REFERENCES

1. Nikhilananda S. *The Upanishads.* London: Phoenix House, 1949.
2. Williams HL, Hammack JT, Daly RL, Dement WC,

Lubin A. Responses to auditory stimulation, sleep loss and the EEG stages of sleep. *Electroencephalogr Clin Neurophysiol* 1964;16:269–279.

3. Aserinsky E, Kleitman N. Regularly occurring periods of eye motility, and concomitant phenomena during sleep. *Science* 1953;118:273–274.

4. Jouvet M, Michel F, Courjon J. Sur un stade d'activite electrique cerebrale rapide au cours du sommeil physiologique. *C R Soc Biol* 1959;153:1024–1028.

5. Dement W, Kleitman N. The relation of eye movements during sleep to dream activity: an objective method for the study of dreaming. *J Exp Psychol* 1957;53: 339–346.

6. Madsen PL, Vorstrup S. Cerebral blood flow and metabolism during sleep. *Cerebrovasc Brain Metab Rev* 1991;3:281–296.

7. Hofle N, Paus T, Reutens D, Fiset P, Gotman J, Evans AC, Jones BE. Regional cerebral blood flow changes as a function of delta and spindle activity during slow wave sleep in humans. *J Neurosci* 1997;17:4800–4808.

8. Steriade M, McCarley RW. *Brainstem control of wakefulness and sleep.* New York: Plenum, 1990.

9. Morison RS, Dempsey EW, Morison BR. Cortical responses from electrical stimulation of the brain stem. *Am J Physiol* 1941;131:732–743.

10. Jasper H. Diffuse projection systems: the integrative action of the thalamic reticular system. *Electroencephalogr Clin Neurophysiol* 1949;1:405–420.

11. Moruzzi G, Magoun HW. Brain stem reticular formation and activation of the EEG. *Electroencephalogr Clin Neurophysiol* 1949;1:455–473.

12. Starzl TE, Magoun HW. Organization of the diffuse thalamic projection system. *J Neurophysiol* 1951;14: 133–146.

13. Steriade M, Jones EG, Llinás R. *Thalamic oscillations and signaling.* New York: Wiley, 1990.

14. Steriade M, Deschênes M. The thalamus as a neuronal oscillator. *Brain Res Rev* 1984;8:1–63.

15. Steriade M, Llinás RR. The functional states of the thalamus and the associated neuronal interplay. *Physiol Rev* 1988;68:649–742.

16. Gucer G. The effect of sleep upon the transmission of afferent activity in the somatic afferent system. *Exp Brain Res* 1979;34:287–298.

17. Coenen AML, Vendrik AJH. Determination of the transfer ratio of cat's geniculate neurons through quasi-intracellular recordings and the relation with the level of alertness. *Exp Brain Res* 1972;14:227–242.

18. Facon E, Steriade M, Wertheim N. Hypersomnie prolongee engendree par des lesions bilaterales du systeme activateur medial. Le syndrome thrombotique de la bifurcation du tronc basilaire. *Rev Neurol* 1958;98: 117–133.

19. Lindsley DB, Schreiner LH, Knowles WB, Magoun HW. Behavioral and EEG changes following chronic brain stem lesions. *Electroencephalogr Clin Neurophysiol* 1950;2:483–498.

20. Guilleminault C, Quera-Salva M-A, Goldberg MP. Pseudo-hypersomnia and pre-sleep behaviour with bilateral paramedian thalamic lesions. *Brain* 1993;116: 1549–1563.

21. Jones BE. Basic mechanisms of sleep-wake states. In: Kryger MH, Roth T, Dement WC, eds. *Principles and practice of sleep medicine.* Philadelphia: WB Saunders, 1994:145–162.

22. Paus T, Zatorre RJ, Hofle N, et al. Time-related changes in neural systems underlying attention and arousal during the performance of an auditory vigilance task. *J Cognitive Neurosci* 1997;9:392–408.

23. Foulkes WD. Dream reports from different stages of sleep. *J Abnorm Soc Psychol* 1962;65:14–25.

24. Maquet P, Peters J-M, Aerts J, et al. Functional neuroanatomy of human rapid-eye-movement sleep and dreaming. *Nature* 1996;383:163–166.

25. Jones BE. Paradoxical sleep and its chemical/structural substrates in the brain. *Neuroscience* 1991;40: 637–656.

26. Jouvet M. Recherches sur les structures nerveuses et les mecanismes responsables des differentes phases du sommeil physiologique. *Arch Ital Biol* 1962;100: 125–206.

27. Jones BE. Elimination of paradoxical sleep by lesions of the pontine gigantocellular tegmental field in the cat. *Neurosci Lett* 1979;13:285–293.

28. Carli G, Diete-Spiff K, Pompeiano O. Presynaptic and postsynaptic inhibition of transmission of somatic afferent volleys through the cuneate nucleus during sleep. *Arch Ital Biol* 1969;105:52–82.

29. Carli G, Diete-Spiff K, Pompeiano O. Transmission of sensory information through the lemniscal pathways during sleep. *Arch Ital Biol* 1967;105:31–51.

30. Pompeiano O. Mechanisms responsible for spinal inhibition during desynchronized sleep: experimental study. In: Guilleminault C, Dement WC, Passonant P, eds. *Advances in Sleep Research.* Vol. 3. Narcolepsy. New York: Spectrum, 1976:411–449.

31. Soja PJ, Oka J-I, Fragoso M. Synaptic transmission through cat lumbar ascending sensory pathways is suppressed during active sleep. *J Neurophysiol* 1993;70: 1708–1712.

32. Chase MH, Morales FR. The control of motoneurons during sleep. In: Kryger MH, Roth T, Dement WC, eds. *Principles and practice of sleep medicine.* Philadelphia: WB Saunders, 1989:74–85.

33. Hobson JA, McCarley RW. The brain as a dream state generator: an activation-synthesis hypothesis of the dream process. *Am J Psychiatry* 1977;134:1334–1338.

34. Jouvet M. The function of dreaming: a neurophysiologist's point of view. In: Gazziniga MS, Blakemore C, eds. *Handbook of psychobiology.* New York: Academic, 1975:499–527.

35. Gadea-Ciria M. *Etude sequentielle des pointes pontogeniculo-occipitales (PGO).* Doctoral thesis. Université Claude-Bernard. Lyon, France, 1972.

36. Kauffman SA. *The origins of order.* Oxford, England: Oxford University Press, 1993.

37. Roffwarg HP, Muzio JN, Dement WC. Ontogenetic development of the human sleep-dream cycle. *Science* 1966;152:604–619.

38. Winson J. The meaning of dreams. *Sci Am* 1990;262: 86–96.

39. Smith C. Sleep states and memory processes. *Behav Brain Res* 1995;69:137–145.

40. Pavlides C, Winson J. Influences of hippocampal place cell firing in the awake state on the activity of these cells during subsequent sleep episodes. *J Neurosci* 1989;9:2907–2918.

41. Buzsaki G. The hippocampo-neocortical dialogue. *Cerebral Cortex* 1996;6:81–92.

42. Wilson MA, McNaughton BL. Reactivation of hippo-

campal ensemble memories during sleep. *Science* 1994;265:676–679.

43. Skaggs WE, McNaughton BL. Replay of neuronal firing sequences in rat hippocampus during sleep following spatial experience. *Science* 1996;271:1870–1873.

44. Larson J, Wong D, Lynch G. Patterned stimulation at the theta frequency is optimal for the induction of hippocampal long-term potentiation. *Brain Res* 1986;368:347–350.

45. Greenstein YJ, Pavlides C, Winson J. Long-term potentiation in the dentate gyrus is preferentially induced at theta rhythm periodicity. *Brain Res* 1988;438:331–334.

46. Bramham CR, Srebro B. Synaptic plasticity in the hippocampus is modulated by behavioral state. *Brain Res* 1989;493:74–86.

47. Kandel ER. Cellular mechanisms of learning and the biological basis of individuality. In: Kandel ER, Schwartz JH, Jessell TM, eds. *Principles of neural science.* New York: Elsevier, 1991:1009–1031.

48. Beebe Smith C, Dang T, Ito M, et al. Local rates of cerebral protein synthesis measured in sleeping monkeys are positively correlated with percent time in deep sleep. *Soc Neurosci Abstr* 1995;21:1495.

49. Llinás R, Ribary U. Coherent 40-Hz oscillation characterizes dream state in humans. *Proc Natl Acad Sci U S A* 1993;90:2078–2081.

50. Maloney KJ, Cape EG, Gotman J, Jones BE. High frequency gamma EEG activity in association with sleep-wake states and spontaneous behaviors in the rat. *Neuroscience* 1997;76:541–555.

51. Parmeggiani PL, Zanocco G. A study of the bioelectrical rhythms of cortical and subcortical structures during activated sleep. *Arch Ital Biol* 1963;101:385–412.

52. Itil TM. Digital computer analysis of the electroencephalogram during rapid eye movement sleep state in man. *J Nerv Ment Dis* 1970;150:201–208.

53. Bressler SL. The gamma wave: a cortical information carrier. *Trends Neurosci* 1990;13:161–162.

54. Ribary U, Ioannides AA, Singh KD, et al. Magnetic field tomography of coherent thalamocortical 40-Hz oscillations in humans. *Proc Natl Acad Sci U S A* 1992; 89:11037–11041.

55. Singer W. Synchronization of cortical activity and its putative role in information processing and learning. *Ann Rev Physiol* 1993;55:349–374.

56. Stumpf C. The fast component in the electrical activity of rabbit's hippocampus. *Electroencephalogr Clin Neurophysiol* 1965;18:477–486.

57. Buzsaki G, Leung L-WS, Vanderwolf CH. Cellular bases of hippocampal EEG in the behaving rat. *Brain Res Rev* 1983;6:139–171.

58. Steriade M, Curro Dossi R, Pare D, Oakson G. Fast oscillations (20–40Hz) in thalamocortical systems and their potentiation by mesopontine cholinergic nuclei in the cat. *Proc Natl Acad Sci U S A* 1991;88:4396–4400.

59. Jones BE, Bobillier P, Pin C, Jouvet M. The effect of lesions of catecholamine-containing neurons upon monoamine content of the brain and EEG and behavioral waking in the cat. *Brain Res* 1973;58:157–177.

60. Jones BE, Moore RY. Ascending projections of the locus coeruleus in the rat. II. Autoradiographic study. *Brain Res* 1977;127:23–53.

61. Jones BE, Harper ST, Halaris AE. Effects of locus coeruleus lesions upon cerebral monoamine content, sleep-wakefulness states and the response to amphetamine. *Brain Res* 1977;124:473–496.

62. Hobson JA, McCarley RW, Wyzinski PW. Sleep cycle oscillation: reciprocal discharge by two brainstem neuronal groups. *Science* 1975;189:55–58.

63. Shute CCD, Lewis PR. The ascending cholinergic reticular system: neocortical, olfactory and subcortical projections. *Brain* 1967;90:497–520.

64. Domino EF, Yamamoto K, Dren AT. Role of cholinergic mechanisms in states of wakefulness and sleep. *Prog Brain Res* 1968;28:113–133.

65. Karczmar AG, Longo VG, Scotti de Carolis A. A pharmacological model of paradoxical sleep: the role of cholinergic and monoamine systems. *Physiol Behav* 1970;5:175–182.

66. Jasper HH, Tessier J. Acetylcholine liberation from cerebral cortex during paradoxical (REM) sleep. *Science* 1971;172:601–602.

67. Celesia GG, Jasper HH. Acetylcholine released from cerebral cortex in relation to state of activation. *Neurology* 1966;16:1053–1064.

68. Webster HH, Jones BE. Neurotoxic lesions of the dorsolateral pontomesencephalic tegmentum-cholinergic cell area in the cat. II. Effects upon sleep-waking states. *Brain Res* 1988;458:285–302.

69. Jones BE. Immunohistochemical study of choline acetyl transferase-immunoreactive processes and cells innervating the pontomedullary reticular formation. *J Comp Neurol* 1990;295:485–514.

70. Ford B, Holmes C, Mainville L, Jones BE. GABAergic neurons in the rat pontomesencephalic tegmentum. Codistribution with cholinergic and other tegmental neurons projecting to the posterior lateral hypothalamus. *J Comp Neurol* 1995;363:177–196.

71. Vertes RP, Colom LV, Fortin WJ, Bland BH. Brainstem sites for the carbachol elicitation of the hippocampal theta rhythm in the rat. *Exp Brain Res* 1993;96: 419–429.

72. Lee MG, Chrobak JJ, Sik A, Wiley RG, Buzsaki G. Hippocampal theta activity following selective lesion of the septal cholinergic system. *Neuroscience* 1994; 62:1033–1047.

73. Kohler C, Chan-Palay V, Wu J-Y. Septal neurons containing glutamic acid decarboxylase immunoreactivity project to the hippocampal region in the rat brain. *Anat Embryol* 1984;169:41–44.

74. Gritti I, Mainville L, Mancia M, Jones BE. GABAergic and other non-cholinergic basal forebrain neurons project together with cholinergic neurons to meso- and isocortex in the rat. *J Comp Neurol* 1997;383:163–177.

75. Saper CB. Organization of cerebral cortical afferent systems in the rat. I. Magnocellular basal nucleus. *J Comp Neurol* 1984;222:313-342.

76. Khateb A, Muhlethaler M, Alonso A, Serafin M, Mainville L, Jones BE. Cholinergic nucleus basalis neurons display the capacity for rhythmic bursting activity mediated by low threshold calcium spikes. *Neuroscience* 1992;51:489–494.

77. Alonso A, Khateb A, Fort P, Jones BE, Muhlethaler M. Differential oscillatory properties of cholinergic and non-cholinergic nucleus Basalis neurons in guinea pig brain slice. *Eur J Neurosci* 1996;8:169–182.

78. McCormick DA. Neurotransmitter actions in the thalamus and cerebral cortex and their role in neuromodulation of thalamocortical activity. *Prog Neurobiol* 1992; 39:337–388.

79. Serafin M, Willimas S, Khateb A, Fort P, Muhlethaler M.

Rhythmic firing of medial septum non-cholinergic neurons. *Neuroscience* 1996;3:671–675.

80. Cape E, Jones BE. Modulation of sleep-wake state and cortical activity following injection of agonists into the region of cholinergic basal forebrain neurons. *Soc Neurosci Abstr* 1994;20:156.

81. Khateb A, Fort P, Serafin M, Jones BE, Muhlethaler M. Rhythmical bursts induced by NMDA in cholinergic nucleus basalis neurones in vitro. *J Physiol (Lond)* 1995;487.3:623–638.

82. Cape EG, Jones BE. Changes in gamma and theta EEG activity and sleep-wake state following microinjections of procaine or glutamate agonists into the basal function (submitted).

83. Soltesz I, Deschênes M. Low- and high-frequency membrane potential oscillations during theta activity in CA1 and CA3 pyramidal neurons of the rat hippocampus under ketamine-xylazine anesthesia. *J Neurophysiol* 1993;70:97–116.

84. Freund TF, Buzsaki G. Interneurons of the hippocampus. *Hippocampus* 1996;6:347–470.

85. Beaulieu C, Somogyi P. Enrichment of cholinergic synaptic terminals on GABAergic neurons and coexistence of immunoreactive GABA and choline acetyltransferase in the same synaptic terminals in the striate cortex of the cat. *J Comp Neurol* 1991;304:666–680.

86. Freund TF, Meskenaite V. Gamma-aminobutyric acid-containing basal forebrain neurons innervate inhibitory interneurons in the neocortex. *Proc Natl Acad Sci U S A* 1992;89:738–742.

87. Jones BE. Reticular formation. Cytoarchitecture, transmitters and projections. In: Paxinos G, eds. *The rat nervous system.* New South Wales, Australia: Academic, 1995:155–171.

88. Friedman L, Jones BE. Study of sleep-wakefulness states by computer graphics and cluster analysis before and after lesions of the pontine tegmentum. *Electroencephalogr Clin Neurophysiol* 1984;57:43–56.

89. Muhlethaler M, Khateb A, Fort P, Jones BE, Alonso A. Forty Hz membrane potential oscillations and theta-like activity in basal forebrain neurones. *Neurosci Abstr* 1992;18:197.

DISCUSSION

Moderated by E. G. Jones

Edward G. Jones: Let me ask you about one of the PET scanning results in which you showed a great reduction in activity in the midline and medial thalamus. In your subsequent discussion, you attributed that, I think, to high activation of the reticular nucleus, yet you did not show us any increased activity, metabolic activity in the reticular nucleus.

Barbara E. Jones: In fact, that was one of the original rationales of the study. As I was to learn myself, the resolution is such that, given the large decrease that we see in the massive central thalamus, this would mask any minor increase that we might see in the very small and narrow reticularis nucleus surrounding the thalamus.

Jeffrey A. Gray: You commented on the similarities and the continuities between the septal and basal forebrain components of the cholinergic projections. We have reported data that are very consistent with this idea of continuity (1). We made lesions in the regions containing each of these two cholinergic nuclei, either separately or combined, and showed that the behavioral effects of the two lesions were qualitatively and quantitatively alike and additive in their combined effects (the observations were made with rats tested in a radial arm maze). Furthermore, cholinergic-rich neural transplants were able to restore function in animals with the combined lesions, whether they were placed in the hippocampus (target of the septal cholinergic projection) or the neocortex (target of the basal forebrain nucleus).

Jonathan Downar: I was wondering if you might be able to put these states and mechanisms into a sort of an evolutionary perspective in terms of their adaptationist role for the organism?

Barbara E. Jones: Well, from my own individual work, I would not pretend to have particular insights into that aspect. But I might mention that Jonathan Winson, as part of his theory concerning the importance of REM sleep to learning and consolidation of memory, attributes great importance to the role of REM sleep in the maintenance of species-specific behaviors and to the incorporation of learned daytime information into what are more fundamental behavioral paradigms of the species.

Discussion Reference

1. Sinden JD, Hodges, H, Gray JA. Neural transplantation and recovery of cognitive function. *Behav Brain Sci* 1995;18:1–35.

Consciousness: At the Frontiers of Neuroscience,
Advances in Neurology, Vol. 77,
edited by H.H. Jasper, L. Descarries,
V.F. Castellucci, and S. Rossignol.
Lippincott–Raven Publishers, Philadelphia © 1998.

7

Temporal Conjunction in Thalamocortical Transactions

Rodolfo R. Llinás and Urs Ribary

Department of Physiology and Neuroscience, New York University School of Medicine,
New York, New York 10016

Given that sensory inputs generate but a fractured representation of universals, the issue of perceptual unity concerns the mechanisms that allow these different sensory components to be gathered into one global image. In recent years, this has been described as binding, to be implemented by temporal conjunction (1–4).

Because the number of possible categories of perceptions is so extensive, it is unlikely that their implementation occur via purely hierarchical connectivity. That is, where a single grandmother neuron or a small group of such neurons represent specific elements of a category. A second problem with the hierarchical proposal is sampling size, i.e., a large number of specific elements in a large number of categories would make the retrieval problem immense. Thus, even considering that neuronal elements transduce and transmit signals at a millisecond rate from the onset of sensory primitives, exhausting all sequential combinations would be awkwardly time intensive. At a more familiar level, however, it takes roughly the same amount of time to recognize that a face is familiar than that it is not. As in any sequential strategy, it takes much longer to conclude nonfamiliarity, because it would require comparison with all known faces with familiar faces, the search would proceed for only as long as necessary to match. From a different perspective, the grandmother neuron hypothesis fails to explain how their unique perceptual insights (the specific elements in a given category) are communicated to the rest of the nervous system. Indeed, how does a grandmother cell tell the rest of their neurons what they know, given their unique position at the top of a hierarchy?

Alternatively, because categorizations are generated by spatial mapping of the primary sensory cortex and its associated cortical structures, a more dynamic interaction based on temporal coherence may generate dissipative functional structures (5) capable of as rapid a change as the perception they generate. Thus, simultaneity mapping may be envisioned that takes advantage of the parallel and synchronous organization of the brain networks in order to generate perception.

The hypotheses discussed here are derived from two areas of research: first, from the investigation of single neuronal elements studied in vitro and in vivo, and second, from measurements made via noninvasive magnetoencephalography in humans. The principal issue to be discussed is the assumption that the intrinsic electrical properties of neurons, and the dynamic events resulting from their connectivity, result in global resonant states that we know as cognition.

THE BRAIN AS AN INTROSPECTIVE REALITY EMULATOR

Several lines of research suggest that the brain is essentially a closed system (5) capable of self-generated activity based on the intrinsic electrical properties of its component neurons and their connectivity. In such a view, the central nervous system (CNS) is a "reality"-emulating system (6), and the parameters of such reality are delineated by the senses (7). The hypothesis that the brain is a closed system follows from the observation that the thalamic input from the cortex is larger than that from the peripheral sensory system (8), suggesting thalamocortical iterative recurrent activity (9) as the basis for consciousness (6). In addition, neurons with intrinsic oscillatory capabilities that reside in this complex synaptic network allow the brain to self-generate dynamic oscillatory states that shape the functional events elicited by sensory stimuli. In this context, functional states such as wakefulness or rapid eye movement (REM) sleep and other sleep stages are prominent examples of the breadth of variation that self-generated brain activity will yield.

The above hypothesis assumes that, for the most part, the connectivity of the human brain is present at birth and "fine-tuned" during normal maturation. This view of a neurologic a priori was suggested in early neurologic research (10,11), with the identification by Broca of a cortical speech center and the discovery of point-to-point somatotopic maps in the motor and sensory cortices (12) and in the thalamus (13,14).

A second organizing principle may be equally important, one that is based on the temporal rather than the spatial relationships among neurons. This temporal mapping may be viewed as a type of functional geometry (15). This mechanism has been difficult to study until recently because it requires the simultaneous measurement of activity from large numbers of neurons and is not a parameter usually considered in neuroscience.

TEMPORAL MAPPING GAMMA RANGE ACTIVITY AND COGNITIVE CONJUNCTION

Synchronous neuronal activation during sensory input has recently been studied in the mammalian visual cortical cells when light bars of optimal orientation and displacement rate are presented (16–18). Furthermore, the components of a visual stimulus corresponding to a singular cognitive object, e.g., a line in a visual field, yield coherent gamma band oscillations in regions of the cortex that may be as far as 7 mm apart (17–19) or may even be in the contralateral cortex. In fact, gamma band oscillatory activity between related cortical columns has a high correlation coefficient under such circumstances. In addition, coherent 40-Hz oscillations throughout the cortical mantle of awake human subjects has been revealed by magnetoencephalography (20). These gamma oscillations display a high degree of spatial organization and thus may be a candidate mechanism for the production of temporal conjunction of rhythmic activity over a large ensemble of neurons.

From a neuronal point of view, the mechanism by which gamma oscillation may be generated has been studied at the level of single neurons and of neuronal circuits. For example, it has been shown that the membrane potential of sparsely spiny inhibitory neurons in cortical layer IV support gamma frequency membrane voltage oscillation (Fig. 1), the mechanism for the oscillation being a sequential activation of a persistent low-threshold sodium current (21) followed by a subsequent potassium conductance (22). The inhibitory input of these sparsely spinous interneurons onto pyramidal cells projecting to the thalamus can entrain 40-Hz oscillation in the reticular nucleus and so entrain, by rebound activation, the specific and nonspecific thalamus. This issue will be treated in the modeling part of this paper. Indeed, because the GABAergic reticular thalamic neurons project to most of the relay nuclei of the thalamus (23), layer IV cells would indirectly make a contribution to the 40-Hz resonant os-

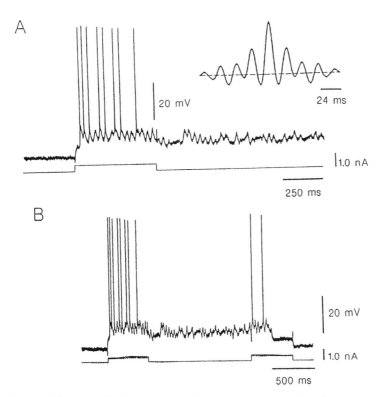

FIG. 1. In vitro intracellular recording from a sparsely spinous neuron of the fourth layer of the frontal cortex of the guinea pig. **A:** The characteristic response obtained in the cell, after direct depolarization, consisting of a sustained subthreshold oscillatory activity on which single spikes can be observed. The intrinsic oscillatory frequency was 42 Hz, as demonstrated by the autocorrelogram shown in the upper right corner. **B:** The same record as in A, but at a slower sweep speed, demonstrating how the response outlasts the first stimuli but comes to an abrupt cessation in the middle of a second stimulus. Modified with permission from Llinás et al. (22).

cillation in the thalamocortical network. It has recently been demonstrated that under in vivo conditions, relay-thalamic and reticular-nucleus neurons and pyramidal cells themselves are capable of close to 40-Hz oscillation on their own, laying out in this manner the possibility for network resonance intrinsically at gamma band frequency (24). The ionic mechanisms underlying this oscillation are similar to those of the spiny layer IV neurons (25).

When the interconnectivity of these nuclei is combined with the intrinsic properties of the individual neurons, a network for resonant neuronal oscillation emerges in which specific corticothalamocortical circuits would tend to resonate at gamma frequency. According to this hypothesis, neurons at the different levels, and in particular those in the reticular nucleus, would be responsible for the synchronization of gamma oscillation in distant thalamic and cortical sites. As we will see later, these oscillations may be organized globally over the CNS, especially because it has been shown that neighboring reticular-nucleus cells may be linked by dendrodendritic and intranuclear axon collaterals (26).

THALAMOCORTICAL RESONANCE AS THE SUBSTRATE FOR CONSCIOUSNESS

Based on research on the minimal temporal interval to sensory discrimination, we may conclude that consciousness is a noncontinuous event determined by synchronous activity in the thalamocortical system (27). Because this activity is present during REM sleep (28) but is not seen during non-REM sleep, we may postulate further that the resonance is modulated by the brain stem and would be given content by sensory input in the awake state and by intrinsic activity during dreaming. These studies addressed issues concerning (a) the presence of gamma band activity during sleep and (b) the possible differences between gamma resetting in different sleep/wakefulness states.

Spontaneous magnetic activity was recorded continuously during wakefulness, delta sleep, and REM sleep using a 37-channel sensor array positioned as shown in Fig. 2A. Because Fourier analysis of the spontaneous, broadly filtered rhythmicity (1-200 Hz) demonstrated a large peak of activity at 40 Hz over much of the cortex, we decided that it was permissible to filter the data at gamma band frequency (35–45 Hz). Large

coherent signals with a high signal-to-noise ratio were typically recorded from all 37 sensors as shown in Fig. 2B for a single 0.6-second epoch of global spontaneous oscillations in an awake individual.

The second set of experiments examined the responsiveness of the oscillation to an auditory stimulus during wakefulness, delta sleep, and REM sleep. The stimulus comprised frequency-modulated 500-millisecond tone bins, triggered 100 milliseconds after the onset of the 600-millisecond recording epoch; recordings were made at random intervals over about 10 minutes. In agreement with previous findings (28–30), auditory stimuli produced well-defined 40-Hz oscillation during wakefulness (Fig. 2C), but no resetting was observed during delta (Fig. 2D) or REM sleep (Fig. 2E) in this or the six other subjects examined (28).

The traces in Fig. 2C through F are a superposition of the 37 traces recorded during a single 600-millisecond epoch. Their align-

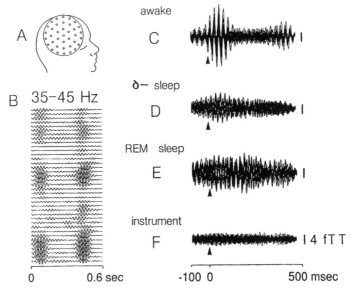

FIG. 2. A 40-Hz oscillation in wakefulness and a lack of 40-Hz reset in delta sleep and REM sleep. Recording using a 37-channel MEG. Diagram of sensor distribution over the head (**A**) and in the spontaneous magnetic recordings from the 37 sensors during wakefulness, shown immediately below (filtered at 35–45 Hz) (**B**). **C–F:** Averaged oscillatory responses (300 epochs) after auditory stimulus. **C:** The subject is awake and the stimulus is followed by a reset of 40-Hz activity. **D and E:** The stimulus produced no resetting of the rhythm. **F:** The noise of the system in femtoteslas (fT). Modified with permission from Llinás and Ribary (28).

ment in panel C indicates the high level of coherence of the 40-Hz activity at all the recording points after the auditory stimulus. A high level of coherence is also typical of spontaneous 40-Hz bursts such as that in Fig. 2B.

These findings indicated that although the awake state and the REM sleep state are electrically similar with respect to the presence of 40-Hz oscillations, a central difference remains: that of the inability of sensory input to reset the 40-Hz activity during REM sleep. By contrast, during delta sleep the amplitude of these oscillators differs from that of wakefulness and REM sleep, but as in REM sleep there is no 40-Hz sensory response. Another significant finding is that gamma oscillations are not reset by sensory input during REM sleep, although clear evoked-potential responses indicate that the thalamoneocortical system is accessible to sensory input (7,31). We consider this to be the central difference between dreaming and wakefulness. These data suggest that we do not perceive the external world during REM sleep because the intrinsic activity of the nervous system does not place sensory input in the context of the functional state being generated by the brain (7). That is, the dreaming condition is a state of hyperattentiveness to intrinsic activity in which sensory input cannot access the machinery that generates conscious experience.

An attractive possibility in considering the morphophysiologic substrate is that the "nonspecific" thalamic system, particularly the intralaminar complex, plays an important part in such coincidence generation. Indeed, neurons in this complex project in a spatially continuous manner to the most superficial layers of all cortical areas, including the primary sensory cortices. This possibility is particularly attractive given that single neurons burst at 30 to 40 Hz (24), especially during REM sleep, which is a finding consistent with the macroscopic magnetic recordings observed in this study, and given that damage of the intralaminar system results in lethargy or coma (32,33).

BINDING OF SPECIFIC AND NONSPECIFIC GAMMA RANGE RESONANT ACTIVITY: THE ISSUE OF COINCIDENCE DETECTION

A schematic of a neuronal circuit that may subserve temporal binding is presented in the left side of Fig. 3. Gamma oscillations in neurons in specific thalamic nuclei (34) establish cortical resonance through direct activation of pyramidal cells and feed-forward inhibition through activation of 40-Hz inhibitory interneurons in layer IV (22). These oscillations reenter the thalamus via layer VI pyramidal cell axon collaterals (34), producing thalamic feedback inhibition via the reticular nucleus (23). A second system is illustrated on the right side of Fig. 3. Here the intralaminar nonspecific thalamic nuclei projection to cortical layers I and V and to the reticular nucleus (12) is illustrated. Layer V pyramidal cells return oscillations to the reticular nucleus and intralaminar nuclei. The cells in this complex have been shown to oscillate at gamma band frequency (24) and to be capable of recursive activation.

It is also apparent from the literature that neither of these two circuits alone can generate cognition. Indeed, as stated above, damage of the nonspecific thalamus produces deep disturbances of consciousness, while damage of specific systems produces loss of the particular modality. Although at this early stage it must be quite simple in its form, the above hypothesis suggests the overall organization of brain function. This rests on two tenets. First, the "specific" thalamocortical system is viewed as encoding specific sensory and motor activity by the resonant thalamocortical system specialized to receive such inputs (e.g., the LGN and visual cortex). The "specific system" is understood to comprise those nuclei, whether sensorimotor or associative, that project mainly, if not exclusively, to layer IV in the cortex. Second, after optimal activation, any such thalamocortical loop would tend to oscillate at gamma band frequency and activity in the "specific" thalamocortical system could be easily "recognized" over the cortex by this oscillatory characteristic.

BINDING BY SPECIFIC 40 Hz RESONANT CONJUNCTION

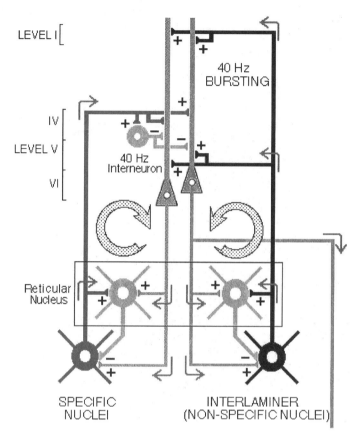

FIG. 3. Thalamocortical circuits proposed to subserve temporal binding. Diagram of two thalamocortical systems. (*Left*) Specific sensory or motor nuclei project to layer IV of the cortex, producing cortical oscillation by direct activation and feed-forward inhibition via 40-Hz inhibitory interneurons. Collaterals of these projections produce thalamic feedback inhibition via the reticular nucleus. The return pathway (circular arrow on the right) reenters this oscillation to specific and reticular thalamic nuclei via layer VI pyramidal cells. (*Right*) Second loop shows nonspecific intralaminar nuclei projecting to the most superficial layer of the cortex and giving collaterals to the reticular nucleus. Layer V pyramidal cells return oscillation to the reticular and nonspecific thalamic nuclei, establishing a second resonant loop. The conjunction of the specific and nonspecific loops is proposed to generate temporal binding. Modified with permission from Llinás and Ribary (28).

In this scheme, areas of cortical sites "peaking" at gamma band frequency would represent the different components of the cognitive world that have reached optimal activity at that time. The problem now is the conjunction of such a fractured description into a single cognitive event. We propose that this could come about by the concurrent summation of specific and nonspecific 40-Hz activ-

ity along the radial dendritic axis of given cortical elements, that is, by coincidence detection. This view differs from the binding hypothesis proposed by Crick and Koch in which cortical binding is attributed to the activation of cortical V4, pulvinar or claustrum (3).

In conclusion, the system would function on the basis of temporal coherence. Such coherence would be embodied by the simultaneity of neuronal firing based on passive and active dendritic conduction along the apical dendritic core conductors. In this fashion, the time-coherent activity of the specific and nonspecific oscillatory inputs, by summing distal and proximal activity in given dendritic elements, would enhance de facto 40-Hz cortical coherence by their multimodal character and in this way would provide one mechanism for global binding. The "specific" system would thus provide the content that relates to the external world, and the nonspecific system would give rise to the temporal conjunction, or the context (on the basis of a more interoceptive context concerned with alertness), that would together generate a single cognitive experience.

ACKNOWLEDGMENT

This work was supported by Grant NS13742 from the National Institutes of Health/National Institute of Neurological and Communicative Disorders and Stroke (NIH-NINCDS) and Charles A. Dana Fd. to R.L.

REFERENCES

1. Bienenstock E, Von der Malsburg C. Statistical coding and short-term synaptic plasticity: a scheme for knowledge representation in the brain. In: Bienenstock E, Fogelman F, Weisbuch G, eds. *Disordered systems and biological organization.* Springer-Verlag, 1986: 247–272.
2. Von der Malsburg C. The correlation theory of brain function. Internal report, Max-Planck Institute for Biophysical Chemistry. Gottingen, Germany, 1981.
3. Crick F, Koch C. Some reflections on visual awareness. *Cold Spring Harb Symp Quant Biol* 1990;55:953–962.
4. Llinás R. Intrinsic electrical properties of mammalian neurons and CNS function. In: *Fidia Research Foundation Neuroscience Award Lectures.* Vol. 4. New York: Raven, 1990:1–10.
5. Llinás R, Paré D. In: Llinás R, Churchland PM, eds. *The mind-brain continuum.* Cambridge, MA: MIT Press, 1996;1:1–18.
6. Llinás R, Ribary U. Perception as an oneiric-like state modulated by the senses. In: *Large-scale neuronal theories of the brain.* Cambridge, MA: MIT Press, 1994.
7. Llinás R, Paré D. Of dreaming and wakefulness. *Neuroscience* 1991;44:521–535.
8. Wilson JR, Friedlander MJ, Sherman SM. Ultrastructural morphology of identified X- and Y-cells in the cat's lateral geniculate nucleus. *Proc R Soc Lond [Biol]* 1984;221:411–436.
9. Edelman GM. *Neuronal Darwinism: The theory of neuronal group selection.* New York: Basic Books, 1987.
10. Cajal SR. *Etude sur la Neurogénese de quelques Vertébrés.* Springfield, IL: Charles C Thomas, 1929.
11. Harris WA. Neurogenetics. In: Adelman G, ed. *Encyclopedia of neuroscience.* Basel, Switzerland: Birkhäuser, 1987:791–793.
12. Penfield W, Rasmussen T. *The cerebral cortex of man.* New York: MacMillan, 1950.
13. Mountcastle VB, Hennemann E. Pattern of tactile representation in thalamus of cat. *J Neurophysiol* 1949;12: 85–100.
14. Mountcastle VB, Hennemann E. The representation of tactile sensibility in the thalamus of the monkey. *J Comp Neurol* 1952;97:409–440.
15. Pellionisz A, Llinás R. Space-time representation in the brain. The cerebellum as a predictive space-time metric tensor. *Neuroscience* 1982;7:2949–2970.
16. Eckhorn R, Bauer R, Jordan W, et al. Coherent oscillations: a mechanism of feature linking in the visual cortex? *Biol Cybern* 1988;60:121–130.
17. Gray CM, Konig P, Engel AK, Singer W. Oscillatory responses in cat visual cortex exhibit inter-columnar synchronization which reflects global stimulus properties. *Nature* 1989;338:334–337.
18. Gray CM, Singer W. Stimulus-specific neuronal oscillations in orientation columns of cat visual cortex. *Proc Natl Acad Sci U S A* 1989;86:1698–1702.
19. Singer W. Synchronization of cortical activity and its putative role in information processing and learning. *Ann Rev Physiol* 1993;55:349–374.
20. Llinás R, Ribary U. Rostrocaudal scan in human brain: a global characteristic of the 40-Hz response during sensory input. In: Basar E, Bullock T, eds. *Induced rhythms in the brain.* Boston: Birkhäuser, 1992: 147–154.
21. Llinás R, Sugimori M. Electrophysiological properties of in vitro Purkinje cell somata in mammalian cerebellar slices. *J Physiol (Lond)* 1980;305:171–195.
22. Llinás R, Grace AA, Yarom Y. In vitro neurons in mammalian cortical layer 4 exhibit intrinsic activity in the 10 to 50 Hz frequency range. *Proc Natl Acad Sci U S A* 1991;88:897–901.
23. Steriade M, Parent A, Hada J. Thalamic projections of reticular nucleus thalami of cat: a study using retrograde transport of horseradish peroxidase and double fluorescent tracers. *J Comp Neurol* 1984;229:531–547.
24. Steriade M, CurróDossi R, Contreras D. Electrophysiological properties of intralaminar thalamocortical cells discharging rhythmic (^{a}40 Hz) spike-bursts at ^{a}1000 Hz during waking and rapid eye movement sleep. *Neuroscience* 1993;56:1–9.
25. Steriade M, CurróDossi R, Paré D, Oakson G. Fast oscillations (20 40 Hz) in thalamocortical systems and their potentiation by mesopontine cholinergic nuclei in the cat. *Proc Natl Acad Sci U S A* 1991;88:4396–4400.
26. Deschênes M, Madariaga-Domich A, Steriade M. Dendrodendritic synapses in the cat reticularis thalami nucleus: a structural basis for thalamic spindle synchronization. *Brain Res* 1985;334:165–168.
27. Joliot M, Ribary U, Llinás R. Neuromagnetic oscillatory activity in the vicinity of 40-Hz coexists with cognitive temporal binding in the human brain. *Proc Natl Acad Sci U S A* 1994;91:11748–11751.
28. Llinás R, Ribary U. Coherent 40-Hz oscillation charac-

terizes dream state in humans. *Proc Natl Acad Sci U S A* 1993;90:2078–2081.

29. Galambos R, Makeig S, Talmachoff PJ. A 40-Hz auditory potential recorded from the human scalp. *Proc Natl Acad Sci U S A* 1981;78:2643–2647.

30. Pantev C, Makeig S, Hoke M, Galambos R, Hampson S, Gallen C. Human auditory evoked gamma-band magnetic fields. *Proc Natl Acad Sci U S A* 1991;88: 8996–9000.

31. Steriade M. In: Peters A, Jones EG, eds. *Cerebral cortex*. New York: Plenum, 1991:279–357.

32. Facon E, Steriade M, Wertheim N. Hypersomnie prolongée engendrée par des lésions bilatérales due systèm activateur médial le syndrome thrombotique de la bifurcation du tronc basilaire. *Rev Neurol* 1958;98: 117–133.

33. Castaigne P, Buge A, Escourolle R, Masson M. Ramollissement pédonculaire médian, tegmento-thalamique avec ophtalmoplégie et hypersomnie. *Rev Neurol* 1962; 106:357–367.

34. Steriade M, Jones EG, Llinás R. *Thalamic oscillations and signalling*. New York: Wiley, 1990.

DISCUSSION

Moderated by E. G. Jones

Stuart R. Hameroff: I was really intrigued by your presentation. Are you saying that consciousness is a sequence of discrete events, as opposed to a continuum?

Rodolfo R. Llinás: Yes, that is our basic hypothesis.

Benjamin Libet: I thought that the different oscillations at different sites were not precisely synchronous. Now does that make a difference in your binding idea?

Rodolfo R. Llinás: How much of a dispersion is there? Well, I will say it again: it is in the range of 12.5 milliseconds. Basically, the 40-Hz coherence wavelength is about twice the size of the head (if the dispersion across the brain is 12.5 milliseconds). In other words, the rising phase of the gamma band will cover all the cortex in one sweep and so generate synchronized coherence between any "n" points in the cortex.

Timothy E. Kennedy: My question relates to neural development and also plasticity. Essentially it is: What is it about 40 Hz? Why 40 Hz? Is there an intrinsic constraint in the way the system is structured that generates this coherence that you see in cortex at 40 Hz?

Rodolfo R. Llinás: The type of answer that one can give is as follows. Given the dielectric properties of lipid bilayer and the kinetics of channels, if the system needs oscillations, i.e., not full spikes, that is about as fast as the system can support. In fact, you can calculate from channel kinetics how fast oscillations can be. What this means, to us, is that the sub-

threshold neuronal oscillations are basically setting the macroscopic rhythm. Now, there are great advantages of having computing in a noncontinuous manner, and it has to do with the amount of energy and information that the brain must handle if computation were to be continuous. It would be immense. The same thing would happen if movement were to be continuous. The problem is vaguely analogous to that encountered with hot body radiation, which must occur in a discontinuous manner (quanta); otherwise, the energy radiated would be infinite. So, 40 Hz apparently is fast enough to integrate information given the gravitational field of earth and how fast things fall, and so on. That is the kind of explanation that comes to mind. Motor rhythmicity must be fast enough to allow proper coordination. As we move at 10 Hz, we must bind sensory input faster than that; otherwise, we will not survive.

Toré A. Nielsen: I wonder if you could clarify the point you were making about the distinctiveness of the 40-Hz cycle. It was not clear from the slide whether you were saying that there is evidence of frequencies falling outside of the 35- to 45-Hz window and having similar characteristics to the 40 Hz.

Rodolfo R. Llinás: Yes there are.

Toré A. Nielsen: It seems to me that the importance of the 40-Hz cycle would rest on its distinctiveness, its discriminant validity.

Rodolfo R. Llinás: We were expecting to see a much narrower band, but in fact it is much wider. Looking at a fast Fourier spectra, there is a peak at 35 to 45. Apparently, the frequency band is not equally rich in all frequencies. But we never found a place where it is zero. That is what we have.

Toré A. Nielsen: Barbara Jones mentioned that she had found evidence for higher coherence in the theta band in REM sleep, I believe it was, and in wakefulness. We have also looked for 40-Hz activity in the EEG power spectrum, and we have not found anything that is very distinctive, either in wakefulness or at sleep onset or even in REM sleep. I am wondering if the concept of greatest interest might not be the concept of coherence itself, and perhaps not of any particular frequency?

Rodolfo R. Llinás: Many people are considering coherence in time as the only real issue in temporal binding. But, how do you ensure that such coherence remains so that you may generate a sense of continuity? That is the advantage that I see with oscillation. Now, it is not surprising that gamma band oscillations are not easily observed. Such activity was not seen by most workers for a long time. In order to see it, one has to reduce the sampling time so that the high-frequency components are not averaged out, because the oscillatory frequency is not precise and occurs in short bursts. If one examines shorter fragments of time (about 250 milliseconds at the time) it comes up beautifully everywhere.

Toré A. Nielsen: Provided that it is filtered properly.

Rodolfo R. Llinás: Yes, it is very important that filtering is done with care as improper filtering can generate spurious oscillations.

Timothy E. Kennedy: Perhaps related to that, and also rephrasing my question: When you looked at 10 Hz, you saw that the activity would dissipate in cortex, whereas at 40 Hz you almost had a resonance that seemed to produce a peak that remained localized. What is it about the circuitry in cortex that generates a coherent resonance at 40 Hz?

Rodolfo R. Llinás: The cellular properties we have been through. The macroscopic oscillation in the cortex seems to involve resonance between input barrages at gamma frequency and the activity of inhibitory interneurons that serves to focus this rhythmicity further and to restrict them to narrow bands.

Jacques Montplaisir: If you give anticholinergic drugs to an animal or to a human, you generate a sleeplike pattern. If you look at single cell unit discharges, you get this bursting pattern even when the animal or the human is awake. So, this is an EEG-behavior dissociation. I was wondering whether anyone has looked at the effects of anticholinergic drugs such as scopolamine or atropine on the 40-Hz activity?

Rodolfo R. Llinás: We plan to do it in slices. And indeed, preliminary experiments suggest that acetylcholine makes column activation become even sharper. The fact is that acetylcholine changes neuronal impedance and gives it different resonant properties. It makes a whole lot of sense.

Barbara E. Jones: Atropine dramatically decreases gamma activity.

Rodolfo R. Llinás: Yes, that is so, and it agrees with what has been said. I would just like to end by saying that if per chance people noticed similarities between what I was saying and the centroencephalic system that Dr. Jasper was talking about, it is not accidental.

Consciousness: At the Frontiers of Neuroscience,
Advances in Neurology, Vol. 77,
edited by H.H. Jasper, L. Descarries,
V.F. Castellucci, and S. Rossignol.
Lippincott–Raven Publishers, Philadelphia © 1998.

8

Corticothalamic Networks, Oscillations, and Plasticity

Mircea Steriade

Laboratory of Neurophysiology, Faculty of Medicine, Université Laval,
Ste-Foy, Quebec, G1K 7P4, Canada

The search for the neuronal substrates of conscious processes has led to divergent views. At one pole is the blunt refusal of reductionistic approaches or vague statements about cooperative phenomena among cerebral structures leading to the emergence of new qualities that do not allow the localization of different mental activities within defined neural circuits. Quite opposite concepts are championed by those who postulate that certain cortical areas and/or thalamic nuclei, or even distinct neuronal types with unusual connections and functional characteristics, are endowed with mysterious properties giving rise to consciousness, self-awareness, or other, more or less ill-defined, global mental functions. An additional problem of attempts at pinpointing the genesis of conscious events within precise cerebral areas or neurons is that such views often stem from studies relying on modern techniques of investigation that impose extreme limitations on brain circuitry. In this age when the brain looks more and more fragmented, it is not trivial to emphasize that functional states are produced by a permanent dialogue among reciprocally related structures in a brain with preserved connectivity.

I take an intermediate position between the two extreme views and consider that a number of components defining mental activities can be studied at the cellular and network levels, even if the present tools are not sophisticated enough to understand the global notion of consciousness on the basis of simple correlative evidence obtained, by necessity, from restricted brain territories. Whether or not solving part(s) of consciousness may help to understand this entity as a whole is an open issue, mostly debated by epistemologists.

At a previous symposium on the role of the cerebral cortex in higher brain function, Jasper (1) asked rhetorically, "Can the melody of the mind be played on a keyboard . . . with rigidly determined functional characteristics?", and considered the role of widely distributed neuronal networks as well as the state-dependency under the control of generalized activating systems. Here, I continue on this track and discuss a series of recent investigations on alterations in intrinsic excitability of cortical neurons as a function of network activity and fluctuations in the state of vigilance, as well as the functional changes resulting from coherent oscillations in the cortex and thalamus. The long- or short-term plastic properties of corticothalamic networks as a consequence of their rhythmic activities are of importance for the understanding of neuronal operations underlying normal and abnormal behavioral states.

Why focus on the cellular substrates of spontaneous brain electrical activity? Although some investigators regard spontaneous rhythms as epiphenomena with little or no functional correlate, it has been long known that, for example, the blockade of alpha waves occurs even in the absence of a visual stimulus, when attempting to "see" in a totally darkened room (2) or when expecting a light stimulus that was omitted (3). These data would seem to indicate that brain waves are related to imagination and attention. Even during deafferented behavioral states, such as slow-wave (quiescent or resting) sleep, that are conventionally thought to be associated with an "abject annihilation of consciousness" (4), cortical and thalamic neurons display an unexpectedly rich spontaneous activity, which suggests a reorganization/specification of networks throughout the cerebrum (5). This view is supported by studies using indicators of neuronal activities during quiescent sleep in humans, showing more marked changes in those cortical areas that are implicated in memory tasks and decision making during wakefulness (6).

Besides providing some clues to shed light on the function of spontaneous brain waves, another aim of our studies has been to reduce the apparent chaos of electroencephalographic (EEG) waves to a few basic neuronal operations. We did this by using intracellular recordings in preparations with intact brain circuitry (including dual simultaneous impalements of cortical and thalamic neurons in vivo), in conjunction with multisite field potential and extracellular single-unit recordings (7,8). Because the stability for such complex recording procedures required anesthetized preparations, the results have been validated through multisite extracellular recordings in naturally sleeping and aroused animals (9) and humans (10–12). The cellular studies of spontaneous brain rhythms led to the knowledge of basic mechanisms underlying a multitude of wave patterns that are widely used in correlative studies of conscious processes (13,14).

The topics discussed in this chapter are enumerated as follows. First, the dynamic properties of certain neocortical cell classes

implicated in the generation of fast (30–40 Hz) oscillations will be documented. Such neurons may play a role in feature binding during cognitive processes. The issue here is that, at variance with some ideas emphasizing the invariant features distinguishing different cell classes, the fast rhythmic bursting cortical neurons display dramatic changes in their intrinsic properties by synaptic activity in local and distant networks. Next, the synchronization of different oscillatory types within corticothalamic networks will be presented during both normal (wake and sleep) and pathologic (epileptic) states. These aspects will finally lead to the discussion of plasticity resulting from repetitive activation of thalamic and cortical neurons and implicated in cognition but also in some perversions of normal states.

DYNAMIC PROPERTIES OF CORTICOTHALAMIC NEURONS PRODUCING FAST OSCILLATIONS

Fast oscillations (20–50 Hz, mainly 30–40 Hz), occurring synchronously in spatially distributed neuronal pools, have been hypothesized to be implicated in consciousness by binding different features of an object into a global percept (15–17). I have an alternative view (18), namely that fast rhythms do not require optimal sensory stimuli and are not necessarily related to higher conscious processes, but are part of the background electrical activity and simply depend on the depolarization of thalamic and cortical neurons in a sustained manner during waking and rapid eye movement (REM) sleep or more episodically during the depolarizing component of the slow sleep oscillation. Experimental studies (9,19) support all these assumptions. The fact that fast oscillations also appear during the state of resting sleep, when thalamocortical gates are closed to external signals (20), does not preclude that the same intrinsic and network properties underlie binding operations during brain-active states. Indeed, weakly synchronized and spatially circumscribed fast oscillations become robustly coherent for a short time, about 0.6 second, after a synchronous brain stem–thalamic volley mimicking the pontogeniculooccipital wave (9,21), a plausible correlate of tempestuous dreaming mentation during REM sleep. Similar effects may be elicited by relevant signals during the wakeful state. The dependency of fast oscillations on ascending activating modulatory systems is demonstrated by the increased incidence and amplitude of these rhythms after stimulation of the brain stem reticular core or upon natural awakening (9,19,21). That fast oscillations are implicated in brain attentive processes, either focused or diffuse, is corroborated by the presence of such oscillations during arousal and highly motivated states in behaving monkeys (22,23).

As shown below, the frequencies of fast oscillations are largely dependent on the level of depolarization in cortical and thalamic neurons. Thus, there is no reason to distinguish the so-called beta from gamma rhythms, on the only basis that the former are below and the latter above a certain frequency. Oscillations above 20 Hz, which I simply call fast, may double their frequencies over periods as short as 0.5 to 1 second (9). At the present time, such changes can hardly be related with subtle mental operations in the performing brain.

What are the best candidates among various neuronal types implicated in the generation and synchronization of fast rhythms? A series of studies has demonstrated the propensity of cortical (24) and thalamic (25) neurons to display fast subthreshold oscillations, occasionally leading to single spikes, upon direct depolarization. The impact exerted by fast-oscillating neurons on target structures is greatly enhanced when, instead of single action potentials, neurons fire spike-bursts at high frequencies. Such cells have been described in the rostral part of thalamic intralaminar nuclei that contain neurons firing spike-bursts with exceedingly high frequencies (900–1,000 Hz) and recurring rhythmically at about 40 Hz (26). Other bursting cells have been found in superficial layers of visual cortex (27) and in motor and association cortical areas (9,28,29). Although the intrinsic properties of fast-oscillating neurons have been intensively investigated, including the ionic nature of different conductances (24,30), their connectivity has remained largely unknown. To clarify the role played by such neurons in the synchronization of fast oscillations, their input–output organization should be identified first. This requirement, particularly the identification of targets of fast rhythmic bursting neurons within reciprocal corticothalamic circuits, was fulfilled in recent experiments (28,29), reported below.

Whether the thalamus plays a role in the synchronization process has been debated, with pro (13,16,19,28,29,31) and con (32) arguments. Studies using multisite intracellular and extracellular recordings indicate that it is decisively implicated (19). Therefore, the best neuronal candidates should be corticothalamic cells receiving back thalamic inputs and having the property of firing high-frequency, fast rhythmic spike-bursts upon imposed or natural depolarization. The presence of such neurons has recently been demonstrated in cat's motor and association cortical areas by intracellular recordings and staining in vivo (28,29). These neurons are located in layers V and VI, which contain corticothalamic neurons (33). They have been physiologically identified as part of the corticothalamocortical loops by antidromic and monosynaptic responses to stimulation of appropriate thalamic nuclei (Fig. 1A, left). Surprisingly, the spontaneous action potentials of these long-axoned glutamatergic cells are extremely brief, 0.3 to 0.4 millisecond at half amplitude (Fig. 1A, right), a feature that is commonly attributed to local-circuit (L-C) GABAergic neurons. Upon intracellular injection of depolarizing current pulses, these corticothalamic neurons discharged rhythmic (20–50 Hz), high-frequency (300–600 Hz) spike-bursts (Fig. 1B). Their increasing number of action potentials upon increasing the intensity of testing pulses stems from depolarizing afterpotentials (Fig. 1B).

Importantly, the intrinsic discharge pattern described above is not an invariant stigma of

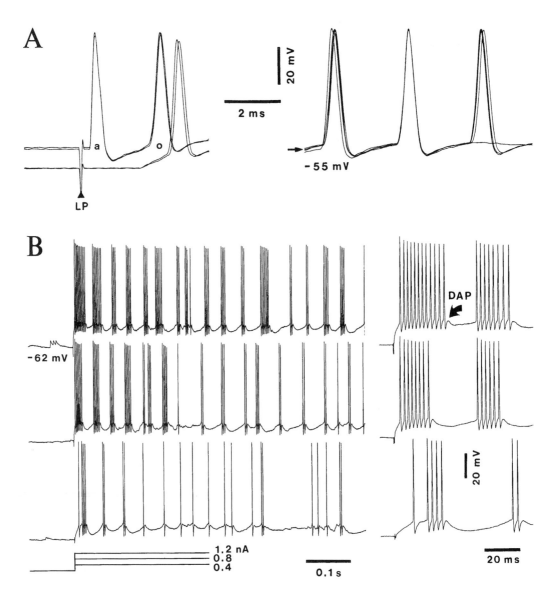

FIG. 1. Fast-rhythmic-bursting (FRB) corticothalamic neurons. Intracellular recordings in cat under ketamine-xylazine anesthesia. **A:** At left, identification of a corticothalamic cell from layer VI in association area 5 of the suprasylvian gyrus. Stimulus (*arrowhead*) to the lateral posterior (LP) thalamic nucleus elicited an antidromic (a) action potential, followed by orthodromic (o) activation (upper trace, resting membrane potential 55 mV). At a hyperpolarized level (lower trace), antidromic response failed and orthodromic response survived. This neuron is an example of a cell interposed in a corticothalamocortical loop. At right, spontaneous action potentials show the brief duration of spikes (<0.4 milliseconds) at half amplitude. **B:** The fast rhythmic spike-bursts in identified corticothalamic neurons from area 5, elicited by direct depolarization of the cell. Responses to three depolarizing steps (0.4, 0.8, and 1.2 nA) are illustrated. The initial part of responses is expanded at right (arrow indicates depolarizing afterpotential, DAP). Note progressive increase in the number of action potentials within bursts (up to 500 Hz) as well as the number of rhythmic bursts (from 20 to 30 Hz) by increasing the direct depolarization. Modified with permission from Steriade et al. (29).

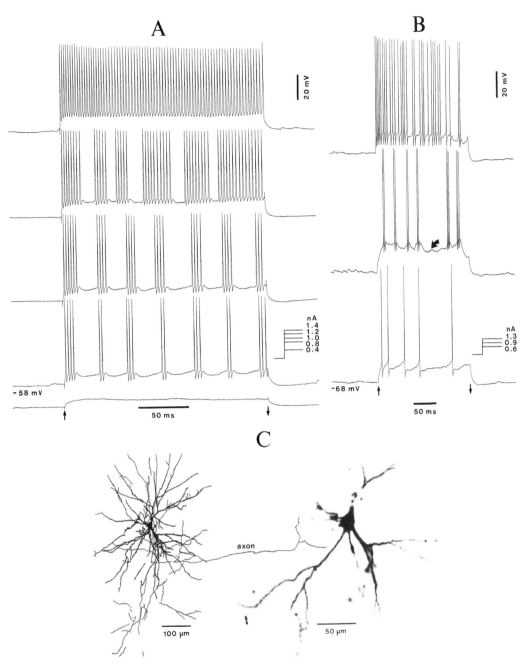

FIG. 2. Changes in discharge patterns of fast-rhythmic-bursting (FRB) neurons by increasing the intensity of direct depolarization (200-millisecond pulses). Intracellular recordings in cats under ketamine-xylazine anesthesia. **A:** A corticothalamic neuron from association area 7 displayed passive response upon subthreshold depolarization (0.4 nA); by increasing the pulse to 0.8, 1, and 1.2 nA, the neuron demonstrated high-frequency spike-bursts with progressively increased rates of repetition (from 30 to 40 Hz) and increased number of action potentials within each burst; finally (1.4 nA), the cell fired tonic action potentials at 450 Hz, without frequency adaptation. Intracellular staining showed its pyramidal shape and location in layer VI (not illustrated). **B:** Sparsely spiny local-circuit cell (see intracellular staining and camera lucida reconstruction in **C**) showing a similar transformation, from single spikes to rhythmic spike-bursts (~40 Hz) and finally tonic firing by increasing the intensity of direct depolarization (values are indicated). Reprinted with permission from Steriade et al. (29).

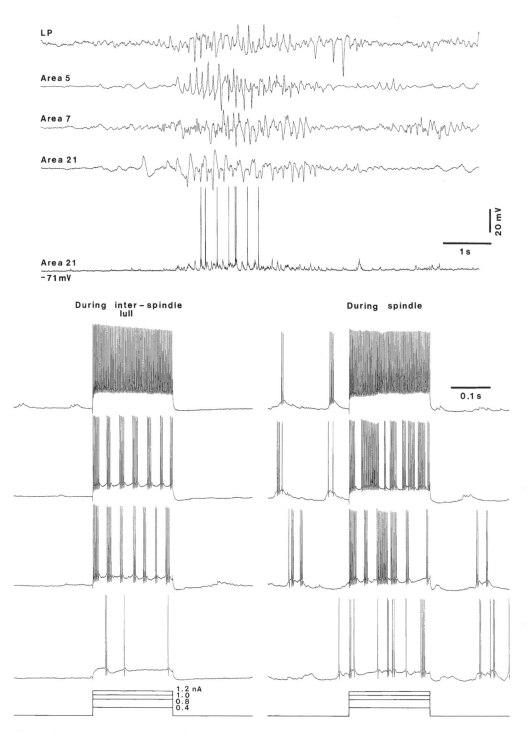

FIG. 3. Changes in responses of corticothalamic neurons from area 21 to depolarizing current pulses with different intensities, during periods poor and rich in synaptic activity. Intracellular recording in cats under barbiturate anesthesia. Field potentials were simultaneously recorded from the thalamic LP nucleus and from the depth of cortical areas 5, 7, and 21 (the latter in the immediate vicinity of the impaled cell). Depolarizing current pulses (duration 200 milliseconds) with four intensities (0.4, 0.8, 1, and 1.2 nA) were applied during interspindle lulls, with negligible or absence of synaptic activity, and during spindle sequences, with rich synaptic activity generated by thalamocortical volleys. Note the transformation from rhythmic (35 Hz) spike-bursts into tonic firing (450 Hz) during neuronal silence, and disruption of intrinsically generated rhythmic spike-bursts by network synaptic activity. Reprinted with permission from Steriade et al. (29).

fast rhythmic bursting corticothalamic neurons. After a passive response to subthreshold current pulses, these neurons fired fast rhythmic spike-bursts, but they eventually reached the pattern of fast tonic firing upon further raising the intensity of stimulation (Fig. 2A). Note that the final pattern of high-rate tonic firing (300–600 Hz), without frequency adaptation (upper trace in Fig. 2A), is conventionally ascribed to L-C GABAergic neurons (34), similarly to the thin action potentials of these cells. A change from fast spike-bursts to tonic firing without frequency adaptation also has been observed in formally identified, intracellularly stained, sparsely spiny L-C neurons (Fig. 2B and C). Fast rhythmic bursting neurons are found throughout the cortical depth, from layer II to layer VI.

The pattern of fast rhythmic spike-bursts mostly occurs in its pure form during periods in which synaptic activity is poor or absent, as in slices. In animals maintained under barbiturate anesthesia, we compared the responses to depolarizing current pulses during the silent periods between sequences of spindle waves (interspindle lulls) with responses elicited by identical stimulus parameters during spindles, i.e., when cortical neurons are submitted to an intense synaptic bombardment from the thalamus. During periods with rich synaptic activity, the fast rhythmic spike-bursts were disrupted and transformed into fast tonic firing (Fig. 3).

These data are at variance with ideas postulating the sharp distinctness between various neocortical cell types characterized by invariant electrophysiologic properties. Instead, a continuum of discharge patterns may appear in the same neuron as a function of membrane potential and network activity. Even in slices, identified GABAergic local interneurons in the neocortex include not only the conventional fast-spiking type but a series of other patterns, such as regular-spiking and bursting patterns (35); in most ways, type 3 regular-spiking cells are similar to intrinsically bursting neurons (36). Moreover, as a consequence of prolonged stimulation, regular-spiking

neurons may become rhythmically bursting (37). Intrinsically bursting neurons develop into the regular-spiking type by activating the animal with a brief pulse-train to the mesopontine cholinergic nuclei in vivo (38) or by applying muscarinic or glutamatergic metabotropic agonists in vitro (39).

Thus, intrinsic electrophysiologic properties may be overwhelmed by synaptic activity in the network and by setting into action generalized modulatory systems. Neurons with identical intrinsic properties may display different oscillatory types because they are embedded within different synaptic circuits (40); conversely, neurons with quite dissimilar intrinsic properties, such as neocortical and GABAergic thalamic reticular, display virtually identical patterns of slow oscillations because they are synaptically connected (5). Although we used depolarizing current pulses to observe the shifts in discharge patterns similar to those of regular-spiking, bursty, and fast-spiking cells (34), the same changes are expected to occur during natural fluctuations in the behavioral state of vigilance because only subtle changes in the membrane potential of thalamic and cortical neurons distinguish brain-active from deafferented states (20,41).

CORTICOTHALAMIC SYNCHRONIZATION AND MODULATION BY BRAIN STEM CORE SYSTEMS

Accumulating data point to the potency of corticothalamic volleys in synchronizing normal and paroxysmal oscillations. With each corticothalamic volley, the oscillatory machinery of the thalamus is set into action, which is of consequence for the long-range coherence of oscillations during both activated and deactivated states. This section considers the corticothalamic synchronization of fast rhythms during activated states, the low-frequency (<15 Hz) oscillations during slow-wave sleep, and finally, the development from sleep to seizures in cortical and thalamic circuits.

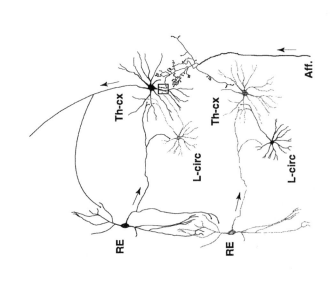

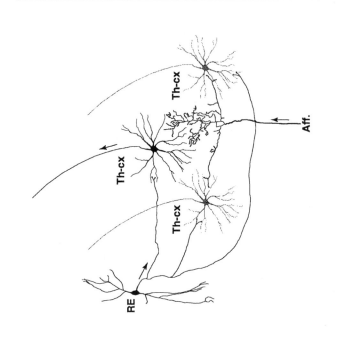

To begin with, it must be emphasized that most investigators consider the intrathalamic circuitry to consist basically of glutamatergic thalamocortical (TC) neurons and GABAergic thalamic reticular neurons. This greatly simplifies the network because the other class of GABAergic cells, L-C neurons in different nuclei of the dorsal thalamus, is not included in intrathalamic circuits. However, L-C cells represent 25% to 30% of the total neuronal population in dorsal thalamic nuclei of felines and primates, and even in the lateral geniculate nucleus of rat (42). It cannot yet be decided whether the effects of reticular neurons on TC cells are exclusively inhibitory, or whether the synaptic contacts made by reticular cells on L-C inhibitory neurons ultimately lead to disinhibition of TC cells under certain conditions (Fig. 4). The reticular axons contacting L-C cells represent a minority (8–10%) of the total number of reticular axons distributed in the corresponding dorsal thalamic nuclei (43), but the arborizations of these axons and their synaptic weight is not yet known. Anyway, disinhibition of TC cells, as a result of reticular-to-L-C connections, has been demonstrated by an increased number of short-lasting, chloride-dependent inhibitory postsynaptic potentials (IPSPs) in TC cells after disconnection from the reticular nucleus (44), as if L-C cells were released

from inhibition. Intrareticular inhibitory synaptic operations, through both axonal collaterals and dendrodendritic contacts, further complicate thalamic operations. This is to stress the oversimplification of circuits in most studies, due to our present ignorance of the functional significance of reticular-to-L-C connection, and to caution against inferences based on only reticular-to-TC contacts. The possible role of the reticular-to-L-C connection in the thalamic inhibitory circuitry involved in sensory discrimination (Fig. 4), as hypothesized (45) on the basis of previous experiments dealing with the activity of reticular neurons in behaving animals (46), remains a tantalizing task for future research.

Corticothalamic Synchronization of Fast Rhythms

Fast oscillations are synchronized within intracortical networks (9,17,21,23,27,32) as well as among different thalamic nuclei (19). The synchronization of fast rhythms is under the control of activating brain stem reticular neurons with projections to thalamocortical systems (9,25,28). The bisynaptic brain stem–thalamic–cortical projection is operational even in preparations in which the parallel activating system involving the nucleus basalis is extensively lesioned (25,38). The

---

FIG. 4. Tentative representation of operations in synaptic networks involving thalamocortical (Th-cx), reticular (RE), and local-circuit (L-circ) thalamic cells. Elements drawn in thick black contours are active, whereas those with dotted somata and thin dendritic-axonal processes are thought to be under inhibitory influences. Left panel represents a network without L-circ elements. Such circuits may exist in species (such as rodents) without intrinsic inhibitory interneurons in most dorsal thalamic nuclei (lateral geniculate nucleus is an exception). The activity in afferent (Aff) prethalamic fiber prevalently excites the Th-cx cell in the center. The inhibition exerted by reticular neurons is distributed equally to the three Th-cx cells, but it mainly affects the two cells at the periphery because of the reduced amount of afferent excitation onto those cells. Right panel represents possible interactions in species (such as felines and primates) that possess a significant number of GABAergic L-circ cells in thalamic nuclei. In the top Th-cx cell (which receives prevalent excitation from the afferent fiber), directly connected reticular neurons may contribute to further enhancing this relevant activity by inhibiting the pool of L-circ inhibitory elements. Simultaneously, the activity in adjacent reticular neurons (bottom reticular neuron) is suppressed by axonal collateralization within the reticular nucleus. The consequence would be the released activity of target L-circ neurons and inhibition of weakly excited Th-cx neurons in thalamic territories adjacent to the active focus. From Steriade (45), redrawn by E.G. Jones. The hypothesis from operations in Th-cx, RE, and L-circ synaptic networks derives from experiments by Steriade et al. (46).

synchronization of fast rhythms upon arousal challenges the term "desynchronization" that was widely used to designate brain-active states. Instead, we should use the term "activation," as was originally proposed (47).

In addition to purely intracortical or intrathalamic synchronizing processes, the reciprocal loops between the neocortex and thalamus introduce a new dimension because the reentrant pathways do not only return to the origin of the corticothalamic projection but also project to different, even distant cortical areas (48). Intracellular recordings from thalamic relay cells in conjunction with field potential recordings from the appropriate cortical areas show a strong coherence of fast oscillations in the motor system (Fig. 5) (19,28). Surprisingly, the fast oscillations in the motor system do not exclusively originate in the thalamus and/or cortex, but also in deep cerebellar nuclei, because lesions of cerebellothalamic axons lead to the diminution or disappearance of these rhythms in the ventrolateral–cortical system (49). These and related data, showing that retinal and lateral geniculate neurons are synchronized within the frequency range of fast oscillations (50), indicate that these oscillations may well arise before the thalamus.

In addition to synchronization among sensory and motor cortical areas and specific thalamic nuclei, as demonstrated by recording from multiple foci that are connected in both ascending and descending directions (19), the long-range coherence of fast oscillations is subserved by reciprocal corticothalamic circuits implicating rostral intralaminar nuclei that possess two important features: they contain neurons with antidromically identified cortical projections that fire rhythmic (~40 Hz) spike-bursts at 900 to 1,000 Hz (26) and have widespread cortical projections (33). The synchronization of fast rhythms through intralaminar nuclei is congruent with the hypothesis (13,16) based on magnetoencephalographic recordings in humans. Instrumental conditioning in behaving cats that were trained to deliver groups of fast oscillations (20–50 Hz) showed coherent activity within this frequency range between rostral intralaminar centrolateral nucleus and lateral geniculate nucleus (Fig. 6) (51). Because there is no direct connection between the two thalamic nuclei, this result can be explained by an intermediate link through the cerebral cortex because the centrolateral nucleus projects to the visual cortex (52) and coherent fast oscillations have been demonstrated within the corticothalamic visual system (19).

Coherent Low-Frequency Sleep Oscillations in Corticothalamic Networks

The effects exerted by the cerebral cortex upon the thalamus are particularly obvious when investigating the influence of the corti-

---

FIG. 5. Episodes of tonic activation are associated with coherent fast rhythms (40 Hz) in cortical EEG and intracellularly recorded thalamocortical neurons. Cats under ketamine-xylazine anesthesia. In top panel, four traces represent simultaneous recordings of surface- and depth-EEG from motor cortical area 4, extracellular discharges of neuron from the rostrolateral part of the thalamic reticular (RE) nucleus, and intracellular activity of relay neuron from the ventrolateral (VL) nucleus. EEG, RE, and VL cells displayed a slow oscillation (0.7–0.8 Hz) during which the sharp depth-negative (excitatory) EEG waves led to IPSPs in VL cell, presumably generated by spike-bursts in cortically driven GABAergic reticular neurons. The part marked by the horizontal bar, taken from a short-lasting period of spontaneous EEG activation, is expanded below (*arrow*), with EEG waves and field potentials from the reticular nucleus filtered from 30 to 50 Hz; the part marked by the horizontal bar in this panel is further expanded on the right to illustrate relationships between action potentials of VL cell and depth-negative waves in cortical EEG, at a frequency of 40 Hz. Cross-correlations (CROSS) between action potentials and depth-EEG show a clear-cut relationship, with opposition of phase between intracellularly recorded VL activity and cortical field potentials. Modified from Steriade et al. (19).

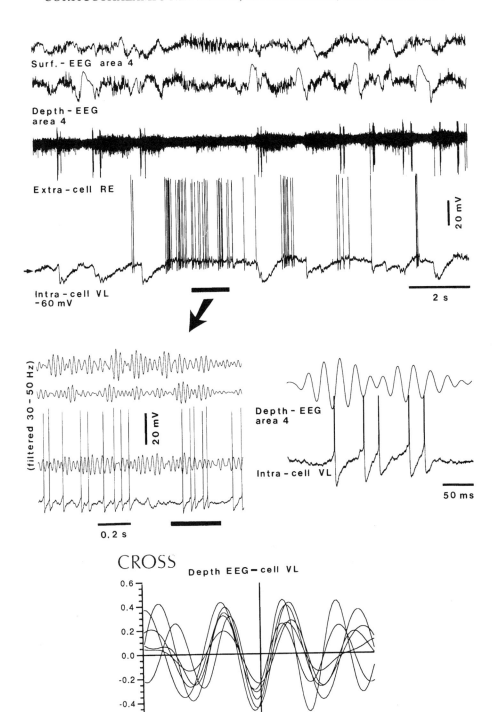

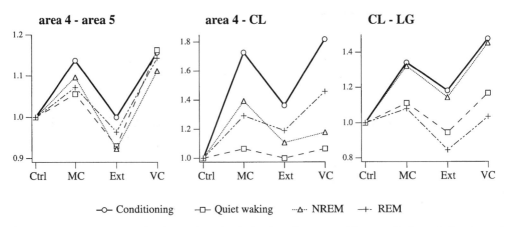

FIG. 6. Intracortical, intrathalamic, and corticothalamic coherence of fast oscillations. Behaving cats were trained to produce groups of fast potentials (20–50 Hz) by instrumental conditioning. Cats also were recorded for 1 hour after the end of the conditioning sessions. Analyzing the quiet waking from this postconditioning period, as well as the slow-wave sleep (NREM) and REM sleep epochs, allowed us to study the expression of the conditioning-induced changes in corticothalamic synchrony during wake-sleep states. These graphs show the evolution of the cross-correlation peak for intracortical (*left*), corticothalamic (*center*), and intrathalamic (*right*) synchrony as a function of behavioral state. Conditioning task period is compared with waking, NREM, and REM (see different symbols). Ctrl, control conditioning session 1; MC, end of conditioning for eliciting fast oscillations from motor cortex; Ext, end of extinction; VC, end of conditioning for eliciting fast oscillations from visual cortex. Data are expressed as ratios to control values. Note similar direction of changes in all behavioral states from one condition to the next. Reprinted with permission from Amzica et al. (51).

cal slow oscillation (<1 Hz) on thalamically generated sleep rhythms, as well as spindle (7–14 Hz) and clocklike delta (1–4 Hz) oscillations. The description of each of these three types of sleep rhythms (slow, spindle, and delta) as distinct phenomena, generated in different networks, may be useful for didactic purposes (Fig. 7). However, in the intact brain the networks are interacting and their rhythms are combined within complex wave sequences. This is due to the powerful depolarizing volleys of corticothalamic neurons during the slow oscillation that can be seen as a conductor for other sleep rhythms.

The newly discovered slow oscillation (10) is generated in the neocortex as it survives thalamectomy (53) and is absent in the thalamus of decorticated animals (54), and its synchronization is disrupted by disconnection of intracortical synaptic linkages (55). The slow oscillation has a frequency of 0.6 to 0.9 Hz during ketamine-xylazine anesthesia (8), or

natural sleep in cats (9) and humans (11,12), and a lower frequency (0.3–0.5 Hz) under urethane anesthesia (10). The two components of the slow oscillation are a prolonged hyperpolarization, associated with a depth-positive field potential, and a prolonged depolarization that is initiated by a sharp potential and leads to a series of low- and high-frequency rhythms (Fig. 8). Typically, the synchronous, rhythmic depolarizing volleys of corticothalamic cells (associated with sharp, depth-negative field potentials) produce sequences of spindle waves by exciting GABAergic reticular neurons and, consequently, triggering rhythmic IPSP-rebound sequences in TC cells (5,7,8). The grouping of thalamically generated sleep rhythms by the slow cortical oscillation is also evident when clocklike delta waves, resulting from the interplay between two inward currents of TC cells (56,57), are periodically interrupted because of the increased conductance produced by the rhyth-

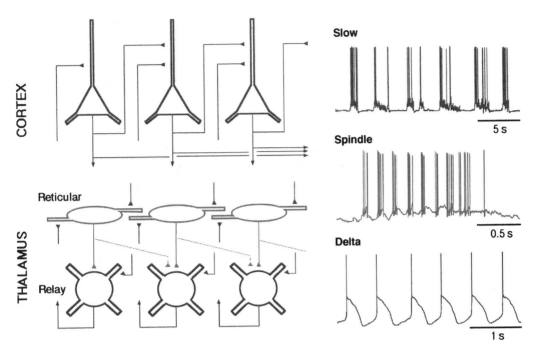

FIG. 7. Building blocks of corticothalamic networks and different types of resting sleep oscillations generated by excitatory glutamatergic neocortical (green), inhibitory GABA reticular thalamic (magenta), and excitatory glutamatergic thalamocortical or relay (blue) neurons. The direction of the axons is indicated by arrows. Short- and long-scale intracortical pathways are illustrated. Divergent reticular thalamic axons are shown as broken lines. Note the different time calibrations in intracellular traces showing the cortical slow oscillation (~0.3 Hz), the reticular thalamic spindles (~7 Hz), and the intrinsic (clocklike) delta rhythm (~1.5 Hz) of thalamocortical cells. These oscillations may be generated at each of these levels, even after their disconnection from afferent sources. Reprinted with permission from Steriade et al. (53).

mic slow oscillation in the corticothalamic projection (5).

The influence of the neocortex on thalamic sleep oscillations is also shown by comparing the pattern of spindle synchronization in the intact cortex and decorticated hemisphere. In the intact cortex, spindles appear nearly simultaneously in widespread thalamic and cortical territories, whereas after decortication this impressive coherence is less organized (58,59). One of the conclusions of these studies is that, in vivo, the slow cortical oscillation, with a frequency similar to that of the slow rhythm of periodic spindle sequences, provides a background corticothalamic activity that triggers burst firing in many thalamic

foci during the narrow time-window of lower threshold at the end of the interspindle lull. The absence of cortex in thalamic slices explains the difference between the propagation of spindles in vitro (60) and the near-simultaneity of spindles in vivo (58,59). Thus, although spindles are generated in the thalamus even after decortication (61), owing to interactions between reticular and TC cells (20, 42,44,62,63), the cortex has an important role in triggering spindles (64,65) and in synchronizing them over widespread territories (58,59).

The role of corticothalamic volleys in spindle generation is also emphasized by analysis of the K complex, a major grapho-

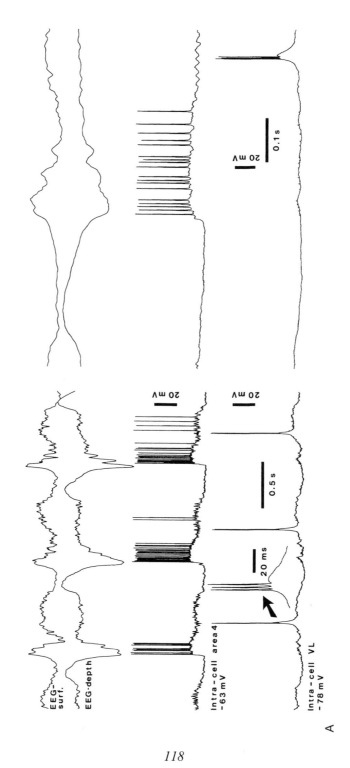

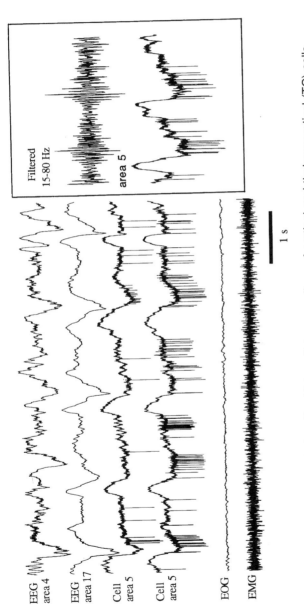

EEG
area 4

EEG
area 17

Cell
area 5

Cell
area 5

EOG

EMG

B

Filtered
15–80 Hz

area 5

1 s

FIG. 8. The slow oscillation. Dual intracellular recordings of cortical and thalamocortical (TC) cells in cats under ketamine-xylazine anesthesia (**A**) and multisite extracellular recordings in chronically implanted, naturally sleeping cats (**B**). **A:** Simultaneous impalements of regular-spiking cells from cortical area 4 and TC cells from the VL nucleus. Left and right parts are at a different time base (at right, an expanded slow oscillatory cycle). At left, three cycles of the slow oscillation, each consisting of a prolonged hyperpolarization in cortical and VL cells (associated with a depth-positive EEG field potential) and a depolarization with discharges in cortical cells (associated with an initial, sharp depth-negative EEG field potential), followed by a spike-burst in VL cells (*arrow*). Note EEG spindle sequence in the third oscillatory cycle. **B:** Pattern of slow oscillation during natural sleep. Six traces represent depth-EEG from motor area 4, visual area 17, unit discharges and focal waves from association area 5, similar activities from an adjacent focus in area 5 (2 mm apart), electrooculogram (EOG), and electromyogram (EMG). The right part shows reduction, up to disappearance, of fast rhythms (filtered 15–80 Hz) during the prolonged depth-positive wave of the slow oscillation that, in intracellular recordings (see A), is associated with hyperpolarization in cortical and thalamic neurons. Data from experiments by M. Steriade and D. Contreras (**A**) and M. Steriade and F. Amzica (**B**). Inset in **B** is modified from Steriade et al. (9).

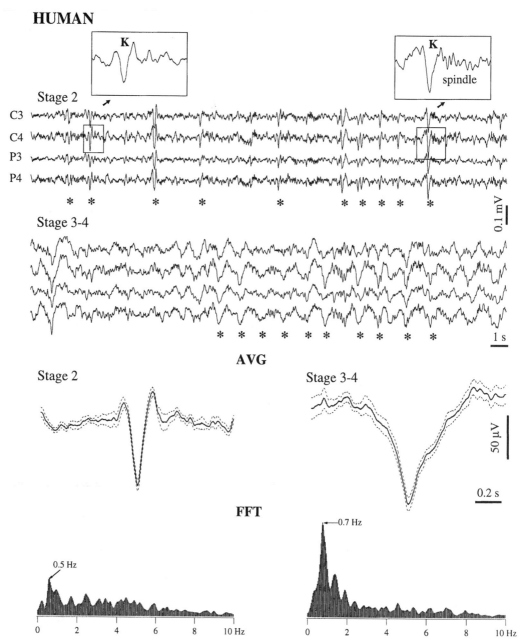

FIG. 9. Rhythmic K-complexes (KCs) in human EEG during natural resting sleep. Top panel represents four leads, recorded from the two hemispheres during stage 2 sleep, showing quasirhythmic (~0.5 Hz) KCs. The expanded insets display a simple KC (*left*) and a KC followed by a spindle (*right*). Stage 3–4 EEG (*below*) is characterized by an oscillation of the KCs at about 0.7 Hz. Asterisks mark the most obvious KCs to suggest their rhythmicity. Middle panel represents averaged (AVG) KCs (n = 200) from stages 2 (*left*) and 3–4 (*right*). The gray surface around the averaged KCs covers the standard deviation. The lowest trace (dotted line) results from the filtering of the average KC in the delta frequency band (1–4 Hz). The bottom panel (FFT) represents power spectra of 2-minute epochs containing the ones displayed above. Note the principal peak at 0.5 Hz for the stage 2 episode (*left*), surrounded by other lower peaks as evidence for distributed rhythmicity. At variance, deep sleep stages 3–4 shows a dominant peak at 0.7 Hz. The two FFT graphs are scaled with the same ordinate. Reprinted with permission from Amzica and Steriade (11).

element of sleep EEG, described since the 1930s (66). The cellular substrates of the K complex were shown recently in intracellular recordings from cats and in field potential recordings from humans (11). Briefly, the surface-positive, depth-negative K complex represents the initial, sharp deflection of the depolarizing component of the slow oscillation that often leads to a sequence of spindle waves (Fig. 9) through the activation of the reticular cell–TC cell circuit in the thalamus. The rhythmicity of the K complex is that of the slow oscillation (see spectral analyses in Fig. 9).

In sum, the neocortex and thalamus constitute a unified oscillatory machine as the slow cortical sleep oscillation groups the thalamically generated rhythms and determines the near-simultaneity of sleep spindles over widespread thalamocortical systems. The major characteristics of cortical and thalamic neurons during sleep patterns are their prolonged hyperpolarizations. These are due to both disfacilitation processes and, in the case of thalamic neurons, to IPSPs generated by GABAergic reticular neurons (5,7,8,41), thus explaining the decrease in regional cerebral blood flow changes observed during slow-wave sleep in humans (6,67; see also Chapter 5) and the obliteration of sensory awareness and motor responsiveness.

Development from Sleep to Paroxysmal Events: Network Interactions Generating Partial Quiescence of Thalamocortical Neurons during Spike-and-Wave Cortical Seizures

That normally synchronized sleep patterns may develop into paroxysmal discharges, characterized by spike-and-wave (SW) complexes at 2 to 4 Hz as in absence epilepsy, is known from animal and human studies. Stimulation at three per second of medial thalamic nuclei, especially under light pentobarbital anesthesia, produces bilateral SW-like cortical responses (68). Occasionally, an SW complex outlasts the stimulation (69). In behaving primates, SW seizures in the pre-

central gyrus preferentially occur during periods of drowsiness, either spontaneously or after single-shock stimulation of related thalamic nuclei (70). These seizures are self-sustained, last for about 10 to 15 seconds, are characterized by tonic eyelid movements at the beginning of the electrical seizure (as in petit mal epilepsy), and are preferentially displayed by cortical bursting neurons that fire during the depth-negative spike component and are silenced during the last part of the depth-positive wave component of the SW complex (Fig. 10A). These relationships between neuronal discharges and SW components are similar to those described intracellularly under anesthesia (71). The dependency of SW seizures on a decreased level of vigilance also has been demonstrated in humans by the preferential appearance of these paroxysms during the spindle stage of resting sleep (72).

The general view is that thalamic neurons are implicated in SW seizures. This is partially true and, indeed, about 40% of TC cells are depolarized and fire in close relation with the depth-negative (excitatory) spike component of cortical field potentials (Fig. 10B) (73). However, dual simultaneous intracellular recordings from cortical and thalamic neurons in vivo have demonstrated that 60% of TC cells display a sustained hyperpolarization during the cortical SW seizure and, additionally, repetitive IPSPs coincident with paroxysmal depolarizing shifts and spike-bursts in cortical neurons (73). After the cessation of cortical SW or poly-SW seizures, TC cells are disinhibited and display tonic firing (Fig. 11A). On the basis of parallel recordings from GABAergic reticular neurons, which exhibit a striking increase in duration of spike-bursts (200–300 milliseconds) during transition from sleep patterns to SW seizures, we have proposed that reticular neurons play a decisive role in the quiescence of TC cells (73). The proposal was that the summated actions of reticular neurons, which can discharge prolonged spike-bursts in response to every corticofugal volley during the seizure, render TC cells to a state that pre-

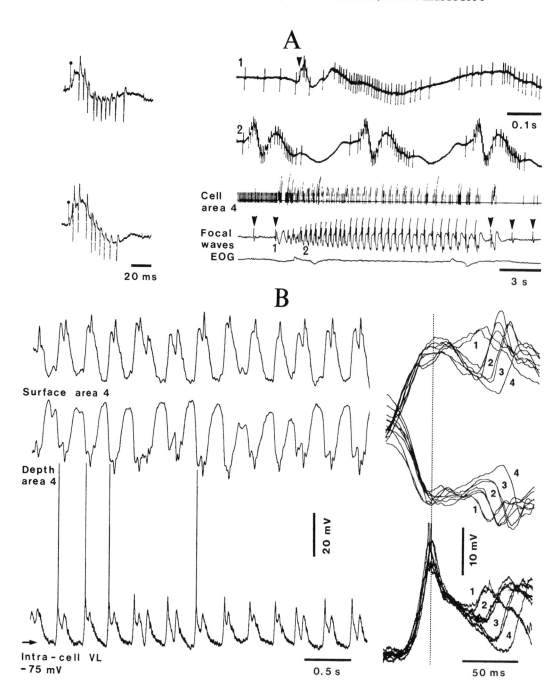

vents their discharges because of strong and repetitive IPSPs. Recent modeling studies of reciprocally connected reticular cell–TC cell neuronal pairs (74) support the conclusion from our experimental data by demonstrating that, in the quiescent mode, TC cells are submitted to coalescing IPSPs due to cortically driven spike-bursts in reticular cells. An additional mechanism for TC quiescence was proposed by a cooperative model of $GABA_B$-mediated responses in TC cells (74).

The inhibition of a great proportion of TC cells during cortical SW seizures suggests that a principal factor responsible for the unconsciousness during absence seizures is the dramatic hyperpolarization of TC cells and their incapacity of relaying messages from the outside world (73). The role of the cerebral cortex in such paroxysms was previously suggested on the basis of typical SW seizures in behaving monkeys that were manifest in the depth of the cortex but had no reflection at the cortical surface (see Fig. 8 in ref. 70). Further evidence for the leading role of the neocortex in such seizures came from multisite, extra- and intracellular recordings from cortical and thalamic neurons showing that SW or poly-SW seizures are initiated in the cortex and are thereafter transferred to the thalamus, and that the buildup of SW seizures obeys the rule of synaptic circuits,

sequentially distributed through short- and long-range linkages (73,75).

At variance with the opinion that SW seizures are suddenly generalized, bilaterally synchronous paroxysms, a view that generally derived from the macroscopic inspection of EEG recordings, cortical neurons display time lags (10 to 100 milliseconds) between their rhythmic spike-bursts and progressively increased synchrony in most SW seizures (75). Paradoxically, the areas that are subject to epileptic overdrive from the cortex will be the areas with the highest percentage of thalamic quiescence due to hyperactivity of GABAergic reticular cells (73). In the penumbra, reticular neurons would produce less intense hyperpolarization in TC cells, allowing the production of low-threshold spikes and the appearance of mutual oscillation (74). The process of progressive synchronization probably involves the spread of an epileptic penumbra of those TC neurons that participate with spike-bursts in the cortically initiated SW seizure, whereas relative TC neuronal quiescence is present in the area of the established seizure. The fact that many TC neurons display inhibition rather than excitation during SW seizures may explain why this type of epilepsy is less detrimental than seizures with higher neuronal involvement.

FIG. 10. Cellular bases of SW seizures. **A:** Chronically implanted behaving *Macaca mulatta.* Extracellular recordings from the precentral gyrus during a period of drowsiness. Left part shows identification of a presumed local-circuit neuron responding with a spike-burst (200–250 Hz) to stimulation of the caudal part in the ventrolateral (VL) nucleus. Right part shows two expanded parts (1–2) from the epoch displayed below; the three traces in the ink-written recording represent unit spikes (cell area 4), focal waves recorded through the same microelectrode, and electrooculogram (EOG). Stimuli to VL are marked by arrowheads. Note tonic eyelid movements during the SW seizure. During the SW seizure, which lasted for about 15 seconds, no stimulus was applied. **B:** Spontaneously occurring SW seizure, with intracellular recording of thalamic VL neuron in cat under ketamine-xylazine anesthesia, together with surface- and depth-EEGs from cortical area 4. Right part shows the striking correlation between excitatory cortical potentials (surface-positive, depth-negative) and EPSPs superimposed by spike-discharges in VL cells. 1-to-4 are different components indicating that small variations in the size of cortical EEG graphoelements are faithfully reflected in the intracellular activity of thalamic VL neurons. **A** is modified with permission from Steriade (69); **B** is based on unpublished data by M. Steriade and D. Contreras.

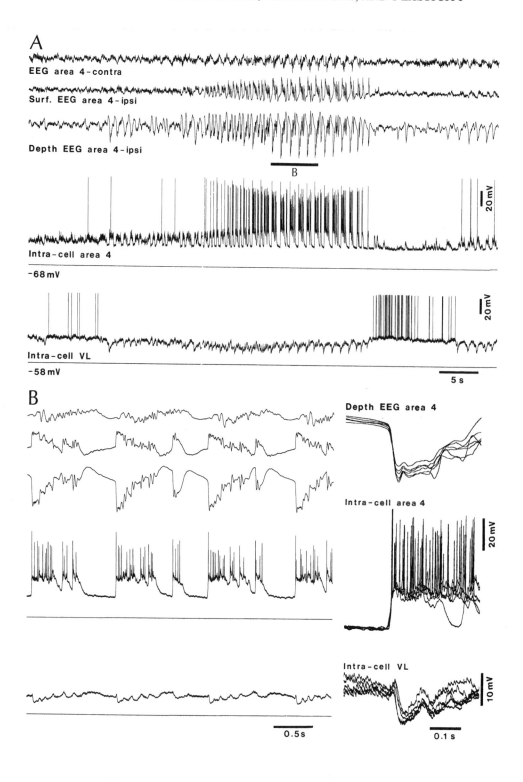

SHORT-TERM PLASTICITY PRODUCED BY RHYTHMIC ACTIVITIES IN CORTICOTHALAMIC NETWORKS

Repetitive stimulation within the frequency range of 5 to 15 Hz, applied to the cortex or thalamus, elicits responses in target neurons that grow in size during the first stimuli. The augmenting responses predispose cortical and thalamic neurons to progressive and persistent changes in membrane properties and synaptic responsiveness, outlasting the stimulation period. Initially, incremental responses were shown to be elicited in the cortex upon thalamic stimulation (76). Although such responses could also be obtained by stimulating the white matter in thalamically lesioned animals (77,78), it was emphasized that cortical responses to white matter stimulation are different from those evoked by thalamic stimuli (77). Nonetheless, in view of the cortical ability to display augmentation in the absence of the thalamus, it was assumed that the basic mechanisms of augmenting potentials are located within the cortex, and studies of rat motor cortex have specifically proposed that augmenting responses depend on the intrinsic properties of, and interconnections among, layer V pyramidal cells (79,80). The fact is that either the cortex of athalamic animals (53) or the thalamus of decorticated animals (81) has the neuronal equipment required to generate augmenting responses leading to plastic cellular phenomena, but when these structures are interconnected, the augmentation is facilitated by thalamically generated spike-bursts transmitted to the cortex as well as by incremental potentials transmitted back to the thalamus. Some of these recent experimental and modeling studies are exposed below.

After virtually complete hemithalamectomy, ipsilateral cortical association neurons display augmenting responses to rhythmic (10 Hz) stimulation of homotopic points in the contralateral cortex. Repetition of pulse trains (every 1–3 seconds) leads to a progressive depolarization of membrane potential, increase in the depolarization area of responses, and increased number of action potentials in response to testing stimuli (53). These progressive changes in membrane and synaptic properties are especially pronounced in deeply lying, intrinsically bursting cells (Fig. 12) but also can be observed, less conspicuously, in more superficial intrinsically bursting cells that can be found in layer III of cat association cortex (10) as well as in other types of cortical neurons. After protracted cortical stimulation, leading to a progressive increase in membrane depolarization and a greater number of action potentials in spike-bursts, cortical neurons reach the status of self-sustained seizures, with spike-bursts at 10 to 12 Hz, a frequency range similar to that of evoked responses dur-

---

FIG. 11. Dual intracellular recording demonstrating hyperpolarization of TC cells from the VL nucleus during seizure depolarization and spike-bursts in area 4 cortical neurons. Cat under ketamine-xylazine anesthesia. **A:** Five traces depict simultaneous recording of EEG from the skull over the right (contra) cortical area 4, surface and depth EEG from the left (ipsi) area 4, and intracellular activities of left area 4 cortical neuron and left VL neuron (below each intracellular trace, current monitor). The seizure was initiated by a series of EEG waves at ~0.9 Hz in the depth of left area 4, continued with discharges at ~2 Hz, and ended with high-amplitude, periodic (~0.9 Hz) EEG sequences consisting of ~14 Hz wavelets. The latter are expanded in **B.** All these periods were faithfully reflected in the intracellular activity of cortical cells, whereas VL thalamic cells displayed a tonic hyperpolarization throughout the seizure, with phasic sequences of IPSPs related to the large paroxysmal depolarizations and spike-bursts occurring at the end of the seizures (**B**). At right, expanded superimpositions of six traces from depth-EEG in area 4, and simultaneous intracellular recordings from area 4 and VL neurons showing IPSPs in VL cells during the cortical seizure. Modified with permission from Steriade and Contreras (72).

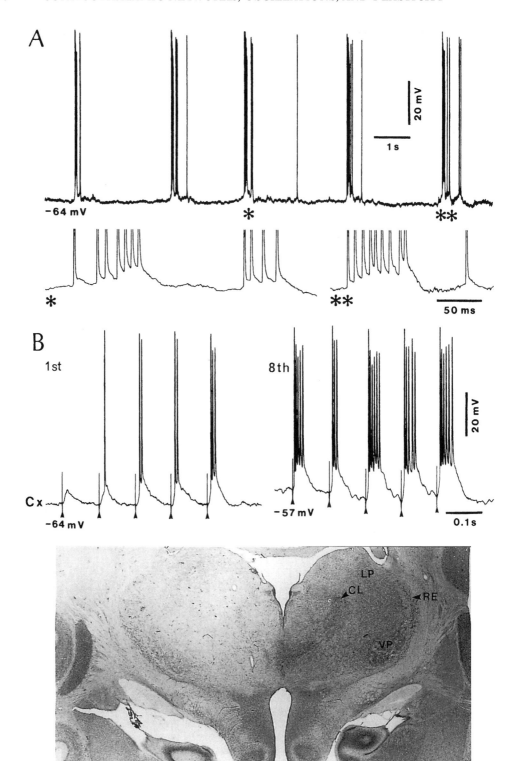

ing the last period of cortical stimulation (see Fig. 14 in ref. 53). This is reminiscent of earlier findings showing that self-sustained afterdischarges are gradually generated from incremental responses in amygdalo–hippocampal circuits (82). In that study, the waveform and frequency of potentials during the self-sustained afterdischarge were nearly identical to those of responses during the final period of stimulation.

The thalamus is also capable of producing augmentation and plasticity, even in the absence of the cerebral cortex. Although this was demonstrated intracellularly only recently (81), the presence of augmentation in the thalamus of a decorticated hemisphere was expected because augmenting responses mimic waxing-and-waning sleep spindles, and spindles occur after decortication (61) by reticular cell–TC cell interactions (41,42). Thus, the thalamic machinery seems necessary and sufficient to develop spindles as well as their artificial model, augmenting responses. We have indeed demonstrated two forms of augmenting responses in TC cells after repetitive (10 Hz) stimulation of dorsal thalamic nuclei in animals with ipsilateral decortication and callosal cut (Fig. 13A). In one form, TC cells exhibit a progressive decrease of IPSPs with repetitive stimuli at 10 Hz, leading to a progressive depolarization associated with high-threshold spike-bursts (Fig. 13B). Although in half the neurons displaying this form of intrathalamic augmentation the incremental responses developed in association with depression of IPSPs, in the remaining neurons augmenting developed im-

mediately after an antidromically elicited spike that depolarized the cell to the level required for the appearance of a high-threshold response, without an intermediate step involving an IPSP leading to a low-threshold spike. The other form of augmenting results from a progressive hyperpolarization, leading to low-threshold activated rebound bursts (Fig. 13C). Dual simultaneous impalements of ventrolateral (VL) cells demonstrate the two forms of augmentation, depending on the membrane potential of the two neurons (81). In some instances, the low-threshold response, deinactivated by hyperpolarization, leads to a high-threshold spike-burst on top of it (see Fig. 7 in ref. 81), as similarly demonstrated in data obtained by applying current pulses in thalamic slices (83).

The two types of intrathalamic augmentation are ascribed to two contrasting patterns of activity elicited in GABAergic reticular neurons by dorsal thalamic stimulation: (a) decremental responses that may account for disinhibition leading to high-threshold responses in TC cells and (b) incremental responses explaining the progressive hyperpolarization and increased postinhibitory rebound spike-bursts in TC cells (84). These experimental data have recently been reproduced with computer models of TC and reticular neurons (85), including voltage- and calcium-dependent currents, which confirmed the in vivo results and showed that the lateral inhibition between reticular cells (86,87) diminishes $GABA_B$ IPSPs and delays the augmenting responses in TC cells (84).

FIG. 12. Changes in properties of cortical neurons after repetitive cortical stimulation in a thalamically lesioned cat (see bottom panel with kainic thalamic lesions, ipsilateral to the recorded cortical neuron). Intracellular recording from intrinsically bursting neuron recorded at a depth of 1.5 mm in area 7. Urethane anesthesia. **A:** Slow oscillation (~0.4 Hz). Spike-bursts marked by one and two asterisks are expanded below (spikes truncated). **B:** Responses of the same cell to repetitive stimulation (five-shock trains at 10 Hz, repeated every 3 seconds) of contralateral area 7. The intracortical augmenting responses to the first and eighth trains are illustrated. Note depolarization by about 7 mV and increased number of action potentials within bursts after repetitive stimulation. CL, LP, and RE, centrolateral, lateroposterior, and reticular thalamic nuclei, respectively. Modified with permission from Steriade et al. (53).

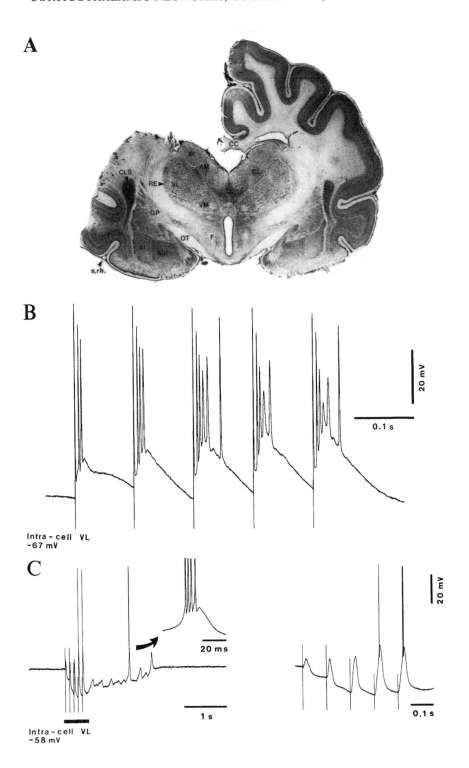

The intrathalamic augmenting responses develop in parallel with a progressive and persistent increase in the area of TC depolarization (Fig. 14) (81). Together with the persistent decrease in IPSPs' amplitudes, this result suggests that such plastic changes may influence the processing of incoming information and may play an important role in the generation of late excitatory postsynaptic potentials (EPSPs), which are usually ascribed solely to intracortical events. Thus, short-term plasticity in the thalamic gateway to the cortex may decisively influence cortical excitability during rhythmic responses.

Finally, in an intact-brain preparation, cortical and thalamic networks are interacting to generate not only more powerful augmentation but also more prolonged consequences. Thus, we did not succeed in eliciting long-lasting, self-sustained epileptic afterdischarges after augmenting responses in the thalamus of a decorticated hemisphere (81), but we did so after thalamocortical (88) or corticothalamic (89) augmenting responses. Evidence for plasticity after rhythmic cortical volleys at 10 Hz, eliciting responses in a bursting thalamic neuron, is illustrated in Fig. 15, showing that, after a series of repetitive responses evoked by pulse trains, the thalamic neuron spontaneously produced spike-bursts similar to the shape and frequencies of those evoked by testing stimuli (45). The "memory" of the circuit, due to resonant frequencies in neocortical areas and thalamic nuclei, may eventually lead to typical, self-sustained SW seizures (89).

The study of intracortical and corticothalamic synchrony during periods of sleep after conditioning sessions has shown that changes in the coherence of rhythmic activities during the behavioral task are also expressed during sleep (Fig. 6) (51). The persistence of plasticity during a behavioral state that is fundamentally different from that in which conditioning took place suggests, as in the hippocampus (90,91), that the reexpression during sleep of information acquired in wakefulness may be related to memory consolidation (5,41).

ACKNOWLEDGMENT

Personal experimental studies mentioned in this chapter were supported by grants from the Medical Research Council of Canada, National Sciences and Engineering Research Council of Canada, and Human Frontier Science Program. Thanks are due to all my Ph.D. students and postdoctoral fellows during recent years, especially F. Amzica, D. Contreras, and I. Timofeev, for their skillful and creative collaboration. Claude was my continuous source of inspiration and this chapter was written with the hope that, at some time, two decades from now, she will be interested in reading how intrinsic and network properties of cortical and thalamic neurons were envisioned at the end of this century.

FIG. 13. Intrathalamic augmenting responses in decorticated cats. Intracellular recordings of TC cells from the thalamic VL nucleus under ketamine-xylazine anesthesia. **A:** Hemidecortication (ipsilateral to thalamic recordings) and cut of corpus callosum. Nissl-stained section. AV, AM, CL, RE, VL, and VM, anteroventral, anteromedial, centrolateral, reticular, ventrolateral, and ventromedial thalamic nuclei, respectively ;CA, caudate nucleus; CC, corpus callosum; F, fornix; Al and Abl, lateral and basolateral nuclei of amygdala; CLS, claustrum; GP, globus pallidus; OT, optic tract; s.rh., rhinal sulcus (*arrowhead*). **B:** High-threshold augmenting responses of VL cells to local VL stimulation, occurring at a depolarized level. Responses consisted of an early antidromic action potential, followed by orthodromic spikes displaying progressive augmentation and spike inactivation. **C:** Low-threshold augmenting responses of VL cells developing from progressive increase in IPSP-rebound sequences and followed by a self-sustained spindle. Arrow indicates expanded spike-burst (action potentials truncated). The part marked by horizontal bar and indicating augmenting responses is expanded at right. Modified with permission from Steriade and Timofeev (81).

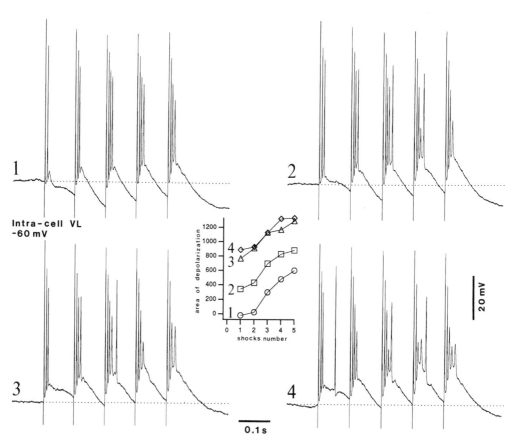

FIG. 14. Plasticity from repetitive high-threshold intrathalamic augmenting responses, as shown by progressive and persistent increase in the area of depolarization by repeating the pulse-trains. Intracellular recording of the VL neuron in cat with ipsilateral hemidecortication and callosal cut (as in Fig. 13A). Ketamine-xylazine anesthesia. Pulse-trains consisting of five stimuli at 10 Hz were applied to the VL every 2 seconds. Responses to four pulse-trains (1–4) are illustrated (1 and 2 were separated by 2 seconds; 3 and 4 also were separated by 2 seconds and followed 14 seconds after 2). With repetition of pulse-trains, IPSPs elicited by preceding stimuli in the train were progressively reduced until their complete obliteration and spike-bursts contained more action potentials with spike inactivation. The graph depicts the increased area of depolarization from the first to the fifth responses in each pulse-train as well as from pulse-train 1 to pulse-trains 3 and 4. Reprinted with permission from Steriade and Timofeev (81).

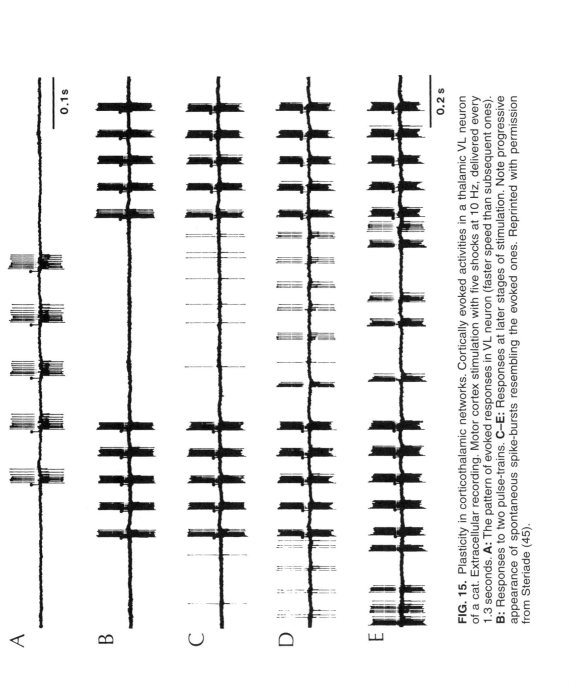

FIG. 15. Plasticity in corticothalamic networks. Cortically evoked activities in a thalamic VL neuron of a cat. Extracellular recording. Motor cortex stimulation with five shocks at 10 Hz, delivered every 1.3 seconds. **A:** The pattern of evoked responses in VL neuron (faster speed than subsequent ones). **B:** Responses to two pulse-trains. **C–E:** Responses at later stages of stimulation. Note progressive appearance of spontaneous spike-bursts resembling the evoked ones. Reprinted with permission from Steriade (45).

REFERENCES

1. Jasper HH. Problems of relating cellular and modular specificity to cognitive functions: importance of state-dependent reactions. In: Schmitt FO, Worden FG, Adelman G, Dennis SG, eds. *The organization of the cerebral cortex.* Cambridge, MA: MIT Press, 1981: 375–393.
2. Adrian ED, Matthews BHC. The Berger rhythm: potential changes from the occipital lobes in man. *Brain* 1934;57:355–384.
3. Jasper HH, Shagass C. Conscious time judgments related to conditioned time intervals and voluntary control of the alpha rhythm. *J Exp Psychol* 1941;28: 503–508.
4. Eccles JC. Chairman's opening remarks. In: Wolstenholme GEW, O'Connor M, eds. *The nature of sleep.* London: Churchill, 1961:1–3.
5. Steriade M, Contreras D, Curró Dossi R, Nuñez A. The slow (<1 Hz) oscillation in reticular thalamic and thalamocortical neurons: scenario of sleep rhythm generation in interacting thalamic and neocortical networks. *J Neurosci* 1993;13:3284–3299.
6. Maquet P, Degueldre C, Delfiore G, Aerts J, Péters JM, Luxen A, Franck G. Functional neuroanatomy of human slow wave sleep. *J Neurosci* 1997;17:2807–2812.
7. Steriade M, Contreras D, Amzica F. Synchronized sleep oscillations and their paroxysmal developments. *Trends Neurosci* 1994;17:199–208.
8. Contreras D, Steriade M. Cellular basis of EEG slow rhythms: a study of dynamic corticothalamic relationships. *J Neurosci* 1995;15:604–622.
9. Steriade M, Amzica F, Contreras D. Synchronization of fast (30–40 Hz) spontaneous cortical rhythms during brain activation. *J Neurosci* 1996;16:392–417.
10. Steriade M, Nuñez A, Amzica F. A novel slow (<1 Hz) oscillation of neocortical neurons in vivo: depolarizing and hyperpolarizing components. *J Neurosci* 1993;13: 3252–3265.
11. Amzica F, Steriade M. The K-complex: its slow (<1 Hz) rhythmicity and relation with delta waves. *Neurology* 1997;49:952–959.
12. Achermann P, Borbély A. Low-frequency (<1 Hz) oscillations in the human sleep EEG. *Neuroscience* 1997;81:213–222.
13. Llinás R, Ribary U. Coherent 40-Hz oscillation characterizes dream states in humans. *Proc Natl Acad Sci U S A* 1993;90:2078–2081.
14. Gevins A, Smith ME, McEvoy L, Yu D. High-resolution EEG mapping of cortical activation related to working memory: effects of task difficulty, type of processing, and practice. *Cereb Cortex* 1997;7:374–385.
15. Crick F, Koch C. Some reflections on visual awareness. *Cold Spring Harb Symp Quant Biol* 1990;55:953–962.
16. Llinás R, Ribary U, Joliot M, Wang XJ. Content and context in temporal thalamocortical binding. In: Buzsáki G, Llinás R, Singer W, Berthoz A, Christen Y, eds. *Temporal coding in the brain.* Berlin: Springer, 1994:251–272.
17. Singer W, Gray CM. Visual feature integration and the temporal correlation hypothesis. *Annu Rev Neurosci* 1995;18:555–586.
18. Steriade M. Central core modulation of spontaneous oscillations and sensory transmission in thalamocortical systems. *Curr Opin Neurobiol* 1993;3:619–625.
19. Steriade M, Contreras D, Amzica F, Timofeev I. Synchronization of fast (30–40 Hz) spontaneous oscillations in intrathalamic and thalamocortical networks. *J Neurosci* 1996;16:2788–2808.
20. Steriade M, Jones EG, Llinás RR. *Thalamic oscillations and signaling.* New York: Wiley-Interscience, 1990.
21. Steriade M, Amzica F. Intracortical and corticothalamic coherency of fast spontaneous oscillations. *Proc Natl Acad Sci U S A* 1996;93:2533–2538.
22. Murthy VN, Fetz EE. Coherent 25- to 35-Hz oscillations in the sensorimotor cortex of awake behaving monkeys. *Proc Natl Acad Sci USA* 1992;89: 5670–5674.
23. Murthy VN, Fetz EE. Oscillatory activity in sensorimotor cortex of awake monkeys: synchronization of local field potentials and relation to behavior. *J Neurophysiol* 1997;76:3949–3967.
24. Llinás R, Grace AA, Yarom Y. In vitro neurons in mammalian cortical layer 4 exhibit intrinsic oscillatory activity in the 10- to 50-Hz frequency range. *Proc Natl Acad Sci U S A* 1991;88:897–901.
25. Steriade M, Curró Dossi R, Paré D, Oakson G. Fast oscillations (20–40 Hz) in thalamocortical systems and their potentiation by mesopontine cholinergic nuclei in the cat. *Proc Natl Acad Sci U S A* 1991;88:4396–4400.
26. Steriade M, Curró Dossi R, Contreras D. Electrophysiological properties of intralaminar thalamocortical cells discharging rhythmic (~40 Hz) spike-bursts at ~1000 Hz during waking and rapid-eye-movement sleep. *Neuroscience* 1993;56:1–9.
27. Gray CM, McCormick DA. Chattering cells: superficial pyramidal neurons contributing to the generation of synchronous oscillations in the visual cortex. *Science* 1996;274:109–113.
28. Steriade M. Synchronized activities of coupled oscillators in the cerebral cortex and thalamus at different levels of vigilance. *Cereb Cortex* 1997;7:583–604.
29. Steriade M, Timofeev I, Dürmüller N, Grenier F. Dynamic properties of corticothalamic neurons and local cortical interneurons generating fast oscillations. *J Neurophysiol* 1998;79:483–490.
30. Pedroarena C, Llinás R. Dendritic calcium conductances generate high-frequency oscillation in thalamocortical neurons. *Proc Natl Acad Sci U S A* 1997;94: 724–728.
31. Ghose GM, Freeman RD. Oscillatory discharge in the visual system: does it have a functional role? *J Neurophysiol* 1992;68:1558–1574.
32. Gray CM, König P, Engel AK, Singer W. Stimulus-specific neuronal oscillations in cat visual cortex exhibit inter-columnar synchronization which reflects global stimulus properties. *Nature* 1989;338:334–337.
33. Jones EG. *The thalamus.* New York: Plenum, 1985.
34. Gutnick MJ, Mody I, eds. *The cortical neuron.* New York: Oxford University Press, 1995.
35. Thomson AM, West DC, Hahn J, Deuchars J. Single axon IPSPs elicited in pyramidal cells by three classes of interneurons in slices of rat neocortex. *J Physiol (Lond)* 1996;496:81–102.
36. Chagnac-Amitai Y, Connors BW. Synchronized excitation and inhibition driven by intrinsically bursting neurons in neocortex. *J Neurophysiol* 1989;62:1149–1162.
37. Kang Y, Kayano F. Electrophysiological and morphological characteristics of layer VI pyramidal cells in the cat motor cortex. *J Neurophysiol* 1994;72:578–591.

38. Steriade M, Amzica F, Nuñez A. Cholinergic and nora-drenergic modulation of the slow (~0.3 Hz) oscillation in neocortical cells. *J Neurophysiol* 1993;70:1384–1400.

39. Wang Z, McCormick DA. Control of firing mode of corticotectal and corticopontine layer V burst-generating neurons by norepinephrine, acetylcholine and 1S, 3R-ACPD. *J Neurosci* 1993;13:2199–2216.

40. Paré D, Steriade M, Deschênes M, Oakson G. Physiological characteristics of anterior thalamic nuclei, a group devoid of inputs from reticular thalamic nucleus. *J Neurophysiol* 1987;57:1669–1685.

41. Steriade M, McCormick DA, Sejnowski TJ. Thalamocortical oscillations in the sleeping and aroused brain. *Science* 1993;262:679–685.

42. Steriade M, Jones EG, McCormick DA. *Thalamus: organization and function.* Oxford: Elsevier, 1997.

43. Liu XB, Warren RA, Jones EG. Synaptic distribution of afferents from reticular nucleus in ventroposterior nucleus of the cat thalamus. *J Comp Neurol* 1995;352: 187–202.

44. Steriade M, Deschênes M, Domich L, Mulle C. Abolition of spindle oscillations in thalamic neurons disconnected from the nucleus reticularis thalami. *J Neurophysiol* 1985;54:1473–1497.

45. Steriade M. Alertness, quiet sleep, dreaming. In: Peters A, Jones EG, eds. *Cerebral cortex.* Vol. 9. New York: Plenum, 1991:279–357.

46. Steriade M, Domich L, Oakson G. Reticularis thalamic neurons revisited: activity changes during shifts in states of vigilance. *J Neurosci* 1986;6:68–81.

47. Moruzzi G, Magoun HW. Brain stem reticular formation and activation of the electroencephalogram. *Electroencephalogr Clin Neurophysiol* 1949;1:455–473.

48. Kato N. Cortico-thalamo-cortical projection between visual cortices. *Brain Res* 1990;599:150–152.

49. Timofeev I, Steriade M. Fast (mainly 30–100 Hz) oscillations in cat cerebellothalamic pathway and their synchronization with cortical potentials. *J Physiol (Lond)* 1997;504:153–168.

50. Neunschwander S, Singer W. Long-range synchronization of oscillatory light responses in the cat retina and lateral geniculate nucleus. *Nature* 1996;379: 728–733.

51. Amzica F, Neckelmann D, Steriade M. Instrumental conditioning of fast (20–50 Hz) oscillations in corticothalamic networks. *Proc Natl Acad Sci USA* 1997;94: 1985–1989.

52. Cunningham ET, LeVay S. Laminar and synaptic organization of the projection from the thalamic nucleus centralis to primary visual cortex in the cat. *J Comp Neurol* 1986;254:65–77.

53. Steriade M, Nuñez A, Amzica F. Intracellular analysis of relations between the slow (<1 Hz) neocortical oscillation and other sleep rhythms of the electroencephalogram. *J Neurosci* 1993;13:3266–3283.

54. Timofeev I, Steriade M. Low-frequency rhythms in the thalamus of intact-cortex and decorticated cats. *J Neurophysiol* 1996;76:4152–4168.

55. Amzica F, Steriade M. Disconnection of intracortical synaptic linkages disrupts synchronization of a slow oscillation. *J Neurosci* 1995;15:4658–4677.

56. McCormick DA, Pape HC. Properties of a hyperpolarization-activated cation current and its role in rhythmic oscillation in thalamic relay neurones. *J Physiol (Lond)* 1990;431:291–318.

57. Soltesz I, Lightowler S, Leresche N, Jassik-Gerschenfeld D, Pollard CE, Crunelli V. Two inward currents and the transformation of low-frequency oscillations of rat and cat thalamocortical cells. *J Physiol (Lond)* 1991; 441:175–197.

58. Contreras D, Destexhe A, Sejnowski TJ, Steriade M. Control of spatiotemporal coherence of a thalamic oscillation by corticothalamic feedback. *Science* 1996; 274:771–774.

59. Contreras D, Destexhe A, Sejnowski TJ, Steriade M. Spatiotemporal patterns of spindle oscillations in cortex and thalamus. *J Neurosci* 1997;17:1179–1196.

60. Kim U, Bal T, McCormick DA. Spindle waves are propagating oscillations in the ferret LGNd in vitro. *J Neurophysiol* 1995;74:1301–1323.

61. Morison RS, Bassett DL. Electrical activity of the thalamus and basal ganglia in deocorticated cats. *J Neurophysiol* 1945;8:309–314.

62. von Krosigk M, Bal T, McCormick DA. Cellular mechanisms of a synchronized oscillation in the thalamus. *Science* 1993;261:361–364.

63. Bal T, von Krosigk M, McCormick DA. Synaptic and membrane mechanisms underlying synchronized oscillations in the ferret lateral geniculate nucleus in vitro. *J Physiol (Lond)* 1995;483:641–663.

64. Steriade M, Wyzinski P, Apostol V. Corticofugal projections governing rhythmic thalamic activity. In: Frigyesi TL, Rinvik E, Yahr MD, eds. *Corticothalamic projections and sensorimotor activities.* New York: Raven, 1972:221–272.

65. Contreras D, Steriade M. Spindle oscillations in cats: the role of corticothalamic feedback in a thalamically generated rhythm. *J Physiol (Lond)* 1996;490:159–180.

66. Loomis AL, Harvey N, Hobart GA. Distribution of disturbance patterns in human electroencephalogram, with special reference to sleep. *J Neurophysiol* 1938;1: 413–430.

67. Hofle N, Paus T, Reutens D, Fiset P, Gotman J, Evans AC, Jones BE. Regional cerebral blood flow changes as a function of delta and spindle activity during slow wave sleep in humans. *J Neurosci* 1997;17:4800–4808.

68. Jasper HH, Droogleever-Fortuyn J. Experimental studies on the functional anatomy of petit-mal epilepsy. *Res Publ Assoc Nerv Ment Disord* 1947;26:272–298.

69. Pollen DA, Perot P, Reid KH. Experimental bilateral wave and spike from thalamic stimulation in relation to level of arousal. *Electroencephalogr Clin Neurophysiol* 1963;15:1017–1028.

70. Steriade M. Interneuronal epileptic discharges related to spike-and-wave cortical seizures in behaving monkeys. *Electroencephalogr Clin Neurophysiol* 1974;37: 247–263.

71. Pollen DA. Intracellular studies of cortical neurons during thalamic induced wave and spike. *Electroencephalogr Clin Neurophysiol* 1964;17:398–404.

72. Kellaway P. Sleep and epilepsy. *Epilepsia* 1985;26 (suppl 1):15–30.

73. Steriade M, Contreras D. Relations between cortical and thalamic cellular events during transition from sleep patterns to paroxysmal activity. *J Neurosci* 1995;15: 623–642.

74. Lytton WW, Contreras D, Destexhe A, Steriade M. Dynamic interactions determine partial thalamic quiescence in a computer network model of spike-and-wave seizures. *J Neurophysiol* 1997;77:1679–1696.

75. Steriade M, Amzica F. Dynamic coupling among neocortical neurons during evoked and spontaneous spike-wave seizure activity. *J Neurophysiol* 1994;72:2051–2069.

76. Morison RS, Dempsey EW. Mechanism of thalamocortical augmentation and repetition. *Am J Physiol* 1943; 138:297–308.

77. Morin D, Steriade M. Development from primary to augmenting responses in primary somatosensory cortex. *Brain Res* 1981;205:49–66.

78. Ferster D, Lindström S. Augmenting responses evoked in area 17 of the cat by intracortical axonal collaterals of cortico-geniculate cells. *J Physiol (Lond)* 1985;367: 217–232.

79. Castro-Alamancos MA, Connors BW. Spatiotemporal properties of short-term plasticity in sensorimotor thalamocortical pathways of the rat. *J Neurosci* 1996;16: 2767–2779.

80. Castro-Alamancos MA, Connors BW. Cellular mechanisms of the augmenting response: short-term plasticity in a thalamocortical pathway. *J Neurosci* 1996;16: 7742–7756.

81. Steriade M, Timofeev I. Short-term plasticity during intrathalamic augmenting responses in decorticated cats. *J Neurosci* 1997;17:3778–3795.

82. Steriade M. Development of evoked responses into self-sustained activity within amygdalo-hippocampal circuits. *Electroencephalogr Clin Neurophysiol* 1964;16: 221–236.

83. Jahnsen H, Llinás R. Ionic basis for the electrorespon-siveness and oscillatory properteis of guinea-pig thalamic neurones in vitro. *J Physiol (Lond)* 1984;349: 227–247.

84. Steriade M, Timofeev I. Intrathalamic mechanisms of short-term plasticity processes during incremental responses. *Soc Neurosci Abstr* 1996;22:2030.

85. Bazhenov M, Timofeev I, Steriade M, Sejnowski T. A computational model of intrathalamic augmenting responses. *Soc Neurosci Abstr* 1997;23:1306.

86. Huguenard JR, Prince DA. Clonazepam suppresses GABAB-mediated inhibition in thalamic relay neurons through effects in nucleus reticularis. *J Neurophysiol* 1994;71:2576–2581.

87. Uhlrich S, Huguenard JR. GABAB receptor-mediated responses in GABAergic projection neurones of rat nucleus reticularis thalami in vitro. *J Physiol (Lond)* 1996; 493:845–854.

88. Steriade M, Yossif G. Spike-and-wave afterdischarges in cortical somatosensory neurons of cat. *Electroencephalogr Clin Neurophysiol* 1974;37:633–648.

89. Steriade M, Oakson G, Diallo A. Cortically elicited spike-wave afterdischarges in thalamic neurons. *Electroencephalogr Clin Neurophysiol* 1976;41:641–644.

90. Buzsáki G. Two-stage model of memory trace formation: a role for "noisy" brain states. *Neuroscience* 1989; 31:551–570.

91. Wilson MA, McNaughton BL. Reactivation of hippocampal ensemble memories during sleep. *Science* 1994;265:676–679.

Consciousness: At the Frontiers of Neuroscience,
Advances in Neurology, Vol. 77,
edited by H.H. Jasper, L. Descarries,
V.F. Castellucci, and S. Rossignol.
Lippincott–Raven Publishers, Philadelphia © 1998.

9

Containing the Contents

Alan J. McComas

Department of Biomedical Studies, McMaster University Medical Centre,
Hamilton, Ontario, L8N 3Z5, Canada

PROLOGUE

It is a singular honor to have been invited to participate in this symposium on consciousness, not only because of the primal nature of the subject under discussion, but also because of the quality of the man, Herbert Jasper, whose work we are celebrating. Dr. Jasper's many and varied contributions to our understanding of the working of the brain are, of course, the reason why he is being honored. Yet, for those of us who work in clinical neurophysiology, it is difficult not to be awed by his impact in the electrodiagnostic field. To give but four examples, there is the early report on the localization of brain tumors by electroencephalography (EEG) (1), the development of the international 10- to 20-Hz EEG electrode system (2), the concept of centrencephalic epilepsy (3), and the introduction of monopolar electromyography (EMG) needle recordings (4). It is remarkable that most of the work that led to the papers cited was conducted over a 10-year period, punctuated by Dr. Jasper's military duties in the Second World War.

INTRODUCTION

The chapters that follow in this part of the text address different aspects of the contents of consciousness. It seems fitting in this introduction to the session, then, to consider the brain as a container for those contents. A central theme will be that the human brain has redundant neuronal capacity for those transactions that emerge into consciousness, and this theme will be illustrated by some clinical observations. The argument will then be carried from one of brain dimensions into one of brain activity. The suggestion will be made that much, indeed most, of the electrical activity in the brain is not only unrelated to consciousness but is quite purposeless.

These two ideas are strongly counterintuitive for two reasons. First, because of the remarkable achievements of the human brain in the understanding of the physics of the universe and of the nature of life, and in the creation of art, poetry, literature, and music. Second, the ideas are unattractive because of the extraordinary precision with which the structural and functional elements of the nervous system are put together and operate. This is true whether one considers the enormously complex branching of a Purkinje cell dendrite, the ultrastructure of a synapse, or the opening and closing of a single ion channel. Perhaps part of our difficulty in understanding the brain is that we are too preoccupied with detail, with the activities of single cells, and with events in the millisecond range.

What, then, are the observations that support the idea of a brain that operates quite roughly and in which only a modest fraction does so purposefully? I shall begin by presenting four clinical problems.

CLINICAL OBSERVATIONS

Hydrocephalus

In congenital hydrocephalus, the cerebrospinal fluid is produced normally in the ventricles but cannot drain properly because of a block in the outflow system. As a result, the lateral ventricles can become enormously dilated, as in the example on the left in Fig. 1. In this computed tomography (CT) scan, taken when the patient was 1.5 years of age and after shunting had been performed, the ratio of ventricle to brain is 80%. Now, however, the patient is 12 years of age and, despite some learning problems, is lively, keeps up a good conversation, and thoroughly enjoys school. The CT scan on the right is taken from an extensive study of the relationship between hydrocephalus and intelligence by Lonton (5), which involved 411 children referred to the Sheffield Children's Hospital (England). The scan is that of a young man with a verbal IQ of 143 and a first-class degree in mathematics. The ventricle-to-brain ratio in this subject was 95%. Table 1 is also from this study and shows the lack of correlation between the dilatation of the ventricles, and hence the thinness of the cerebral cortex, and IQ.

Frontal Lobe Lesions

Recently there have been two detailed clinical descriptions of behavioral changes after massive frontal lesions. One is a brilliant reconstruction, by Damasio (6), of the case of Phineas Gage, the young railway engineer

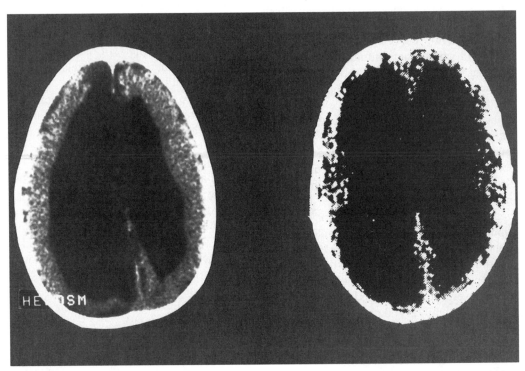

FIG. 1. Left: Horizontal CT scan of the brain of an 18-month-old girl, showing severe hydrocephalus. Shunting was performed soon after birth. Courtesy of Dr. R. Hollenberg. **Right:** CT brain scan of a young male subject with high intellect despite the presence of marked hydrocephalus. Reprinted with permission from Lonton AP. In infantile hydrocephalus how much brain mantle is needed for normal development? In: Warlow C, Garfield J, eds. *Dilemmas in the management of the neurological patient.* Edinburgh, Scotland: Churchill-Livingstone, 1984:267 (fifth panel). Copyright 1984 by Churchill-Livingstone.

TABLE 1. *Lack of correlation between intelligence quotient and degree of hydrocephalus*

VBR range (%)	IQ		
	Verbal	Performance	Full Scale
0–10	104	90	95
11–20	106	90	94
21–30	100	86	94
31–40	101	86	92
41–50	101	82	91
51–100	96	76	86
p	NS	0.001	NS

VBR, ventricle:brain percentage ratio; NS, not significant.

Altered with permission from Lonton AP. In infantile hydrocephalus how much brain mantle is needed for normal development? In: Warlow C, Garfield J, eds. *Dilemmas in the management of the neurological patient.* Edinburgh, Scotland: Churchill-Livingstone, 1984:263. Copyright 1984 by Churchill-Livingstone.

who had a metal tamping rod driven right through, and out of, an orbit and frontal lobe. Yet he was apparently able to carry on a perfectly lucid conversation 1 hour later. The other case is that reported by Sacks (7) of a young man, Greg, with a large meningioma compressing the frontal lobes and optic chiasm. Both of these subjects showed behavioral changes, carefully and beautifully described by the authors, but the most important observation is surely that the behavioral changes were remarkably mild is relation to the enormous amount of brain tissue that must have been destroyed. Of the two cases, Phineas Gage is the more striking, and the more important, for his behavior was observed immediately after the accident, before any compensatory effects could have arisen from structural plasticity, nor was there the complication of total blindness. In my own practice I am familiar with a 44-year-old physician who recently had her right frontal lobe resected for a small glioma. Although she feels that she is not quite the same as before the operation, it is quite impossible to detect any change in her. In a related vein, Penfield (8) described removing the right frontal lobe of his sister for a symptomatic calcified oligodendroglioma. At the end of the opera-

tion, which was performed under local anesthesia, his sister "apologized for having made so much trouble" and, after convalescence, was able to continue looking after her home and six children. The extensive nature of the resection is evident in Fig. 2.

Multiple Sclerosis

Although some brain is destroyed in multiple sclerosis, the clinical problem is compounded by the effect of the characteristic plaques in delaying impulse conduction in the partially or totally demyelinated axons. This effect is readily detected in the clinical neurophysiology laboratories and shows up as prolonged latencies of the cortical responses evoked by visual, somatic, or auditory stimuli. However, despite the temporal dispersion and the delayed and disordered arrival of the impulse messages, many patients are found to be free of any sensory loss. Indeed, many patients are symptom free during life and the plaques are only discovered postmortem (9) or via brain imaging undertaken for other reasons.

Sensory Neuropathy

It is a common experience for an electromyographer to encounter a patient with a severe general peripheral neuropathy, say from Charcot-Marie-Tooth disease or diabetes, yet in whom no sensory loss can be detected by clinical testing. Clearly, some nerve fibers must still be conducting, but measurements of sensory nerve action potential amplitude indicate that this number must be less than 5% of the normal population. We have noticed a similar preservation of function in an ongoing study in which we are looking for cognitive defects in children who have had restricted use of an arm in infancy because of an obstetric brachial palsy (10).

Comment

How are we to interpret these different types of observations? First, the observations

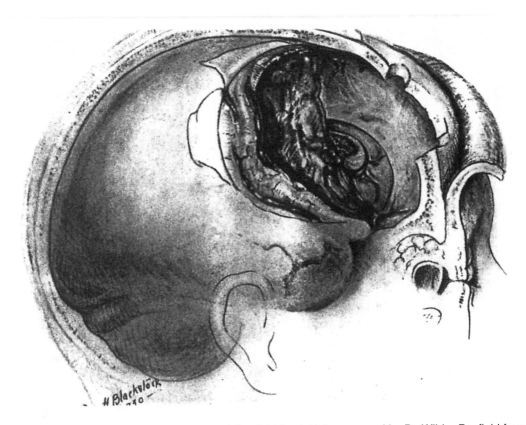

FIG. 2. Artist's impression of the extent of the right frontal lobe removed by Dr. Wilder Penfield from his sister. Reprinted with permission from Penfield W, Evans J. Functional defects produced by cerebral lobectomies. *Res Publ Assoc Nerv Ment Disord* 1934;13:352–377. Copyright 1934 by The Williams & Wilkins Co.

on hydrocephalus and partial sensory denervation show that, under certain circumstances, the human brain can still manage to function quite well, even when only a small fraction of the normal neuropil is able to participate. There is, in other words, a considerable safety margin, which is presumably a consequence both of the large number of neurons performing the same or similar tasks and, in the face of injury or disease, of the ability of surviving neurons to take on additional functions. There is a simple analogy with the motor system, in which motor unit number estimation has shown that normal strength and muscle bulk can remain when up to 80% of the motoneurons or their axons have degener-

ated (11). This remarkable compensation is mostly achieved by collateral sprouting of the remaining axons (Fig. 3).

Next, there is the issue of good function in the presence of widespread demyelination in multiple sclerosis, despite the slowing and dispersion of impulse messages within the central nervous system (CNS). This is an important observation, and one that suggests that the excitatory and inhibitory events in the CNS, which underlie motor and sensory processes, normally occur with considerable latitude in their timing. Indeed, one sees examples of this, as demonstrated in Fig. 4. At the top are the discharges of a single neuron in one of the somatosensory receiving nuclei

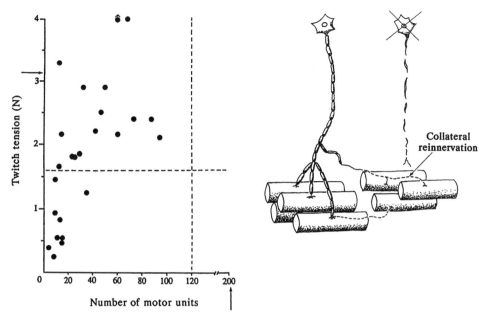

FIG. 3. Effect of collateral reinnervation in compensating for chronic denervation of human skeletal muscle. **Left:** Maximum twitch tensions in the extensor digitorum brevis are maintained until fewer than 20 motor units remain. The horizontal and vertical dashed lines indicate the lower limits of the respective normal ranges, whereas the control mean values are indicated by arrows. Data from McComas et al. (11). **Right:** Collateral sprouting by a surviving motor axon.

(V.c.i and V.im.c. in Fig. 5, lower), after weak stimulation of the contralateral median nerve. Even though the stimuli, being electrical, are precisely timed, and even though there are only two synapses interposed between the wrist and the thalamus, it can be seen that there is already a variation of several milliseconds in the discharges. However, this scatter is small in relation to the responses of neurons in the somatosensory cortex, and particularly of cells in the upper layers (layers II and III). This scatter is evident in Fig. 4 (middle), which shows, in an awake monkey, the responses of superficial cortical neurons to electrical stimulation of the contralateral hand (12). In this figure, the latencies have a bimodal distribution, with most activity in the later firing. Dr. Cynthia Cupido and I have suggested that the later firing is, in effect, a readout of excitatory postsynaptic activity in the apical dendrites of the layer II and III neu-

rons, by a recurrent input from the layer V pyramids (Cupido and McComas, unpublished observations). The recurrent input would arise at the end of an inhibitory postsynaptic potential (IPSP) in the layer V cells.

At the bottom of Fig. 4 is the distribution of latencies for a more complex neural situation, one also involving electrical stimulation of the hand, but this time with the addition of a conscious perception and a motor output. The subject was required to reach forward and to tap a target on the table in front of her as soon as she received an electrical stimulus delivered to the contralateral median nerve. A verbal warning was given within the preceding 2 seconds. In 100 consecutive trials, the reaction time was measured to the appearance of EMG activity in the anterior fibers of the deltoid muscle. Despite the apparent simplicity of the task, there was a fivefold range of values, from 63 to 320 milliseconds. This large

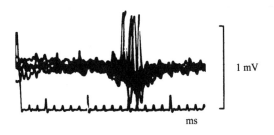

1 mV

ms

Impulse
activity

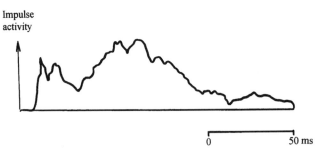

0   50 ms

Number (%)

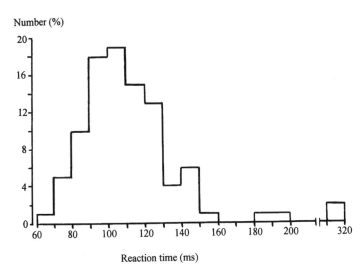

Reaction time (ms)

FIG. 4. Top: Superimposed responses of human thalamic neuron to electrical stimulation of contralateral median nerve. Small time markers indicate milliseconds (McComas, unpublished observations). **Middle:** Aggregated impulse activity in multiple neurons of monkey superficial somatosensory cortex, after electrical stimulation of contralateral hand. Note the wide scatter in the timing of the discharges, and the bimodal distribution of values. Reprinted with permission from Kulics AT, Cauller LJ. Cerebral cortical somatosensory evoked responses, multiple unit activity and current source-densities: their relationships and significance to somatic sensation as revealed by stimulation of the awake monkey's hand. *Exp Brain Res* 1986;62:53. Copyright 1986 by Springer-Verlag. **Bottom:** Distribution of simple reaction times in 100 consecutive trials in a human subject who was required to reach forward and tap in response to an electric stimulus to the opposite wrist (McComas and Scarfone, unpublished observations).

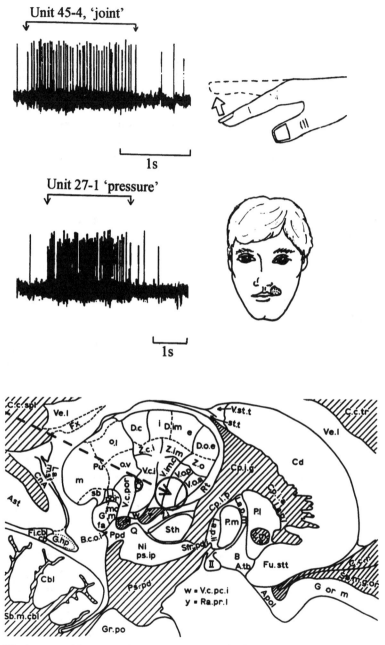

FIG. 5. Top: Discharges of two somatosensory neurons in the human thalamus, one responsive to touching above the lip and the other to passive extension of the second metacarpophalangeal joint (McComas, unpublished observations). **Bottom:** Track of recording electrode in sagittal plane of thalamus, terminating in the target area (*circled*) for a therapeutic lesion to relieve parkinsonian tremor. Abbreviations are as in the nomenclature of Hassler (30).

scatter is, we suggest, due to inclusion of a variable number of IPSP and excitatory post-synaptic potential (EPSP) cycles in the cortical neurons.

Finally, we are left with the study of Phineas Gage and the minimal consequences of surgical frontal lobectomy. These observations are especially challenging for those who hold that the entire brain is normally occupied in purposeful activity. Do they mean, in fact, that the prefrontal area is functionally inert? To answer this question, it would be necessary to remove the prefrontal areas on both sides of the brain. Thus, it is well known that, in the case of the temporal lobe, whereas unilateral removal for intractable epilepsy is functionally acceptable (13), bilateral damage through injury or disease is devastating. In the case of the prefrontal areas, however, the answer is very different, for the operation of prefrontal leukotomy was widely practiced for many years for psychiatric disorders. Although there were definite behavioral changes after surgery, with a reduction in anxiety and depression, and in compulsive and obsessive activity, a reading of the literature indicates that there was no impairment of consciousness, of sensory discrimination, or of motor performance.

Even more impressive are the rare reports of bilateral frontal lobectomy, reviewed in detail by Freeman and Watts (14). To be sure, there were significant changes in behavior, usually with a lack of emotional restraint, and with impairment of judgment, loss of initiative, and difficulty in planning. More recently, Damasio (6) has emphasized the importance of the prefrontal areas in providing emotional weighting in decision making. Nevertheless, one is left with the strong suspicion that, bearing in mind the large size of the prefrontal areas, only a small percentage of their activities contribute to the purposive functions of the brain.

Neurophysiologic Observations

I would now like to report two different types of studies that would be consistent with the presence of such purposeless activity in the human brain. First, thalamic recordings. In the 1960s our laboratory was involved in recording from the human thalamus during sterotaxic operations for parkinsonism and intractable pain (15). The aim was to provide the neurosurgeon with precise topographic information that would enable a small destructive lesion to be placed accurately in the appropriate thalamic nucleus. At that time several other groups were making similar recordings; one of them was at the Montreal Neurological Institute and included Dr. Jasper (16). In our own experience, it was quite easy to detect neurons that responded to touching small areas of skin on the opposite side of the body, or to the passive movement of joints (Fig. 5, upper). However, what might be called the negative findings in this type of study were never reported. Thus, in our system, the recording electrode was advanced through the thalamus from behind, and the trajectory crossed several nuclei, commencing with the pulvinar (Fig. 5, lower). What was so striking, especially in the patients who had undergone surgery for pain, was the profuse impulse activity in these more posterior nuclei and the total inability to influence this activity by such interventions as touching, reading, looking in different directions, other voluntary movements, sounds, speaking, arithmetic calculations, and so on. It is possible that this impulse activity was concerned with some other brain functions, too subtle to be detected through the maneuvers described.

It is possible to go one step further and suggest that, even when neural activity is evoked by a stimulus, much of it is redundant and unrelated to a conscious experience. As an example, consider event-related potentials (ERPs), detected via a scalp electrode on the vertex and elicited by a weak electrical stimulus to the wrist. These waves, which are widely distributed over both cerebral hemispheres, have been described by numerous investigators. Great significance has been attached to the different components, shown by the use of averaging techniques. For example, Hillyard (17) made the following assertion:

Separate ERP components demarcate processes of stimulus selection, evaluation, and classification, thus providing a window into the timing of complex mental operations.

It turns out that if the stimuli are given infrequently and irregularly, the main components are sufficiently large that averaging can be dispensed with. It is then immediately obvious that the response is extremely variable, especially the amplitude and latency of the main positive wave (P 300), and this is true despite the constancy of the somatic perception. In some experiments we have asked whether it is possible to perceive an electrical stimulus that is barely perceptible (liminal) when given by itself and which is delivered when the ERP evoked by an earlier stimulus is at its positive or negative maximum (Fig. 6, upper). The presumption, a reasonable one, is that the large waves at the cortical surface reflect polarization along the apical dendrites of the pyramidal cells in the cortex. Our finding was that, regardless of whether the stimuli were delivered during the P 300 or the subsequent negative wave, they were still detected and felt no different to those stimuli delivered without the conditioning shock.

Along similar lines, we delayed the test stimulus a little more (to 500 milliseconds), after the conditioning shock, and increased the intensity slightly, noting that the averaged ERP was only half the size of that evoked by the same stimulus given alone (Fig. 6, lower). Despite the reduction in size of the ERP, the weak stimuli still felt the same as when presented alone.

DISCUSSION

The implication from the last type of experiment would seem to be that most (although obviously not all) of the electrical activity evoked in the cortex by certain stimuli is unrelated to the conscious perception of the latter. For this reason there is a need to be especially careful in the interpretation of nonligand functional brain imaging studies, which now appear so frequently in the scientific journals. The picture of a red focus of cogni-

tive activity on a gray–green background of (noncognitive) brain is extraordinarily seductive, but how firm are these extracted features? Is there not a danger in the sampling procedures, such as that which caused a reputable laboratory to make the extraordinary claim that water could retain a molecular memory of solutes that had since been removed (18)? The story of this particular saga, which was apparently resolved in a remarkable way (19), should be compulsory reading for all scientific laboratories.

What, then, are we left with? At first sight, all the negative observations that have been put forward seem disappointing, as if the search for the neural mechanisms underlying consciousness is likely to remain unsuccessful because of the elusive nature of the target. In fact, the very opposite is true. Let me suggest an alternative way of looking at the problem, by going back to the embryonic brain. Although the main fiber connections between different cortical areas are presumably specified in the genetic plan for the brain, the situation at a regional level is more complex. For example, Molnár and Blakemore (20) have studied explants of fetal rat cortex and thalamus that are grown together in culture. They have shown that axons from the future lateral geniculate nucleus will readily invade cortex that would normally become frontal lobe, and will terminate appropriately in cortical layer IV.

Also related are experiments in which embryonic cortex is transplanted between the frontal and occipital areas in fetal rats. With further development, it can be shown, by dye tracer techniques, that the transplanted frontal cortex acquires the characteristics of normal visual cortex, in that the deeper pyramids project to the superior colliculus. Conversely, the transplanted occipital cortex comes to resemble the normal motor cortex, in that its neurons project into the pyramidal tract (21). These and other findings, including observations on cortical sensory territories in mole rats and on rats with focal surgical lesions of the fetal thalamus, all indicate that each thalamic nucleus determines the area of cortex to

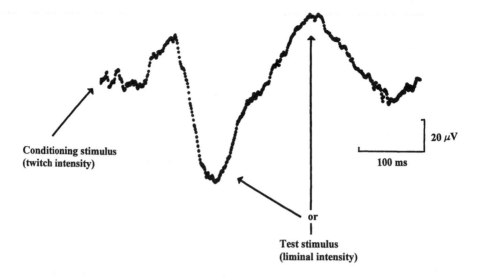

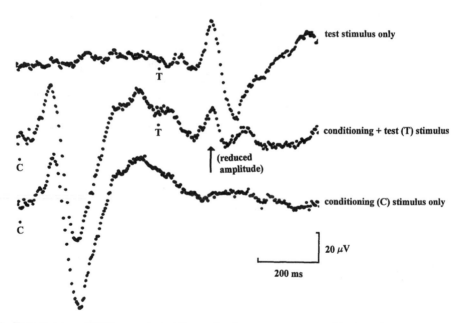

FIG. 6. Top: Averaged ERP recorded at the vertex in response to conditioning electric stimulation of median nerve and showing times at which a weak test stimulus was delivered. The perception of the test stimulus was not affected by the polarization of the cortex from the conditioning stimulus. **Bottom:** Averaged ERPs after conditioning and test stimuli given alone or together. The interval between the two stimuli was 500 milliseconds. Although the conditioning stimulus reduces the size of the response to the test stimulus by half, the perception of the test stimulus is unchanged (Brown et al., unpublished observations). Negativity upward in both the upper and lower figures.

be innervated and the regional differentiation within that field (22). It is rather as if the thalamic axons are an invading army, imposing rules and patterns of conduct on the conquered population of cortical neurons. But although this subjugation would be most complete in the territories initially invaded, where the lines of communication remain strongest, it would be less complete further afield. The analogy of the Roman Empire, and its inability to dominate completely the warring tribes of Gaul and Northern Britain, is not inappropriate.

Returning to the brain, all of the cortical areas are seen as engaging in spontaneous activity, just as explants, or reaggregations of dissociated neurons, from the rodent cerebral cortex, medulla, and spinal cord develop spontaneous activity when grown in culture (23,24). Although some might make the (implausible) argument that the cells in such explants have knowledge of themselves and of each other (25), it is certain that, in the absence of information from receptors, they can have no knowledge of their environment, and in this context their spontaneous activity is meaningless. So, I believe, is much of the spontaneous activity in the human brain, with the caveat that the activity is obviously influencing the general level of excitability of the cortex.

The preceding arguments and speculations have been summarized in Fig. 7. At the top is the lateral view of an adult cerebral hemisphere. The filled symbols represent clusters of pyramidal neurons, and their profusion reflects the generally held view that all cortical cells are engaged in purposive activity and that most neurons contribute to consciousness. According to this view, only activity in the motor cortex, although purposive, would be unable to evoke conscious phenomena directly; for this reason, the neuron clusters in the motor area in the precentral gyrus have been given a different (half-filled) symbol in Fig. 7.

In contrast, the brain in the middle section of Fig. 7 is one in the immediate postnatal period, and the absence of filled symbols de-

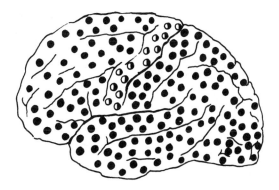

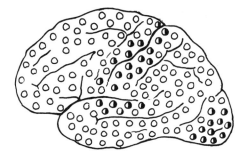

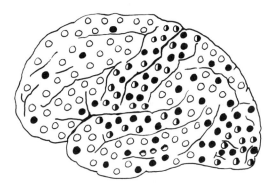

FIG. 7. The concept of functional occupancy in the human cerebral cortex, as shown in the adult (**top and bottom**) and the neonate (**middle**). Filled, half-filled, and open symbols denote consciousness-evoking, non–consciousness-evoking but purposive, and nonpurposive neuron clusters, respectively.

picts the absence of consciousness, as we would normally understand that term. However, because the thalamofugal axons have already established connections within the cortex, the various sensory receiving areas will be fed with information about the infant and its environment. The activities in the recipient cortical neurons can therefore be said to be purposive, even though, at this early stage, there may be no resulting perception at a conscious level. This last statement is recognized as a major assumption and depends largely on how consciousness is to be defined. There would probably be general agreement, nevertheless, that at this relatively early stage in brain development, much of the cortex has yet to acquire function; this situation is shown in Fig. 7 by the preponderance of neuron clusters identified by open symbols.

The lower part of Fig. 7 shows an adult hemisphere again, this time as conceived on the basis of the clinical and neurophysiologic observations presented earlier. Several differences from the previous scheme (Fig. 7, upper) are immediately obvious. Thus, many of the neuron clusters, especially in the prefrontal areas, are depicted with open symbols, indicating that, as in the neonate, they are still without function. These areas can be spoken of as exhibiting low functional occupancy. In contrast, the various sensory receiving areas (auditory, visual, somatic) have expanded their territories. Within these areas the neuron clusters imparting consciousness (filled symbols) are mostly at the periphery, a trend that reflects the ability of the sensory areas to analyze events and situations in ways that are more detailed and complete than in the infant. However, the initial (primary) sensory areas, which deal with elementary analyses, are still envisaged as capable of evoking conscious perceptions. For example, a bar of light, an appropriate stimulus for simple cells in area 17, the primary visual cortex (26), is still seen as a bar of light, even though analytic development in the visual cortex has progressed to the point that neuron clusters in the inferior temporal gyrus have acquired the ability to recognize individual faces (27). The enhanced analytic power of the sensory areas raises an interesting point, however. Why is it that when we look at a face or, for that matter, a table or chair, we see only the finished object and not the imperfect lines and edges to which cells are responding earlier in the analytic process?

The explanation might be that each stage of cells in the analytic pathway inhibits the preceding one, so that only the activity of the ultimate feed-forward stage is left to be read out. The well-developed feedback connections among the stages in the visual pathway would provide an anatomic basis for such an inhibition. In Fig. 7 (lower), some consciousness-evoking neuron clusters are shown in the motor cortex. This, again, is speculation, but there seem no good reasons for viewing the motor cortex as unable to generate conscious perceptions as well as voluntary movements. Not only do these cells receive information from the opposite half of the body (28), but activity in the superficial cortical layers (II and III), evoked by recurrent inputs from the layer V cells might provide the corollary discharges of motor commands (29).

The final question, and the most important one of this symposium, is what causes the output of a particular neuron cluster (depicted by a filled symbol in Fig. 7) to give a conscious perception. The answer may be that some neurons, during infant development, evolved the ability to manipulate the activities of other neurons in the sensory receiving areas, ultimately making possible thinking and imagining, and the preparation of voluntary movements. If so, where are these manipulative neurons? Some may be in the prefrontal areas, but the relatively benign consequences of frontal lobectomy suggest that they are only a small fraction of the total population. The majority of the manipulative neurons, perhaps, are in the posterior parietal area. Although there have been excisions of individual frontal, temporal, and occipital lobes, all without disturbances of consciousness (8), the parietal lobes have not been treated in this way, for obvious reasons. Instead, it is necessary to obtain information from the results of injury or tumor or, more tellingly, of sudden stroke. Of all the losses of cognitive function that may ensue from posterior parietal lesions, none is more fascinating and dramatic than the loss of awareness of the opposite side of the body and of extracorporeal space on that side. This syndrome, spatial hemiagnosia, is best seen after a lesion of the right posterior parietal lobe, but contralateral sensory extinctions also can occur when the lesion is in the dominant left hemisphere, although they may be more difficult to detect because of language impairment. Suppose, then, that both areas, right and left, were to be destroyed in the same individual. Would there not be total unawareness of self and surroundings, and would it then be possible for such a person to be conscious? It is largely on account of this sort of reasoning, contrasted with the benign effects of frontal lobectomy, that the incidence of consciousness-evoking neurons (filled symbols) is shown as being higher in the posterior parietal areas than in the prefrontal areas in Fig. 7 (lower). In keeping with the results of cognitive studies in patients who have undergone surgical sectioning of the corpus callosum (see Chapter 12), there should be many more of the consciousness-evoking neurons in the left hemisphere than in the right.

CONCLUSIONS

In summary, the journey taken to arrive at these conclusions has been a long and circuitous one, but it is one that enables a number of otherwise puzzling clinical and electrophysiologic findings to be viewed with a fresh perspective.

ACKNOWLEDGMENTS

I thank Jane Butler and Heidi Scarfone for technical assistance, and the Natural Sciences and Engineering Research Council for financial support.

REFERENCES

1. Jasper HH, Hawke WA. Electroencephalography. IV. The localization of seizure waves in epilepsy. *Arch Neurol Psychiatry* 1938;39:885–901.
2. Jasper HH. Report of the committee on methods of clinical examination in electroencephalography. *Electroencephalogr Clin Neurophysiol* 1958;10:370–375.
3. Jasper HH, Droogleever-Fortuyn J. Experimental studies on the functional anatomy of petit mal epilepsy. *Res Publ Assoc Nerv Ment Disord* 1947;26:272–298.
4. Jasper HH, Ballem G. Unipolar electromyograms of normal and denervated human muscle. *J Neurophysiol* 1949;12:231–244.
5. Lonton AP. In infantile hydrocephalus how much brain mantle is needed for normal development? In: Warlow C, Garfield J, eds. *Dilemmas in the management of the neurological patient.* Edinburgh, Scotland: Churchill-Livingstone, 1984:260–269.
6. Damasio AR. *Descartes' error. Emotion, reason and the human brain.* New York: Putnam, 1994.
7. Sacks O. *An anthropologist on Mars: seven paradoxical tales.* New York: Alfred A Knopf, 1995.
8. Penfield W, Evans J. Functional defects produced by cerebral lobectomies. *Res Publ Assoc Nerv Ment Disord* 1934;13:352–377.
9. Charcot JM. *Lectures on the diseases of the nervous system.* London: New Syndenham Society, 1877.
10. McComas AJ, Pape K, Kirsch S. Apraxia in congenital brachial palsy. *Can J Neurol Sci* 1993;20:362
11. McComas AJ, Sica REP, Campbell MJ, Upton ARM. Functional compensation in partially denervated muscles. *J Neurol Neurosurg Psychiatry* 1971;34:453–460.
12. Kulics AT, Cauller LJ. Cerebral cortical somatosensory evoked responses, multiple unit activity and current source-densities: their relationships and significance to somatic sensation as revealed by stimulation of the awake monkey's hand. *Exp Brain Res* 1986;62:46–60.
13. Penfield W, Jasper HH. *Epilepsy and the functional anatomy of the human brain.* Boston: Little, Brown, 1954.
14. Freeman W, Watts JW. *Psychosurgery. Intelligence, emotion and social behaviour following prefrontal lobotomy for mental disorders.* Springfield: Charles C Thomas, 1942.
15. McComas AJ, Wilson P, Martin-Rodriguez J, Wallace C, Hankinson J. Properties of somatosensory neurones in the human thalamus. *J Neurol Neurosurg Psychiatry* 1970;33:716–717.
16. Bertrand G, Jasper H, Wong A, Mathews G. Microelectrode recording during stereotactic surgery. *Clin Neurosurg* 1969;16:328–348.
17. Hillyard SA. Electrophysiology of human selective attention. *Trends Neurosci* 1985;8:400–405.
18. Davenas E, Beauvias F, Amara J, et al. Human basophil degranulation triggered by very dilute antiserum against IgE. *Nature* 1988;333:816–818.
19. Maddox J, Randi J, Stewart WN. "High dilution" experiments a delusion. *Nature* 1988;334:287–290.
20. Molnár Z, Blakemore C. How do thalamic axons find their way to the cortex? *Trends Neurosci* 1995;18: 389–396.
21. O'Leary DDM, Stanfield BB. Selective elimination of axons extended by developing cortical neurons is dependent on regional locale: experiments utilizing fetal cortical transplants. *J Neurosci* 1989;9:2230–2246.
22. O'Leary DDM. Do cortical areas emerge from a proto-cortex? *Trends Neurosci* 1989;12:400–406.
23. Crain SM, Bornstein MB. Organotypic bioelectric activity in cultured reaggregates of dissociated rodent brain cells. *Science* 1972;176:182–184.
24. Corner, MA, Crain SM. Patterns of spontaneous bioelectric activity during maturation in culture of fetal rodent medulla and spinal cord tissues. *J Neurobiol* 1972;3:25–45.
25. McGinn C. Could a machine be conscious? In: Blake-

more C, Greenfield S, eds. *Mindwaves*. Oxford, England: Blackwell, 1987:279–288.

26. Hubel DH, Wiesel T. Receptive fields of single neurones in the cat's striate cortex. *J Physiol (Lond)* 1959; 148:574–591.

27. Bruce C, Desimone R, Gross CG. Visual properties of neurons in a polysensory area in superior temporal sulcus of the Macaque. *J Neurophysiol* 1981;46:369–384.

28. Butler EG, Horne MK, Rawson JA. Sensory characteristics of monkey thalamic and motor cortex neurones. *J Physiol (Lond)* 1992;445:1–24.

29. McClosky DI. Corollary discharges: motor commands and perception. In: Brooks VB, ed. *Handbook of physiology*. Section 1, Vol. 2. Motor control. Bethesda, MD: American Physiological Society, 1981:1415–1447.

30. Hassler R. Anatomy of the thalamus. In: Schaltenbrand G, Bailey P, eds. *Introduction to stereotaxis with an atlas of the human brain*. Vol. 1. Stuttgart: Thieme, 1959:230–290.

Consciousness: At the Frontiers of Neuroscience,
Advances in Neurology, Vol. 77,
edited by H.H. Jasper, L. Descarries,
V.F. Castellucci, and S. Rossignol.
Lippincott–Raven Publishers, Philadelphia © 1998.

10

The Emergence of Consciousness

Philip R. Zelazo* and Philip D. Zelazo†

*Department of Psychology, McGill University and The Montreal Children's Hospital,
Montreal, Quebec, H3H 1P3, Canada
†Department of Psychology, University of Toronto, St. George Campus,
Toronto, Ontario, M5S 1A1, Canada

A scientific inquiry into the nature of consciousness might usefully begin with an examination of behavioral development from birth through early childhood. There are at least three reasons to justify this approach. First, mind apparently emerges from matter in the course of ontogeny; with the unification of an egg and sperm, eventually comes consciousness. Thus, the evolutionary miracle of emergence is (in a sense) recapitulated routinely in a way that is amenable to systematic observation. Second, there are changes in the control of behavior that imply that consciousness itself develops in humans during the early years of life. A developmental study allows us to disentangle different aspects of consciousness that may be resistant to analysis in a mature organism. A developmental approach therefore helps us to carve nature at its joints. Third, consideration of behavioral data is necessary both because behavior can be observed directly (unlike consciousness) and because a theory of consciousness must eventually account for the way in which consciousness is related to behavior.

In this chapter, we will describe a functional model of consciousness and its development—called the Levels of Consciousness Model (1,2)—along with empirical support for the key features of the model. To begin, we will present a characterization of the initial state of the neonate. This is followed by a review of behavioral developments during the first year that culminate in a cognitive–behavioral metamorphosis that has been described as the "dawn of active thought" (3). The radical improvement in both the specificity and diversity of cognitive and neuromotor ability at year 1 is accounted for in the model by the onset of recursive consciousness. Further developmental changes in the control of thought and behavior are accounted for by postulating additional levels of recursion.

THE STARTING STATE: MINIMAL CONSCIOUSNESS

It would appear to be fashionable among psychologists to attribute sophisticated forms of consciousness to neonates. For example, Meltzoff and Moore (4,5) have argued that the neonate is capable of true imitation, consciously and deliberately matching the actions of an adult model. On the other hand, others, such as Piaget (6), have argued that neonates are strictly sensorimotor organisms that lack mental representations altogether, and for those who hold that language is a criterion of consciousness, then infants are by definition unconscious. The construct of minimal consciousness (7) is meant to be an alternative to the rather simplistic notion that infants either are or are not conscious in an adultlike sense.

Minimal consciousness is the simplest, conceptually coherent kind of consciousness that we might grant to neonates. P.D. Zelazo (7) outlined the characteristics of minimal consciousness. He argued that minimal consciousness is characterized by intentionality in Brentano's (8) sense; that is, it is about things. As shown in Fig. 1, the baby creates a mental representation for an object (the pacifier), and this mental representation (or description) is the proper content of consciousness (i.e., it is what consciousness is of).

Moreover, minimal consciousness is conative, or willful, in that it motivates approach and avoidance behavior. However, it is unreflective, present oriented, and makes no reference to an explicit sense of self. While minimally conscious, one would be conscious of what one sees, but would not be conscious of seeing what one sees. Moreover, one would not recall seeing what one saw, although one might learn about what one saw.

Minimal consciousness is precisely the kind of consciousness that ought to underlie implicit information processing. Although it is often mistakenly suggested that implicit processing is unconscious, implicit processing does not occur in a zombielike fashion (see Chapter 12); it is simply unreflective. Thus, environmental stimuli are registered or recognized in a minimally conscious way, and these stimuli may elicit behavioral routines directly and automatically. If one assumes the presence of minimal consciousness in neonates, then it seems possible to account for the construction of more sophisticated forms of consciousness—to account for additional aspects of consciousness that have implications for the development of cognition and behavioral control throughout development.

One fundamental implication of the Minimal Consciousness Model and Brentano's (8) description of intentionality as a ground-

FIG. 1. A baby with a mental representation of a pacifier—an intentional object. (Prepared by P. Leclerc.)

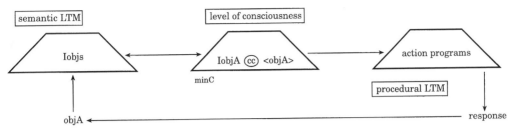

FIG. 2. Model of minimal consciousness. An object in the environment (objA) triggers a corresponding intentional representation of that object (IobjA) from a set of intentional objects (Iobjs) that is stored in semantic long-term memory (LTM); this IobjA, which is causally connected (cc) to objA, becomes the content of minimal consciousness (minC), by way of which it triggers an action program stored in procedural LTM. Adapted with permission (1).

level characteristic of even the simplest possible conscious state is that an account of neonatal behavior must include a capacity for creating mental representations. Fortunately, a vast array of evidence has accumulated over the past 40 years to support this claim for infants 2 months of age and older. The evidence for the neonatal period itself is more recent but clearly implies that neonates have the capacity to create mental representations for both visual (9) and auditory (10) experiences. The Minimal Consciousness model, illustrated in Fig. 2, indicates that with repeated exposure to an object, a mental representation (the description or intentional object) is formed and stored in long-term memory. Minimal consciousness is illustrated in the second box, indicating an awareness of what is seen (the pacifier in Fig. 1) which, in turn, is linked to a prepotent action program (sucking in the case of the pacifier).

We assume the existence at birth of two basic types of process illustrated in this Levels of Consciousness Model. First, there is long-term memory, which has both a semantic and a procedural component. The semantic component stores (potentially) declarative knowledge, whereas the procedural component does not; instead, it stores sensorimotor schemata—initially reflexivelike components. The second process is consciousness, which will later operate on multiple levels that correspond to degrees of recursion or reflection. However, the theoretical primitive, and thus the nonreflective level of consciousness, is minimal consciousness.

Consider first how an infant can act in the absence of reflection. An object in the environment can trigger a description that is "stored" in long-term memory. This particular description can then become an object of minimal consciousness. The infant would be aware of the stimulus only, and even this minimal awareness would be fleeting and unrecoverable. All objects are represented by the organism under a description; that is to say, within the system, there exist only mental representations—intentional objects, objects that have aspectual shape (11) because they are interpreted from a particular (and necessarily limited) perspective. When a description becomes the object of minimal consciousness, it triggers an associated action program that is stored in procedural memory. Thus, in the case of automatic, unreflective responding, there is a circuit that runs along the first and lowest level of the model. Behavior at this minimally conscious level would be stereotypical. The presence of a toy within the infant's line of sight may elicit a habitual stereotypical response; the infant may put the toy in his or her mouth, for example.

EMPIRICAL SUPPORT

What evidence is there for minimal consciousness? Does the neonate have the ability to create mental representations that are modifiable through experience and that have affective and conative properties? The data strongly support these claims, both at the neonatal level and throughout most of the first year. Consider the phenomena of neonatal habituation and recovery of head turning toward sounds. We asked whether habituation and recovery of head turning fit predictions from an information-processing view or more closely conform to predictions from a view that does not implicate mental representations, such as a neuronal fatigue view. According to a neuronal fatigue view, habituation reflects the firing and fatigue of receptor cells and need not involve mental representation of objects or a comparison of present stimuli with these mental representations.

Muir and Field (12) demonstrated that neonates turn their heads unambiguously toward sounds if they are presented repeatedly (as opposed to a single pulse) and time is allowed for the response to be elicited and executed. In most studies, two infrequently occurring words—"tinder" and "beagle"— were presented using an infant-controlled procedure in which criteria for orientation and habituation were achieved at the neonate's own rate (10). Two additional experimentally induced phases generally followed this orientation–habituation phase: (a) recovery, during which a novel sound is presented, and (b) dishabituation, during which the previously familiarized sound is reintroduced after the novel sound. Three responses, shown in Fig. 3, are coded: no turn, turn toward, or turn away. A turn was coded when the neonate rotated the sagittal midline of his or her head 45 degrees to either side and held it for 3 seconds. If no turn occurred within 30 seconds, the trial was terminated. The two principal dependent variables examined in most studies were the percentage of trials in which head turning occurred using blocks of three or five trials and a "difference score" contrasting the frequency of head turns toward the stimulus with head turns away from the sound source.

Three results from a series of studies are sharply at odds with predictions from a neuronal fatigue perspective. First, neonates who were presented with a redundant stimulus during and after the criterion of habituation did not simply cease turning toward the sound source. In six separate studies (10), presentation of a redundant stimulus produced active turning away from the sound source as shown in Fig. 4 (13). Turning away would not happen if receptor cells were fatigued; instead it implicates something akin to boredom. Second, neonates experiencing orientation and habituation to the same stimulus over two consecutive days showed evidence of retention of the information over the 24-hour period (14). On day 2, neonates hearing the redundant stimulus began at a lower initial level of orientation than same-age neonates hearing the sound and experiencing the procedure for the first time. More dramatically, neonates hearing the redundant stimulus on day 2 remained habituated after the 145-second delay that was used to produce recovery on day 1. This result showed that newborns retained a memory for the stimulus over the 145-second delay on day 2. In contrast, neonates hearing a new stimulus on day 2 displayed recovery after the 145-second delay, presumably because they did not remember the stimulus. Retention of information over a 24-hour period greatly exceeds even the most liberal interpretation of a refractory period for fatigued receptors. Moreover, these data showing long-term retention confirm an earlier finding (15) using eye-widening as the dependent variable—a seemingly more ambiguous, but since-vindicated response.

A third finding at odds with a neuronal fatigue view is the neonate's differential cognitive, affective, and conative reactions to stimuli of varying degrees of discrepancy from the standard stimulus to which the neonate was habituated. Weiss and colleagues (16) habituated five groups of neonates to the same computer-generated word, "titi." The recovery stimulus differed from this standard by one of five dif-

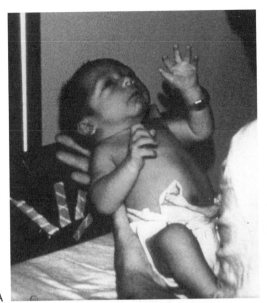

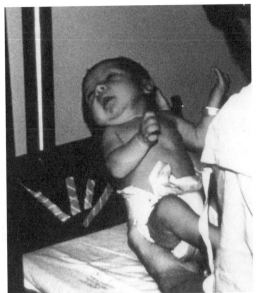

A

B

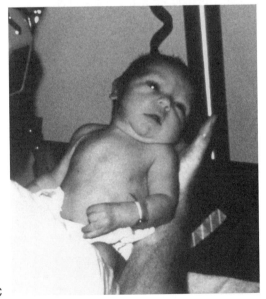

C

FIG. 3. Neonate with head at midline (**A**), turning 90 degrees to the right (**B**), and 90 degrees to the left (**C**). Reproduced with permission (10).

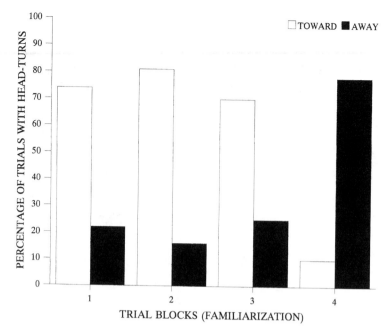

FIG. 4. Percentage of trials with head turns toward and away from a sound source per quartile during the familiarization phase (orientation and habituation). Reproduced with permission (13).

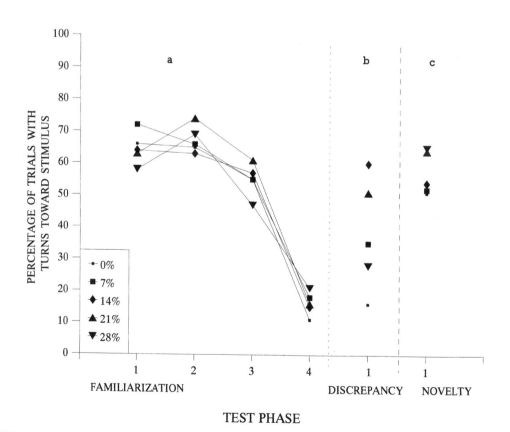

FIG. 5. Mean percentage of trials with headturns toward the sound during the orientation and habituation (**a**), discrepancy (**b**), and novelty phases (**c**). Reproduced with permission (16).

ferent levels of discrepancy (0%, 7%, 14%, 21%, and 28%) in fundamental frequency. The results (Fig. 5) showed that recovery of head turning toward the sound source was a curvilinear function of degree of discrepancy. Greatest recovery of attention occurred to moderate degrees of discrepancy (changes in fundamental frequency of 14% and 21%). There was no recovery to the control group (0%) and only modest recovery to the slight (7%) and large (28%) discrepancies. These findings showed that 2-day-old infants show greatest sustained attention to moderate discrepancies and least attention to redundant and extreme discrepancies, supporting an information-processing view. These data indicate that the unambiguous dependent variable—head turning toward the sound source—is directed by a comparison among mental representations of the experimental stimuli. This result, along with clear turning away (avoidance) during habituation and to the control stimulus, illustrate both the affective (17) and conative qualities of the mental representations that figure in the Minimal Consciousness Model.

BEHAVIOR OVER THE FIRST YEAR

Information Processing

What is the nature of change in information processing and neuromotor ability over the first year of life? Cohen (18) inquired about information processing changes over this period and further examined why infants look longer at some stimuli than others. He relied exclusively on research with visual stimuli, consistent with the vast majority of research on infant information processing. Cohen synthesized a vast body of research and described four empirically driven attentional principles (APs) to characterize the development of information-processing ability. The last two principles are most relevant to this age range. AP3 holds that "as infants develop, they become able to process relations among lower-order units and in so doing are able to form a single more abstract or more complex higher-order unit. The highest unit available becomes the level the infants initially attempt to process" (18). Cohen and Younger (19,20) found clear support for the AP3 using 6- to 30-week-old infants. These investigators found that older infants processed stimuli as whole units, whereas younger infants processed the stimuli as relatively separate components. Older infants also demonstrated less looking to the stimuli overall, implying faster information processing, as would be expected if they processed larger units of information.

Cohen (18) addressed the pervasive finding of increasingly more rapid habituation with age (21) in AP4. He postulated that "the time needed for an infant to process and remember a unit should remain, approximately, the same over age. Speed of habituation or degree of familiarity should be a function of the number of units to be remembered" (18). The strongest support for this principle comes from a study by Younger and Cohen (20). They presented drawings of animals to 4- and 7-month-old infants. Four different animals with some shared features, such as feet and tails, were presented over 12 trials—too few trials for the animals to be "learned" if whole animals were the unit processed. On the other hand, shared features resulted in redundancy over trials and could be acquired within 12 familiarization trials. Infants were tested with a familiar animal, an animal with familiar attributes but a new configuration, and a novel animal. Four-month-old infants habituated rapidly to the animals with familiar attributes and recovered only to the novel animal. In contrast, 7-month-old infants showed no evidence of habituation or differential responding to the test items. Seven-month-old infants performed more poorly than 4-month-olds on this task because the older infants processed the whole animal and there were too few trials (only three per animal) to create mental representations for the four different animals. If 4-month-olds processed specific attributes rather than whole animals, they would have had sufficient trials of exposure for habituation to occur. These results show that, in part, the unit of processing influences the rate of habituation and functional speed of processing.

In addition to these results, there are overwhelming data showing that speed of processing increases with age, not only over the first year, but steadily over the first 26 years of life (22). Miller and Vernon (23) showed clear age-related increases in processing speed among 4-, 5-, and 6-year-olds using a nonverbal reaction time task. Age-related changes in processing speed were not paralleled by changes in accuracy rates. Zelazo and colleagues (24) demonstrated that measures of processing speed—latencies to first clusters of expressive physiologic and behavioral responses on complex attentional tasks—get increasingly shorter from 22 to 27 to 32 months of age. More relevant to the immediate argument, Lewis (21) amassed an extensive array of studies to demonstrate that speed of processing of static stimuli—inferred from trials to criterion or the slope of habituation—increased over the first year of life.

Together, these data sets indicate that functional processing speed increased steadily over the first year. It is reasonable to propose that increased processing speed is due in part to improved myelination, as Yakovlev and Lecours (25) have shown, and in part to the processing of higher order units as demonstrated by Cohen (18). Additional influences on the functional speed of processing are likely, including increased inhibition of extraneous stimuli (26,27) and decreased proactive inhibition (24). Thus, these data show that during the first year to the cusp of the child's first birthday, higher order units of information are processed and functional speed of processing increases. There appears to be improved use of existing mechanisms, but no evidence of qualitative changes, at least to the end of the first year.

Neuromotor Development

A similar pattern emerges for neuromotor development. Piaget's (6) conception of circular reactions leading to improved use and expansion of existing neuromotor behaviors has long been accepted because it corresponds to what is seen in the baby. The fact that the infant's neuromotor ability expands along existing dimensions before changing qualitatively at around 12 months is seen most clearly in systematic observations of the child's play.

Zelazo and Kearsley (28) examined object use during a 15-minute free play sequence with a cross-sectional sample of 9.5-, 11.5-, 13.5-, and 15.5-month-old children. Six different sets of toys were used, including a tea set, telephone, large doll with a brush and bottle, a small doll with furniture, a dump truck with blocks and a garage, and a baseball set. A total of 36 unambiguous adult-defined functional uses were identified such as brushing the doll's hair, bringing the telephone to one's ear, and stirring the spoon in the cup. The objects could be used in less mature ways as well. Thus, immature stereotypical play, defined as mouthing, waving, banging and fingering objects, and relational play defined as bringing two or more objects together in a manner that was not clearly functional (putting the cup to the baseball glove, for example) were coded as well.

The percentages of each form of play are illustrated in Fig. 6. The behavior of greatest interest for this period of development is stereotypical play. At 9.5 months, 88% of all object use involved indiscriminate mouthing, waving, and banging of objects. It is important to remember that these behaviors are chained or integrated versions of reflexive behaviors: grasping, the Babinski reflex, rooting, and sucking, for example, just as Piaget (6) described.

Thus, behavior of the infant during the first 9 months of life consists of expansion and refinement of an existing repertoire both in terms of neuromotor behavior and mental representations. Indeed, data on smiling while stepping and sitting after 4 weeks of daily practice imply that mental representations also are formed for neuromotor acts as infants gain control over those complex patterns (29). Moreover, the evidence implies that information processing and neuromotor development occur with the same level of im-

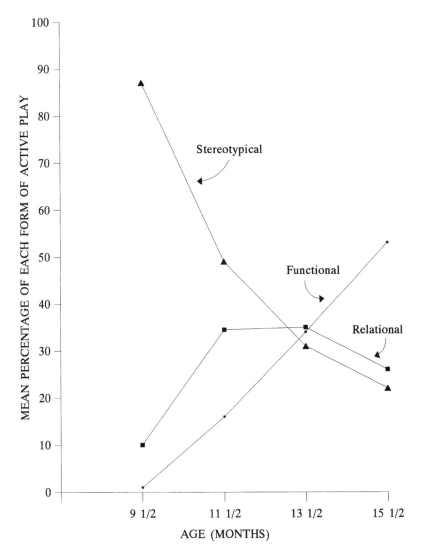

FIG. 6. Mean percentage of stereotypical, relational, and functional play and the means for the incidences of the three forms of play at each of the four ages. Reproduced with permission (28).

plicit learning assumed in the Minimal Consciousness Model for the neonate.

THE DAWN OF ACTIVE THOUGHT

At the end of the first year, profound behavioral changes occur. A host of qualitatively new abilities appear with high interval synchrony (3,30), implying a common determinant. In the space of 2 months, between about 10 and 12 months of age, the child dis-

plays a number of abilities that define our species, including his or her first spoken words, first bipedal steps unaided, and first functional uses of objects. The child first displays protodeclarative pointing, searching for hidden objects, deferred imitation, social referencing, and joint attention. Finally, for the first time, the child also reliably reacts with distress and protest when left with a stranger in an unfamiliar place. We argue that the basis for these ontogenetic changes (and perhaps the analogous phylogenetic ones, as well) is a change in the nature of consciousness.

These numerous changes in behavior appear to reflect the child's newly emergent capacity to generate two or more associations rapidly, allowing the infant to perform two-step functions (3,31,32). The nature of these changes is revealed most clearly in a study of object use by Zelazo and Kearsley (28). The finding of greatest theoretical significance in this study is the appearance of functional object use in all children at 11.5 months and its linear increase through 15.5 months (Fig. 6). Not only did the frequency of functional play increase steadily, but the number of different appropriate uses increased linearly over the four ages from a mean of 0.38 at 9.5 months to 10.38 at 15.5 months.

In concrete terms, the appearance of functional play allows the child to put the telephone to his or her ear rather than into his or her mouth. For the first time, the child associates two separate mental representations: a function and an object. Similarly, with first words, the child sees a round object and names it (e.g., "ball"). This cognitive change permits a paradoxical increase in both specificity and diversity of behavior. The toddler is freed from the reflexive-based repertoire of the infant. It is not the infant's motor dexterity per se that changes; it is the cognitive program that guides the child's manipulatory skills that has transformed.

This capacity to generate two associations rapidly was also tested with a cross-sectional sample of 8-, 12-, and 16-month-old children with the training of five swimming behaviors (31): four one-step behaviors (kicking, arm flexions, turning over, and traversing a distance of 5 feet unaided) and one two-step behavior (turning toward and reaching for the pool wall). Only the two-step behavior distinguished the groups. The 8-month-olds required an average of 25 timed training sessions to acquire this ability, whereas 12- and 16-month-olds mastered the behavior in 11 and five sessions, respectively.

The fact that these behavioral changes occurring at 1 year are strongly age related and exhibit such high-interval synchrony implicates a maturational basis to the underlying cognitive change. However, maturation itself is not an explanation; it is necessary to identify the maturing capability and suggest plausible mechanisms that may bring it about. We suggest that increased speed of processing is the most likely mechanism, but it is also necessary to postulate a psychological window—effectively the temporal span of the infant's minimal consciousness—for this explanation to make sense. Both the psychological (18,21) and neurologic (25) evidence indicates that speed of processing increases linearly. How then can two-step functions emerge from a steady linear increase? If one imagines a slow pulse passing through an infant's relatively fixed psychological window, only one object can be processed at a time, even if that object has multiple features. However, if the speed of the pulse is doubled, two objects can be considered simultaneously, including associations from memory. Two associations can be held in consciousness simultaneously, and two-step functions, such as turning toward and reaching for the pool wall, become possible for the infant.

RECURSIVE CONSCIOUSNESS

Can the Levels of Consciousness Model account for the cognitive changes occurring at a year? We argue that the ability to exhibit two-step functions can be explained by a process of recursion. Recursive consciousness (1) captures the capacity to hold two mental representations associations in memory simultaneously (Fig. 7).

The contents of minimal consciousness (namely, a description) are reprocessed and related to another token of the same description from long-term memory (via a first-order identity relation). The prototypes here are pointing and labeling. Protodeclarative pointing indicates, "[That thing, whatever it is] *is* that," just as the word "mama" says (effectively), "[Mama, over there, or wherever] *is* mama."

Recursive consciousness also permits the subjective phenomenal character of an experience because mental representations are retained in a kind of "remembered present" (33). One important consequence of recursion is the opportunity to use the third basic process in the model: working memory (34,35). Working memory is understood to be a short-term buffer for maintaining contents of consciousness in an activated state and treated as if they were "presentations" despite the fact that they are "re-presentations." With recursive consciousness, it is possible to use working memory because the declaration ("That is that") permits the description to be decoupled from the representation of the thing described. As we will see, generally, when the contents of consciousness become an object of reflection, they may be considered in relation to (and integrated with) other contents of consciousness. The results of this integration can then be deposited into working contents of consciousness or used as a representational proxy for the immediate perception of a stimulus. Crucially, maintaining something in working memory elicits action

programs so that an organism is not restricted to responses that are elicited directly by the perception of an immediately present stimulus. That is, the representation of something in working memory permits mediated (or indirect), rather than direct, action. It is at this point, when the infant is able to keep an object in mind as a goal and use that goal to trigger an action plan, that search for hidden objects becomes possible.

Because recursive consciousness permits retention of information (in the form of a description) in working memory, a description can override the initially reflexive action program. For example, an object, such as a telephone, triggers an intentional object, and through the recursive process this description is described. This associated description directs a functional action (telephone to ear) to override the stereotypical action of placing the telephone into one's mouth. The toddler is only conscious of the object as described, not yet of him- or herself as the actor. There is no research evidence for self-awareness at this age (36,37).

As we ascend levels, which is just minimal consciousness depicted in different functional phases, we move away from an impetus to an action. Thus, levels of consciousness vary in

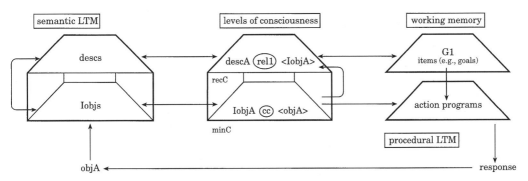

FIG. 7. Model of recursive consciousness. When the entire contents of minimal consciousness (MinC) are fed back into MinC, a higher level of consciousness is achieved, namely recursive consciousness (RecC). The contents of RecC can be related (rel1) to a corresponding description (descA), which can then be deposited into working memory, where it can serve as a goal (G1) to trigger an action program (stored in procedural LTM). See text and Figure 2 for additional definitions. Adapted with permission (1).

what has been called psychological distance (38). More reflective levels are psychologically more distant.

SELF-CONSCIOUSNESS

The next level of reflection in the model is called self-consciousness. Consistent with research on children's self-recognition in mirrors (37), research on children's understanding of means and ends (39), and research on children's rule use (40,41), we suggest that self-consciousness first appears toward the end of the second year of life (36). This state of self-consciousness is what allows a 2-year-old to use a single arbitrary rule. Knowledge of a rule is knowledge of one's own behavioral potential in a situation, i.e., knowledge of a conditionally-specified means that one has at one's disposal. It can be argued that all self-understood actions are conditionally specified because we act only when the situation permits (1). Research indicates that 2.5-year-olds can take as an object of consciousness a self-description of his or her knowledge of a single rule (R1). Moreover, this self-description may be activated from long-term memory or placed in reflective consciousness via perceptual input (e.g., by being told the rule).

REFLECTIVE CONSCIOUSNESS I

Zelazo and Reznick (40) presented 2.5-year-olds with a pair of arbitrary (ad hoc) rules for sorting pictures. The fact that the rules were arbitrary ensured that if children sorted correctly, they were representing the rule and using it to guide their behavior. One pair of rules that children were told was, "If I show you something that goes outside the house, put it here; things that go inside, go over here. Here's a snowman, which box does that go in? How about this refrigerator?" Two-year-olds started to use one of these rules, but perseverated on it. Sometimes they put the snowman in the right box,

but then assimilated the refrigerator to that rule. If they were able to step back from their knowledge, and consider one rule in relation to the other, they would recognize the need to choose carefully between the rules and avoid assimilating test cards to only one of them. However, 2.5-year-olds do not seem to be able to do this.

In contrast to a 2.5-year-old child, a 3-year-old (36 months) can successfully use a pair of arbitrary rules to sort things that go inside versus outside, things that make noise versus being quiet, animals that can fly versus those that run, etc. To do so requires that children not only know a rule but know that they know it, so that they can consider it in relation to another rule that they know. In terms of the Levels of Consciousness Model, this corresponds to a higher level of consciousness, which we call reflective consciousness I (1) (Fig. 8). Three-year-old children can reflect on a self-description (SdescB) of another rule (R2). This relation (Re12) is a second-order contrastive relation (as opposed to a first-order identity relation). Both of these rules can then be deposited into working memory, where they can be used contrastively to control the elicitation of an action program.

Of course, there are still limitations on children's self-awareness and self-control. The limitation at this level is perhaps best illustrated using the Dimensional Change Card Sort Task, but it could be illustrated using a false belief task, a representation change task, or other tasks that put two perspectives into conflict (42).

Zelazo and Frye (42,43) have proposed that 3-year-olds can represent a pair of rules but they cannot reflect on their representation of a pair of rules and, consequently, cannot represent a higher order relation between two incompatible pairs of rules. In the Dimensional Change Card Sort Task, children are given target cards (e.g., red rabbit and blue boat) and then test cards that would be sorted differently by color and shape (e.g., blue rabbits and red boats). They are first told one pair of rules, such as, "Red ones go here, blue

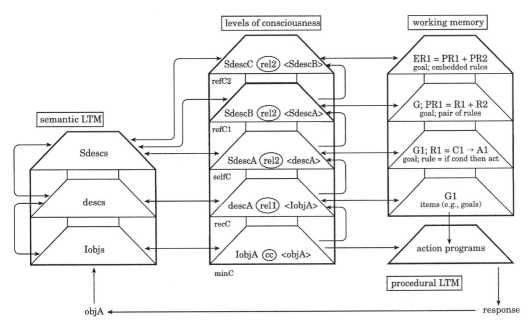

FIG. 8. A Levels of Consciousness Model of the role of reflection in cognitive control. rel2, second-order contrastive relation; rules (R1, R2) that link conditions (C1) to actions (A1); PR1, pairs of rules; ER1, embedded rule systems. See text and Figs. 2 and 7 for additional definitions. Adapted with permission (1).

ones go there." Three-year-olds can successfully use a pair of rules, but they cannot switch between two incompatible pairs of rules: "Red here, blue there," and then "rabbits here, boats there." When told to switch between rule pairs, they perseverate on the first pair of rules.

It is theoretically revealing that 3-year-old children can verbally express their knowledge of the postswitch rules but are unable to implement the rule correctly (44). If asked, "Where do the rabbits go?", 3-year-olds will point to the correct box, or name the correct box. However, when given a test card and asked, "So where does this rabbit go?", they will sort it incorrectly. They know the rabbit versus boat rules, which is why they can state them, but they do not know that they know them, which is why they cannot make a deliberate decision to use them in contradistinction to the color rules (red versus blue), which are now prepotent.

REFLECTIVE CONSCIOUSNESS II

At the next level of reflective consciousness, reflective consciousness II (RefCII), the entire contents of reflective consciousness I can be considered in relation to a self-description of comparable complexity. At this level, children know that they know one pair of rules for responding to a situation, and they know that they know another pair of rules for responding to the same situation. This level of consciousness is attainable by 5-year-olds, and it allows them to consider two (or more) embedded rules in relation to a goal that occasions their use. By stepping back from a situation, and from one's own knowledge (1,43), 5-year-olds are able to construct a representation of the entire system of rules in the hierarchical tree structure depicted in Fig. 8. This system of rules (abbreviated in Fig. 8 as ER1) can then be put into working memory where it can serve to control behavior. By recognizing that they know two pairs of rules, 5-year-old children are able to use a higher-order rule for determining which pair of rules to use.

Levels of consciousness vary in a way that is directly proportional to the degrees of embedding illustrated in Fig. 8. Each level of embedding in the tree structure requires a new degree of recursion and therefore demands a new level of consciousness.

CONCLUDING COMMENT

The main points of this chapter and the Levels of Consciousness Model may be summarized as follows. First, the model includes a characterization of minimal consciousness. This is an alternative to the notion that infants either are or are not conscious in an adultlike sense. The fundamental problem of first emergence is temporarily side-stepped, but postulating minimal consciousness allows us to trace the emergence of adultlike consciousness and construct increasingly sophisticated forms of conciousness using very few theoretical tools (mainly, minimal consciousness plus recursion).

Second, there is considerable evidence that neonates understand the world in terms of mental representations—intentional states— that can direct behavior in predictable ways and have conative properties.

Third, at the end of the first year of life, there is the rapid emergence of behaviors that require two steps: functional play, naming, and protodeclarative pointing, to name a few. This cognitive metamorphosis is accommodated in the model by the addition of a recursive process to minimal consciousness, permitting associations to perceptual input that ultimately influence and liberate the reflexive action programs. The recursion permits the decoupling of a description from the thing described and allows behavior to be controlled by the description (stored in working memory) rather than by the presentation of environmental stimulation.

Finally, from infancy through early childhood there are continuing developments in controlled behavior that imply corresponding changes in consciousness; there are developments in self-recognition, self-knowledge of intention, and rule use. The connection to rule use illustrates how this approach captures the importance of language to consciousness and action control. According to the model, age-related changes in controlled processing are accounted for by increasingly higher order degrees of recursion that put distance between the child and his or her rule-based representations. Expansion of the phenomenologic window referred to above may occur not so much in terms of breadth (i.e., temporal span) but depth (distance from the environment). With increasing psychological distance, there is a deeper level of awareness and greater complexity of consciousness. A developmental approach thus allows for an expanded conception of consciousness. The evidence from early human development indicates that consciousness itself is something that develops.

ACKNOWLEDGMENT

We thank Peta Leclerc for help with and comments on this chapter. P.R. Zelazo's research was supported in part by grants from the Natural Sciences and Engineering Reseach Council of Canada (to P.R. Zelazo and P. Robaey) and from the Montreal Children's Hospital/McGill University Research Institute and the Gustav Levinschi Foundation (to P.R. Zelazo). P.D. Zelazo's research was supported in part by a grant from the Natural Sciences and Engineering Reseach Council of Canada. The authors contributed equally to the preparation of this chapter.

REFERENCES

1. Zelazo PD, Jacques S. Children's rule use: representation, reflection and cognitive control. *Ann Child Dev* 1996;12:119–176.
2. Zelazo PD. Self-reflection and the development of consciously controlled processing. In: Mitchelll P, Riggs KJ, eds. *Children's reasoning and the mind.* Hove, UK: Psychology Press, 1998 (in press).

3. Zelazo PR, Leonard EL. The dawn of active thought. In: Fisher K, ed. *Levels and transitions in children's development.* San Francisco: Jossey-Bass, 1983:37–50.

4. Meltzoff AN, Moore MK. Imitation of facial and manual gestures by human neonates. *Science* 1977;198: 75–78.

5. Meltzoff AN, Moore MK. Imitation in newborn infants: exploring the range of gestures imitated and the underlying mechanism. *Developmental Psychol* 1989;25: 954–962.

6. Piaget J. *The origins of intelligence in children.* New York: International Universities Press, 1952.

7. Zelazo PD. Towards a characterization of minimal consciousness. *New Ideas Psychol* 1996;14:63–80.

8. Brentano F. *Psychology from an empirical standpoint.* In: Kraus O, ed. Rancorevilo AC, Terrell DB, McAllster LL, translators. London: Routledge & Kegan, Paul, 1874/1973.

9. Slater A, Morison V. Visual attention and memory at birth. In: Weiss MJ, Zelazo PR, eds. *Newborn attention: biological constraints and the influence of experience.* Norwood, NJ: Ablex, 1991:256–277.

10. Zelazo PR, Weiss MJS, Tarquinio N. Habituation and recovery of neonatal orienting to auditory stimuli. In: Weiss, MJS, Zelazo PR, eds. *Newborn attention: biological constraints and the influence of experience.* Norwood, NJ: Ablex, 1991:120–141.

11. Searle JR. *The rediscovery of the mind.* Cambridge, MA: MIT Press, 1992.

12. Muir D, Field J. Newborn infants orient to sound. *Child Dev* 1979;50:431–436.

13. Tarquinio N, Zelazo PR, Gryspeerdt DM, Allen KM. Generalization of neonatal habituation. *Infant Behav Dev* 1991;14:69–81.

14. Swain IU, Zelazo PR, Clifton R. Newborn infants' memory for speech sounds retained over 24 hours. *Dev Psychol* 1993;29:686–691.

15. Ungerer J, Brody L, Zelazo PR. Long-term memory for speech in 2-4-week-old infants. *Infant Behav Dev* 1978; 1:177–186.

16. Weiss MJ, Zelazo PR, Swain IU. Newborn response to auditory stimulus discrepancy. *Child Dev* 1988;59: 1530–1541.

17. Zelazo PR. Infant habituation, cognitive activity and the development of mental representations. *Eur Bull Cognitive Psychol* 1988;8:649–654.

18. Cohen L. Infant attention: an information processing approach. In: Weiss MJS, Zelazo PR, eds. *Newborn attention: biological constraints and the influence of experience.* Norwood, NJ: Ablex, 1991:1–21.

19. Cohen LB, Younger, BA. Infant perception of angular relations. *Infant Behav Dev* 1984;7:37–47.

20. Younger BA, Cohen LB. Developmental change in infants' perception of correlations among attributes. *Child Dev* 1986;57:803–815.

21. Lewis M. Individual differences in the measurement of early cognitive growth. In: Hellmuth J, ed. *Exceptional infant.* Vol. 2. New York: Brunner/Mazel, 1971.

22. Kail R. Developmental change in speed of processing during childhood and adolescence. *Psychol Bull* 1991; 109:490–501.

23. Miller LT, Vernon P. Developmental changes in speed of information processing. *Dev Psychol* 1997;33:549–554.

24. Zelazo PR, Kearsley RB, Stack DM. Mental representations for visual sequences: increased speed of central processing from 22 to 32 months. *Intelligence* 1995;20: 41–63.

25. Yakovlev PI, Lecours AR. The myelogenetic cycles of regional maturation of the brain. In: Minkowski A, ed. *Regional development of the brain in early life.* Oxford, England: Blackwell Scientific, 1967:3–70.

26. Dempster FN. Inhibitory processes: a neglected dimension of intelligence. *Intelligence* 1991;15:157–173.

27. McCall RB. What process mediates predictions of childhood IQ from infant habituation and recognition memory? Speculations on the roles of inhibition and rate of information processing. *Intelligence* 1994;18:107–125.

28. Zelazo PR, Kearsley RB. The emergence of functional play in infants: evidence for a major cognitive transition. *J Appl Dev Psychol* 1980;1:95–117.

29. Zelazo PR. Infant-toddler information processing assessment for children with PDD and autism. *Infants Young Children* 1997;10:1–14.

30. Fischer KW, Bullock D. Patterns of data: sequence, synchrony and constraint in cognitive development. In: Fischer KW, ed. *Cognitive development. New directions for child development.* No. 12. San Francisco: Jossey-Bass, 1981:69–78.

31. Zelazo PR. The year-old infant: a period of major cognitive change. In: Bever T, ed. *Regressions in development: basic phenomena and theoretical alternatives.* Hillsdale, NJ: Erlbaum, 1982:47–79.

32. Zelazo PR. The development of walking during infancy: new findings and old assumptions. *J Motor Behav* 1983;15:99–137.

33. Edelman GM. *The remembered present.* New York: Basic Books, 1989.

34. Baddeley AD. Working memory. *Science* 1992;255: 556–559.

35. Goldman-Rakic PS. The prefrontal contribution to working memory and conscious experience. In: Eccles JC, Creutzfeldt O, eds. *The principles of design and operation of the brain.* New York: Springer-Verlag, 1990:389–407.

36. Kagan J. *The second year.* Cambridge, MA: Harvard, 1981.

37. Lewis M, Brooks-Gunn J. *Social cognition and the acquisition of the self.* New York, NY: Plenum Press, 1979.

38. Sigel I. The centrality of a distancing model for the development of representational competence. In: Cocking RR, Renninger KA, eds. *The development and meaning of psychological distance.* Hillsdale, NJ: Erlbaum, 1993:91–107.

39. Frye, D. The origin of intention in infancy. In: Frye D, Moore C, eds. *Children's theories of mind.* Hillsdale, NJ: Erlbaum, 1991:15–38.

40. Zelazo PD, Reznick JS. Age-related asynchrony of knowledge and action. *Child Dev* 1991;62:719–735.

41. Zelazo PD, Reznick JS, Pinon DE. Response control and the execution of verbal rules. *Dev Psychol* 1995;31: 508–517.

42. Frye D, Zelazo PD, Palfai T. Theory of mind and rule-based reasoning. *Cognitive Dev* 1995;10:483–527.

43. Zelazo PD, Frye D. Cognitive complexity and control: a theory of the development of deliberate reasoning and intentional action. In: Stamenov M, ed. *Language structure, discourse and the access to consciousness.* Philadelphia: John Benjamins, 1997:113–153.

44. Zelazo PD, Frye D, Rapus T. An age-related dissociation between knowing rules and using them. *Cognitive Dev* 1996;11:37–63.

DISCUSSION
Moderated by Alan J. McComas

Benjamin Libet: This is a very nice accounting of the development in babies and infants, but I object to the idea that functional behaviorism can be a description of conscious experience. All of the functional behaviors that anyone can produce can be accomplished unconsciously in adult humans where you can tell more clearly that it is unconscious because they report no awareness whatsoever. So, my approach or suggestion is that the basic function is awareness per se. The things that are happening in your so-called levels of consciousness could be described as elaboration of the contents of awareness which can take place. But it is simpler, I think, to view the basic process as one of awareness which the brain can produce, and add contents to it. Mental representations, for example, need not be viewed as an evidence of conscious experience. The great mathematicians, for example, describe their creative solutions of very complicated problems which involve enormous mental representations accomplished completely unconsciously.

Philip D. Zelazo: Well, I agree with you that the basic process is awareness and that is part of the point of suggesting that what we are taking for granted is minimal consciousness. It really is the contents of consciousness that are changing with development. The contents of minimal consciousness then become the contents of minimal consciousness again, so that is a way in which you might say that the contents of consciousness might develop. The question about the functional significance of consciousness—whether consciousness is actually required for the production of certain behaviors or not—is an interesting one I think, and I think that it has not been adequately answered. I think that there are suggestions that you can do a lot of things that we previously thought consciousness might be necessary for in a way that seems not to involve the types of consciousness at least that we formerly thought was necessary. But I would argue, even in those cases of implicit information processing, that there is some consciousness. There needs to be some minimal consciousness, at least, of the stimulus that triggers the conditioned response, or something like that. It is just that not everything that you might expect to be conscious or to be reportable is conscious or reportable in those cases of implicit processing.

Giuseppe Trautteur: What about the number of levels of recursion? Is there a fixed bound upon them as in recursive piles in computing technique? Are

those physical structures or functional recalls as happens in computational technique? Is this a metaphor in a sense or something real in the brain?

Philip D. Zelazo: The model is a functional model. And the question about how this function is accomplished in the brain is not something that we are attempting to address. So yes, it is a metaphor in a sense, or it is meant to provide some functional constraints on an account of the development of consciousness. The question about whether there is a limit or not to the degree of recursion, that remains to be determined. I would imagine that practically, in the majority of cases, there is a limit.

Vernon B. Brooks: I want to disagree with my friend Ben Libet, and point out that what the two speakers have described in a baby can be seen in all of us when we have to learn a new rule in a manual motor task (as opposed to learning a new skill, which is scaling the motor execution). We described this a couple of years ago in learning and memory, when we tested adults on a motor task that required normal subjects to learn a fairly difficult new rule (1). We found that about a third of the subjects could not learn the task even though some had had a few successful trials about which they gave verbal reports at the time. Yet, those isolated trials did not reach what the speakers called a "recursive" stage, which for successful learners was triggered and made long-lasting by approaching repeated successes in which the new rule was carried out with newly acquired skill.

Philip R. Zelazo: I want to emphasize that the main point that we are making over the first year is to try to describe the limits or the constraints on the baby's behavior. I think that is useful in terms of breaking down the problem and simplifying the pieces of what we are calling conscious acts.

Benjamin Libet: I will just add in response to Vernon Brooks that I did not say that consciousness is ruled out for these processes. I only said that it is not necessarily there.

Dan Khuong Huynh: I would like to know if there have been any studies with congenitally blind babies, and what would then be your predictions on the emergence of consciousness. Would you expect any difference in this particular state of development?

Philip R. Zelazo: I would say no, that you obviously would not expect them to create images for visual stimuli, but you would expect it through other modalities, and I would include proprioceptive and tactile modalities.

Paul Cisek: You mentioned something about children being able to recognize lines first and triangles later. Are there studies showing that babies can discriminate these simple primitives before more complicated things like shapes or gestures, or is it the other way around through their development?

Philip D. Zelazo: The studies about attending to simpler elements in a configuration before attending to the configuration are based on habituation studies where the baby is habituated to an angle and then is either shown different line configurations producing the same angle or a different angle composed of the same line configuration. The question is to which of those two test stimuli do you show greater recovery of attention. And there are age differences such that the younger babies appear, when you show them an an-gle, to be paying attention to the components, the separate line segments, rather than the overall configuration. So, I am just trying to contextualize it to say that this is the situation in which you see that kind of age-related change, but there are also indications that even very young babies (work by Robert Fantz and others) can perceive forms.

Discussion Reference

1. Brooks VB, Hilperath F, Brooks M, Ross H-G, Freund H-J. Learning "what" and "how" in a human motor task. *Learning Memory* 1995;2:225–242.

Consciousness: At the Frontiers of Neuroscience,
Advances in Neurology, Vol. 77,
edited by H.H. Jasper, L. Descarries,
V.F. Castellucci, and S. Rossignol.
Lippincott–Raven Publishers, Philadelphia © 1998.

11

Language Contrivance on Consciousness (and Vice Versa)

André Roch Lecours

Institute universitaire de geriatrie de Montréal, Department of Medicine, Université de Montréal,
Montreal, Quebec, H3W IW5, Canada

It is clear that language is a fabulous (same root as "fable") enhancer of human consciousness, as well as of human imagination, which should lead one to infer that the impact of language on one's representation of reality is at times straightforward and at times somewhat kabbalistic.

It is said that, after having occupied the liver, then the heart, then the whole brain (1), then the corpus callosum, the human soul restricted itself for a while to the pineal gland. Maybe it felt safer within a calcified cocoon. In any event, the soul was later perceived to have lost its biologic accomodation, hence warranting the reductionism necessary to the neurosciences. Yet, there are weekends when, after a glass of good wine, I wonder if the soul has not for a while migrated somewhere into the right hemisphere, with the intention of escaping the digital constraints of language and concocting its metaphors (among other things).

It seems to me, as long as brain and mind are not consciously reduced to oneness, that Mario Bunge's emergent materialism (2,3) is the most acceptable philosophical option to the neurosciences, if only because Bunge considers himself to be reductionist. Perhaps the soul was the first and most primitive of Bunge's animated emergences.

In more concrete terms, I perceive language both as a product and as an evolutional transformer of human brain function (but not of its genetic program). I have no idea how this can happen and evolve at the molecular, synaptic, neuronal, convolutional, and net levels. My own belief in this respect, probably related to clinical observations of which I am aware that they have no empirical link to the neurosciences beyond brain autopsy or imaging, is that certain neural nets could be dedicated to consciousness. But I was told that this is hardly compatible with current knowledge of the human brain. I will nevertheless get back to observations of this sort at a later point.

In this chapter, I will discuss the phylogenesis and ontogenesis of consciousness and language. I will also discuss the role of consciousness in the recuperation from language diseases. My awareness of this role has increased to an astounding level as a result of the stress I experienced upon being invited to participate in this homage to Herbert Jasper. I will conclude with a summary of my postulates.

PHYLOGENESIS

Consciousness is perceptibly not a prerogative of the human species. If its memories did not provide awareness that dinner is ready, how could a wolf detect a sheep to be eaten? Yet, can a very hungry wolf imagine the smell of a lamb where there is none? And is a wolf aware of being conscious? Well, wolves can communicate among themselves, and their presence sends information to other animals. But language—as linguists define it, with its Babylonian architecture sequencing segments into gradually more complex arbitrary significant entities—is unique to the human species (4).

WORDS

This is all I wish to say on phylogenesis, but before turning to ontogenesis, I will try to disentangle some of the words we cannot avoid binding to language and consciousness, words such as "memory" and "attention," "semantics" and "cognition." Indeed, we play with many words and imbricated concepts in this field. They are not synonyms but they overlap, more in certain cases and less in others. One can ponder over their meanings without any knowledge of the brain, and even believing that language is an emergence of the liver.

Memory and attention must precede cognition, semantics, and consciousness, in the order of emergences, and semantics must precede language. In other words, there are Bungian entities that emerge at least in part from other emergences, which does not make it easier to detect their neural roots (5).

The notion of consciousness and that of cognition have a lot in common, but not everything, given that cognition can be unconscious. Both depend on memory but, up to a point, in different manners. I have no idea whether the difference is qualitative or quantitative, nor whether the game is played bottom up or top down (maybe both in succession, and in that order).

ONTOGENESIS

Although cognition can be unconscious, as implicitly hinted a century ago by Théodule Ribot (6), only certain specialized memories have access to consciousness. I wonder if Francis Crick (7) included proprioception

when he suggested that there probably is not one consciousness but rather as many consciousnesses as there are perceptual modalities. This being said, proprioception is essential to the ontogenesis of language, whether it is spoken or written or otherwise.

Proprioceptive memories, in my opinion the first to emerge (in utero), and the ones that resist Alzheimer's disease the longest, usually do not reach consciousness unless one is a yogi or a fakir. Proprioceptive information doubtless partakes in cognition, but I am not conscious of what the activities of my muscles tell my brain, especially when movement is not accessible to the eyes. For instance, every time I produce an arbitrary nasal sound while speaking, my velum palati relaxes so that air can resonate within my nasal cavities, but I am not conscious of this event. Likewise, the semic difference between taking a bath and taking a path depends on the deliberate or unconscious proprioceptive memories guiding the degree of contraction of the little muscles around one's vocal cords.

Stored exteroceptive information shapes cognition but can take time reaching consciousness within a healthy brain. I will say a few words on both ears and eyes in this respect, but my remarks on each will be very different.

Myelogenesis occurs early in the lateral lemniscus (8). At the 29th week of gestation, it dominates the picture within the brain stem (Fig. 1). This is compatible with the notion that auditory cognition (not consciousness) starts building subthalamically during gestation. Human fetuses hear lots of different noises, coming from inside or from outside. Some of them are rhythmic, for instance those from the mother's heart and lungs, and the rhythms are different. Others are unpredictable, for instance the mother's borborygmi. Incoming noises from the outside can vary depending on where the mother lives. They can be music, a slamming door, a vibrating motor, an exploding bomb, and so forth. Of course, there is also the mother's

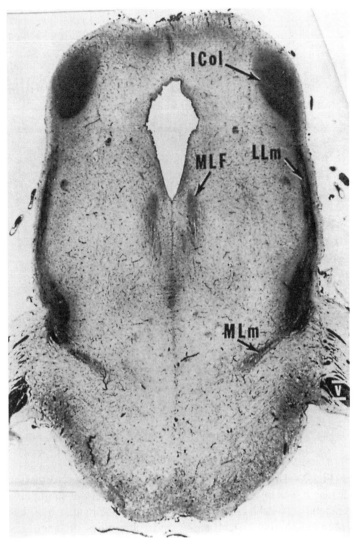

FIG. 1. Advanced myelination of the lateral lemniscus (LLm) and the inferior colliculius (ICol) at 29 weeks of gestation (plus 1 postnatal week). MLm, medial lemniscus; MLf, medial longitudinal fasciculus; V, motor root of the fifth cranial nerve.

voice and speech (and those of other people). With regard to incoming speech information, it has been shown, in particular through research conducted in the laboratory of my friend Jacques Mehler, that human newborns are already interested in potentially syllabic sounds and as a rule they already process this information with their left hemisphere more than with their right one (9).

I will be more anecdotal with regard to eyes. Recently, I played with drawing gadgets on the screen of my laptop. The end result was vertical and it was entirely meaningless to me. At that point, and for some reason, I had in mind Athen's first vowel and Jerusalem's first consonant. Anyway, I printed my blurb a few days later, turned the sheet to the left, and became conscious that I had drawn an elephant

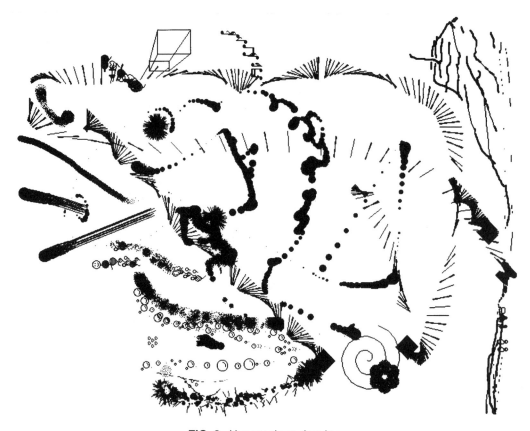

FIG. 2. Unconscious drawing.

and other images (Fig. 2). This flabbergasted me, somehow, because it was my first experience of this type (maybe I should mention that the elephant has long been the unofficial emblem of my laboratory).

Let me now turn to ontogenesis from the collective point of view. Our species initiated the invention of spoken language at least 40 thousand years ago, maybe much more (10). Why this happened is no doubt because the needed genetic program was in place and I do not see how anything but environmental pressures could have acted as triggers.

I do not know if there were one or several languages to begin with, and I doubt that one could find an unquestionable answer to this question. On the other hand, I am quite convinced that the invention of language was a progressive venture. Osiris and Zeus, Shiva, Elohim, Allah, and others are human words,

and I cannot conceive that everything began with the pluperfect subjunctive.

On the one hand, we all know that families and subfamilies of languages are numerous, although many are also extinct. On the other hand, according to Louis Hjelmslev (11), there are only four types of spoken languages: the isolating ones, the agglutinating ones, the inflectional ones, and the polysynthetic ones.

In isolating languages, each word has a single syllabic form[1] and it cannot be transformed by even a single affix. There is no morphology (no closed class bound morphemes), and syntactic rules depend only on word order. Thus, plural can be represented by a word meaning

---

[1]Increasing the number of syllabic words can be accomplished by borrowing from music (tonal heights), and composition is of course authorized (as in English "humbug" and French "garde-fou").

more than one, present tense by a word meaning actual, and so forth. Such words are not perceived as belonging to the closed class (the open-closed class dichotomy—roots versus function words or morphemes—is not recognized in such languages). Classical Chinese was isolating. Modern Chinese languages are somehow less so, although they have retained much of the isolating tradition. Hjelmslev (11) suggested that modern English is also somewhat isolating. I share this opinion, but only up to a point. It is true that inflectional endings are not very numerous in English, but English does comprise a lot of derivational words, that is, words with affixes. It certainly is not as isolating as modern Chinese if only because its games on tonal heights do not go further than its often irregular tonic accents.

In agglutinating languages, all derivational and inflectional appendages to a root are expressed by suffixes. The root always comes first in a word. In line with the Altaic and Uralian traditions, Turkish remains an agglutinating language. If a Turkish word is singular, the fact is indicated by the absence of a suffix. On the other hand, plural always comes first in the order of suffixes. Other suffixes will be situated according to established rules. For instance, one bird is *kus* in Turkish, and two birds or more are *kuslar.* If one bird is ablative, it is *kusdan,* but if two or more birds are ablative, they are *kuslardan* (11), And so forth.

With regard to inflectional languages, I should first say that the meaning of the term here refers to both derivation and inflection, and to both prefixes and suffixes. Now, in such languages, words can be limited to a root or comprise one or more than one prefix and/or one or more than one suffix. Moreover, the boundary between root and suffix is not always clear. This is because the phonemic end of roots can change depending on an appended suffix, as in English "delude" and "delusion." Root modifications related to annexed suffixes also can be more complex, as in French *doigt* and *digital* (a trace of Latin history). Another manner is that suffixes can

embody several functions, a phenomenon known in linguistics as fusion: in the word "bonus," for instance, the suffix "-us" indicates nominative, masculine, and singular (11). Ancient Indoeuropean languages are considered models of inflectional languages, and several of their offsprings, Polish for instance, as well as Spanish, Italian, and Portuguese, have retained much of this tradition. This is less obvious in certain languages, French for instance, and far less obvious in others, such as English.

In polysynthetic languages, a single root can be preceded by a large number of prefixes and followed by a large number of suffixes, in a manner such that what would be perceived as a sentence in other languages becomes a single word. The order in which affixes are placed is strictly rule governed and unchangeable. Moreover, a prefix and a suffix can share a combined inflectional function (the opposite of fusion). Many Amerindian languages are of this type. For instance, the Cree *kekawewetche etuchekamikowanowow* (meaning "I wish this gift remains with you") (12) is a striking example. It comprises a single root, *tucheka,* the meaning of which is "to remain." The other sounds are there to progressively specify it. The first syllable and the last two, *ke* and *owow,* mean second person plural; the second syllable, *ka,* means future tense; the third syllable, *we,* designates imperative mode; the following two, *wetche,* mean conjunction between subject and object; the syllable immediately after the root, *mik,* means verb in agreement with third person subject and second person objects; and the *owan* between *mik* and *owow* means subject inanimate and objects animate.

It is said that this typology of spoken languages can be misleading and that one can perceive isolating, inflectional, and agglutinating traces in French and in English.

This being said, let me talk about the extremes. With regard to normalcy and from the synchronic point of view, my intuition is that a child who is learning a language that is mostly isolating does not build his consciousness of the world (13) exactly the same way as a child who is learning a polysynthetic language. The number of abstract conventional sounds each will master, say at the age of 4, will be more or less the same. Nonetheless, in the first case, most sounds will relate to roots, whereas in the second, an astounding number will relate to affixes attuning a root. Context and inference abilities are essential in both cases, but the manner is somewhat different.

The brains of both children had the same genetic potential to begin with, but certain connections have been strengthened and others less so, and they are not the same given what local culture has requested of neuronal interactions. My main reason for making this postulate comes from empirical observation. There exists a clinical type of aphasia in which affixation procedures are severely impaired, whereas this phenomenon is not observed in another type of aphasia in which speech production is fluent but makes no sense to the listener because roots are often ill chosen or replaced by neologistic entities. Facing identical brain lesions and sharing a comparable educational background, an isolating and a polysynthetic right-hander would not display the same clinical agrammatic manifestations (14).

In my opinion, language keeps framing certain neural activities and consciousness as long as the human brain can learn new words, process new sentences, and reshape its discourse. This aspect of ontogenesis keeps going on as long as the brain remains healthy.

This being said, and beyond prosody, all languages are, from my point of view as a neurologist (linguists might not agree), processed at three main levels. The primary one is sublexical. It deals with phonetics and phonology. Words are not yet there. The second administers lexical to semantic interactions. As to the third, it is supralexical and it masters morphology, when present, and syntax in all cases. I should underline that the third level often has a significant retroactive impact on the second.

With regard to their neural bases, the first and third levels are usually of the left-sided

type and they are governed by automatons. Their sophisticated functional manners are learned and applied unconsciously, although they are created in line with arbitrary social conventions.

At the age of 4, children master the phonology and, for the essential, the morphology (if present), and the syntax of the language they keep learning. On the other hand, they have no idea of the arbitrary rules engendered by their enfolding culture and governing their brain–mind automatons. In adults, some of the rules guiding the automatons may have been learned at school, but they are almost never consciously summoned while one talks (it would disrupt speech).

The lexical semantic level often uses both the left and right hemispheres. If I properly interpret the results of research that I led in Brazil with my friends Jacques Mehler and Maria Alice Parente, the functional threshold at which the right hemisphere is needed can be lower for those without school education. Although not diagnosed as aphasics, right brain–damaged illiterates often had significant difficulties in picture naming, although not in picture pointing (15).

This brings us back to the interactions between the inborn genetic program of humans and the manners in which it actualizes itself sensing outside. Let us go further in this respect and talk about the linguistic commitments of the right hemisphere at more sophisticated levels. Think of the potential meanings of the word "tip" (from fingers to gratuity to information). Even if aphasia (16–32), as medicine defines it, nearly always results from left brain lesions, right brain ones can also puzzle language and perplex it. Conceivably, through different alchemistries, the digital hemisphere and the analogic one both are involved in language and, thus, in human consciousness. There is one level of consciousness that no doubt depends exclusively on memories dedicated to language and on the changes that language keeps bringing to those of semantics, its mother. Let us take metaphor as a prime example. Several of my colleagues advocate that right brain damage can interfere with inference abilities (33,34) and thus with the patient's neural skills to process metaphor. I endorse this assertion.

It is true that metaphor is not necessarily language within the human species and that it is accessible to other species. When the time comes, peacocks can produce amazing metaphors for peacoquettes. But raising your back feathers, dancing, and showing your behind is not the same as arbitrarily representing the same through rule-governed and multilevel sets of sounds or scripts. The convention is more abstract in the second case. It reaches consciousness with greater subtlety and details.

All of this does not facilitate the elucidation of functional modes within the neural substrates of language and consciousness. Nevertheless, spoken language has engendered written language as demography led to the creation of cities and as commerce became more symbolic with the concurrent invention of money (35). Saying words on clay and to the eyes, rather than to the ears and in the air, safeguarded transactions. Some say that this took place before Mesopotamia, but given what I have read, I will stay between the Tigris and Euphrates rivers as to the origins.

The invention of writing also petitioned supplemental resort to the genetic program, occipitally this time, and the destiny of written language was not limited to money. In this case, we do know that the invention was progressive (36–39) and that it diversified itself. The first well-known logographic writing systems emerged in Uruk about 5,300 years ago, and it took some time to perfect. The first syllabic writing system was invented more than 1,000 years later in Babylon, and the first consonantic one in Ugarit about 3,400 years ago. The Greeks invented their alphabet about 600 years later, and the Indians their very regular pseudosyllabic systems about 300 years after the Greeks.

Beyond the forms of signals, humanity has not forsaken any of the engendered conventions related to written language. Although most contemporary writing systems are composite (40,41), logographic, syllabic, consonantic, alphabetic, tonal, and featural writing systems are still in use to this day. It is apparent that, memory helping, written language has expanded consciousness to an amazing extent by thinning the space and time dimensions.

One might also point out that written language has recently engendered a new form of speech: E-mail. With this new gadget, the space dimension has thinned to near nothingness, and spoken language can be addressed to the eyes in nearly no time.

LANGUAGE DISEASES

I shall at this point turn to disasters. If human consciousness is to a large extent shaped by language, there are circumstances in which it can do without it, even for some of its components that could simply not have emerged without it. What I mean to suggest is that the neural substrate of consciousness and that of language are at least partially autonomous even if both probably must resort to nonspecific associative cortices.

I am thinking of an amazing and somewhat whimsical case of paroxystic aphasia (with aberrant left temporal electricity). The patient, Brother John, was 50 years old when my friend Yves Joanette and I began to observe him (42). He was then in charge of answering the numerous letters that were received daily by the editorial board of a religious journal, and he therefore had very regular reading and writing habits. His aphasic spells had begun 30 years earlier. As far as we could tell, and we were meticulous, his epilepsy impaired language almost electively, internal and overt at the same pace, and both spoken and written. Some of his language impairment episodes lasted up to 11 hours and began with global aphasia, thereafter evolving toward Wernicke's aphasia, then conduction aphasia, then word-finding difficulties, and back to normal. During the early phases of such spells, when he could neither speak conventionally nor comprehend language, Brother John performed tasks we had verbally instructed him to perform weeks before (tasks such as convincing the nurse of his convent that she should get in touch with us by phone, tape recording his own jargon, listening to the radio to find out if he could understand, etc.). I do not known if he was then able, without internal language, to ponder over the teachings of Thomas Aquinas, but I suspect he could not and did not wish to try.

Aphasia is not the only pathetic condition, supporting the fact that language and consciousness do not share all of their synaptic games. Take glossomaniac schizophasia, for instance (43,44). In this condition, language often is overexploited in a spectacular manner and lexicon is far from being exiguous. Sentences can be long and splendidly built, as in the following example:

Et alors, il y a des joues, jours, des j'ouvre-ferme qui sont des fermes de campagne . . . à cette organisation de travail, il y donc des plans d'heure et un calendrier du plan de secondes, de minutes, d'heures, d'horlogerie et d'orage. Vous appelez ça des heures-âges, d'où des tonnages qui, de l'âge du début d'un certain âge, par rapport au calendrier, et caetera.

The problem is that words are serialized in view of their kinships rather than with the intention of giving information or lying to friend or foe. Awareness is necessary but tightly restricted to affinities between the phonic and/or semic worth of words.

I should say that this phenomenon is also sometimes observed in subjects with damage to the left angular gyrus. A patient I observed in Paris many years ago (45) was exemplary in this respect. My question to him was, "What do you think of the last American election?" He answered as follows:

On s'est surtout occupé de la partie intérieure et on s'est aperçu que, partout ailleurs, ils ont mis de petits colporteurs et ils ont pu, avec un veston . . . avec de la poudre, avec un manteau colporté de la meilleure poudre, et caetera.

In such cases, there is transcortical sensory aphasia, and the lexicons are both fuzzy and tough to access. Nonetheless, and of course to the exclusion of etiology, one cannot in my opinion exclude a potential kinship between the biologic disorders behind these two nosologic entities.

I shall continue my discussion of acquired language pathology and include the three levels of language that I outlined above. The exercise will be limited to standard adult right-handers with a long school education background and the calamity of a focal left sylvian or occipital stroke.

In prototypical Broca's aphasia, resulting, for instance, from damage to and around the caudal half of the third frontal convolution in the left hemisphere, the patient is conscious of his or her language disorder (and often depressed). Oral comprehension can be normal or nearly so. Favorable evolution sometimes leads to agrammatism (14,31,32) and deep dyslexia (46,47). With regard to speech production, the functions of the second and third levels (more precisely, producing words from output lexicons and including function items in serial ordering) are still impaired at this point. However, what the patient can utter makes sense to listeners, often more so than a standard political speech about the globalization of the free-market system.

Now, if patients remain conscious of their embarrassments in evoking words and combining them, they are usually not conscious of the semantic paralexias that they often vocalize when reading aloud. Their visual access to the form of words is obviously normal, but they are then unaware of their occasional mismatches. The case of Dr. Archibald (48), a patient whom I observed at La Salpêtrière, supports these assertions.

Dr. Archibald was an obstetrician by profession and an archeologist by interest. He was not far from reaching his 50th birthday when he presented with increasing headaches. The surgeon cured him of his (left) Foster-Kennedy syndrome (49), but clips were placed in such a manner that Dr. Archibald woke up with right hemiplegia and absolute Broca's aphasia. Evolution was favorable toward agrammatism and deep dyslexia. With regard to the latter, he read *porc* (pig) when I showed him the word *verrat* (boar); he also read *perdu* (lost) for *égaré* (missing), *jamais* (never) for *toujours* (always), *huit* (eight) for *six* (six), and so forth. Unless his paralexias were pointed out to him, he remained sure of having read in line with the conventions of the French writing system. One of the telencephalic modules of his consciousness was shut off.

Because left anterior brain scars are usually large in such cases, this type of reading behavior might have something to do with right hemisphere functional takeover. Let us see what the third phrenology[2]—functional brain imaging—will perhaps have to say on that in years to come.

In normal speech production, and except for the initial decision to talk about something in particular, consciousness plays only a vague role at the lexical semantic level. As to the other two levels, cognition keeps the automatons going, but consciousness usually plays no role whatsoever.

The scenario is different for a brain-damaged individual. The first time I became somewhat aware of this was when I read a paper by Alajouanine et al. (50) after having found by chance their patient's file at La Salpêtrière, and his brain in a jar of formol. The paper was on pure phonetic disintegration, and the cortical lesion I saw was almost limited to the lower third of the left precentral gyrus (51).

The patient had a severe spoken sublexical disorder. At one point, he wrote a most interesting letter to Alajouanine, a letter saying that consciousness was of great importance in the partial recovery of his wreck:

Docteur, Je vais essayer de vous expliquer la raison que j'ai de syllaber. À l'état normal, la pensée s'exprime, par la parole, automatiquement. On ne s'occupe pas ou peu de l'articulation; par la force de l'habitude, l'articulation devient "machinale." . . . Il me faut syllaber parce que l'articulation est paresseuse, elle n'est plus automatique mais doit être commandée, dirigée. Je dois penser au mot que je vais dire et à la façon de le dire, de l'articuler. . . . En raison de cela, il faut que j'articule chaque voyelle, chaque consonne, en somme chaque syllabe.

Let me translate part of what this patient wrote:

I have to speak syllabically because my articulation is lazy, it is no longer automatic but has to be commanded, directed. I have to think of the word I am going to say and how to say it, how to articulate it.

In a way, what he meant was that his problem was related to loss of an unconscious proprioceptive memory and that his awkward recovery depended on resorting to an exteroceptive memory of sublexical sounds that was stubbornly fashioning new modes of access to his consciousness.

The scenario is quite different in prototypical Wernicke's aphasia, which can be the result of damage that is limited to the caudal half of the first left temporal convolution. The lexical semantic impairment is such that, although the automatons governing the other two levels are in good shape, there is an overwhelming production of paraphasias of various types and of neologisms. The patient is unaware of his jargon. Auditory feedbacks do not access his consciousness, and conventional language comprehension is impaired (there is no evidence of depression).

Consciousness can otherwise be intact, a phenomenon that I have observed in the case of Professor Jérôme (52), a right-handed man who had scarlatine and Bouillaud's disease at age 15, a transient (about 1 hour) right hemiparesis and speech disorder at age 37, a second episode of transient right hemiparesis with long-lasting Wernicke's aphasia at age 43, and a transient left hemiparesis and global

---

[2]According to my ancient Greek dictionary, the meaning of ψυχη evolved from "breath" to "soul," whereas that of φρην evolved from "diaphragm" to "viscera" to "heart" to "thought" and thereafter to "mind." We now talk of psychology and keep phrenology in mind. I sort of like the latter word, even if the first phrenology referred to cranial humps. As to the second, it evolved from "skull" to "convolutions."

aphasia at age 53. During the period when he was jargonaphasic (age 43+) and unaware of his language disorder, Professor Jérôme scored in the 90th percentile on the adult form of Raven's progressive matrices. At that point, he continued to enjoy classical music, he could play chess and usually won, and he could draw very sharp cartoons of fellow patients.

In jargonaphasic speech, cognition escorts the automatons and everything goes fine in this respect. As to the second level, it is blasted to begin with, and favorable evolution implies regression of the anosognosia and, unlike what occurs in standard speech, a need for conscious word-by-word lexical semantic processing (for the open class). The latter will gradually lead the patient to speak much slower, to produce aborted sentences, and to drop jargon. This is what occurred in the case of Professor Jérôme before his last stroke and his death soon after as a result of myocardial infarction. The autopsy suggested that there had been a right temporal takeover before the last cerebrovascular accident (52).

Although this happens rarely and, to my knowledge, only in very old and very educated persons, Wernicke's jargonaphasia also can forever destroy the second and the third levels (45,53). Jargon is then glossolalic, that is, fluid but wordless. I once asked a patient with this problem how long he had had it, to which he replied:

sẽ dikte di tRɔ kɔdeRe dRikɔdedeRe digœRe dis tis ti lavektoRe tRykœs œ œ ledø tRɔke di ki dedoRe dis tekodegoRe dil kɔdeteRe.

As far as I know, such patients do not recover comprehension and the anosognosia is final; auditory feedbacks will never again access consciousness. It seems to me that glossolalic behavior of this type indicates that the sublexical level for spoken speech has its own dedicated substrate within the human internet, and that Wernicke's area proper might not be an essential component of it. If not, the patient quoted above could only have moaned or groaned.

This anecdote leads me to another. Although they remain unconscious, proprioceptive memories can, in certain cases and after a left occipital lesion, help reshape a specialized module with potential access to consciousness. I am thinking of those patients with pure word blindness (20,24,31,32), in whom recovery occurs as the lesion transforms into a scar.

What led Jean-Baptiste Charcot (the son of Jean-Martin) to devise his rehabilitation contraption[3] (54) before he boarded the *Pourquoi pas?* and became a famous explorer of the poles was no doubt his observation of instinctive right-sided finger movements in subjects with pure word blindness who were facing scripts that they could not read with their eyes.

This reminds me of another case. Previous to his left occipital lesion, the patient earned his living as a proofreader. After a period of total word blindness, and despite a persisting right hemianopia, his proprioceptive finger memories entered into action and he gradually regained his ability to read; but he could no longer work as a proofreader. My interpretation of this case is that right hemisphere takeover occurred at the occipital level (and the right hemisphere of right-handers is not necessarily conscious of literal errors).

In patients having mastered an intricate writing system, say Mandarin or Kannada (Fig. 3), better than an alphabetic system, say English, recovery of pure word blindness has twice been shown to begin with the latter (55,56). Given the interactions between brain and cultures, it seems clear to me that this is related to the lesser complexity of stored proprioceptive and visual information in alphabetic, as opposed to pseudosyllabic and logographic writing systems.

---

[3]The patient (with pure verbal blindness) holds a long pencil at the bottom and the therapist holds it at the top while guiding the patient's writing hand movements in front of a word to be read and written from block to cursive letters.

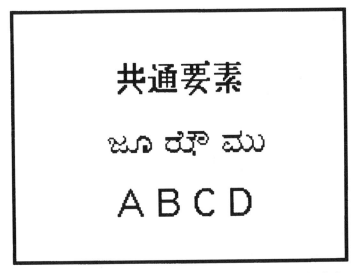

FIG. 3. Mandarin logograms, Kannada pseudosyllables, and Latin letters.

CONCLUSION

I will briefly discuss Alzheimer's disease before I conclude. One might suggest that the paramount symptoms of this calamity, including those crippling language, stem from a gradual loss of conscious cognition. One might label Alzheimer's disease as progressive unconsciousness. Braak and Braak (57) recently reported on Alzheimer's disease as it relates to myelogenesis, which fascinated me because I had the privilege of defining myelogenetic cycles with my mentor, Paul Ivan Yakovlev (8). According to Braak and Braak, Alzheimer's disease first strikes those neurons located where myelogenesis keeps working for a highly protracted period, that is, those located in nonspecific associative cortices. This might indicate that those cortices where genesis begins late and lasts very long in the neuropil (58), those which are no doubt the most sophisticated in their functions, are also the most fragile when the unknown root of Alzheimer's disease crops up.

Last September, my friend Peter Fox told me by E-mail that, in his opinion, consciousness is a distributed property. He meant biologically distributed of course, within the matter inside one's head. Having trained as a neurologist, I must agree with that. Moreover, I think that the distribution has two levels, at least in the human brain. The first is single, mesencephalic, and not very sophisticated (although it can turn off the second). The latter is multiple, telencephalic, and far more refined, and its modules are specialized. If I say multiple with regard to the second level of consciousness, it is of course because I am thinking of these right parietal lesions resulting in left hemiasomatognosia, of these occipital lesions at the origin of prosopagnosia, of these left temporal lesions with jargonaphasia lasting as long as the unfortunate is unaware of it, and so forth.

My goal has been to make the following seven points (Fig. 4):

1. Consciousness is not a prerogative of the human species.
2. To be conscious of cognition is to know that cognition includes unconscious modules.
3. Language is the chief builder in the genesis of human consciousness (and it can play a long-lasting role in this respect, as long as one's brain remains healthy).
4. One's perception of reality is perhaps influenced to some extent by the typology of one's spoken language.

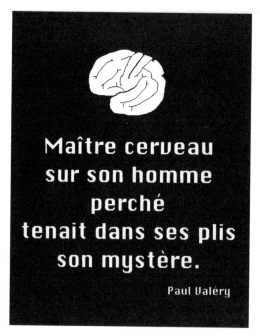

FIG. 4. Paul Valéry's option.

5. There are cases of aphasia in which favorable evolution depends on consciousness, and conciousness then performs in a manner different from that linked to normal adult language.

6. The biologic substrate of consciousness and that of language are, at least in part, autonomous.

7. Certain components of nonspecific associative cortices might at the second level play a dedicated role in the structure of consciousness.

With regard to the fifth point, functional recovery, although partial in most cases, cannot be attributed to scars. In my opinion, this tells us that the human genetic program can attempt to thwart the effects of certain focal brain lesions provided consciousness gets into the game.

What I have also tried to suggest is that language has its role in modeling not only consciousness but also phantasms, that it permits sharing information consciously, consciously helps or annoys kins, and it propagates falsehood consciously.

REFERENCES

1. Lordat J. *Exposition de la doctrine de P.-J. Barthez et mémoire sur la vie de ce médecin.* Paris: Gabon, 1818.
2. Bunge M. *The mind-body problem.* Oxford, England: Pergamon, 1980.
3. Jimenez M. Dualisme, monisme et émergence. In: Seron X, ed. *Psychologie et cerveau.* Paris: PUF, 1990.
4. Terrace HS, Petitto LA, Sanders RJ, Bever TG. Can an ape create a sentence? *Science* 1979;206:891–902.
5. Jasper HH. Problems of relating cellular or modular specificity to cognitive functions: importance of state-dependent reactions. In: Schmitt FO, Worden FG, Edelman G, Dennis SG, eds. *The organization of cerebral cortex.* Cambridge, MA: MIT Press, 1981:375–393.
6. Ribot T. *Les maladies de la mémoire.* Paris: Alcan, 1894.
7. Crick F. *The astonishing hypothesis.* New York: Scribner, 1994.
8. Yakovlev PI, Lecours AR. The myelogenetic cycles of regional maturation of the brain. In: Minkowski A, ed. *Regional development of the brain in early life.* Oxford, England: Blackwell, 1967:3–70.
9. Bertoncini J, Morais J, Bijeljac-Babic R, McAdams S, Peretz I, Mehler J. Dichotic perception and laterality in neonates. *Brain and Language* 1989;37:591–605.
10. Reichholf JH. *L'émergence de l'homme.* Paris: Flammarion, 1991.
11. Hjelmslev L. *Le langage.* Paris: Éditions de Minuit, 1966.
12. Lashley, KS. The problem of serial order in behavior. In: Jeffress LA, ed. *Cerebral mechanisms in behavior.* New York: Wiley, 1951:112–136.
13. Carrol JB, ed. *Language, thought and reality: selected writings of Benjamin Lee Whorf.* Cambridge, MA: MIT Press, 1967.
14. Menn L, Obler LK, eds. *Agrammatic aphasia: a cross-language narrative sourcebook.* Amsterdam: Benjamins, 1990.
15. Lecours AR, Mehler J, Parente MA. Illiteracy and brain damage. 3. A contribution to the study of speech and language disorders in illiterates with unilateral brain damage (initial testing). *Neuropsycologia* 1988;4:575–589.
16. Lordat J. Leçons tirées du cours de physiologie de l'année scolaire 1842–1843: analyse de la parole pour servir à la théorie de divers cas d'alalie et de paralalie que les nosologistes ont mal connus. *J Soc Med Pratique Montpellier* 1843;7:333–353.
17. Lordat J. Leçons tirées du cours de physiologie de l'année scolaire 1842–1843: analyse de la parole pour servir à la théorie de divers cas d'alalie et de paralalie que les nosologistes ont mal connus. *J Soc Med Pratique Montpellier* 1843;7:417–433.
18. Lordat J. Leçons tirées du cours de physiologie de l'année scolaire 1842–1843: analyse de la parole pour servir à la théorie de divers cas d'alalie et de paralalie que les nosologistes ont mal connus. *J Soc Med Pratique Montpellier* 1843;8:1–17.
19. Taylor J, ed. *Selected writings of John Hughlings Jackson.* New York: Basic Books, 1958.
20. Charcot JM. *Differenti forme d'afazia.* Milano: Vallardi, 1883.
21. Broca P. Du siège de la faculté de langage articulé. *Bull Soc Anthropol* 1865;6:377–393.

22. Trousseau A. De l'aphasie. In: Trousseau A, ed. *Clinique médicale de l'Hôtel-Dieu de Paris*. Paris: Baillière, 1877:669–729.
23. Wernicke C. *Der aphasische symptomenkomplex*. Breslau, Germany: Cohn & Weigert, 1874.
24. Dejerine J. *Séméologie des affections du système nerveux*. Paris: Masson, 1926.
25. Freud S. *Zur Auffassung der Aphasien Eine Kritische Studie*. Leipzeig, Germany: Deuticke, 1891.
26. Marie P. *Travaux et mémoires*. Tome 1. Paris: Masson, 1926.
27. Head H. *Aphasia and kindred disorders of speech*. Cambridge, England: Cambridge University Press, 1926.
28. Ombredane A. *L'aphasie et l'élaboration de la pensée explicite*. Paris: PUF, 1951.
29. Alajouanine T. *L'aphasie et le langage pathologique*. Paris: Baillière, 1968.
30. Geshwind N. *Selected papers on language and the brain*. Boston: Reidel, 1976.
31. Lecours AR, Lhermitte F. *L'aphasie*. Paris: Flammarion, 1979.
32. Lecours AR, Lhermitte F, Bryans B. *Aphasiology*. London: Baillière-Tindall, 1983.
33. Joanette Y, Goulet P, Hannequin P. *Right hemisphere and verbal communication*. New York: Springer-Verlag, 1990.
34. Joanette Y, Brownell HH, eds. *Discourse ability and brain damage. Theoretical and empirical perspectives*. New York: Springer-Verlag, 1990.
35. Jurdant B. *Ecriture, monnaie et connaissance*. Doctoral thesis. Strasbourg, France: Université Louis-Pasteur, 1984.
36. Cohen M. *La grande invention de l'écriture et son évolution*. Paris: Klincksieck, 1958.
37. Sampson G. *Writing systems*. Stanford, CA: Stanford University Press, 1985.
38. Coulmas F. *The writing system of the world*. Oxford, England: Blackwell, 1992.
39. Lecours AR. *Langage écrit: histoire, théorie et maladie*. Molinghem, France: Ortho, 1996.
40. Gelb IJ. *A study of writing*. Chicago: University of Chicago Press, 1963.
41. DeFrancis J. *Visible speech: the diverse oneness of writing systems*. Honolulu: University of Hawaii Press, 1989.
42. Lecours AR, Joanette Y. Linguistic and other psychological aspects of paroxysmal aphasia. *Brain Language* 1980;10:1–23.
43. Lecours AR, Vanier-Clément M. Schizophasia and Jargonaphasia: a comparative description with comments on Chaika's and Fromkin's respective looks at schizophrenic language. *Brain Language* 1976;3:516–555.
44. Lecours AR. Schizophasia: the glossomanic and the glossolalic subtypes. In: Sims ACP, ed. *Speech and language disorders in psychiatry*. London: Gaskell, 1995:81–95.
45. Lecours AR, Osborn E, Travis L, Rouillon F, Lavallée-Huynh G. Jargons. In: Brown JW, ed. *Jargonaphasia*. New York: Acadamic Press, 1981:9–38.
46. Marshall JC, Newcombe F. Patterns of paralexia: a psycholinguistic approach. *J Psycholinguistic Res* 1973;2:175–200.
47. Colheart M, Patterson K, Marshall JC, eds. *Deep dyslexia*. London: Routledge & Kegan Paul, 1980.
48. Lecours AR, Lupien S, Bub D. Semic estraction behavior in deep dyslexia: morphological errors. In: Nespoulous JL, Villard P, eds. *Morphology, phonology and aphasia*. New York: Springer-Verlag, 1990:60–71.
49. Adams RD, Victor M. *Principles of neurology*. New York: McGraw-Hill, 1985.
50. Alajouanine Th, Pichot P, Durand M. Dissociation des altérations phonétiques avec conservation relative de la langue la plus ancienne dans un cas d'anarthrie pure chez un sujet français bilingue. *Encéphale* 1949;28:245–265.
51. Lecours AR, Lhermitte F. The pure form of the phonetic disintegration syndrome (pure anarthria): anatomo-clinical report of a historical case. *Brain and Language* 1976;3:88–113.
52. Lhermitte F, Lecours AR, Ducarne B, Escourolle R. Unexpected anatomical findings in a case of fluent jargon aphasia. *Cortex* 1973;9:433–446.
53. Lecours AR, Travis L, Osborn E. Glossolalia as a manifestation of Wenicke's aphasia: A comparison glossolalia in schizophasia and in possession. In, Taylor Sarno M, Höök O, eds. *Aphasia assessment and treatment*. Stockholm: Almqvist & Wiksell, 1980:212–230.
54. Charcot JB. Sur un appareil destiné à évoquer les images motrices graphiques chez les sujets atteints de cécité verbale. *Soc Biolo* 1892;39:235–241.
55. Lyman RS, Kwan ST, Chao WH. Left occipito-parietal brain tumor with observations on Alexia and Agraphia in Chinese and in English. *Chin Med J* 1938;6:491–516.
56. Karanth P. Pure alexia in a Kannada-English bilingual. *Cortex* 1981;17:187–198.
57. Braak H, Braak E. Development of Alzheimer-related neurofibrillary changes in neocortex inversely recapitulates cortical myelogenesis. *Acta Neuropathol* 1996;92:197–201.
58. Kaes T. *Die Grosshirnrinde des Menschen in ihrem Massen und in iherm Fasergehalt*. Jena, Germany: Fischer, 1907.

DISCUSSION
Moderated by Edward G. Jones

John C. Fentress: I perhaps missed one of the lessons that you would like to give us. When you spoke of the various neurological disorders and the effects on speech that would sort of knock out different layers of consciousness, would it not be useful to supplement that type of thinking with the fact that when I articulate a sentence speaking to you, at some level I am not really aware of the particular sounds that I am going to make. I have sort of a general idea. And when I concentrate on a sentence, I might lose the overall idea, and when I concentrate on the articulation of a particular sound I might lose the ability to string certain words together, the notion being that in a relatively normal nervous system, we can move up and down and change the focus of what I think we call consciousness. And the only question I had is whether you believe that studies that would deal with this sort of dynamics in the production of speech in a normal nervous system are feasible, and whether there might be some selective disorders of this process in some of your patients? Does that make sense to you?

André Roch Lecours: Yes, it does make sense to me. Especially if you refer to someone who is talking his native language, which is not my case at this point. But I do agree with you, with what you say. And I think that it was sort of implicit in what I said. There are three levels of processing in all languages and there is also the semantic level. Clinical obser-vation tells us that each is at least in part au-tonomous within our brain's lipids. But everything is not at the same level. If semantic knowledge is in disarray, the lexicosemantic procedures (second level) to lexical memories become perplexed, and therefore the lexicons are also perplexed as to their choices of words. Of course, semantic conscious-ness does not have to be there all the time: one can keep talking a long time about a chosen topic with-out having in conscious memory the words repre-senting the topic.

Consciousness: At the Frontiers of Neuroscience,
Advances in Neurology, Vol. 77,
edited by H.H. Jasper, L. Descarries,
V.F. Castellucci, and S. Rossignol.
Lippincott–Raven Publishers, Philadelphia © 1998.

12

Brain and Conscious Experience

Michael S. Gazzaniga

Center for Cognitive Neuroscience, Dartmouth College,
Hanover, New Hampshire 03755

As we stumble forward into the next century, groping for a way to think about the problem of conscious experience, it is good to remember we do know something about the brain and psychological process. There are a set of facts, of observations that can help guide our thinking about how the brain enables the mind. I would like to outline these milestones and argue that progress on the mind–brain issue is being made (1).

We start with the simple realization that our mind is the product of natural selection. This fact has many implications for how we should think about the nature of conscious experience.

THE EVOLUTIONARY PERSPECTIVE

The central nervous system did not spontaneously arise in mammals. The function and structure of the extant mammalian brain is the consequence of millions of years of interaction with the environment. For a species to have survived, let alone evolve, it had to come to terms with the challenges of its niche. To cope with those challenges, it had to develop specialized neural circuitry that supports adaptations and programs for response to an environmental challenge. In short, any organism from *Escherichia coli* to a human has built-in responses that are ready to be applied to environmental challenges.

This position is part of a large issue in biology that has to do with whether information from the environment instructs biologic systems or that biologic systems select information it already has built into it. The best example of this distinction has come from immunology. For years it was thought that when a foreign substance (antigen) invaded the body, its unique structure instructed the lymphocyte cells to form an antibody. The antigen–antibody response subsequently occurred, and the foreign element would be neutralized.

For almost 30 years we have known this is not how the system works. Human beings are born with all their antibodies, and when an antigen is tied up by an antibody, it is because that antibody had been selected from the millions already present in the body. This immunologic fact was first applied to the nervous system by Niels Jerne (2), who proposed that perhaps all the nerve circuits we will ever need to perform tasks are already built into the brain. This would imply that more complex organisms, which possess more complex behaviors (language, abstract thought), must possess complex and specialized circuits. As William James noted (3), humans must have more instincts, not fewer, than lower animals.

Peter Marler reported many years ago on a fascinating aspect of bird song that directly relates to Jerne's suggestion (4). Young males learn their song from their fathers, and although there are all kinds of parameters for correct song learning, the most intriguing is that the young male can learn only a limited song. It must hear the adult males' song of its own species or only a slight dialect, but it cannot learn a related song. In short, the environment triggers the expression of a song pattern, but a pattern is selected from a small array of possibilities built into the young male; it cannot learn any random song. A related example from human research is the reduced ability to not only produce but also to perceive phonemes of different languages (5) if a child is not exposed to the language early in life.

These examples set the stage for a view of the nervous system that suggests the cerebral cortex is not a dynamic, general purpose, learn-anything, anytime, anywhere kind of device. It has built-in constraints, huge ones. Although some investigators believe that constant Darwinian competition is ongoing in the cerebral cortex (6), my view is that during learning, selection processes are at work to find the built-in circuit, the already existing adaptation, to meet the environment challenge at hand. Although all researchers studying reorganizations of cortical maps are aware of what their work may or may not mean, it is represented as showing that synapses constantly reorganize to handle new environmental circumstances (7,8). The evolutionary view would indicate little or no recrafting of synapses; the cerebral cortex is hard wired with circuitry crafted to meet specific challenges. If the brain was not hard wired, why would the same bird be able to learn one song pattern but not another?

TIMING AND AUTOMATIC ACTIONS

Timing is everything. With our brains chock full of marvelous devices, one would think they do their duties more or less automatically and before we are truly aware of the act. As reviewed by Libet in Chapter 14, that is precisely what happens in the brain. Recent research confirms that not only are there mechanisms that seem to create this illusion, there are modern studies on the primate brain that show how cells are preparing for decisive

action way before the animal is even thinking about making its decision (9).

It is also clear that, when activated, these automatic processes give rise to illusions, as in Roger Shepard's turning table illusion (10). The explanation for this striking phenomenon can be found in how the brain computes information residing on a two-dimensional structure, the retina, and transforms it into a three-dimensional reality. The cues that give perspective, the long axis lines, suggest that the table on the left is going back in depth. The long axis cues for the table on the right are at right angles to the line of sight, and now the brain reacts to these cues. The image on the retina of these two tables is exactly the same. However, the brain automatically responds to depth cues of the left table and infers (for us) that because the table is going back in depth, the image is foreshortened, and because it is foreshortened as a real table in real depth, it must be longer. The same is true for why the horizontal table appears wider. Even though one can fully understand that the images are exactly the same and that at a level of personal consciousness one knows this to be true, it has no effect on perception. The brain automatically supplies the inference, and there is nothing one can do about it.

There are also demonstrations that our motor system, the system that makes operational any decision about the world our brains might make, works with a high degree of independence from our conscious perceptions (11). Too often our perceptions are in error, and it would be disastrous in many instances to have our lives depend on those perceptions. It would be better if our brains reacted to real sensory truths, not illusory ones.

CONSCIOUS VERSUS UNCONSCIOUS PROCESSES

If so many processes are automatic, it would seem logical to think they could function outside the realm of conscious awareness. And yet we have come to think that the part of our brain that has grown so large, the cerebral cortex, is reserved for our conscious activities. It now seems clear that brain scientists have been wrong about this issue. The cortex is involved in all sorts of unconscious processes.

A series of reports over the past 20 years indicates that although a patient suffering damage to the primary visual system may not consciously see in a blind field of vision, the hand or even the mouth might be able to respond to stimuli presented in the blind field. Patients who exhibit this condition, which has been dubbed "blindsight," can actually respond to such stimuli without being consciously aware of the stimulus. The hope of this research was that the site of unconscious processing had been discovered and could now be examined.

Ever since the psychodynamic ideas of Freud, there has been a fascination with the unconscious. There in that great platform for our mental life, ideas are sewn together, true relationships between information are seen, and plans are made. Although Freud never really suggested which parts of the brain might be involved in managing the unconscious, there has been a tacit assumption and sometimes an explicit claim that such things go on in the older and more primitive regions.

In the collective enthusiasm for this view, we all have missed a fundamental point. It is a fact that 98% of what the brain does, it does outside of conscious awareness. Starting with basics, no one would argue that virtually all of our sensory-motor activities are unconsciously planned and executed. As I sit here and type this sentence, I have no idea how the brain actually pulls off the task of directing my fingers to the correct keys on the keyboard. I have no idea how the bird, sitting on the outside deck, a glimpse of which I must have caught in my peripheral vision, just caught my attention, while I nonetheless continue to type these words. Furthermore, the same goes for rational behaviors. As I sit and write, I am not aware of how the neural messages arise from various parts of my brain and are programmed into something resembling a rational argument. It all just sort of happens.

Surely we are not aware of how much of anything gets done in the realm of our so-called "conscious" lives. As we use one word and find that suddenly a related word comes into our consciousness with a greater probability than another, do we really think that we have such processes under conscious control? Do we really think that we have consciously achieved an understanding of what a logarithm represents? Indeed, only a few members of our species possess such an understanding and among those who do, it just sort of happened.

It is easy to see why very clever psychologists began to wonder if formal cognitive psychology had missed the boat. Perhaps the challenge is to study that great platform of life, the unconscious. It was in this context that my colleagues and I became interested in the work of Weiskrantz and the phenomeon of blindsight (12).

The unconscious now seemed to be explorable in scientific terms. It looked as though various subcortical and parallel pathways and centers could now be studied in the human brain. A large body of subhuman primate literature on the subject also developed. Monkeys with occipital lesions were reported as being not only able to localize objects in space but were also able to perform color and object discriminations.

As the early reports on blindsight accumulated, we began to examine related issues in other types of brain patients (13,14). Damage to the parietal lobe of the brain, for example, causes strange symptoms to appear. If it occurs on the right side of the brain, most patients experience neglect. Thus, when looking straight ahead, they deny seeing anything to the left of where they are looking, even though their primary visual system is perfectly intact. A milder symptom of damage to the right parietal lobe is extinction, which is often present when both visual fields are stimulated at the same time.

When all of these behaviors are considered, it becomes clear that the parietal lobe somehow is involved with the attentional mechanism. Something distinct is at work from the parts of the brain that simply represent visual information. Information is getting into the brain, but it operates outside the realm of conscious experience. We showed this basic fact in a number of ways. In one study, we asked patients with neglect to judge whether two lateralized visual stimuli, one appearing in each visual field, were the same or different. So, a patient might see an apple in one part of the visual field and an orange in the other. Conversely, two apples or two oranges might be presented, one in each half visual field. The patients were able to perform this task accurately. However, when questioned as to the nature of the stimuli after a trial, they could easily name the stimulus in the right visual field but denied having seen the stimulus presented in the neglected left field.

These studies were the first in a long series that have now been conducted by several laboratories. Taken together, they show that the information presented in the neglected field could be used to make decisions, even though it could not be consciously described. A decision was correctly made that two objects were different, but the patient could name only one of them.

We discovered other related phenomena while studying split-brain patients, who have had the cortical connections between the two halves of their brains severed in an attempt to control their epilepsy. In consequence of this surgery, information presented to one half of the brain can no longer consciously influence information presented to the other half of the brain (15). Thus, an apple held in one hand will not help the patient find a matching apple with the other hand. J.W., a patient we have been studying for some 15 years, was the first to provide insight into how a visual stimulus is transmitted from the visual cortex into the realm of conscious awareness. We tested J.W. during all phases of his recent medical history: before his first surgery, between the two surgeries when only the posterior half of the corpus callosum had been sectioned, and dozens of times since the callosum was completely sectioned. Before his initial surgery, J.W. performed normally on all tests of

whether information presented to the right hemisphere could be named by the left. Clearly, his corpus callosum was functioning normally, and conscious unity was intact.

We were astounded by J.W.'s behavior after only the posterior half of his callosum had been sectioned, the portion of the brain that connects the primary visual areas (16). After posterior callosal sectioning, the brain messages that encode the visual images from the left visual field are no longer directly connected to the left, speech-dominant hemisphere. Thus, we expected that pictures of objects presented to J.W.'s left visual field would not be named, and that was indeed the case, but only for a couple of weeks. Unlike previous split-brain patients, who had undergone complete callosal sectioning, J.W. began to name pictures presented solely to his right hemisphere. Somehow, information was being transferred to the left brain via the remaining callosal fibers. What proved to be most interesting was the nature of this information.

Upon careful analysis of J.W.'s spoken commentary after a picture was presented to his right hemisphere, it was clear that attributes of the original stimulus were being communicated to the left hemisphere, not the actual stimulus itself. For example, when the word "knight" was flashed to the right hemisphere, J.W. would initiate with himself a process not unlike a game of 20 questions. He would avert his eyes after the word had been presented and report, "I have a picture in mind but can't say it . . . two fighters in a ring . . . ancient, wearing uniforms and helmets . . . on horses trying to knock each other off . . . knights?"

As the partial information was being communicated from the right hemisphere to the left through the uncut part of his callosum, the left hemisphere pieced each clue together until an intelligent guess was possible. Observing this behavior, trial after trial, was a very powerful experience. These observations showed that the brain's cortical pathways handle identifiable and qualitatively different information. In this case, a communication channel in the brain was transmitting abstract information about a stimulus, not the stimulus itself. These processes are largely unconscious, and yet they go on at the level of the cortex, not among the older, subcortical parts of the brain.

In a series of studies on these same patients, we began to see that one hemisphere could influence the attentional properties of the other. Somehow, through remaining neural connections, one half of the brain was manipulating the state of the other half of the brain in an unconscious way (17). It appeared that perceptual information presented to one hemisphere subtly influenced the decision processes of the other. In light of blindsight reports, it hardly seemed surprising that subjects could make use of visually presented information not accessible to consciousness. Subcortical networks, with their interhemispheric connections, seemed to be the anatomic structures that allowed for this transfer of information. It would be difficult to argue against the concept that perceptual decisions or cognitive activities routinely result from processes outside of conscious awareness, and it looked as if we were observing such processes in the form of subcortical, interhemispheric semantic transfer.

As our studies progressed, however, we were not able to support our original hypothesis that higher order, perceptual information interacts between the hemispheres after surgical sectioning of the corpus callosum. There were also new reports of high-level hemispheric interactions after full commissurotomy. These studies prompted us to carefully reexamine our split-brain patients, and when we did so, we could find no interhemispheric interactions of this kind. This was the case even when we used stabilized images to permit extended stimulus presentations. Moreover, we could not reproduce our original findings on semantic priming, and we have been forced to conclude that this report was in error. It also has become apparent that there are grounds for uncertainty regarding an interpretation of blindsight in terms of subcortical systems (12,18). If the subcortex was the

answer, split-brain patients should be able to show interactions of perceptual information, which they cannot. At this point, we began to suspect that the multitudinous reports of the subcortical basis of blindsight were in error.

In the early 1980s, Jeffrey Holtzman began to study blindsight in my laboratory. We were fortunate to have a piece of equipment that allowed for the very careful assessment of the position of the eye in relation to where a stimulus might appear, allowing for the precise presentation of stimuli within the scotoma.

We first studied a 34-year-old woman who had undergone surgery to clip an aneurysm in the right half of her brain (18). The surgery was expected to have the consequence of producing blindness in part of the patient's vision, because damage would occur to her right occipital lobe, the brain area with the aneurysm. Sure enough, after surgery, there was a dense, left homonymous hemianopia. Magnetic resonance imaging (MRI) showed an occipital lesion that clearly spared both extrastriate regions as well as the main midbrain candidate for residual vision, the superior colliculus. These intact areas should have been able to support many of the blindsight phenomena commonly reported.

Holtzman started out by presenting the patient with a very simple task. In each visual field, he presented a matrix of four crosses. The patient was asked to fixate a point in the middle of a visual monitor and to move her eyes to the point in the matrix that flashed. The four crosses were randomly highlighted. Of course, the patient had no problem doing the task when the matrices were flashed into her intact field of vision. What Holtzman wanted to see was good performance in her blind field. He wanted her to be able to move her eyes accurately but not be able to claim that she actually saw the lights.

The patient was shown to be blind even though she had the brain structures intact that should support the phenomenon of blindsight; he studied her for months and got nothing. Holtzman moved on to several other studies. He studied other patients who had been reported to show the phenomenon, and when he did the experiments correctly, none had it. Working with Steven Hillyard at the University of California, San Diego, he also showed that none of these patients had what are called evoked responses to light flashed into their blind fields.

We left the problem alone for a few years. It was not until a new graduate student, Mark Wessinger, came along to the laboratory that my colleague Robert Fendrich and I renewed our interest in this issue (19,20). By this time, we had moved to Dartmouth Medical School and were calling on a different kind of patient. Our first case was a woodsman from New Hampshire who had had a stroke involving his right primary visual cortex. Nonetheless, he pursued life with vigor and was quite a marksman. Before studying what could or could not be done in the blind visual field, basic perimetry was performed to discover the exact character of the scotoma.

For these tests, we were able to use a newly acquired image stabilizer, which allowed us to keep images steady on the retina despite observer eye motions. Our woodsman's scotoma was carefully explored using high-contrast black dots on a white background. In fact, a whole matrix of dots was presented in an area of his scotoma. Hundreds of trials were presented over many testing sessions.

The efforts paid off. In the sea of blindness, we found what we called a "hot spot," an island of vision. In one small area, about 1 degree in diameter, the woodsman could detect the presence of visual information. If it were truly a 1 degree window, a 2 degree stimulus that was either a square or a diamond shape should not be detected. Even though a 2 degree stimulus is larger and under normal conditions would be easier to detect, the patient should not be able to see it because the black dot would be larger than the window the island provided. In fact, the patient could not see the larger stimulus. Follow-up testing showed that the patient could detect differences between light of different wavelengths in the "hot spot." Could it be that the island was the source of so-called blindsight?

There are many aspects of our finding that correspond directly to the original reports. First, the woodsman was not at all confident of his decisions about the lights he could detect. On a scale of 1 to 5, his confidence hovered around 1. When a spot had been presented in his good field of vision, it was closer to 5. At some level, therefore, he was responding above chance but outside of conscious awareness, which is the very definition of blindsight phenomena. But like everything else, the true answer is in the details. Our findings suggested that blindsight was not a property of subcortical systems taking over the visual function because vision was not possible in the vast majority of the blind area. Our patient could see only in the islands of vision, whereas the original reports had maintained that patients could detect visual information throughout their visual fields.

Without an eye-tracking device of the kind we used, there are real problems with interpreting the results using standard testing procedures of the type used by Weiskrantz and colleagues. One simply cannot be sure what part of the patient's visual field one is stimulating with any kind of precision. His extensively studied patient also had a shrinking blind spot; although it started out large, by the time many studies were done, it was quite small. Overall, the smaller the blind spot, the less certain one is that discrete stimulation of the blind area, and only the blind area, is occurring. Moreover, an area approximately 10 degrees in diameter of partially preserved vision was embedded within the scotoma that remained in his patient. Many of the studies on case D.B. were conducted without any eye motion monitoring or control, so one simply must have faith that stimuli were properly placed.

There is another way of examining the issue of whether residual vision is supported by visual cortex or by subcortical structures. Through advances in modern brain imaging, one can take pictures of a patient's brain and look for spared cortex. Our woodsman had several studies done of this kind. First, using

MRI, a method of taking a picture that shows the basic anatomic structure of the brain, there was the clear suggestion that part of his visual cortex was spared. Yet, MRI does not show if the remaining tissue is functional; it might be in place but damaged.

We followed up these studies on case C.L.T. with a positron emission tomography study. We tested the woodsman using that method, and discovered his spared cortex as detected with MRI was also metabolically active. We also recently confirmed and extended the finding of islands of vision in other patients who have suffered lesions to the primary visual system (21). Thus, before one can assert that blindsight occurs due to subcortical structures, one first must be extremely careful to rule out the possibility of spared visual cortex.

Finally, we have studied two patients who underwent either partial or complete functional hemispherectomy (22). Neither patient showed any evidence of residual vision even though both patients had collicular systems intact.

None of this, of course, is to suggest that unconscious processes are not of constant and primary importance to our vision. It is yet another demonstration of the truth that most of what our brain does, it does outside of the realm of conscious awareness. However, my colleagues and I do reject the proposition that because blindsight demonstrates vision outside the realm of conscious awareness, it supports the view that perception can occur in the absence of sensation, as sensations are presumed to be our experiences of impinging stimuli. Because it is the role of the primary visual cortex to process sensory inputs, advocates of this view have found it useful to attribute blindsight to alternative visual processing pathways. I submit that this formulation is unnecessary and implausible. It is commonplace to design demanding perceptual tasks where non-neurologic subjects routinely report low confidence values for tasks they are performing above chance. However, it is not necessary to propose secondary visual systems to account for such data because

the primary visual system is intact and fully functional.

As previously noted, it is also the case that patients with parietal lobe damage but spared visual cortex can perform perceptual judgments outside the realm of conscious awareness. These subjects can compare two stimuli, although they deny awareness of one of them. The failure of these patients to consciously access the information used to compare the stimuli should not be attributed to processing within a secondary visual system because the geniculostriate pathway was still intact. Many other examples of phenomena can be found where, as the M.I.T. philosopher Ned Block has said, conscious access to brain events is impaired or nonexistent. The vast staging for our mental activities happens largely without our monitoring, and it is to be expected that this situation can be identified by various experimental means.

THE CONCEPT OF MODULARITY AND THE ROLE OF THE INTERPRETER

Human brains are large because of the great number of things they can do. The uniquely human skills we possess may well be produced by minute and circumscribed neuronal networks sometimes referred to as modules. And yet our highly modularized brain generates this feeling in all of us that we are integrated and unified. How does that come about, even though we are a collection of specialized modules?

The answer appears to be that there is a specialized left hemisphere system we have designated as the "interpreter," a device that seeks explanations for why events occur. The advantage of having such a system is obvious. By going beyond observing contiguous events and asking why they happened, a brain can cope with these same events more effectively, should they happen again.

We first showed the interpreter using a simultaneous concept test. The patient is shown two pictures, one exclusively to the left hemisphere and one exclusively to the right, and is asked to choose from an array of pictures placed in full view in front of him or her, the ones associated with the pictures lateralized to the left and right brain. In one example of this kind of test, a picture of a chicken claw was flashed to the left hemisphere and a picture of a snow scene to the right. Of the array of pictures placed in front of the subject, the obviously correct association is a chicken for the chicken claw and a shovel for the snow scene. Split-brain subject P.S. responded by choosing the shovel with the left hand and the chicken with the right. When asked why he chose these items, his left hemisphere replied, "Oh, that's simple. The chicken claw goes with the chicken, and you need a shovel to clean out the chicken shed." Here, the left brain, observing the left hand's response, interprets that response into a context consistent with its sphere of knowledge—one that does not include information about the right hemisphere snow scene.

There are many ways to influence the left brain interpreter. As already mentioned in the foregoing example, we wanted to know whether or not the emotional response to stimuli presented to one half of the brain would have an effect on the affective tone of the other half. Using an optical computer system that detects the slightest movement of the eyes, we were able to project an emotion-laden movie to the right hemisphere. If the patient tried to cheat and move the eye toward the movie, it was electronically shut off.

We studied patient V.P. The movie her right hemisphere saw was about a vicious man pushing another off a balcony and then throwing a fire bomb on top of him. It then showed other men trying to put the fire out. When V.P. was first tested on this problem, she could not access speech from her right hemisphere. When asked what she had seen, she said, "I don't really know what I saw. I think just a white flash." When I asked, "Were there people in it?", V.P. replied, "I don't think so. Maybe just some trees, red trees like in the fall." I asked, "Did it make you feel any emotion?", and V.P. answered, "I don't really know why, but I'm kind of scared. I feel jumpy. I think maybe I don't like this room, or maybe it's you, you're getting me nervous." Then V.P. turned to one of the research assistants and said, "I know I like Dr. Gazzaniga, but right now I'm scared of him for some reason."

The foregoing experimental evidence represents a commonly occurring event in all of us. A mental system sets up a mood that alters the general physiology of the brain. The verbal system notes the mood and immediately attributes cause to the feeling. It is a powerful mechanism, and once so clearly seen, it makes you wonder how often we are victims of spurious emotional/cognitive correlations.

There have been recent studies that examine further the properties of the interpreter and how its presence influences other mental skills. There are, for example, hemisphere-specific changes in the accuracy of memory process (23). The predilection of the left hemisphere to interpret events has an impact on the accuracy of memory. When subjects were presented with a series of pictures that represented common events (i.e., getting up in the morning or making cookies) and then asked several hours later to identify whether pictures in another series had appeared in the first, both hemispheres were equally accurate in recognizing the previously viewed pictures and rejecting the unrelated ones. Only the right hemisphere, however, correctly rejected pictures in the second set that were not previously viewed but were related or semantically congruent with pictures from the first. The left hemisphere incorrectly "recalled" significantly more of these pictures as having occurred in the first set, presumably because they fit into the schema it had constructed regarding the event. This finding is consistent with the view of a left hemisphere interpreter that constructs theories to assimilate perceived information into a comprehensible whole. In doing so, however, the elaborative processing involved has a deleterious effect on the accuracy of perceptual recognition. This result has been extended to include verbal material (24).

A more recent example of the interpreter in action comes from studies that now document the patient J.W. who can speak out of his right hemisphere as well as his left. In brief, naming of left field stimuli appears to be increasing at a rapid rate (25,26). An interesting phenomenon that occurred during these naming tasks was J.W.'s tendency to sometimes report that he saw a stimulus in his right visual field that was actually presented to his left visual field. Although there is no convincing evidence of any genuine visual transfer between the hemispheres, on trials where he was certain of the name of the stimulus, he maintained that he saw the stimulus well. On trials where he was not certain of the name of the stimulus, he maintained that he did not see it well. This is consistent with the view that the left hemisphere's interpreter actively constructs a mental portrait of past experience, even though that experience did not directly occur in that hemisphere. We speculate that this experience was caused by the left hemisphere interpreter giving meaning to right hemisphere spoken responses, possibly by activating the left hemisphere mental imagery systems.

A related phenomenon is seen in patients with cochlear implants. Implant surgery can enable patients who have become deaf after experiencing normal development of language to regain their capacity to hear (27). The cochlear implant transduces auditory information into discrete patterns of stimulation on an eight-electrode array that is implanted on the cochlear nerve. After 3 months of practice, subjects begin to be able to decode the implant's output as speech. As they become adept at this decoding task, they report that the speech they hear sounds normal. Because the eight electrodes are unlikely to be stimulating the cochlear nerve in the way it was naturally activated before their hearing loss, the new auditory code must undergo a transformation such that the patients feel they are hearing undistorted speech. In short, a new kind of auditory input is converted to a form that resembles the patients' stored representations. Observations of this kind are consistent with our present findings concerning visual input. J.W.'s left hemisphere maintains that he sees the objects presented to the right hemi-

sphere; because the evidence suggests that there is no actual sensory transfer, J.W.'s interpretive system appears to be constructing this reality from speech cues provided by the right hemisphere.

The left hemisphere's capacity for continual interpretation suggests that it is always looking for order and reason, even where there is none. Nowhere has this been more dramatically realized than in a recent study by George Wolford at Dartmouth College. In a simple test that requires one simply to guess if a light is going to appear on the top or bottom of a computer screen, we humans perform in an inventive way. The experiment manipulates the stimulus to appear on the top 80% of the time. Although it quickly becomes evident the top button is being illuminated more often, we keep trying to figure out the whole sequence and deeply believe we can. Yet by adopting this strategy we are rewarded only 68% of the time. If we simply always pressed the top button, we would be rewarded 80% of the time. Rats and other animals are more likely to "learn to maximize" and only press the top button. It turns out the right hemisphere behaves in the same way. It does not try to interpret its experience and find the deeper meaning but continues to live only in the thin moment of the present. And when the left is asked to explain why it is attempting to figure out the whole sequence, it always comes up with a theory, even though it is spurious.

SUMMARY AND CONCLUSIONS

There is a deep belief that we can attain not only a neuroscience of consciousness but a neuroscience of human consciousness. It is as if something terribly new and complex happens as the brain enlarges to its human form. Whatever this is, it triggers our capacity for self-reflection, for ennui, and for lingering moments,

I would like to propose a simple, three-step suggestion. First, we should focus on what we mean when we talk about conscious experience. It is merely the awareness we have of our capacities as a species, but not the capacities themselves—only the awareness or feelings we have about them. The brain is clearly not a general purpose computing device but is a collection of circuits devoted to quite specific capacities. This is true for all brains, but what is wonderful about the human brain is that we have untold numbers of these capacities. We have more than the chimp, which has more than the monkey, which has more than the cat, which runs circles around the rat. Because we have so many specialized systems and because they can frequently do things they were not designed to do, it appears our brains have a single, general computing device. But we do not. Thus, step 1 requires that we recognize we are a collection of adaptations and, furthermore, we recognize the distinction between a species' capacities and its feelings about those capacities. Now consider step 2.

Can there be any doubt that a rat at the moment of copulation is as sensorially fulfilled as a human? Of course it is. Do you think a cat does not enjoy a good piece of cod? Of course it does. Or, a monkey does not enjoy a spectacular swing? Again, it has to be true. Each species is aware of its special capacities. So, what is human consciousness? It is the very same awareness, save for the fact that we can be aware of so much more, so many wonderful things. A circuit—perhaps a single system or one duplicated over and over again—is associated with each brain capacity. The more systems a brain possesses, the greater the awareness of capacities.

Think of the variations in capacity within our own species; they are not unlike the vast differences between species. Years of split-brain research have informed us that the left hemisphere has many more mental capacities than the right one. The left is capable of logical feats that the right hemisphere cannot manage. Although the right has capacities such as facial recognition systems, it is a distant second with problem-solving skills. In short, the right hemisphere's level of awareness is limited. It knows precious little about a lot of things, but the limits to human capacity are everywhere in the population. No one

need be offended to realize that just as someone with normal intelligence can understand Ohm's law, others, like yours truly, are clueless about Kepler's laws. I am ignorant about them and will remain so. I am unable to be aware about what they mean for the universe. The circuits that enable me to understand these things are not present in my brain.

By emphasizing specialized circuits that arise from natural selection, we see that the brain is not a unified neural net that supports a general problem-solving device. With this being understood, we can concentrate on the possibility that smaller, more manageable circuits produce awareness of a species' capacities. Holding fast to the notion of a unified neural net means we can understand human conscious experience only by figuring out the interactions of billions of neurons. That task is hopeless. My scheme is not.

Hence step 3. The very same split-brain research that exposed shocking differences between the two hemispheres also showed that the human left hemisphere has the interpreter. The left brain interpreter's job is to interpret our behavior and our responses, whether cognitive or emotional, to environmental challenges. It constantly establishes a running narrative of our actions, emotions, thoughts, and dreams. It is the glue that keeps our story unified and creates our sense of being a unified, rational agent. It brings to our bag of individual instincts the illusion that we are something other than what we are. It builds our theories about our own life, and these narratives of our past behavior ooze into our awareness.

The problem of consciousness, then, is tractable. We do not have to find the code of one huge, interacting neural network. Instead, we must find the common and perhaps simple neural circuit(s) that allows vertebrates to be aware of their species-specific capacities, and the problem is solved. The same enabling circuit(s) in the rat is most likely present in the human brain, and understanding that basic point makes the problem scientifically tractable. What makes us so grand is that the basic circuit has so much more to work with in the human brain.

Finally it becomes clear. The insertion of an interpreter into an otherwise functioning brain delivers all kinds of by-products. A device that begins to ask how one thing relates to another, a device that asks about an infinite number of things, and a device that can get productive answers to those questions cannot help give birth to the concept of self. Surely one of the questions the device would ask is, who is solving these problems? Let us call that me, and away it goes! The device that has its rules for solving a problem of how one thing relates to another must be reinforced for such an action, just as solving where the evening meal is for an ant reinforces the ant's food-seeking devices.

Our brains are automatic because physical tissues perform what we do. How could it be any other way? That means they do it before our conceptual self knows about it. But the conceptual self grows and grows and reaches proportions that find the biologic fact of interest but not paralyzing. The interpretation of things past has liberated us from the sense of being tied to the demands of the environment and has produced the wonderful sensation that our self is in charge of our destiny. All of our everyday success at reasoning through life's data convinces us of our centrality. Because of that we can drive our automatic brains to greater accomplishment and enjoyment of life.

ACKNOWLEDGMENT

This work was supported by National Institutes of Health Grants NIND S 8 R01, NS22626-09, NINDS 5 PO1, and NS1778-014, and by the James S. McDonnell Foundation. Parts of this chapter have appeared in *The Cognitive Neurosciences,* ed. by M.S. Gazzaniga, MIT Press, Cambridge, MA.

REFERENCES

1. Gazzaniga MS. *Interpretations of things past.* Berkeley, CA: University of California Press, 1998.
2. Jerne N. Antibodies and learning: selection versus instruction. In: Quarton G, Melnechuck T, Schmidt FO, eds. *The neurosciences: a study program.* Vol. 1. Rockefeller University Press, 1967:200–205.
3. James W. *The principles of psychology.* Vol. I. New York: Dover, 1890.
4. Marler P. An ethological theory of the origin of vocal learning. *Ann N Y Acad Sci* 1976;280:386–395.
5. Kuhl PK. Learning and representation in speech and language. *Curr Opin Neurobiol* 1994;4:812–822.
6. Edelman GM. *Neural Darwinism: the theory of neuronal group selection.* New York: Basic Books, 1987.
7. Merzenich MM, Kaas JH, Wall JT, Nelson RJ, Sur M, Felleman DH. Topographic reorganization of somatosensory cortical areas 3b and 1 in adult monkeys following restricted deafferentation. *Neuroscience* 1983;10:33–55.
8. Merzenich MM, Schreiner C, Jenkins WM, Wang X. Neural mechanisms underlying temporal integration, segmentation, and input sequence representation: some implications for the origin of learning disabilities. *Ann N Y Acad Sci* 1993;682:1–22.
9. Platt (manuscript in preparation).
10. Shephar RN. *Mindsights.* San Francisco: WH Freeman, 1992.
11. Goodale MA, Milner AD. Separate visual pathways for perception and action. *Trends Neurosci* 1992;15:20–25.
12. Weiskrantz L. *Blindsight: a case study and implications.* Oxford, England: Oxford University Press, 1986.
13. Gazzaniga MS, Ledoux JE. *The integrated mind.* New York: Plenum, 1978.
14. Volpe BT, LeDoux JE, Gazzaniga MS. Information processing of visual stimuli in an extinguished field. *Nature* 1979;282:722–724.
15. Gazzaniga MS. Principles of human brain organization derived from split-brain studies. *Neuron* 1995;14:217–228.
16. Sidtis JJ, Volpe BT, Holtzman JD, Wilson DH, Gazzaniga MS. Cognitive interaction after staged callosal section: evidence for a transfer of semantic activation. *Science* 1981;212:344–346.
17. Holtzman JD, Sidtis JJ, Volpe BT, Wilson DH, Gazzaniga MS. Dissociation of spatial information for stimulus localization and the control of attention. *Brain* 1981;104:861–872.
18. Holtzman JD. Interactions between cortical and subcortical visual areas: evidence from human commissurotomy patients. *Vision Res* 1984;24:801–813.
19. Gazzaniga MS, Fendrich R, Wessinger, CM. Blindsight reconsidered. *Curr Directions Psychol Sci* 1994;3:93–96.
20. Gazzaniga MS, Fendrich R, Wessinger CM. Blindsight reconsidered. *Curr Directions Psychol Sci* 1994;3:93–96.
21. Wessinger CM, Fendrich R, Gazzaniga MS. Islands of residual vision in hemianopic patients. *J Cognitive Neurosci* 1997;9:203–221.
22. Wessinger CM, Fendrich R, Gazzaniga MS. Residual vision with awareness in the field contralateral to a partial or complete functional hemispherectomy. *Neuropsychologia* 1996;34;1129–1137.
23. Phelps EA, Gazzaniga MS. Hemispheric differences in mnemonic processing: the effects of left hemisphere interpretation. *Neuropsychologia* 1992;30:293–297.
24. Metcalfe J, Funnell M, Gazzaniga MS. Right hemisphere superiority: studies of a split-brain patient. *Psychol Sci* 1995;6:157–164.
25. Baynes K, Wessinger CM, Fendrich R, Gazzaniga MS. The emergence of the capacity of the disconnected right

hemisphere to control naming: implications for functional plasticity. *Neuropsychologia* 1995;33:1225–1242.

26. Gazzaniga MS, Eliassen JC, Nisenson L, Wessuger CM, Baynes KB. Collaboration between the hemispheres of a callosotomy patient—emerging right hemisphere speech and the left brain interpreter. *Brain* 1996;119: 1255–1262.

27. Schindler RA, Kessler DK. The UCSF/Storz cochlear implant: patient performance. *Am J Otol* 1987;8: 247–255.

DISCUSSION

Moderated by Alan J. McComas

Vincent F. Castellucci: In the case where you have multiple lexicons, is it possible to have some lexicons on the right and some on the left?

Michael S. Gazzaniga: Yes. In the split-brain literature, there are about six or seven of these patients, not out of the hundreds of split-brain patients, but out of the 60 or 70 that have been tested carefully. About 10% of them have a lexicon in the right hemisphere in addition to the left. It is different; it is organized differently and has different properties.

Vincent F. Castellucci: For the people that have the dominant brain on the right and have a complete inversion, are all properties that you described for the left brain found on the right?

Michael S. Gazzaniga: Largely yes, but there are so few cases that I am sure there are going to be variations. In fact, one case that we have studied with Dr. Kathy Baynes is a patient from California (case V.J.). The patient can speak out of her left hemisphere, cannot speak out of her right hemisphere, but can write out of her right hemisphere and not out of her left.

Jeffrey A. Gray: What happens when a split-brain patient tries to play a game with complex nonverbal skills, like tennis, or tries to ski or something like that?

Michael S. Gazzaniga: Years ago, one of the patients remained able to play the piano, which was some sort of measure that they are capable of doing bimanual tasks.

Jeffrey A. Gray: What happens if you try to challenge the two hemispheres separately, such as try to play the left hand bit or the right hand bit of the piano part. What you said was that the right hemisphere is devoid of all high-level complex function, whereas most of the things you have tested involve high-level verbally based complex functions. Well, what is happening in the right hemisphere if you have a complex nonverbal task?

Michael S. Gazzaniga: Well, for instance, the right hemisphere is very good at the apprehension of faces, of reading the aesthetic quality of faces. The left hemisphere is terrible at that. One could say that those are high-level things, but they are very specific.

Yves Joanette: Do split-brain patients have split minds and split consciousness, particularly in view of some phenomenon like diagonistic apraxia?

Michael S. Gazzaniga: What I was trying to say was that each hemisphere possesses, at the level that it is competent, an awareness of those capacities. When we first started reporting on these split-brain phenomena, it was so dramatic to see these functions go on outside of awareness of the left, we just dubbed it "doubly conscious." But when you really get into it and map out what mental representations are present, it would be impossible to confer the same level of "consciousness" to each side.

Benjamin Libet: Following on the last question a bit, do the split-brain patients show any evidence of loss of personal identity? That is, do they feel like they are split identities?

Michael S. Gazzaniga: Absolutely not. They feel just like you and me. You would think that the left brain would miss the right, but it does not. This goes along with, in the clinic if you have a disorder—we were discussing this yesterday at Dr. Lecours' talk—that produces a dysfunction, the cortex that is damaged is damaged, and therefore your awareness of the system, the behaving system, is not behaving correctly. If it is due to a cortical damage, you do not seem to be aware of the deficit. So, people can have huge lesions in their occipital lobes, and they are really not aware of the huge scotoma. Whereas if the lesion were in the optic track, they are immediately aware of the scotoma because the cortex is there getting ready to process the visual input. It is not getting any information and you become aware of the scotoma. So, it is as if each little zone or packet of capacity in the cortex has its own enabling circuits that allow for the conscious awareness of that sensory field or cognitive activity.

Benjamin Libet: I am not sure that I understood your answer to Jeffrey Gray. Are your split-brain patients able to play the piano properly with both hands?

Michael S. Gazzaniga: Well, I am being light about it because she plays the piano like I do. But we do not have a baseline to compare it to. It was just a little rote piano playing, but it was coordinated and bilaterally integrated.

Ante L. Padjen: Speaking of duality of left and right, I remember reading about a case in the 1980s about a boy whose brain was split around the age of 5.

Testing at 10 indicated that the hemispheres were able to verbally communicate and that these two hemispheres showed evidence of being two personalities. Now, one of the expected responses would be that my left brain fooled me, but would not that be a case of dual personality? I believe there was an additional finding that one side, the right side, was quite aggressive and often had been antagonistic to the surrounding, and in that case the left brain showed some hyperactivity and there was a whole story made out of this as a possible cause of hyperactivity. Did I remember that right?

Michael S. Gazzaniga: Yes, I wrote it. Sounds familiar, believe it or not! That was the case of P.S., who was operated on when he was 15. It was one of the cases that I mentioned that went on to develop right hemisphere speech. But it never was—at least not so far—seen that when you get right hemisphere speech, you do not get a chattering, dialogue-building system. You get a system that can utter a word, can say apple, instead of pointing to apple. You do not have a full bilateral system. What we did do with him was go in and see how he evaluated, put a valence on, a set of objects, people, foods that we knew he liked and did not like. On a day when he was agitated, behaviorally disruptive and agitated, we then went in and nonetheless carried out these valence analyses of each hemisphere. One hemisphere liked an apple, the other one hated it, one hemisphere liked a pizza, the other one hated it. It was just a total conflict of his evaluation of a common stimulus. You test on a day when everything is tranquil and he is at peace with himself and you give him another set of things, they would always match the evaluations of the stimulus. So, the notion was that yes you can have two evaluative systems putting different valences on the same stimulus and when that happens there is a conflict. And when that does not happen, you do not see the conflict behaviorally.

Ante L. Padjen: In this case, the right hemisphere knew something about the left one?

Michael S. Gazzaniga: Well, it knows because it is an emotive thing. The valence of an emotion, as I pointed out earlier, seems to remain communicable between the hemispheres. And yes, it does know that. It does not know what is driving it, but it knows that there is a different mood state, switching between one and the other.

John C. Fentress: When you talk about the phylogeny of consciousness as a layman would use the term, I get the feeling that there is a very strong social force, social contact, in the way we tend to use consciousness. Do you think consciousness could have evolved if we had lived as hermits, as independent creatures?

Michael S. Gazzaniga: There is a lot of thinking on that, and I do not know what I think about it! The notion is that we quickly evolved to work in groups because working in groups would protect us from predators so we could coordinate our defenses, coordinate our food-gathering efforts. So, we work best socially when we are interacting with others, and this interaction produces a state that is quite different from when you are home in your study at night when you are trying to put your day together. Those have got to be powerful forces, and the people that study this make observations about what the group size has to be before information starts to break down. For example, you should never manage more than 50 people. You get to 50 and the whole infrastructure of information flow in an office just crumbles, social relationships get funny, etc. So, it is like there is something in there and we have adapted to a set number of parameters. I think there is going to be something to that story, but I just do not have a feel for it other than reading about it at this point.

Consciousness: At the Frontiers of Neuroscience,
Advances in Neurology, Vol. 77,
edited by H.H. Jasper, L. Descarries,
V.F. Castellucci, and S. Rossignol.
Lippincott–Raven Publishers, Philadelphia © 1998.

13

Abnormal Contents of Consciousness: The Transition from Automatic to Controlled Processing

Jeffrey A. Gray

Department of Psychology, Institute of Psychiatry, London, England SE5 8AF, United Kingdom

I am among those who believe that there is a "hard question" of consciousness (1–4). Put in its most general form, this question arises because the following three statements all appear at present to be true. First, we already have in principle a well-articulated scientific understanding of how the brain gives rise to behavior, with only the details (difficult as they are bound to be) still to fill in. Second, we know as a matter of first-person, but widely agreed, fact that the transactions between brain and behavior involve conscious experiences or qualia (things like the sight and smell of a rose, the touch of velvet, the sound of a violin, the sound of a word spoken in the head, a mental image of a face, a feeling of sadness, etc.). Third, there is nothing in our scientific understanding of brain, behavior, or the connections between them that is related in any principled way to the occurrence of conscious experiences. The strongest relationships currently available between these disparate entities consist of "where" statements. Generally, they are of the following form: conscious experiences A, B, C . . . are mediated by brain structures or circuits X, Y, Z . . . (so-called brute correlations). But we have no answers to the much harder "how" question (what is it about these brain circuits that accomplishes the remarkable trick?) or

"why" question (what functional consequences of conscious experience contribute to Darwinian survival?). A true solution to the overall hard question of consciousness would provide answers to both the how and the why questions (2).

An important aspect of the why question, concerning the functional value of consciousness, lies in the fact that, for most purposes, conscious experiences occur too late to affect the behavior with which they are apparently connected. A dramatic example of this phenomenon comes from competition tennis. The speed of play in a Wimbledon final is so great, and the speed with which percepts enter consciousness so slow, that the response to a typical serve has to be completed before the player has consciously seen the ball come over the net (I owe this example to John McCrone). Although it is logically impossible that the whole of consciousness could be an illusion, it is certain that much about conscious experience is illusory. In the tennis example, there is an illusory experience that one consciously sees the ball and then hits it. What actually happens is that one hits the ball (based on a great deal of extremely rapid unconscious processing of visual information), consciously sees it, and then consciously experiences the hitting, thus preserving in con-

TABLE 1. *Conscious awareness is not necessary for:*

Analysis of sensory input
Analysis of speech input
Learning
Memory
Selection of response
Control of action
Production of speech output

Data from Velmans (5).

sciousness the temporal order of events that actually took place unconsciously. From the functional point of view, therefore, it remains mysterious what conscious seeing adds to the unconscious processing of visual information that is on its own sufficient to permit the extraordinarily high-precision performance seen in competition tennis. However, dramatic as the tennis example is, it is nonetheless but one of many. Velmans (5) has summarized evidence concerning a whole array of highly complex psychological processes that all appear to be (to a thoroughly counterintuitive degree) completely free of any on-line influence of conscious experience (Table 1).

In an effort to find something useful for consciousness to do, I recently (2) proposed the hypothesis that the contents of consciousness consist of the outputs of a comparator system (Fig. 1), which acts as a late error-de-

tection device, on a slower time base than that which subserves the fast on-line processing upon which most actual behavior is based. The function discharged by this system was proposed to be that of identifying motor programs as faulty, in the sense that they result in error, failure, or punishment, and of ensuring that they undergo modification for better future performance. This hypothesis, if correct, would get around the lateness problem and so allow consciousness the possibility of contributing to Darwinian survival (as in some way it must, since, having arisen in biologic systems, it must presumably have been subject to the same evolutionary processes and pressures as the rest of the biologic world). Note, however, that we would still be faced with a deeper version of the why question: because the brain is capable of doing so many complex and interesting things without making use of the consciousness trick, why could it not set up a late error-detection device in the same way? This deeper version of the why question needs to be—and so far has not been—answered in relation to any such proposal as to the function of consciousness.

I first proposed the comparator hypothesis in the context of a model of the neuropsychology of anxiety (6,7) which, however, at that time took no account of the conscious aspects of this emotion. Subsequently, my colleagues and I extended this model into a the-

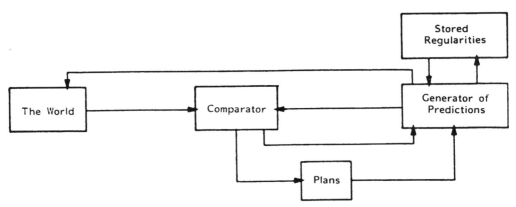

FIG. 1. The kinds of information processing required for the successful functioning of the hypothetical comparator.

ory of the neuropsychology of the positive symptoms of schizophrenia (8,9). Despite the fact that these symptoms consist almost entirely of aberrations of conscious experience, we still did not explicitly tackle the relationship of such experiences to the rest of the model, following in this respect the policy of benign neglect that is currently normal scientific practice (10). Here, however, I revisit the theory of schizophrenia to see whether the proposed link between the outputs of the comparator and the contents of consciousness (2) can throw useful light on the special features of conscious experience that form part of this condition.

THE NEUROPSYCHOLOGY OF SCHIZOPHRENIA

The theory of the neuropsychology of schizophrenia that guides our current research in this field was developed in collaboration with groups in Tel Aviv and Oxford (8,9,11). The theory is intended to span the complete range of explanation from a malfunction in the brain to the psychological symptoms of the condition, although it is limited to positive symptoms (12) (Table 2). It can be regarded as integrating four levels of description (Fig. 2). (a) A structural abnormality in the brain (Fig. 3) (specifically in the limbic forebrain, affecting the hippocampal formation, amygdala, and temporal and frontal neocortex), gives rise to (b) a functional neurochemical abnormality in the brain (specifically, hyperactivity of transmission in the ascending mesolimbic dopaminergic pathway). (c) This, in turn, disrupts a cognitive process (specifically, the integration of past regularities of experience with current stimulus recognition,

TABLE 2. *Positive psychotic symptoms*

Auditory hallucinations
Delusional beliefs
Enhanced sensory awareness
Overattention
Visual illusions
Racing thoughts

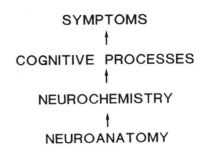

FIG. 2. An integrative theory (8) of positive schizophrenic symptoms (*top*), seen as arising from a structural abnormality in the brain (*bottom*), which gives rise to a functional neurochemical abnormality, and hence abnormality in cognitive processing.

learning, and action), and so produces (d) the positive symptoms characteristic of acute psychosis.

At the first, neuroanatomic, level, the theory draws on evidence (8) from the postmortem schizophrenic brain that shows pathology in the limbic forebrain. At the second, neurochemical, level, it draws on evidence from drugs with psychotomimetic or antipsychotic properties, indicating a relationship between dopaminergic transmission and the positive symptoms of schizophrenia. The third and fourth levels, linking symptoms to underlying cognitive processes, rests on Hemsley's hypothesis (13–15) and supporting arguments that positive psychotic symptoms derive from an impairment in the ability to use stored, past regularities of experience to aid in the interpretation of elements in current information processing. Integration across these levels of the theory is obtained by a proposed correspondence (Fig. 4) between: (a) the stored regularities and current information processing of Hemsley's hypothesis (Fig. 4A); (b) the links (Fig. 4B and C) between the subicular area (origin of the major output from the hippocampal formation) and the nucleus accumbens, a major gateway to the basal ganglia and recipient of a dopaminergic projection that ascends (in the mesolimbic pathway) from nucleus A 10 in the ventral tegmental area; and (c) inputs from a com-

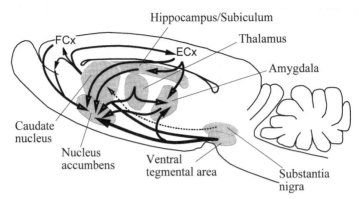

FIG. 3. Schematic representation of the ascending dopaminergic projections from nucleus A 10 in the ventral tegmental area to the nucleus accumbens, amygdala, frontal (FCx) and entorhinal (ECx) cortex, together with the descending glutamatergic projections from the subiculum (carrying hippo-campal output), FCx, ECx, and the thalamus to the nucleus accumbens. Also shown (*dotted arrow*) is the ascending dopaminergic projection from the substantia nigra to the caudate nucleus (courtesy of Dr. A. Young).

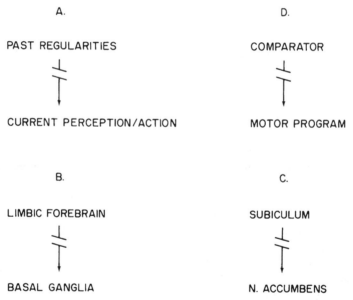

FIG. 4. A further illustration of the theory of schizophrenia proposed by Gray et al. (8). **A:** The abnormality of cognitive processing consists of a failure to integrate past regularities of experience with the current control of perception and action. **B:** This reflects a dysfunctional connection between the limbic forebrain and the basal ganglia. **C:** The specific pathway carrying the dysfunctional connection is from the subiculum (in the limbic forebrain) to the nucleus accumbens (in the basal ganglia). **D:** The computing functions thus disrupted are the passage of information from a comparator system using stored traces of past regularities (limbic forebrain) to a motor programming system (located in the basal ganglia) controlling perception and action.

parator system (6) to a motor programming system (Fig. 4D).

The proposed correspondence relies on several assumptions. First, the limbic forebrain uses stored regularites of previous input to compute a prediction as to the next state of the perceptual world, given the subject's current motor program; to this end, time is divided into quanta of approximately 0.1 second, as discussed further below. Second, the limbic forebrain compares this prediction to the actual state of the world in the following time quantum. Third, the outcome of this matching operation is transmitted via the projection from the subiculum to the nucleus accumbens. Fourth, this nucleus forms part of a motor programming system in the basal ganglia (8,16); the motor programming system uses a match message from the subiculum to continue the current motor program and a mismatch message ("something novel/unexpected has occurred") to interrupt it. Fifth, schizophrenia entails a disruption of the normal input from the subiculum to the nucleus accumbens, leading, neurochemically, to a functional imbalance equivalent to hyperactivity in the mesolimbic dopaminergic pathway and, psychologically, to an overoccurrence of apparently novel events. Sixth and finally, these apparently novel events give rise to positive psychotic symptoms, as considered in detail by Hemsley (13–15) and reconsidered below.

EXPERIMENTS ON LATENT INHIBITION

This model of schizophrenia has been subjected to intensive experimental (11,17,18) and theoretical (19) investigation in recent years. Much of the relevant evidence has been gathered in studies of the phenomenon of latent inhibition (LI). If a stimulus is repeatedly presented without other consequence (preexposure) and is subsequently used as the conditioned stimulus (CS) in a standard Pavlovian conditioning paradigm, the preexposed CS develops a weaker association with the unconditioned stimulus (US), as measured by

the strength of the ensuing conditioned response (CR), than does a nonpreexposed CS. This difference between the CRs evoked by preexposed and nonpreexposed CS, respectively, constitutes LI (20).

LI has been demonstrated in many species, including humans (21). The experiments from our own laboratory have used both rats and human subjects. In the former case, we typically assess LI using an off-the-baseline conditioned emotional response procedure in animals licking for water (22). In this procedure, after initial baseline training to lick in animals on restricted water, CS preexposure and CS-footshock pairings are both conducted without access to water, and the CS is then presented to the rat while it is again licking; CR magnitude is measured by the degree of lick suppression during the CS. LI consists of lower supression of licking in response to the CS in the preexposed as compared with the nonpreexposed animals. With human subjects, our usual procedure is based on that of Ginton et al. (23). Subjects first listen to a tape recording of nonsense syllables, with instructions to count the number of times one of them recurs. In the preexposed condition, bursts of low-intensity white noise (the CS) are randomly superimposed on the recording. Subsequently, still listening to the tape recording, subjects are asked to predict when a counterdisplay will be incremented; increments (the US) are preceded for all subjects by the white noise CS, and the number of trials taken to detect this contingency is the measure of conditioning. LI is shown as a larger number of trials to criterion in the preexposed than in the nonpreexposed condition.

The relevance to schizophrenia of LI (or, more exactly, of disruption of LI) lies in its resemblance to the deficit in the ability to ignore irrelevant stimuli that has been extensively documented in schizophrenia (13). This resemblance was initially pointed out by groups in Massachusetts (24) and Tel Aviv (25,26). These groups both reported that LI is attenuated or abolished in the rat by systemic administration of the indirect dopamine (DA) agonist, amphetamine. This effect has since been extensively replicated both with amphetamine and other indirect DA agonists; and it is reversed by concomitant treatment with DA receptor antagonists (17). Neurochemically, the relevance to schizophrenia of these observations derives from the fact that indirect DA agonists, including amphetamine (27), have psychotomimetic effects, whereas DA receptor antagonists are used therapeutically as antipsychotics (16,27). Furthermore, the effects of both the psychotomimetic and antipsychotic drugs are exerted specifically on the positive (Table 2), not the negative, symptoms of schizophrenia. Psychologically, the relevance of these observations derives from the fact that at least some positive psychotic symptoms (12) can be regarded as reflecting a diminished tendency to screen out redundant stimuli from processing (28,29); this description also seems to apply well to an amphetamine-treated rat learning about a CS despite preexposure, which in a (placebo-treated) control rat leads to its relative disregard. Within Hemsley's (13) framework, LI can be treated as a case in which the initial regularity, *to-be-CS leading to no consequence,* is followed by the requirement to learn a conflicting regularity, which in our standard conditioned suppression paradigm with rats is *CS–shock* or, in our human paradigm (30–32), *CS–counter increment.* In the absence of pathology or drug treatment, this sequence of conflicting regularities normally leads to retarded learning of the CS–US association (i.e., to LI). In animals that fail to show LI or show reduced LI (e.g., after amphetamine treatment), the influence of the past regularity is diminished, and they are controlled by the most recent (i.e., the CS–US) regularity.

Recent studies using these and related paradigms have demonstrated several findings that are relevant to the argument pursued in the remainder of this paper. First, in human subjects, as in rats, amphetamine abolishes LI; that is, this drug prevents preexposure from having its usual adverse effect upon subsequent learning about the CS (32,33). Second, in unmedicated schizophrenic patients (34) or patients in the

first 2 weeks of medication (30,31), LI is absent, due to fast learning in the preexposed condition relative even to normal controls. Third, DA is released in the nucleus accumbens by a novel CS but not if the CS has first been preexposed (35). Fourth, abolition of LI by indirect DA agonists such as amphetamine has been clearly related to release of DA specifically in the nucleus accumbens, whereas blockade of DA transmission in this nucleus has the converse effect, potentiating LI (17, 18). Fifth, both increases and decreases in DA transmission within the nucleus accumbens exert their effects on LI at the time of conditioning (i.e., formation of the CS–US association), not at the time of CS preexposure or at the time of testing for the presence of the conditioned response (17,18). Sixth, LI is abolished by lesions of the hippocampal formation and entorhinal cortex (regions that show pathology in the schizophrenic brain) and by disconnection of these structures from the nucleus accumbens; because these effects are reversed by systemic administration of DA receptor antagonists, it is likely that the lesions result (as predicted by the model) in (the equivalent of) dopaminergic hyperactivity in the nucleus accumbens (17).

THE TRANSITION FROM AUTOMATIC TO CONTROLLED PROCESSING

Taken together, these results support a model (8,9,11) in which positive schizophrenic symptoms result from heightened dopaminergic transmission in the nucleus accumbens, probably as a secondary consequence of structural damage in the temporal lobe, especially in the hippocampal formation and those parts of the temporal neocortex that are closely related to the hippocampal formation. Furthermore, because so many of the critical results have been obtained in experiments on LI, they allow a fairly detailed transference of inferences from the neurophysiologic basis of this phenomenon to the symptomatology of schizophrenia, especially to the positive symptoms of this condition.

Because these symptoms consist essentially of aberrations of conscious experience (Table 2), it is possible that the inferences so made also will be applicable to an understanding of the basis in brain function of at least certain aspects of such experiences. Accordingly, the last part of this chapter is devoted to the attempt to draw out these inferences.

The nucleus accumbens is usually regarded as a key interface between the limbic system and the motor programming circuits of the basal ganglia (16,36), an assumption that is almost certainly correct. However, blockade of LI, e.g., by release of DA in the nucleus accumbens as a result of amphetamine administration (17,18), suggests rather a change in sensory processing, one that allows a stimulus that would otherwise by ignored to reenter current information processing. The symptoms of schizophrenia that Gray et al. (8,9) attempted to relate to blockade of LI similarly suggest changes in perceptual experience rather than motor programming. However, a solution to this problem recently has become apparent from work in Grace's laboratory.

Lavin and Grace (37) have studied what happens to the outputs from the nucleus accumbens farther downstream. Using electrophysiologic and tract-tracing techniques, these workers demonstrated that the inhibitory gamma-aminobutyric acid (GABA)-ergic output from the nucleus accumbens projects, in the ventral pallidum, upon further GABA-ergic inhibitory neurons that project to the nucleus reticularis thalami (NRT). The NRT is unusual among thalamic nuclei in that it consists mainly of inhibitory GABA-ergic neurons; these project to a number of the surrounding thalamic nuclei, whose job is to relay impulses originating in peripheral sense organs to the appropriate sensory regions of the cerebral cortex (38). The possible role of the NRT in the selection of stimuli for attention and conscious processing was first pointed out by Crick (39) and has been incorporated into a neural network model by Taylor and Alavi (40). Because the pallidal output to these neurons is itself inhibitory, its activation

has the effect of disinhibiting these sensory relay pathways, i.e., increasing the entry to the cerebral cortex of those stimuli that are currently engaging the thalamocortical sensory processing loops. Figure 5 presents this circuitry in diagrammatic form.

Let us consider how the circuitry of Fig. 5 would be likely to work under the conditions of an experiment in which an indirect DA agonist is used to block LI by causing DA release in the nucleus accumbens. As we know, the basic phenomenon of LI consists in the fact that a preexposed CS is slow to enter into an association with a Pavlovian US. One way to interpret this (2,41) is as reflecting a lack of access to conscious processing by the preexposed CS. However, if presentation of this CS is accompanied by enhanced DA release in the nucleus accumbens (as induced pharmacologically or during acute psychosis), LI is overcome, indicating that the preexposed CS has regained the capacity to engage conscious processing. The circuitry of Fig. 5 constitutes a mechanism by which this effect can be produced. DA release within the nucleus accumbens inhibits, by acting on DA D2 receptors (42), the GABA-ergic pathway to the ventral pallidum, thus disinhibiting the pallidal GABA-ergic pathway to NRT, which in turn inhibits the GABA-ergic projections from NRT to the ascending thalamocortical sensory relay projections, so disinhibiting the latter. In this way, accumbal DA release should lead to an intensification of processing in whichever thalamocortical sensory relay projections were already operative in the prior instant of time (as defined by the basic comparator circuitry briefly outlined above) (6,8). In the LI experiment, this intensification of sensory processing will allow the preexposed CS (which otherwise would not have been fully processed) to enter more readily into association with the US.

Let us now consider in greater detail the specific hypothesis I have proposed (2,41) as to the neuropsychology of the contents of consciousness. According to this hypothesis, these consist of the successive outputs of the

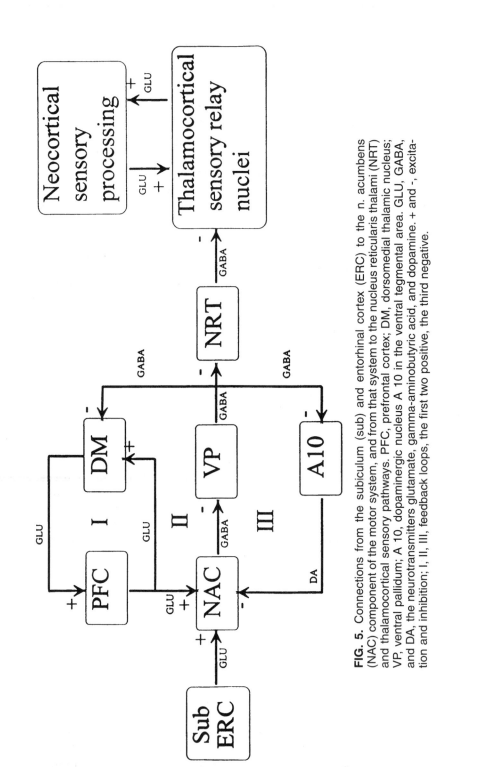

FIG. 5. Connections from the subiculum (sub) and entorhinal cortex (ERC) to the n. acumbens (NAC) componcont of the motor system, and from that system to the nucleus reticularis thalami (NRT) and thalamocortical sensory pathways. PFC, prefrontal cortex; DM, dorsomedial thalamic nucleus; VP, ventral pallidum; A 10, dopaminergic nucleus A 10 in the ventral tegmental area. GLU, GABA, and DA, the neurotransmitters glutamate, gamma-aminobutyric acid, and dopamine. + and -, excitation and inhibition; I, II, III, feedback loops, the first two positive, the third negative.

limbic comparator system (6,7) (Figs. 1 and 6), tagged according to the degree to which the different elements making up these outputs are variously expected (i.e., predicted by the comparator circuitry) or unexpected. In neural terms, it is proposed that the outputs of the comparator system are determined by its feedback to the cortical sensory systems whose inputs to the comparator system have just (i.e., in the preceding instant, with a duration of approximately 100 milliseconds) entered into the process of comparison. Applying the hypothesis to schizophrenia, we are able to make contact—but in a more fully specified and testable manner—with an older tradition (28,43,44) in understanding this disorder. According to this tradition, schizo-

phrenic symptoms reflect, using Schneider and Shiffrin's (45) widely accepted terminology, a failure in automatic processing, with a consequent breaking into conscious processing of material that would not normally figure there (9). In terms of the model outlined here, this transition to conscious processing would, in neural terms, be due to abnormalities in the functioning of the limbic–basal ganglia interface constituted by the projection from the hippocampal formation and retrohippocampal region (i.e., entorhinal cortex plus subicular area) to the nucleus accumbens. The consequent overactivity in the dopaminergic projection to the nucleus accumbens (whether direct, or due to imbalance between this input and that from the hip-

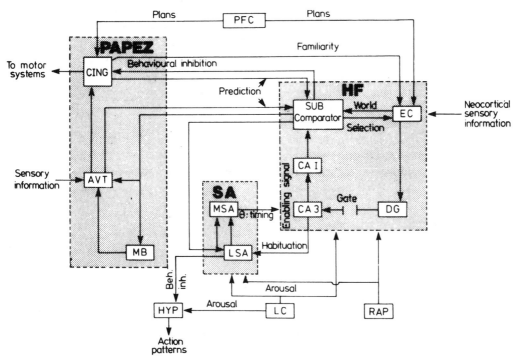

FIG. 6. A summary of the theory developed by Gray (6). The three major building blocks are shown in heavy print. The hippocampal formation (HF) is made up of the entorhinal cortex (EC), the dentate gyrus (DG), CA 3, CA 1, the subicular area (SUB), and the septal area (SA), containing the medial septal area (MSA) and the lateral septal area (LSA), as well as the Papez circuit, which receives projections from and returns them to the subicular area via the mammilliary bodies (MB), anteroventral thalamus (AVT), and cingulate cortex (CING). Other structures shown are the hypothalamus (HYP), the locus coeruleus, the raphe nuclei (RAP), and the prefrontal cortex (PFC). Arrows show the direction of projection; the projection from SUB to MSA lacks anatomic confirmation. Words in lower case show postulated functions. beh. inh., behavioral inhibition.

pocampal system) would then, via the NRT and the thalamocortical sensory relays (Fig. 5), boost back into conscious processing parts of the perceptual world that would otherwise receive only automatic processing.

It is instructive to consider the temporal parameters that may govern this circuitry. The comparator hypothesis of the contents of consciousness (2) may be understood as offering a solution to the binding problem: that is, it proposes a way in which perceptual features represented by widely distributed populations of neurons may be synchronously activated (namely, by feedback from the comparator to the cortical regions that have just provided it with input) so as to form a single coherent conscious scene. Most other physiologically based discussions of the binding problem (39,46,47) ignore the problem posed by the lateness of conscious experience. Instead, they focus on the construction of a neuronal gestalt in the immediate period (approximately the first 100 to 200 milliseconds; let this be *t1*) after sense organs first receive stimuli from the environment. But in this period, as is well documented (5), the brain is capable of a high degree of perceptual analysis, extraction of meaning, cognitive processing, and organization of action, all of which remain entirely unconscious, at least by all normal tests. For this initial solution to the binding problem then to lead to the conscious experience of a complex, multimodally specified, coherent scene of some kind, something further has to happen (in approximately the next 100 to 200 milliseconds; *t2*), for it takes a period of about *t1 + t2* after the onset of initial stimulation for the appropriate experience to enter consciousness (5).

Putting these temporal considerations together with the circuitry of Fig. 5, we may suppose that there are two passes through the thalamocortical system on which the formation of a perceptual description of the world depends. The first pass solves the initial binding problem but leaves the solution at an unconscious level (although one still eminently capable of providing highly processed guidance for the next step in a complex and fast-moving on-

line action program, as in the tennis example considered above). Only at a second pass, when the outcome of that step in the program is compared with the expected outcome, predicted by reference to memory stores of previous regularities of past experience as described by Gray and colleagues (6,8,9), does consciousness come into play. As described above, a critical role is played in the initiation of this second pass by the pathway that links the output from the hippocampal formation (via the subiculum; Figs. 5 and 6) to the nucleus accumbens and its dopaminergic afferents from nucleus A 10 in the ventral tegmental area (Fig. 3). What enters consciousness at the second pass is a mixture of elements that are surprising (i.e., mismatched within the comparator system) and not surprising, but with priority given to the former. *Ex hypothesi,* stimuli are more easily tagged as surprising in the state of acute, positively symptomatic schizophrenia (due to dopaminergic overactivity, whether direct or indirect), so leading to an excess of conscious, controlled processing relative to normal individuals.

This analysis of the way in which the circuitry of Fig. 5 would be expected to function when a supranormal pulse of DA is injected into it via the nucleus accumbens needs to be understood in the context of its likely continuing activity under more normal conditions. A striking feature of this circuitry is the imbalance between the lengths of, on the one hand, the accumbens output to the thalamocortical sensory loops (comprising three successive inhibitory steps) and, on the other hand, the dorsomedial thalamic–prefrontal motor loop (comprising two such steps). This imbalance has the consequence that, assuming that these pathways are activated either by the same initial output from the nucleus accumbens to the ventral pallidum or by two such outputs simultaneously, the one set of thalamocortical loops will always be excited when the other is inhibited. This arrangement seems ideally suited to produce a rapid oscillation between (a) the taking in of information from the environment and (b) the organization of a step in a motor program (8,9). Given other considerations as to the time-scale of events in these loops (2,6–9), we may suppose that these oscillations between sensory-dominant and motor-dominant processing occur every 50 milliseconds or so. Figure 5 suggests furthermore that, in agreement with a hypothesis proposed by Weiner (48), the switch between the one and the other form of processing is controlled by the feedback loop from the ventral pallidum via A 10 back to the nucleus accumbens. When the inhibitory step from the nucleus accumbens to the ventral pallidum is operated (leading to sensory-dominated processing), this simultaneously disinhibits the ventral pallidal input to A 10 and so inhibits the pathway from A 10 to the nucleus accumbens. In this way, accumbens inhibition of the ventral pallidum would be reinstated, switching dominance back to the thalamic–prefrontal loop.

It is assumed in this account that conscious experience is linked to processing in the sensory but not the motor component of these linked loops, together with widespread activity in the overall comparator system and its associated cortical input and feedback regions, as described by Gray (2,41). This assumption is motivated by the fact that one is conscious only of the goals and consequences of motor programs, not of the running of the motor program itself (2). However, interpreted in this way without further gloss, this understanding of the circuitry of Fig. 5 would seem to predict that conscious experience would be interrupted by recurrent periods of 50-millisecond blanks in every 100 milliseconds, and this is clearly not the case. Therefore, we also must suppose that, once the sensory processing that fills conscious experience is initiated in the thalamocortical sensory loops, it continues until it is replaced, approximately every 100 milliseconds, by a new set of selected elements. Many of these will presumably be the same as elements in the previous set, so resulting in an apparently seamless stream of consciousness. This smoothing process also is likely to be aided by the ability of the comparator system to engage in predictive extrapolation in time (49)—so to some extent

compensating for the lagging of conscious experience behind behavior—as well as space (50).

APPLYING THE MODEL TO SYMPTOMS

I doubt that, even in the heyday of radical behaviorism, anyone has ever proposed that the strange subjective experiences so characteristic of schizophrenia can be dismissed as mere oddities of verbal behavior. Freedman (51) has distilled a summary of some of these experiences from about 60 autobiographic accounts written by schizophrenics during or after their psychotic episodes. They include feelings of enhanced sensory awareness, visual illusions, changes in depth perception, racing thoughts each with an increased range of associations, loss of meaning of words or objects, difficulty in focusing attention and concentrating, not to mention the classic symptoms of auditory hallucinations and delusional beliefs.

The framework developed here offers a reasonably plausible explanation for at least some of these symptoms. Enhanced sensory awareness is one such: a failure of the comparator system to correctly indicate that an event in the perceptual world is familiar/expected should lead directly to enhanced sensory awareness of that event, just as the occurrence of a genuinely novel event does for normal individuals. Apparently more basic changes in perceptual experience, as in visual illusions or changes in depth perception, fit less readily with the model. One possibility, however, is that specification of the contents of consciousness depends on the process of differentiation of figure from ground; disturbance in this process would be expected to give rise to a range of abnormal perceptual experiences. In line with this possibility, a role for the hippocampus (a key structure in the proposed comparator circuitry) in linking events to their context (especially the spatial context) often has been suggested (6); Gaffan (52) recently presented evidence that, in monkeys, the hippocampal system is essential for the analysis of visually perceived scenes, i.e, objects presented against complex backgrounds.

An increase in the range of associations also falls out naturally from the model. LI, precisely, is a process by which redundant stimuli are normally prevented from entering into associations. A second process that appears to have the same effect is Kamin's (53) blocking effect. This phenomenon is demonstrated in a Pavlovian conditioning paradigm in which a CS1–US association is first set up, and then compound conditioning trials are conducted in which CS1 and CS2 are jointly presented and followed by the US. This procedure blocks the development of the CR that would occur if CS2 were paired with the US on its own. Like LI, the Kamin blocking effect appears to work to limit the formation of associations to those environmental relationships that are of greatest importance (54); if an event, the US, is already fully predicted by CS1, then the additional CS2 adds nothing to the subject's capacity to prepare appropriate behavior. Also like LI (although the data base is much less extensive), the Kamin blocking effect depends on the integrity of the hippocampal system and normal dopaminergic transmission (8), and it is absent in acute, but not chronic, medicated schizophrenics, thus showing a similar time course to that of LI (55). Disruption of LI and/or Kamin blocking would have the effect that, in accounting for the occurrence of a significant event (a US), a schizophrenic would be likely to attribute causal efficacy to stimuli that normal individuals would ignore, either because these were familiar and had previously occurred without being followed by the significant event, or because the significant event was already predicted by other, existing associations. These abnormalities of stimulus processing could clearly give rise to delusional beliefs concerning the importance in the causal structure of the environment of what are in fact trivial events.

A further process of potential importance is that of sensory preconditioning. In experiments using intracerebral microdialysis, we (56) have recently shown that sensory preconditioning (in which a Pavlovian association is formed between two biologically neutral stimuli, such as a tone and a light) is accompanied by increased DA release in the nucleus accumbens. Therefore, it is possible that excess accumbens DA release would increase the range over which the phenomenon of sensory preconditioning would come into play. Thus, if I have an existing association between the smell of roses and the color red, and come to form an association between the color red and stopping at traffic lights, might I then interpret the smell of roses as indicating that I should slam on the brakes? This is a dramatic (albeit fictitious) example of the kind of "clang" associations that are well known in schizophrenic speech. Given this possibility, it may be productive to study sensory preconditioning in schizophrenia.

As indicated in our first description of the model of schizophrenia (8), an account of auditory hallucinations requires a slight elaboration of the model. This elaboration is based on Frith's (57) suggestion that such hallucinations arise because of a failure to distinguish between stimulus and willed intentions, i.e., between behavior that is instigated directly by environmental input and behavior that arises from an internal motor program. In consequence, internal speech that is in fact part of an internal motor program is not recognized by the schizophrenic as such but is treated as alien. Frith further suggests that failure in recognizing willed intentions is due to a disruption in the efferent copy of the motor program that would normally be sent from the frontal cortex to limbic structures. This hypothesis fits naturally with the general comparator model proposed by Gray et al. (8,9) because this treats the projection from the frontal cortex via entorhinal cortex to the hippocampal system as conveying information about current steps in the motor program (Fig. 6), which the comparator then uses to compute the next predicted state of the perceptual world.

CONCLUSION

The comparator hypothesis was first proposed in the context of a theory of the neuropsychology of anxiety (6) and then extended to a treatment of the positive symptoms of schizophrenia (8). Although these conditions both involve phenomena that are clearly of a subjective nature, there was initially no attempt to use the comparator hypothesis to account directly for these phenomena. Only subsequently (2) was the hypothesis used to generate a possible account of a range of features of the contents of consciousness, motivated by considerations that were almost entirely independent of the origins of the comparator hypothesis in these earlier treatments of psychopathology. This chapter represents a first attempt to combine these different uses of the comparator hypothesis into a unified account. It has sought to show how the subjective phenomena of schizophrenia can perhaps be understood in terms of the brain machinery that determines the events selected to form the contents of consciousness. I hope that the arguments advanced have succeeded in throwing some light on the neuropsychology of the contents of consciousness or the nature of schizophrenic symptoms. I have little hope, however, that they are likely to contribute to the solution of the "hard question" (1–4) of consciousness.

ACKNOWLEDGMENT

I am grateful to many of my colleagues who have contributed much to the ideas in this chapter, especially David Hemsley, Nestor Schmajuk, Michael Joseph, and Andrew Young. Most of the empirical data on which the neuropsychological concepts are based was gathered in research supported by the Wellcome Trust, Grants 036927/Z/92/Z and 042038/Z/94/Z, and the European Comission, Contract CI/*CT93-0005.

REFERENCES

1. Gray JA. The mind-brain identity theory as a scientific hypothesis. *Philos Q* 1971;21:247–253.
2. Gray JA. The contents of consciousness: a neuropsychological conjecture. *Behav Brain Sci* 1995;18:659–722.
3. Chalmers DJ. Facing up to the problem of consciousness. *J Consciousness Studies* 1995;2:200–219.
4. Chalmers DJ. *The conscious mind.* New York: Oxford University Press, 1996.
5. Velmans M. Is human information processing conscious? *Behav Brain Sci* 1991;14:651–726.
6. Gray JA. *The neuropsychology of anxiety: an investigation into the functions of the septohippocampal system.* Oxford, England: Oxford University Press, 1982.
7. Gray JA, McNaughton N. The neuropsychology of anxiety: reprise. In: Hope DA, ed. *Perspectives on anxiety, panic and fear.* Vol. 43. Nebraska Symposium on Motivation. Lincoln, NE: University of Nebraska Press, 1996:61–134.
8. Gray JA, Feldon J, Rawlins JNP, Hemsley DR, Smith AD. The neuropsychology of anxiety. *Behav Brain Sci* 1991;14:1–20.
9. Gray JA, Hemsley DR, Feldon J, Gray NS, Rawlins JNP. Schiz bits: misses, mysteries and hits. *Behav Brain Sci* 1991;14:56–84.
10. Gray JA. Consciousness, schizophrenia and scientific theory. In: Marsh J, Bock G, eds. *Experimental and theoretical studies of consciousness.* Ciba Foundation Symposium 174. Chichester, England: Wiley, 1993:263–281.
11. Weiner I. Neural substrates of latent inhibition: the switching model. *Psychol Bull* 1990;108:442–461.
12. Crow TJ. Positive and negative schizophrenic symptoms and the role of dopamine. *Br J Psychiatry* 1980;137:383–386.
13. Hemsley DR. An experimental psychological model for schizophrenia. In: Hafner H, Fattaz WF, Janzavik W, eds. *Search for the causes of schizophrenia.* Stuttgart, Germany: Springer-Verlag, 1987.
14. Hemsley DR. A simple (or simplistic?) cognitive model for schizophrenia. *Behav Res Ther* 1993;31:633–645.
15. Hemsley DR. Cognitive disturbance as the link between schizophrenic symptoms and their biological bases. *Neurol Psychiatry Brain Res* 1994;2:163–170.
16. Swerdlow NR, Koob GF. Dopamine, schizophrenia, mania and depression: toward a unified hypothesis of cortico-striato-pallido-thalamic function. *Behav Brain Res* 1987;10:215–217.
17. Gray JA, Joseph MH, Hemsley DR, et al. The role of mesolimbic dopaminergic and retrohippocampal afferents to the nucleus accumbens in latent inhibition: implications for schizophrenia. *Behav Brain Res* 1995;71:19–31.
18. Gray JA, Moran PM, Grigoryan GA, Peters SL, Young AMJ, Joseph MH. Latent inhibition: the nucleus accumbens connection revisited. *Behav Brain Res* 88:27–34.
19. Schmajuk NA, Lam Y-W, Gray JA. Latent inhibition: a neural network approach. *J Exp Psychol* 1996;22:321–349.
20. Lubow RE, Moore AU. Latent inhibition: the effect of non-reinforced preexposure to the conditioned stimulus. *J Comp Psychol* 1959;52:415–419.
21. Lubow RE. *Latent inhibition and conditioned attention theory.* Cambridge, England: Cambridge University Press, 1989.
22. Feldon J, Weiner I. An animal model of attention deficit. In: Boulton AA, Baker GB, Martin-Iverson MT, eds. *Neuromethods.* Vol. 18. Animal models of psychiatry, Clifton, NJ: One Humana Press Inc, 1991:313–361.
23. Ginton A, Urca G, Lubow RE. The effects of preexposure to a non-attended stimulus on subsequent learning:

latent inhibition in adults. *Bull Psychonom Soc* 1975;5: 5–8.

24. Solomon PR, Crider A, Winkelman JW, Turi A, Kamer RM, Kaplan LJ. Disrupted latent inhibition in the rat with chronic amphetamine or haloperidol-induced supersensitivity: relationship to schizophrenic attention disorder. *Biol Psychiatry* 1981;16:519–537.

25. Weiner I, Lubow RE, Feldon J. Chronic amphetamine and latent inhibition. *Behav Brain Res* 1981;2:285–286.

26. Weiner I, Lubow RE, Feldon, J. Abolition of the expression but not the acquisition of latent inhibition by chronic amphetamine in rats. *Psychopharmacology* 1984;83:194–199.

27. Meltzer HY, Stahl, SM. The dopamine hypothesis of schizophrenia: a review. *Schiz Bull* 1976;2:19–76.

28. Frith CD. Consciousness, information processing and schizophrenia. *Br J Psychiatry* 1979;134:225–235.

29. Anscombe F. The disorder of consciousness in schizophrenia. *Schiz Bull* 1987;13:241–260.

30. Baruch I, Hemsley DR, Gray JA. Differential performance of acute and chronic schizophrenics in a latent inhibition task. *J Nerv Mental Dis* 1988;176:598–606.

31. Gray NS, Hemsley DR, Gray JA. Abolition of latent inhibition in acute, but not chronic, schizophrenics. *Neurol Psychiatry Brain Res* 1992;1:83–89.

32. Gray NS, Pickering AD, Hemsley DR, Dawling S, Gray JA. Abolition of latent inhibition by a single 5 mg dose of *d*-amphetamine in man. *Psychopharmacology* 1992; 107:425–430.

33. Thornton JC, Dawe S, Lee C, Frangou S, Gray NS, Russell MAH, Gray JA. Effects of nicotine and amphetamine on latent inhibition in human subjects. *Psychopharmacology* 1996;127:164–173.

34. Gray NS, Pilowsky LS, Gray JA, Kerwin RW. Latent inhibition in drug naive schizophrenics: relationship to duration of illness and dopamine D$_2$ binding using SPET. *Schiz Res* 1995;17:95–107.

35. Young AMJ, Joseph MH, Gray JA. Latent inhibition of conditioned dopamine release in rat nucleus accumbens. *Neuroscience* 1993;54:5–9.

36. Mogenson GJ, Nielsen M. A study of the contribution of the hippocampal-accumbens-subpallidal projections to locomotor activity. *Behav Neural Biol* 1984;42:52–60.

37. Lavin A, Grace AA. Modulation of dorsal thalamic cell activity by the ventral pallidum: its role in the regulation of thalamocortical activity by the basal ganglia. *Synapse* 1994;18:104–127.

38. Jones EG. Some aspects of the organisation of the thalamic reticular complex. *J Comp Neurobiol* 1975;162: 285–308.

39. Crick F. The function of the thalamic reticular complex: the searchlight hypothesis. *Proc Natl Acad Sci U S A* 1984;81:4586–4590.

40. Taylor JG, Alavi FN. Mathematical analysis of a competitive network for attention. In: Taylor JG, ed. *Mathematical approaches to neural networks*. Amsterdam: Elsevier, 1992:341–382.

41. Gray JA. Consciousness and its (dis)contents. *Behav Brain Sci* 1995;18:703–722.

42. Robertson GS, Jian M. D$_1$ and D$_2$ dopamine receptors differentially increase fos-like immunoreactivity in accumbal projections to the ventral pallidum and midbrain. *Neuroscience* 1995;64:1019–1034.

43. Venables PH. Cerebral mechanisms, automatic responsiveness and attention in schizophrenia. In: Spaulding

WD, Cole JK, eds. *Theories of schizophrenia and psychosis*. Lincoln, NE: University of Nebraska Press, 1984.

44. Knight RA. Converging models of cognitive deficit in schizophrenia. In: Spalding WD, Cole JK, eds. *Theories of schizophrenia and psychosis*. Lincoln, NE: University of Nebraska Press, 1984.

45. Schneider W, Shiffrin RM. Controlled and automatic human information processing. I. Detection, search and attention. *Psychol Rev* 1977;84:1–66.

46. Crick F, Koch C. Towards a neurobiological theory of consciousness. *Semin Neurosci* 1990;2:263–275.

47. Llinas R, Ribary U, Joliot M, Wang T. Content and context in temporal thalamocortical binding. In: Buzsaki G et al., eds. *Temporal coding in the brain*. Berlin: Springer-Verlag, 1994.

48. Weiner I. The accumbens-substantia nigra pathway, mismatch and amphetamine. *Behav Brain Sci* 1991;14: 54–55.

49. Nijhawan R. Visual decomposition of colour through motion extrapolation. *Nature* 1997;386:66–69.

50. Dennett DC. *Consciousness explained*. Boston: Little, Brown, 1991.

51. Freedman BJ. The subjective experience of perceptual and cognitive disturbances in schizophrenia. *Arch Gen Psychiatry* 1974;30:333–340.

52. Gaffan D. Scene-specific memory for objects: a model of episodic memory impairment in monkeys with fornix transection. *J Cognitive Neurosci* 1994;6:305–320.

53. Kamin LJ. Predictability, surprise, attention and conditioning. In: Campbell BA, Church RM, eds. *Punishment and aversive behavior*. New York: Appleton-Century-Crofts, 1969:279–296.

54. Dickinson A. *Contemporary animal learning theory*. Cambridge, England: Cambridge University Press, 1980.

55. Jones SH, Gray JA, Hemsley DR. Loss of the Kamin blocking effect in acute but not chronic schizophrenics. *Biol Psychiatry* 1992;32:739–755.

56. Young AMJ, Ahier RG, Upton RL, Joseph MH, Gray JA. Associative learning of neutral stimuli increases dopamine release in the nucleus accumbens of the rat. *Neuroscience* 83:1175–1183.

57. Frith CD. The positive and negative symptoms of schizophrenia reflect impairments in the perception and initiation of action. *Psychol Med* 1987;17:631–648.

DISCUSSION

Moderated by Alan J. McComas

Christof Koch: I take issue with your statement that consciousness typically arrives too late to play any role in sensory processing. In the example of the tennis player that you gave, visual consciousness does not play a role because by the time the player can so effortlessly return the serve before he was aware of the ball, he had to train for 10 years 8 hours a day so that this task has become completely automated. When the player first started playing as a little kid, I would submit that he needed consciousness. When I show you a cartoon you have never seen before and you have to recognize Margaret Thatcher in it, the visual processing will be much much slower compared to the tennis player seeing the ball, and it will involve consciousness. So, I think your examples all involve training and learning.

Jeffrey A. Gray: I fully accept what you are saying. Clearly, I am certainly not saying that consciousness does nothing. It has got to do something because we have it. That is a basic evolutionary postulate. What is quite difficult is to find something that it does that is conducive to survival.

Christof Koch: Planning!

Jeffrey A. Gray: Planning maybe, but not fast running and things like that.

Christof Koch: The idea is very similar to what Milner and Goodale have proposed in their monograph (1). They argue for the existence of one or more on-line systems that respond very rapidly in a fairly stereotyped manner (e.g., for eye or for arm movements). So, while early on you need consciousness to perform a task like returning a volley in tennis, later on you train up one of these on-line systems bypassing consciousness, but only for these training tasks.

Jeffrey A. Gray: I have a very strong hunch, and it is not more than a hunch, in answer to the evolutionary question, that consciousness is just too big a phenomenon, too important a phenomenon, to have just evolved recently. I believe it must have been around a long time.

Christof Koch: Well, monkeys can plan.

Jeffrey A. Gray: When I say a long time, I mean long before monkeys. That is my hunch. And when you look at other species, including people, there is very little they ever go through that would count as skilled learning, that would be important for their survival. Most of the things that rats do do not depend on skilled learning, and I cannot believe that my rats are not conscious because they show the same behavior, they respond the same way to drugs; the whole hypothesis is based upon what we study in the rat. The rat in the wild does a lot of interesting things, but none of it would count as skilled learning of how to do things like play the piano.

André Achim: I would just like to share an intuition I had a few weeks ago that fits quite well with what you are saying about the slowness of consciousness, the comparator with the real world. It seems to me that one possible use of consciousness might not be primarily related to its role in perception, the here and now. Rather, consciousness could be viewed as a marker that would differentiate speculations about the world, essentially generating predictions not about the things about the world but about things that could be, things that could happen. And so, if consciousness allowed to differentiate the here and now that we need to act upon to escape if something comes at us, to differentiate that from anticipation about the future, that would fit quite well into the timing that it comes too late for the here and now. It seems that in artificial intelligence, people could have come across this problem if someone would have been studying, a system whereby the same thing at the same time would keep its integrity in real time and plan for actions. It is very simple for a system to play chess; it is always in the planning state so that you do not need to discriminate what is speculation and what is the real thing.

Jeffrey A. Gray: I agree with a great deal of what you said. At this point, the particular wiring diagrams in Figs. 1, 4, and 5 of this chapter become relevant. If the comparator hypothesis is correct, and it is the hippocampal system that plays a key role in the comparator function, then there is a great deal of relevant evidence about what the hippocampus does in both experimental animals and in people. There is a reasonable hypothesis (2) about what the core hippocampal cognitive function might be that is able to make sense of both the relationship of the hippocampus to episodic memory and to spatial cognition, as well as integrating the relationship I have postulated with the comparator function. Essentially, this core function would be that of detecting error and modifying motor programs, memory, and future goal-oriented plans in light of the error that has been detected. And this, indeed, is central to planning for the future, in line with your suggestion.

Burton Vorhees: I wonder if you have considered the possibility that, when this process of comparison that you hypothesize is going on, consciousness might be provoked by the appearance of discrepancies and might have some sort of relation to a startle response.

Jeffrey A. Gray: Let me give you an anecdotal answer. I think what you suggest is absolutely right. It is clear that the unexpected is much more important in terms of what gets instantiated into consciousness. My answer is in the form of the following anecdote. I am a keen skier. I have my own skis, and have had them for years. I went out to ski one morning, picked up my skis with my left hand without looking at them and carried them walking forward. Then, my eyes still forward, suddenly a little blue light started winking in my left eye. I looked around, and there was this tiny, tiny blue thing on this pair of skis which were not my own, on the binding. Something in my brain was analyzing and detecting that, "Hey! something is different, no blue on your skis." So, that came straight through to my consciousness, but it had to have been done after the first pass analysis. Yes, you are absolutely right.

Paul Cisek: I think that the idea of the comparator is good because it potentially explains things like visual illusions or the kind of confabulations that Gazzaniga's or Ramachandran's patients go through. But as far as the phenomenal experience of things, if the predictions affect our experience of things, then why does pain feel the same whether we expect it or not?

Jeffrey A. Gray: Pain, I think, is the ultimate interrupter. It is the ultimate thing that says, "Interrupt this motor program, it is going wrong." It is not performing the function of something we check up on; it is the alarm that tells you that anything you are doing at the moment is wrong. So, it is not like everything else in the sense that you do not predict it and compare it. It is an interruption.

Benjamin Libet: Of course, I agree that the fast actions are initially unconscious because in my proposals it takes time to develop awareness. On the other hand, I do not think it is true that in all cases consciousness follows after the action. In the voluntary act that we studied, there was a delay in the appearance of conscious intention, but it did appear before the action, and in fact it is able to control the outcome.

Jeffrey A. Gray: There is obviously a very important compensatory mechanism which, for lack of time, I have not mentioned. Consciousness being too late means, and especially with a predictive system, that you gain a lot of mileage by extrapolating forward in time if you have a sufficiently regular predictable set of events. That may or may not apply to the example you are talking about. There was a very interesting paper in *Nature* a few months ago, in which a stationary red line was briefly flashed so that it was directly superimposed onto a green bar (3). If the bar was also stationary, the two colors were fused, as is normal, into a perceived yellow. If, however, the bar was moving, even though the two stimuli were still directly superimposed, the viewer saw them as a separate red line trailing the green bar. This is a very nice analysis of the capacity of the predictive system to extrapolate forward in time. So, the smoothness with which we experience the world is almost certainly, at least in part, due to such forward extrapolation of the predictive system.

Stuart R. Hameroff: One explanation for the evolutionary survival advantage of consciousness comes from Roger Penrose's suggestion of noncomputability in conscious thought. In predator–prey relationships, it is well known that unpredictability, seemingly random behavior, is a tremendous advantage. So, organisms that first developed the noncomputable actions would have a tremendous advantage. Similarly, humans, up until at least recently, could still beat a computer at chess, despite a tremendous disadvantage in brute processing.

Jeffrey A. Gray: I am absolutely out of my depth when somebody talks about noncomputability because I then really have to remind myself what Penrose did say. But, yes, I am of the opinion that our ignorance of how it is that the neuroscientific theories we currently have could be linked up to what consciousness does is so total that I am quite prepared to accept that the solution could come from any direction, including (though it seems extremely implausible to me as it does to most others) some quite radical new physics in the brain and noncomputability. I do not think we can exclude any of those possibilities. Equally, I do not personally put any bets on any of them being right.

Keith Schneider: Your model places the emphasis on the hippocampal system in consciousness, but how do you account for the apparent normal conscious functioning of patients with extensive hippocampal lesions like HM?

Jeffrey A. Gray: I have two answers. The first is that we have to take very seriously the "zombie" notion. Because people can do so many wonderful things without being conscious, it is actually quite possible that people might be doing things in a manner which is unconscious and we would not actually be able to detect a difference. If we had a theory, we could have a scalpel, as David Chalmers says, we would have a consciousness meter. We do not have a theory as yet, so I think we have to take seriously the possibility that people with various brain lesions might be able to do things which simulate what we would do if we were conscious. That is the first possible answer. The second is that we are dealing with a highly complex, distributed system. You would need very considerable brain lesions to get rid of it all. We saw very nice examples in Michael Gazzaniga's chapter (Chapter 12) of what isolated bits of tissue could still do in the scotoma case. There is one patient that I described, not my own but he has been described in the literature, in the reply in my article in *Behavioral and Brain Sciences* (1995), who had massive damage to this whole system and whose self-report is quite extraordinary. He was a musician, a highly skilled musician, and among other things he used to conduct choirs. He was still able to play the piano, but we know that that can go on unconsciously, and among other things he conducted a choir perfectly well, sight reading and doing all the right things. And in the end he said, "I just waved my hands and they sang. What happened?" He had no conscious understanding at that point of what he was doing. And the other critical thing he said of himself, over and over again, was quite painful. He wrote diaries. Every quarter of an hour or so, the diary entry would be, "I have been unconscious, I just woke up." "There were no colours, there were no sounds." "I have just woken up from being unconscious." And then he does it again 15 minutes later. So, I do not think we should exclude the possibility that, if you made the right brain damage, you could produce a zombie.

Giuseppe Trautteur: You made a passing remark about the 40-Hz phenomenon. Now, your 100 milliseconds are 10 Hz, which is a little out of range. I am not clear how this 100 milliseconds arises. Is it a neural phenomenon or a systemic phenomenon? Since the 40 Hz hypothesis is strongly correlated with consciousness, it would be interesting to relate those two temporal activities.

Jeffrey A. Gray: I will only take up the last point. The 40-Hz rhythm as far as I see cannot be strongly correlated to consciousness because, unless I am mistaken, it occurs in the anesthetized rat or cat . . . does it not?

Barbara E. Jones: Although gamma is always present during either anesthesia or natural sleep, the amplitude and coherence of gamma is much diminished during these states as compared to waking and is thus state dependent.

Jeffrey A. Gray: Well, I have obviously gone straight out of my depth in that answer. But the key question is where does the lower frequency come from? I started my modeling from the theta rhythm in the hippocampal system. This is a very prominent feature in the hippocampus of subprimates, but it is also there in primates. The theta rhythm has a frequency range of approximately 6 Hz to approximately 12 to 13 Hz. The general comparator hypothesis includes the notion that it is a system for gating the passage of information. We already had talked of quantizing in Llinás' talk, and for me the quantizing is the same in principle but on a slower time base, paced by the theta rhythm. The theta rhythm is present in the conscious animal, but not invariably, absent in slow-wave sleep, and very strongly present in REM sleep. So, from that point of view I think it has slightly better characteristics than the faster rhythms. But I think you need both. I think you need a fast coherence for the first binding prior to consciousness but you need something slower then to keep track of what is coming in and out of conscious experience.

Barbara E. Jones: I just want to recall that in the hippocampus, the 40-Hz rhythm was very early shown to be riding on the theta rhythm, and that is exactly what we are seeing in our electroencephalographic readings across large areas of the cortex. Gamma and theta vary together with higher amplitude, higher coherence, across broad regions during active or attentive waking states. So, the slow oscillations may be carrying the faster oscillations which otherwise could not be carried across such large distances.

Jeffrey A. Gray: I am aware of the data you are talking about and of course that is actually consistent with the notion that they are both doing the same thing in an integrated manner but on two different time bases.

Discussion References

1. Milner D, Goodale M. *The visual brain in action.* Oxford, England: Oxford University Press, 1995.
2. Gray J, McNaughton N. The neuropsychology of anxiety: reprise. In: Hope DA, ed. *Perspectives on anxiety, panic, and fear.* Volume 43. *Nebraska Symposium on Motivation.* Lincoln NE, University of Nebraska Press, 1996:61–134.
3. Nijhawan R. Visual decomposition of colour through motion extrapolation. Nature 1997;386:66–69.

Consciousness: At the Frontiers of Neuroscience,
Advances in Neurology, Vol. 77,
edited by H.H. Jasper, L. Descarries,
V.F. Castellucci, and S. Rossignol.
Lippincott–Raven Publishers, Philadelphia © 1998.

14

Do the Models Offer Testable Proposals of Brain Functions for Conscious Experience?

Benjamin Libet

Department of Physiology, University of California, San Francisco, California 94143

CRITERIA FOR SCIENTIFIC MODELS

The question of how the brain may produce conscious experience is fundamental to our views of who we are as humans, and fascinating in its challenge. So it is not surprising that there have been many models or theories proposed to address that question. But if a model is to have some potential validity, it must meet at least two criteria: (a) it must deal with the stubborn fact that conscious experience is a subjective phenomenon, and (b) it should be at least potentially testable.

Conscious subjective experience or awareness is accessible only to the subject having the experience, not to an external observer. Consequently, only an introspective report by the subject can provide valid operational information about the subjective experience. Conscious experience is a primary phenomenon not definable or describable by or reducible to any other observable physical event, whether molecular or behavioral. Even a complete knowledge of the observable neural processes in the brain of an individual would not in itself tell us what the subject is experiencing or feeling (unless correlative relationships with conscious experiences have been established by simultaneous introspective reports from the subject).

It follows that behavioral responses or actions, other than introspective reports, would not provide valid indications of subjective experience. This would include even those behavioral responses that depend on cognitive and decision-making processes. Such behavioral events can be and often are performed by human subjects without any introspective reportable awareness of them (1–3). Therefore, we cannot safely assume that such behaviors in animals indicate conscious thought and experience (without denying that animals may indeed have conscious experiences). However, Cowey and Stoerig (4) have designed a unique test that appears to provide some convincing evidence of subjective experience in the monkey's responses. Monkeys with lesions of the primary visual cortex were tested in a signal-detection task in which half of the trials were blank trials with no visual stimulus. When visual stimuli were presented in the defective visual field, the monkeys classified them as blank, even though in a forced-choice paradigm they detected these stimuli 100% of the time; this resembled the "blindsight" in human patients, not a degraded real vision.

A model or theory must be testable, at least in principle, if it is to have scientific merit. As Karl Popper pointed out, the test must be potentially capable of falsifying the theory. Otherwise, one can propose any kind of speculative model without any fear of its being contradicted; in that case, one model is no better scientifically than any other. On the other hand, untestable models could provide potentially useful metaphors that may stimulate imaginative approaches to the problem. Metaphors do not, of course, describe the real situation. In order not to be misleading, these (and other) proposals and their assumptions and premises should be clearly stated.

Some Tested and Testable Models

I have myself proposed models relating brain functions to conscious experience. I shall briefly outline a few of these, partly to review their contributions to the real condition and partly to show that such models can be experimentally testable even when they propose rather outrageously radical solutions to some fundamental issues. There have, of course, been other testable proposals (5).

We had produced strong evidence for the view that a conscious sensory experience does not appear immediately; there is a delay of up to 500 msec for neuronal activities to achieve adequacy for the awareness (6,7). But sensory events are subjectively perceived with no discernible delay after the stimulus. (Exceptions are, of course, sensations of deep pain for which the slowly conducting sensory C fibers can impose a discernible delay of seconds.)

Subjective Antedating of Sensory Experience

How could one address the paradox of a subjective timing with no delay, of an experience that does not actually appear until about 500 milliseconds later? We had to recognize that subjective timing need not be identical with the neuronal time for an experience. We also established that for a stimulus to the somatosensory cortex (S-I) there was in fact a substantial subjective delay, in contrast to the subjective time for stimuli at any point in the subcortical sensory pathway, from skin to thalamus. That led to our hypothesis of subjective referral backwards in time. In this case, the normal experience is actually delayed up to about 500 milliseconds by the

neuronal requirements; but it is then subjectively and automatically antedated back to the time of the initial primary evoked potential response of S-I cortex. This response is elicited by the first sensory input arriving at the cortex in about 10 to 25 milliseconds.

It was possible to put this rather startling hypothesis to an experimental test. Near-threshold stimuli in the fast specific projection pathway, e.g., medial lemniscus (ML), do require the same roughly 500 milliseconds of repetitive pulses as does the stimulus at the S-I cortex to elicit sensory awareness. But each stimulus pulse in the ML also produces a primary evoked potential at the S-I cortex, unlike the surface stimuli at the S-I cortex. The hypothesis predicted, therefore, that the experience elicited by a stimulus in the ML would be referred back to the putative timing signal produced with the first pulse, even though it was factually demonstrable that the experience could not have appeared before the end of the 500-millisecond train of pulses. That prediction was confirmed by tests that matched the subjective timing of sensations elicited by stimuli at the skin, ML, and S-I cortex (8).

Subjective referrals of the temporal or spatial content of a sensory experience appear to be mental phenomena. There are no neural representations that exhibit the subjectively referred experience and from which one could have predicted or described that experience.

Conscious Versus Unconscious Mental Functions

There is the question of how the brain distinguishes between conscious and unconscious mental functions. (Unconscious functions even include creative problem-solving, as has been proven by the great mathematicians and many others). We had found that a 500-millisecond cortical stimulus train of repetitive pulses, required to elicit a sensory experience, produced substantial neuronal responses with each pulse in the train. It had been shown that animals could be conditioned to respond behaviorally to virtually any neuronal action in the brain. That led us to propose a time-on theory to explain the transition between unconscious and conscious mental functions (9).

In this theory, appropriate neuronal activities must persist for a minimum time (time-on) to elicit a conscious experience; but similar activities that have a shorter time-on than that minimum could support or mediate the mental function without awareness, i.e., unconsciously. We designed an experimental test of the theory insofar as it applied to a somatosensory function (1).

Patients with permanent implants of stimulating electrodes in ventrobasal thalamus (for relief of intractable pain) were available for study. The duration of the stimulus train was randomly varied in the successive trials, from 0 to 750 milliseconds (at the constant intensity that elicited a sensory experience with a train duration of about 400 milliseconds). In a forced choice paradigm, subjects reported in which of two periods the stimulus was presented, even if they felt nothing. Analysis of the thousands of trials in nine subjects yielded the following results:

1. Correct detection of the stimulus was well above the 50% chance level, even when subjects reported feeling nothing, just guessing.
2. To go from a correct-but-guessing response to a correct-with-minimal-awareness response required an *additional* 375 milliseconds of stimulus train duration.

These results provided strong evidence for the time-on theory.

Unconscious Initiation of a Voluntary Act

How the conscious will to act is mediated by brain activity is another fundamental issue of special relevance to the question of free will. One approach to this issue is to ask whether conscious intention to act precedes or follows the specific brain activity that leads to a voluntary act. An experimental entry into this crucial question became possible (a) with finding of recordable brain activity (the readi-ness potential [RP]) that precedes a freely voluntary act, and (b) with the design of a method for measuring the time of the first awareness of the intention to act (10,11).

A rigorous study of the relative timings showed that (a) specific brain activity (RP) preceded a freely voluntary act by about 550 milliseconds, whereas (b) the first awareness of that intention did not appear until 200 milliseconds before the act (corrected to 150 milliseconds). These results have been confirmed by others (12). It appeared, then, that the volitional process was *initiated* unconsciously in the brain, about 350 to 400 milliseconds before the subject was aware of his/her intention to act. However, the appearance of conscious intention 150 milliseconds before the act allowed for the possibility of a role for the conscious function. That role would appear to be one of potentially blocking or vetoing the volitional process so that no actual motor action occurs. Veto of an urge to act is a common experience for individuals generally. Additionally, we demonstrated that a subject could veto an expectation to act within the 100- to 200-millisecond period before an expected action. Veto or self-control of the conscious urges or intentions to act is in accord with the ethical doctrines of major religions.

How Is Subjective Experience Unified?

One of the mysteries in the relationship between brain and conscious experience lies in the phenomenon of the unified, integrated subjective experience. How can such a unified subjective phenomenon emerge from or be causally related to the activities of a brain with an estimated 100 billion nerve cells, each with thousands of interconnections to other nerve cells?

A correlational solution to this so-called binding problem has been proposed based on finding of synchronization of electrical oscillations in structures related to a given function (13). However, a causal relationship in this model has yet to be experimentally established. Also, one must be careful not to equate binding in a behavioral function with unity of a conscious experience. Subjective phenomena are not predictable by or reducible to purely behavioral events.

My own view has been that conscious experience is an independent phenomenon in nature. It is certainly related to brain function and it may be regarded as an emergent property of the brain. But conscious experience should be viewed as a unique natural phenomenon, not describable a priori by the nerve cell activities. Other natural phenomena, like gravity associated with mass or magnetism associated with electric current flow, are also fundamental phenomena whose existences are accepted as givens in nature (14).

I have proposed a theory to address the unified nature of conscious experience (15). Subjective experience could be viewed as if it were a field, emerging as a property of appropriate nerve cell activities. This conscious mental field (CMF) would be a new fundamental natural phenomenon. The CMF is not reducible to or explainable by any known physical processes, just as the known characteristics of the subjective experience it represents are not reducible. On the other hand, the CMF is a function of the brain system from which it emerges; it is not the separable entity envisioned in Cartesian dualism. It is not a ghost in the machine any more than a magnetic field emerging from electric current in a wire is a ghost.

The CMF would have the attribute of the integrated subjective experience. It is also proposed that the CMF could act back on the brain so as to influence certain neural activities. That ability may be viewed as analogous to the ability of a magnetic field to influence the electric current in a wire, from which the field initially emerged. The putative CMF capability would provide a basis for conscious modulation of some neuronal activities, i.e., for the operation of conscious will. An ability to influence physical neuronal activities would make the CMF a kind of force field. (The issue of mental force fields has been creatively dealt with by Popper et al.) (16,17). However, the postulated CMF force field would be different from all known physical forces.

The CMF theory is radical and speculative. But it makes a testable experimental prediction. The detailed experimental design for this has been described by me (15). This design could potentially confirm or falsify the theory. The CMF theory is thus in accord with the recommended features for scientific models.

The design of that experimental test is relatively simple in principle and it is doable, although it is technically challenging. If, as proposed, local areas of cerebral cortex could contribute to or alter the larger unitary CMF, it should be possible to demonstrate such contributions when (a) that cortical area is completely cut off from all neuronal communication with the rest of the brain, but (b) the area remains in situ, alive, and maintained in a functional state that sufficiently resembles its normal behavior.

Viable isolated slabs of cortex can be produced by subpial cuts that retain the blood supply. This procedure was used some decades ago in both animals (18) and humans (19). For testing of the CMF theory, one would want to isolate a cortical site known to elicit a reportable conscious experience with electrical stimulation. The obvious candidates are sites in any primary sensory area, although some others may be possible (in the temporal lobe). Also, the isolated slab of cortex would have to be awakened from the abnormal comatose state that follows loss of subcortical afferent inputs. Methods for restoring the awakened state have been suggested (15). I hope that a neurosurgeon, who may have patients who require excision or isolation of a bit of sensory cortex, and who is motivated to take on the designed experimental test, will come forward to perform the test.

It is, of course, easy to argue that only a negative result would ensue. But that is based on current views of requirements for behavioral activities. Existing models do not satisfactorily account for conscious subjective experience, especially for its unitary nature and for the operation of conscious will. The proposed CMF offers a possible fundamental re-orientation of our views of the mind–brain relationship and, I submit, merits a test of its validity.

REFERENCES

1. Libet B, Pearl DK, Morledge DE, Gleason CA, Hosobuchi Y and Barbaro NM. Control of the transition from sensory detection to sensory awareness in man by the duration of a thalamic stimulus: the cerebral time-on factor. *Brain* 1991;114:1731–1757.
2. Velmans M. Is human information processing conscious? *Behav Brain Sci* 1991;14:651–669.
3. Weiskrantz L. *Blindsight: a case study and implications.* Oxford, England: Clarendon, 1986.
4. Cowey A, Stoerig P. Blindsight in monkeys. *Nature* 1995;373:247–249.
5. Jasper HH. Current evaluation of the concepts of centrencephalic and cortico-reticular seizures. *Electroencephalogr Clin Neurophysiol* 1991;78:2–11.
6. Libet B. Electrical stimulation of cortex in human subjects, and conscious sensory aspects. In: Iggo A, ed. *Handbook of sensory physiology.* Vol. 2. Somatosensory system. New York: Springer-Verlag, 1973:743–790.
7. Libet B. *Neurophysiology of consciousness.* Boston: Birkhäuser, 1993.
8. Libet B, Wright EW, Feinstein B, Pearl DK. Subjective referral of the timing for a conscious sensory experience: a functional role for the somatosensory specific projection system in man. *Brain* 1979;102:191–222.
9. Libet B. Conscious subjective experience vs unconscious mental functions: a theory of the cerebral processes involved. In: Cotterill RMJ, ed. *Models of brain function.* Cambridge, England: Cambridge University Press, 1989.
10. Libet B, Gleason CA, Wright EW, Pearl DK. Time of conscious intention to act in relation to onset of cerebral activities (readiness-potential): the unconscious initiation of a freely voluntary act. *Brain* 1983;106:623–642.
11. Libet B. Unconscious cerebral initiative and the role of conscious will in voluntary action. *Behav Brain Sci* 1985;8:529–566.
12. Keller I, Heckhausen H. Readiness potentials preceeding motor acts: voluntary vs involuntary control. *Electroencephalogr Clin Neurophysiol* 1990;76:351–361.
13. Singer W. Response synchronization of cortical neurons: an epiphenomenon or a solution to the binding problem. *IBRO News* 1991;19:6–7.
14. Chalmers DJ. Facing up to the problem of consciousness. *J Consciousness Studies* 1995;2:200–219.
15. Libet B. A testable field theory of mind-brain interaction. *J Consciousness Studies* 1994;1:119–126.
16. Popper KR, Lindahl BIB, Århem P. A discussion of the mind-brain problem. *Theoret Med* 1993;14:167–180.
17. Lindahl BIB, Århem P. Mind as a force field: comments on a new interactionist hypothesis. *J Theoret Biol* 1994;171:111–112.
18. Burns BD. Some properties of the isolated cerebral cortex in the unanesthetized cat. *J Physiol (Lond)* 1951;112:156–175.
19. Henry CE, Scoville WB. Suppression-burst activity from isolated cerebral cortex in man. *Electroencephalogr Clin Neurophysiol* 1952;4:1–22.

Consciousness: At the Frontiers of Neuroscience,
Advances in Neurology, Vol. 77,
edited by H.H. Jasper, L. Descarries,
V.F. Castellucci, and S. Rossignol.
Lippincott–Raven Publishers, Philadelphia © 1998.

15

Recordings from the Striate Cortex in Awake Behaving Animals

David H. Hubel

Department of Neurobiology, Harvard Medical School, Boston, Massachusetts 02115

Perhaps I should begin by confessing that I am here on false pretensions because I am no expert on the subject of consciousness. My field is the visual cortex. I started out working on sleep and wakefulness back in 1956, but after a year or so switched over to vision, for reasons that I will soon recount.

My career in neurophysiology began one day in the spring of 1949, when I was a second-year medical student at McGill. I had done my undergraduate work in mathematics and physics (also at McGill) and went into medicine with the idea of trying both research and clinical work, to see if I was any good at either. Francis MacNaughton's second-year course in neuroanatomy got me interested in the nervous system, so one day, grabbing the bull by the horns, I called Wilder Penfield's secretary and made an appointment to see him. On the day of the appointment I borrowed the family car, parked it on University Street, and in a state of acute anxiety climbed the hill to the famous Montreal Neurological Institute (MNI). Penfield was most charming and friendly. When he realized that neurophysiology was one of my main interests, he walked me upstairs to Herbert Jasper's office. My introduction to Herbert 48 years ago marked the beginning of a long and great friendship. In the course of our conversation, Herbert asked what I had read in neurophysiology. I mentioned Norbert Wiener's book on

cybernetics. With a grin, Herbert asked if I had understood it. When I said that I thought I had, more or less, I could see that Herbert was surprised, but was too nice to press me further. That was my first exposure to Herbert's honesty, judgment, and clarity of mind, which have continued to impress me right up to the present.

Herbert took me down to meet Les Geddes, the MNI electronics engineer, and made arrangements for me to work there in the summers. That way I met most of the fellows at the Institute, learning about the equipment, watching experiments and witnessing many of Penfield's temporal lobe operations. (When I returned to the car, later that day, I found it locked with the keys inside and the motor running. Getting back home for spare keys involved a round trip on the all-too-familiar Westmount-NDG bus and the 65 streetcar, by which time my nervousness had considerably abated.)

On Herbert's advice I began a neurology residency at the MNI in 1952, after a year's rotating internship at the old Montreal General Hospital on Dorchester Street. The year of neurology was followed by a year of clinical neurophysiology, mainly electroencephalography (EEG). Cosimo Ajmone-Marsan was Herbert's assistant then and was responsible for much of my EEG training, but he left for the National Institutes of Health in Bethesda after

3 months, and suddenly I found myself reading most of the Institute's EEGs, except for those of the Penfield service. By the end of that year I felt pretty competent in EEG, and very tired of turning EEG pages. I made a solemn resolution, which I have kept, never to read one again.

I left Montreal in 1954 for a second year's residency in neurology at Johns Hopkins Hospital. I knew that as a dual citizen (U.S. through my parents, Canadian by birth) I would be subject to the Doctor's Draft and 2 year's service in the U.S. Armed Forces—there was a shortage of medical people in the era between Korea and Vietnam—but I saw no sense in basing career choices on such possibilities. I was indeed drafted into the U.S. Army, and by a piece of marvelous good luck was assigned in July 1955 to the Neuropsychiatry Division of the Walter Reed Army Institute of Research in Washington, DC, where I was at last able to start research at the late age of 29.

My main advisor at Walter Reed was M.G.F. Fuortes. Fuortes had a a wonderful feel for biology and for experiments, and a wonderful sense of humor. The small but strong neuropsychiatry group at Walter Reed was headed by David Rioch, with Robert Galambos in auditory neurophysiology, Walle Nauta in neuroanatomy, and Fuortes in spinal cord. Soon after my arrival, Mike Fuortes drew up a list of possible research projects for me to choose from, one of which consisted of chronically inserting tiny insulated wires into the brain to record from the cerebral cortex. I found this most appealing and ambitious: no one had ever recorded single cells in awake behaving animals. It soon became obvious that the problem was not simple, and I determined to begin by designing an electrode tough enough to go through dura and arachnoid. The head of instrumentation at Walter Reed was a man named Leon Levin, who had got his Ph.D. in electrochemistry. He produced a roll of tungsten wire and a recipe for electropolishing it, and soon I had a wire sharp and strong enough to go through my thumbnail. Finding an insulation to coat it

with was the next problem. General Electric could supply an insulation called Formvar, but only in tank-car amounts. A helpful colleague in the next laboratory, Guy Sheatz, suggested a lacquer that was used in industry to coat the insides of tin cans. This turned out to have just the right viscosity and adhesiveness to cover the wire to within 15 to 25 microns of the tip, and soon I found myself recording from a variety of central nervous system (CNS) structures, from dorsal cochlear nuclei to the olfactory bulb. It was around that time that Herbert Jasper visited me at Walter Reed, to learn to make these electrodes. His group, too, was setting out to record from chronically prepared cats, and in fact they finally succeeded, a short time before I did. I resolved to build a hydraulic advancer that attached to a peg that mounted on the cat or monkey's skull, and to do this I had to take a course in machining at night school in Washington, DC, an effort that has brought huge dividends in the years that followed, since I have continued to design and build much of my own equipment.

The next question, a crucial one, was what part of the brain to record from. I had a long-standing interest in sleep, stemming from my experience in Montreal, and had also developed an interest in vision, stemming from the time that Herbert asked me to cover vision in a neurophysiology course at the MNI; it was then that I got to know the papers of Hartline and Stephen Kuffler. The cat visual cortex was easily accessible, with almost no muscle between the overlying skull and the outside world, so I began to record there, turning on and off the room lights as a stimulus. It was easy to confirm the work of Richard Jung and Günter Baumgartner that the cat visual cortex contained five types of cells, A, B, C, D , and E, of which B, D, and E were on, off, and on-off, respectively, C was inhibited by light, and A cells were unresponsive. One day, using a method I had devised for making electrolytic lesions by passing tiny currents through the recording electrodes, I discovered to my amazement a lesion in the subcortical white matter. Amazement, because at that time it was not known that metallic electrodes could record impulses from fibers. It dawned on me that some of my records of visual responses could be coming from afferents from the lateral geniculate. It finally turned out that the B, C, D, and E cells were all afferent fibers from the lateral geniculate, and that A cells were cortical cells. Striate cortical cells respond poorly or not at all to changes in levels of diffuse light, which the Freiburg group had been using exclusively; visual cortical cells require spatially restricted forms, especially moving objects, as I first found out by standing in front of the cat waving my hands (Fig. 1). This record, made around 1957, may be the first direct indication that the cerebral cortex was contributing something new toward reorganizing information it received from lower levels.

My first efforts were directed toward learning what changes if any occurred in the visual pathway when a sleeping cat was aroused. I soon found that the spontaneous firing of cortical cells could increase or decrease, depending on the cell, but that almost always, after arousal, the activity became smoother, less bursty.

I also developed a rather elaborate but effective means of recording stereotaxically from deep brain structures in behaving cats and was able to study lateral geniculate cells directly. It was relatively easy to show that geniculate cells had center-surround receptive fields, like those Kuffler had seen in retinal ganglion cells in the early 1950s. What interested me most was the characteristic bursting pattern these cells showed when a cat was drowsy or asleep, which disappeared whenever the cat was aroused.

I was beginning to find it frustrating to have so little control over my visual stimuli in these freely viewing cats. I did some recordings from the auditory cortex, but hesitated to abandon vision completely.

In 1958 my time at Walter Reed came to an end. Vernon Mountcastle had invited me to join the Physiology Department at Johns Hopkins Medical School, and I eagerly accepted. The catch was that the laboratories in physiology were being remodeled and would not be ready for about a year. One day Steve Kuffler phoned to ask if I would be interested in joining his group at the Wilmer Institute at Johns Hopkins for the intervening months to work with Torsten Wiesel. This was obviously a good solution, so Torsten and I joined forces in the spring of 1958, not for 8 or 9 months as we then thought, but for what turned out to be 25 years. All our work was performed in acutely prepared cats and monkeys, and through our efforts and those of many other laboratories the striate cortex has become the best understood of all cortical areas, perhaps all areas of the CNS, possibly excepting the retina and spinal cord.

Awake behaving techniques were meanwhile taken up by Ed Evarts and many others and adapted for work with primates. A few years ago it became clear that I would no longer be able to continue to perform experiments that lasted all day and all night, and I decided to return to single-cell studies in awake monkeys. It was a decision made reluctantly because I hated to give up the combined anatomy–physiology approach that Torsten and I had found so fruitful. But to be free of worries over the possible effects of anesthetics was a strong compensating advantage.

Margaret Livingstone and I began to tool up for the change about 2 years ago. We wanted, as far as possible, to free ourselves from long arduous periods of monkey training, so we decided to try to outline receptive fields indirectly, in freely viewing macaque monkeys. The method of attaching a small wire coil to the equator of an eye, and recording radiofrequency currents induced by two pairs of large external coils, devised first by David Robinson, allowed us to track eye position to within several arc minutes, with a time resolution of several milliseconds. The animal sits in a large box facing a TV monitor and is rewarded for fixating on a small spot with the usual fruit juice. On this screen we display various forms; meanwhile, we have our own monitor on which we display a spot that indicates the center of the animal's gaze. We be-

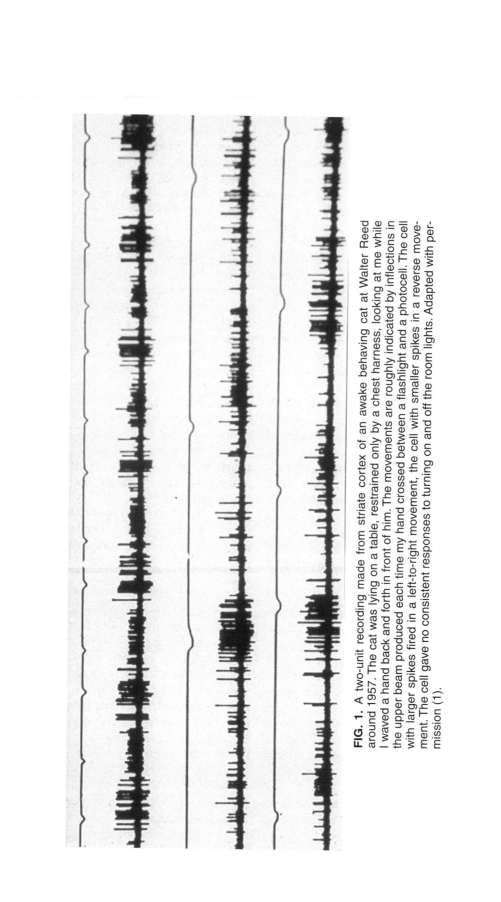

FIG. 1. A two-unit recording made from striate cortex of an awake behaving cat at Walter Reed around 1957. The cat was lying on a table, restrained only by a chest harness, looking at me while I waved a hand back and forth in front of him. The movements are roughly indicated by inflections in the upper beam produced each time my hand crossed between a flashlight and a photocell. The cell with larger spikes fired in a left-to-right movement, the cell with smaller spikes in a reverse movement. The cell gave no consistent responses to turning on and off the room lights. Adapted with permission (1).

gin a typical study of a cell by presenting the monkey with a succession of parallel-line arrays whose orientations change at random every 200 milliseconds (Fig. 2, left half). We ask, for each impulse, what the orientation was a certain number of milliseconds before. We then plot orientation against number of impulses in a polar histogram (Fig. 2, right half).

Next we try to obtain a record of responses. Our computer keeps track of the animal's eye position at all times, and of the impulses. Then for each impulse we plot a pixel on our TV monitor, indicating the position of the animal's gaze a given number of milliseconds before the impulse. This delay can be varied, and we simply play with the delay setting until we get a constellation of pixels that bears some relationship to the stimulus. In principle this can be done with the animal just looking around, if one allows enough time so that its gaze samples all of the monitor screen it faces. In practice it turns out to be far less time-consuming to have the monkey fixate on a spot whose position changes to a new random position every second or so. Figure 3 shows the result for a square, oriented so as to correspond to the orientation of the cell determined as in Fig. 2. It is important to realize that the pixels represent not the receptive field of the cell, but the eye positions at which impulses occurred. Clearly, impulses will tend to occur whenever the eyes are so positioned that the cell's receptive field is intersected by a contour to which the cell is sensitive, in this case the near-vertical left and right edges of the square. At first we wished to know if the act of fixation, as opposed to simply letting the eyes wander around, would make a difference in the behavior of cells in V1. To our delight, is seemed to make no difference, indicating that all the previous work in anesthetized animals, or fixating awake animals, probably did bear on the actual normal functioning of the cells.

A surprising early finding was that in some cells, especially those with high spontaneous activity, we saw nothing but a cloud of pixels that seemed to have no clear relationship to a stimulus such as a square or circle (Fig. 3, upper left). What puzzled us was that by waving our hands (as in Fig. 1) we could make the cell respond. It soon became clear that in some cells the responses took the form of high-frequency bursts of impulses. We decided to take the raw spike records that we had stored in the computer, along with eye position, and reevaluate them by applying a spike filter that plotted a pixel at each occurrence of a burst of spikes, ignoring the isolated impulses. Our engineer, David Freeman, arranged things so that we could set the filter to accept a given number of impulses in a given span of time (say, three or more impulses in 15 milliseconds), at a particular delay. By taking a set of observations on a cell, we could then play with these parameters to see if we could bring out something related to the cell's receptive field. Figure 3 (upper right) shows the result for the same set of records, now filtered to represent bursts of two or more impulses in 26 milliseconds, at a delay of 50 milliseconds. The lower left panel represents an even more stringent setting (bursts of three or more spikes in 26 milliseconds). In the lower right the square is included. Clearly the cell was most sensitive to the square's left edge. (The offset between the row of pixels and this edge corresponds to the distance between the cell's receptive field and the center of gaze.) Thus in such cells we could see a receptive field equivalent where none had been evident without the filter. For most cells we see a constellation of eye positions associated with responses in the unfiltered record, but striking improvement in definition in the filtered record.

We are still working to understand why bursts so frequently tell us more about a cell's properties than the raw unfiltered record. One possibility has to do with adaptation: the fact that in many cells the very high frequency of discharge seen at the onset of a stimulus declines over time, to noise levels or to a plateau far below the initial discharge rate. We see adaptation in most cells in the visual cortex when a stimulus is appropriately directed in the visual field and kept in the same place.

FIG. 2. Procedure for determining orientation selectivity of a cell in striate cortex of an awake behaving macaque monkey. The animal's gaze was fixated on a small circle (*center of left panel*) and was rewarded with fruit juice every second provided its gaze did not wander outside the square. The monkey viewed a series of sets of parallel lines, each set of lines lasting about 0.25 second, whose orientations varied randomly. The computer recorded the orientation 50 milliseconds before each impulse and plotted the result in a polar histogram, shown to the right. (The symmetry of this plot is artificial because each pixel is plotted twice.)

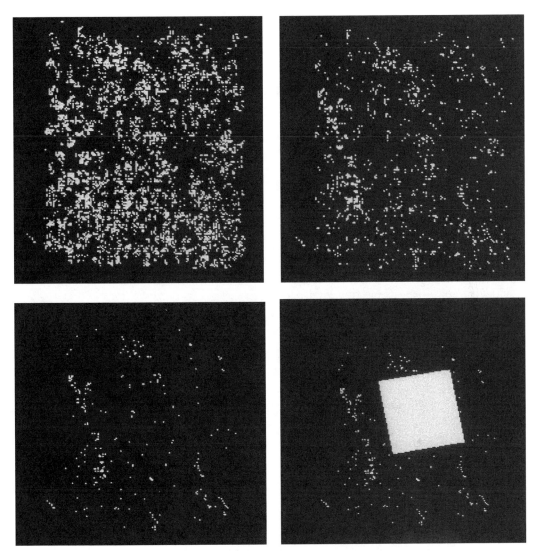

FIG. 3. Monkey gaze is fixated on a spot whose position is changed to a new position every 5 seconds in random fashion so that all points on the screen are sampled every few minutes. The cell's receptive field was a few degrees above and to the right of the point of fixation. The stimulus was a stationary square, shown in the bottom right panel but for purposes of illustration eliminated from the other three panels so that one can see the pixels. In each panel the pixels represent the position of the eyes 50 milliseconds before each impulse (*upper left panel*) or each burst of impulses (*remaining panels*). Upper left panel, no filter, so that each pixel represents gaze position 50 milliseconds before an impulse. Upper right panel, pixels represent eye position 50 milliseconds before bursts of two or more impulses occurring in 26 milliseconds. Lower two panels, same, but for bursts of three or more impulses.

Moving the stimulus within the receptive field of a cell generally leads to steady maintained discharge as long as the movement is kept up, and long ago Torsten Wiesel and I learned that moving stimuli were the most effective way of activating cells in our anesthetized, paralyzed cats and monkeys. One had always assumed that neural adaptation was the cause of the fading of images stabilized on the retina, discovered by Riggs and Ratliff (2) and Ditchburn and Ginsburg (3) in 1952.

It is tempting to think that bursts may be important in transmitting information to the next stage in a sensory pathway, by making use of the temporal summation associated with a rapid sequence of impulses. Bursts would then constitute a kind of neural code over and above the simple frequency code we have recognized since the time of Adrian.

If we have the monkey fixate on a spot and place a stationary edge or line so that it crosses the receptive field of a cell in the optimum orientation, and we listen to the impulses and watch the spot that indicates eye position on our monitor, we can immediately see a clear correlation between the activity of the cell and the microsaccades: the tiny, roughly 0.5 degree movements that occur about once or twice a second. In cells whose resting activity tends to occur in high-frequency bursts, these movements tend to trigger bursts, with a latency of about 30 milliseconds. We are now in the process of correlating in a quantitative way the bursts and the movements.

CONCLUSION

I have described how my own research has come full circle, beginning and ending with work in awake behaving animals. I admit that I regret leaving acute experiments, because I see no other way, at present, of obtaining the physiologic and anatomic correlations that are necessary to understand fine structures such as cortical columns. But to understand the brain will take many different approaches, and what we learn from these different ap-

proaches will be mutually reinforcing. For years my main interest has been the understanding of perception. Understanding consciousness is a tougher question, in part because understanding perception is, in my opinion, a prerequisite. So perhaps, after all, I am not at this meeting entirely on false pretenses.

REFERENCES

1. Hubel DH. Cortical unit responses to visual stimuli in nonanesthetized cats. *Am J Ophthalmol* 1958;46: 110–122.
2. Riggs LA, Ratliff F. The effects of counteracting the normal movements of the eye. *J Opt Soc Am* 1952;42: 872–873.
3. Ditchburn RW, Ginsburg BL. Vision with a stabilized image. *Nature* 1952;170:36–37.

DISCUSSION

Moderated by Benjamin Libet

Barbara E. Jones: I know your first paper very well on single unit recording in monkeys in association with sleep, at the same time that Evarts and Moruzzi had also performed such recordings in the cortex. And the surprise, I think, that was expressed in all that work, was the fact that with the onset of sleep, bursting occurred that thus looked like an increase in neuronal discharge. In some ways, it still remains a mystery that this bursting can occur for example in the motor system, carried down through the pyramidal tract fibers at a time when there is no motor inhibition and yet there is no movement. There is one illustrative piece of recent work by Lindstrom in the thalamus, where he demonstrated that high-frequency stimulation, particularly around 20 to 30 Hz, is followed very faithfully by thalamic relay cells, whereas low-frequency, 1- to 3-Hz stimulation, which we would presume might evoke a burst type of activity, was not followed but instead resulted in an attenuation of the thalamic cell discharges. I am wondering if you have any ideas as to why bursting during waking would presumably be associated with a strong response whereas bursting during sleep would not?

David H. Hubel: It is in sleep that you see the bursts in geniculate cells. In the fully awake animal, you can see firing whose normal rate is the same as that of the bursting firing in sleep. So, I do not have the slightest idea what advantage it is to the animal, that the firing is in bursts during sleep. It may be in some sense simply an epiphenomenon and not have any beneficial effects. But we cannot know that, at least I do not know that.

Alan J. McComas: I very much like your comment on a suggestion made by Crick and Koch that perhaps the primary visual receiving area, area 17, is not amenable to a conscious equivalent. To me, it would be rather odd if we could not see the sort of linear stimulus that you could create. But also there is this. About 2 years ago I had my first migrainous aura, and I saw these shimmering zig-zag lights, and it suddenly occurred to me: could this not be a wave of depolarization advancing over the primary visual area and eliciting those linear detector cells? What do you think of that?

David H. Hubel: I would have thought that you cannot be sure. You cannot negate the idea that consciousness does not occur in the primary visual cortex on those grounds because almost certainly the migrainous aura leads to firing of cells in the primary visual cortex, whose activity is related to what you see. But you may very well be seeing the lights by virtue of the projections from those cells to the next area and the next and so on down the stream. I have a hard time linking up in my mind the idea of consciousness residing in some area, though I think I understood Crick and Koch's paper and I do not have any ready argument against it. It is just a bit hard to understand how you can have firing in an area and not have firing in the area that this area projects to. So, it is a bit hard for me to think of consciousness residing anywhere, because anywhere projects to somewhere else. But I think that Christof probably has a good argument against that, and certainly Francis too. I would be absolutely confident that what goes on in our primary visual cortex most of the time leads to a conscious sensation. Of course, V1 is just one link in a very long chain.

Consciousness: At the Frontiers of Neuroscience,
Advances in Neurology, Vol. 77,
edited by H.H. Jasper, L. Descarries,
V.F. Castellucci, and S. Rossignol.
Lippincott–Raven Publishers, Philadelphia © 1998.

16

The Neuroanatomy of Visual Consciousness

Christof Koch

Division of Biology, California Institute of Technology, Pasadena, California 91125

What is the relationship between a sensory percept and the underlying neuronal activity in some part of the brain? This chapter summarizes our theoretical framework for answering the question based on the neuroanatomy and physiology of the mammalian cortex and associated subcortical structures. Increasing data suggest that primates are not directly aware of neural activity in the primary visual cortex, although they are likely to be aware of such activity in extrastriate cortical areas. Psychophysical and electrophysiologic evidence supporting this hypothesis is discussed.

BASIC ASSUMPTIONS

What is the relationship between "consciousness" or "awareness,"[1] particularly visual awareness, and neuronal activity in the nervous system? Within a larger context, this question is frequently known as the mind–body problem and has been asked since antiquity. Over the past 8 years, Francis Crick and I have attempted to understand this relationship by focusing on the neuronal correlate of consciousness (NCC). Note that whenever information is represented in the NCC, it is represented in consciousness. This chapter provides an overview of the framework we advocate and provides some of our more recent speculations. We have previously (1–4) described our general approach to the problem of visual awareness. In brief, we believe the next important step is to find experimentally the neuronal correlates of various aspects of visual awareness; that is, how best to explain our subjective mental experience in terms of the behavior of large groups of nerve cells. At this early stage in our investigation, we will not worry too much about many fascinating but currently unrewarding aspects of the problem, such as what species do and what species do not have awareness, different forms of awareness (such as dreams, visual imagination, etc.), and the deep problem of qualia.[2] We here restrict our attention mainly to results on humans and on the macaque monkey because their visual systems appear to be similar and, at the moment, we cannot obtain all the information we need from either of them separately.

Our main assumption is that, at any point in time, the firing of some but not all the neurons in what we call the visual cortical system

---

[1]Although some philosophers (64) distinguish "access" awareness from "phenomenal" awareness for logical and ontologic reasons, we see no reason at the moment to do so (e.g., what would it mean to have phenomenal awareness without access awareness?) and will continue to consider them to be the same unless a distinction can be made on either neuronal or psychological grounds.

[2]At the moment, Chalmer's "hard problem" (65) of qualia is indeed a hard problem. Only the future will show whether it will remain a truly hard epistemologic one.

(which includes the neocortex and the hippocampus as well as a number of directly associated structures, such as the visual parts of the thalamus and possibly the claustrum) correlates with visual awareness. However, visual awareness is highly unlikely to be caused by the firing of all neurons in this system that happen to respond above their background rate at any particular moment. If at any given point in time only 1% of all the neurons in the cortex fire significantly, about one billion cells in sensory, motor, and association cortices would be active and we would never be able to distinguish any particular event within this vast sea of active nerve cells. We strongly expect that the majority of neurons will be involved in performing computations, whereas a much smaller number will express the results of these computations. It is probably only a subset of the latter that we become aware of.

There is already preliminary evidence from the study of the firing of neurons during binocular rivalry that in area MT of the macaque monkey only a fraction of neurons follow the monkey's percept (5). We can thus usefully ask the question, what are the essential differences between those neurons whose firing does correlate with the visual percept and those whose firing does not? Are these "awareness" neurons of any particular cell type? Exactly where are they located, how are they connected, and is there anything special about their patterns of firing? Given the specificity inherent in individual neurons, it is possible that the neurons that directly cause visual consciousness are relatively sparse and share some unique combination of molecular, pharmacologic, biophysical, and anatomic properties.

At this point, it may be useful to state our fundamental assumptions:

1. To be aware of an object or an event, the brain has to construct an explicit, multilevel, symbolic interpretation of part of the visual scene.

By explicit, we mean that such a neuron— and a few closely associated ones—must be firing above background at that particular time in response to the feature they symbolize. The pattern of color dots on a television screen, for instance, contains an "implicit" representation of, say, a person's face, but only the dots and their locations are made explicit here; an explicit face representation would correspond to a light that is wired up in such a manner that it responds whenever a face appears somewhere on the TV screen.

By multilevel we mean, in psychological terms, different levels such as those that correspond, for example, to lines or to eyes or to faces. In neurologic terms we mean, loosely, the different levels in the visual hierarchy (6).

By symbolic, as applied to a neuron, we mean that the neuron's firing is strongly correlated with some feature of the visual world and thus symbolizes it (this use of the word "symbol" should not be taken to imply the existence of a homunculus that is looking at the symbol). The meaning of such a symbol depends not only on the neuron's receptive field (i.e., what visual features the neuron responds to), but also to what other neurons it projects to (its projective field). Whether a neural symbol is best thought of as a scalar (one neuron) or a vector (a group of closely associated neurons as in population coding in the superior colliculus) (7) is a difficult question that we shall not address here.

2. Awareness results from the firing of a coordinated subset of cortical (and possible thalamic) neurons that fire in some special manner for a certain length of time, probably for at least 100 or 200 milliseconds. This firing needs to activate some type of iconic memory.

We are assuming that the semiglobal activity that corresponds to awareness has to last for some minimum time (on the order of 100 milliseconds) and that events within that time window are treated by the brain as approximately simultaneous. An example would be the flashing for 20 milliseconds of a red light followed immediately by 20 milliseconds of a green light in the same position. The observer sees a transient yellow light (corresponding to the mixture of red and green) and not a red light changing into a green light (8). Other psychophysical experiments demonstrate that visual stimuli of less than 120 to 130 milliseconds produce perceptions having a subjective duration identical to those produced by stimuli of 120 to 130 milliseconds (9,10).

3. Unless a neuron has an elevated firing rate and unless it fires as a member of such an assembly (usually temporary), its firing will not directly symbolize some feature of awareness at that moment.

These ideas, taken together, place restrictions on what sort of changes can reach awareness. An example would be the visual awareness of movement in the visual scene. Both physiologic and psychophysical studies have shown that motion is extracted early in the visual system as a primitive (by the so-called short-range motion system) (11). We can be aware that something has moved (but not what has moved) because there are neurons whose firing symbolizes movement as such, being activated by certain changes in luminance. To know what has moved (as opposed to a mere change of luminance), there must be active neurons somewhere in the brain that symbolize, by their firing, that there has been a change of that particular character.

4. As a corollary, we formulate our activity principle: Underlying every direct perception is a group of neurons strongly firing in response to that stimulus that come to symbolize it. An example is the Kanizsa triangle illusion, in which three "Pacmen" are situated at the corners of a triangle, with their open mouths facing each other. Human observers see a white triangle with illusory lines, even though the intensity is constant between the Pacmen. As reported by Crow (12), cells in V2 of the awake monkey strongly respond to such illusory

lines. Another case is the filling-in of the blind spot in the retina (13). Because we do not have neurons that explicitly represent the blind spot and events within it, we are not aware of small objects whose image projects onto the blind spot and can only infer such objects indirectly.

A semiglobal activity that corresponds to awareness does not itself symbolize a change within that short period of awareness unless such a change is made explicit by some neurons whose firing makes up the semiglobal activity (because what else but another group of neurons can express the notion that a change has occurred?). These ideas are counterintuitive and are not easy to grasp on first reading because the "fallacy of the homunculus" slips in all too easily if one does not watch out for it.

THE NEURONAL CORRELATE OF CONSCIOUSNESS

It follows that active neurons in the cortical system that do not take part in the semiglobal activity at the moment can still lead to behavioral changes but without being associated with awareness. These neurons are responsible for the large class of phenomena that bypass awareness in normal subjects, such as automatic processes, priming, subliminal perception, learning without awareness, learning to recognize complex sequences and changes in the rules underlying these sequences, and so on (14–16), or take part in the computations leading up to awareness. In fact, we suspect that the majority of neurons in the cortical system at any given time are not directly associated with awareness!

The elevated firing activity of these neurons would explain blindsight and similar clinical phenomena under circumstances in which patients with cortical blindness can point fairly accurately to the position of objects in their blind visual field (or detect motion or color) while strenuously denying that they see anything (17–19).

We have argued from the experiments on binocular rivalry (20,21) that the firing of some cortical neurons does not correlate with the percept. It is conceivable that all cortical neurons may be capable of participating in the representation of one percept or another, although not necessarily doing so for all percepts. The secret of visual awareness would then be the type of activity of a temporary subset of them, consisting of all those cortical neurons that represent that particular percept at that moment. An alternative hypothesis is that there are special sets of "awareness" neurons somewhere in the cortex (e.g., layer V bursting cells). Awareness would then result from the activity of these special neurons. We are interested in finding such neurons, the ultimate NCC.

It is quite possible that these neurons are characterized by a unique combination of molecular, biophysical, pharmacologic, and anatomic traits. Indeed, if such neurons exist, it is only a question of time before specific molecular markers, such as antibodies that label them, are found. It is likely that the set of NCC neurons will be distributed throughout the cortical system.

Note that finding and identifying these NCC neurons will only constitute one step in understanding the neuronal basis of consciousness. Others include finding their projection patterns, in particular into what parts of the brain they project, their developmental time course, how these are affected in various diseases that affect consciousness, and so on.

Such neurons must project directly to some part of the front of the cortex, particularly to the premotor and prefrontal areas anterior to the primary motor area (22). We recently (23) discussed the need for projections from the visual system to the front of the brain. Our basic argument assumes that in moving from one visual area to another farther up in the visual hierarchy, that is, farther away from the retina (6,24,25), the information is recoded at each step. This is certainly broadly compatible with the known fact that the features to which a neuron responds become more complex in going from the primary visual cortex, V1 (also called striate cortex, or area 17), to the higher levels in the visual hierarchy, such as the inferotemporal cortical areas (26,27).

The hypothesis that the NCC corresponds to a relatively small but spatially distributed set of neurons contrasts with the ideas put forth by many scientists that ascribe consciousness to very large ensembles of neurons interacting in ill-defined, collective ways (28).

THE FUNCTION OF CONSCIOUSNESS

Why should the NCC be directly involved with the frontal areas? This assumption is based on the broad idea of the biologic usefulness of visual awareness (or, strictly, of its neuronal correlate). This is "to produce the best current interpretation of the visual scene, in the light of past experience either of ourselves or of our ancestors (embodied in our genes), and to make it available, for a sufficient time, to the parts of the brain which contemplate, plan and execute voluntary motor outputs (of one sort or another)" (23).

This hypothesis is compatible with the experimental evidence—alluded to above—that complex cognitive processing can occur in the absence of consciousness. Our viewpoint holds that consciousness is necessary for planning nontrivial and nonstereotypical behaviors. It is perfectly compatible with the evidence summarized so elegantly by Milner and Goodale in their 1995 monograph (29,30).

Briefly, they argue for two systems operating in parallel in the primate brain, one (or more) on-line system as well as a conscious one. The on-line system can be primed beforehand, responds rapidly and in a stereotype and unconscious manner, is probably inactivated by imposing a delay (on the order of 1 to 10 seconds) between stimulus and response, works in egocentric coordinates, lacks certain perceptual "constancy" illusions, and probably contains no explicit neuronal representation. Two examples of on-line systems include the visuomotor systems controlling certain types of eye and hand movements (31).

Milner and Goodale (29) identify these on-line systems with the dorsal stream of information originating in primary visual cortex and terminating in posterior parietal areas. In their view the system mediating conscious vision is closely associated with the ventral stream of information (from V1 to the inferior temporal cortex).

PREFRONTAL BRAIN AREAS AND PLANNING

Exactly how the premotor and prefrontal cortical areas operate is currently unknown, although there is now fragmentary evidence about the behavior of some of them. Even in the macaque, the details of neuroanatomic connections between all of these areas have not yet been worked out in as much detail as they have for most of the visual areas of the macaque (22,32–35).

It is probably a general rule that the farther (connectionwise) a prefrontal area is from the primary motor area, the longer the time scale of the planning it is engaged in (32,36). Moreover, these cortical areas are all heavily involved with the basal ganglia (which include the neostriatum, the globus pallidus, and the substantia nigra), whose main function, we speculate, is to provide a bias back to these areas (as well as to the superior colliculus in the mid-brain) to influence the next step in their processing; that is, to assist some behaviors that involve a sequence of activities. The subject is additionally complicated for humans because of our highly developed language system and its usefulness for expressing our thoughts (e.g., in silent speech).

Fortunately, at this stage, the details of the behavior of these frontal areas need not concern us. All we need to postulate is that unless a visual area has a direct projection to at least one of them, the activities in that particular visual area will not enter visual awareness directly.

PRIMARY VISUAL CORTEX AND ITS CONNECTIONS

The lack of any projection from V1 to frontal areas appears to hold true in the macaque monkey. V1 is, of course, the almost exclusive recipient of the output of the lateral geniculate nucleus (LGN). V1 has no direct projections to the frontal eye fields (part of area 8), nor to the broad prefrontal region surrounding and including the principal sulcus (see Table 3 in ref. 6); nor, as far as we know, to any other frontal area (Fig. 1). Nor, for that matter, does primary visual cortex in the monkey project to the caudate nucleus of the basal ganglia (37), nor to the intralaminar nuclei of the thalamus, the claustrum (38), or the brain stem (with the exception of a small projection from peripheral V1 to the pons) (39). V1 does, of course, provide the dominant visual input to most of the posterior visual cortical areas, including V2, V3, V4, and area MT (40). Among subcortical targets, the lower layers of V1 strongly project to the superficial layers of the superior colliculus (41) and lateral geniculate nucleus, as well as to the inferior and lateral pulvinar nuclei of the thalamus (26,42). We therefore conclude (23) that while activity in V1 may be necessary for vivid and visual activity, the firing of none of the neurons in V1 directly correlates with what we consciously see.

We think it unlikely that information sent along the pathway from V1 to the superior colliculus, responsible for controlling and initiating eye movements, can produce conscious visual awareness. There is a multistage pathway from V1 to the colliculus, from there to the (inferior) pulvinar and thence to higher visual areas. This pathway may be involved in visual attention (42), but according to our arguments, it is not sufficiently direct or strong to produce, by itself, vivid visual awareness of the neural activities in V1.

The pathway from V1 to the colliculus might possibly be used to produce involuntary eye movements so that psychophysical tests, using eye movements as the response, might

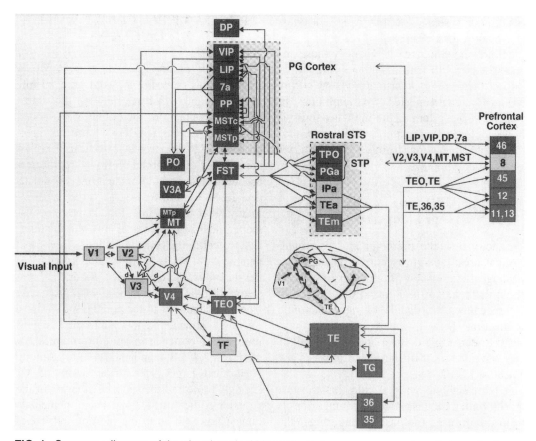

FIG. 1. Summary diagram of the visual cortical hierarchy in the macaque monkey. Only cortical connections are shown. The primary visual cortex (V1) receives a strong projection from both eyes via the lateral geniculate nucleus (not shown). Solid arrowheads indicate feedforward connections, open arrows indicate feedback connections. Almost all connections among cortical areas are reciprocal. (See colorplate 2.) Red indicates areas that are part of the inferior temporal (the so-called object vision) processing stream, whereas green indicates areas belonging to the parietal (the so-called spatial vision) processing stream. Areas shown in yellow receive input or project their outputs into both of these functional distinct streams (Leslie Ungerleider, personal communication). Adapted with permission (66).

show a form of blindsight in which subjects respond above chance while denying that they see anything. It is also possible that this or other pathways can produce vague feelings of some sort of awareness.

PRIMARY VISUAL CORTEX AND AWARENESS

Our hypothesis is too speculative to be convincing as it stands because we are not yet confident as to how to think correctly about most of the operations of the brain, especially about the detailed function of the so-called back pathways. Many readers will find these suggestions counterintuitive. We would ask, do you believe that you are directly aware of the activity in your retina? Of course, without your retinas, you cannot see anything. If you do not believe this, what is the argument that you are directly aware of the neural activity in V1?

To avoid misunderstanding, let us underline what our hypothesis does not say. We are not

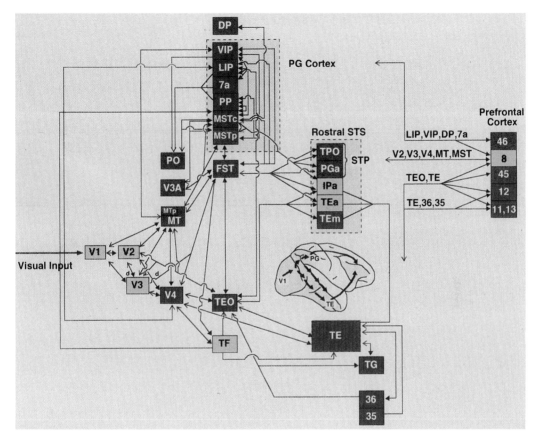

COLORPLATE 2. Summary diagram of the visual cortical hierarchy in the macaque monkey. Only cortical connections are shown. The primary visual cortex (V1) receives a strong projection from both eyes via the lateral geniculate nucleus (not shown). Solid arrowheads indicate feedforward connections, open arrows indicate feedback connections. Almost all connections among cortical areas are reciprocal. Red indicates areas that are part of the inferior temporal (the so-called object vision) processing stream, whereas green indicates areas belonging to the parietal (the so-called spatial vision) processing stream. Areas shown in yellow receive input or project their outputs into both of these functional distinct streams (Leslie Ungerleider, personal communication). Adapted with permission (66).

suggesting that the neural activity in V1 is unimportant. On the contrary, the detailed processing in V1 is crucial for normal vision, although recent work (43) has shown that V1 in at least one patient is not essential for some limited form of visual awareness related to motion perception. All we are hypothesizing is that the activity in V1 does not directly enter awareness. What does enter awareness, we believe, is some form of the neural activity in certain higher visual areas because they do project directly to prefrontal areas. This seems well established for cortical areas in the fifth tier of the visual hierarchy, such as MT and V4. For areas in the intervening tiers, such as V2, V3, V3A, VP, and PIP, we prefer to leave the matter open for the moment (see Table 3 in ref. 6).

Our hypothesis was suggested by neuroanatomic data from the old-world macaque monkey. For humans, we are less certain, due to the present miserable state of human neuroanatomy (44), but we surmise that our hypothesis, if true for the macaque monkey, is also likely to be true for apes and humans. To be established as correct, it also needs to fit with all the neurophysiologic and psychological data. What kind of evidence would support it?

WHAT IS THE RELATIONSHIP BETWEEN SINGLE NEURONS AND PERCEPTION?

Our strategy is to relate the receptive field properties of individual neurons to perception in a quantitative manner. Given the similarity at the quantitative level between the visual behavior of macaque monkeys and humans on the one hand and the structure of their visual systems on the other, we adopt the working hypothesis that it is at the moment useful to relate the receptive field properties of V1 cells in the macaque to human perception. Ultimately, the link between neurons and perception will need to be made in humans.

If the structure of perception does not map to the receptive field properties of V1 cells, it is unlikely that these neurons directly give rise

to consciousness. In the presence of a correlation between perceptual experience and the receptive field properties of one or more groups of V1 cells, it is unclear whether these cells just correlate with consciousness or directly give rise to it. In that case, further experiments (most likely involving invasive lesion or stimulation experiments) need to be conducted to untangle the exact relationship between neurons and perception.

A possible example may make this clearer. It is well known that the color we perceive at one particular visual location is influenced by the wavelengths of the light entering the eye from surrounding regions in the visual field (45,46). This mechanism acts to partially compensate for the effects of differently colored illumination. A white patch surrounded by patches of many colors still looks fairly white even when illuminated by pink light. This form of (partial) color constancy is often called the Land effect.

It has been shown in the anesthetized monkey (47,48) that neurons in V4, but not in V1, exhibit the Land effect. As far as we know, the corresponding information is lacking for alert monkeys. Because we cannot ourselves turn the Land effect on or off, it would follow—if the same results could be obtained in a behaving monkey—that we would not be directly aware of the "color" neurons in V1. Notice that if neurons in both V1 and V4 in the alert monkey did turn out to show the full Land effect, this would not by itself disprove our hypothesis, because we do believe that we are visually aware of certain neural activity in V4 that could be triggered by activity in V1.

Likewise, when two isoluminant colors are alternated at frequencies beyond 10 Hz, humans perceive only a single fused color with a minimal sensation of brightness flicker. Despite the perception of color fusion, color opponent cells in primary visual cortex of two alert old-world macaque monkeys follow high-frequency flicker well above heterochromatic fusion frequencies (49). In other words, neuronal activity in V1 can clearly represent retinal stimulation yet it is not perceived. Very recently, functional imaging in humans has demonstrated that brain activity in V1 and V2—as assessed via functional magnetic resonance imaging—is in quantitative agreement with the perception of colors at temporal frequencies of 1 and 4 Hz but is orthogonal to perception at flicker frequencies of 10 Hz (50).

Another example are neurons in V1 whose firing depends on which eye the visual signal is coming through. Neurons higher in the visual hierarchy do not make this distinction; that is, they are binocular. We are certainly not vividly and directly aware of which eye we are seeing with (unless we close or blink one eye), although whether we have some weak awareness of the eye of origin is more controversial (51–54). These well-known facts suggest that we are not vividly aware of much of what goes on in V1.

Psychophysical experiments would support our hypothesis if they demonstrate that we are not aware of neuronal activity that is highly likely to occur in V1. A number of such psychophysical experiments performed within the past few years have accumulated much evidence that, indeed, is compatible with the idea that the neuronal correlate of consciousness must be located beyond primary visual cortex (53,55,56).

As one example, let us briefly review the experiment of He and colleagues (57). Their basic design is so simple that it is bound to be widely replicated. It is based on a common visual aftereffect (related in kind to the well-known waterfall illusion or motion aftereffect). If a subject stares for a fraction of a minute at a horizontal grating and then looks at a faint test grating to decide whether it is oriented vertically or horizontally, the subject's sensitivity for detecting a horizontal grating will be reduced. This adaptation is orientation specific—the sensitivity for vertical

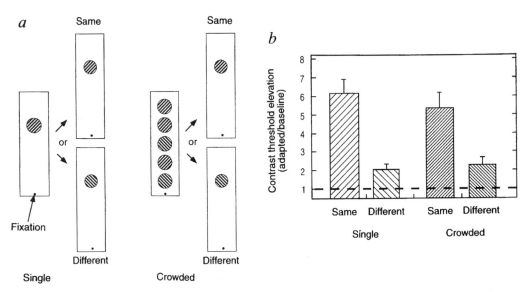

FIG. 2. Psychophysical displays (schematic) and results pertaining to adaptation by "crowded" grating patches. **A:** Adaptation followed by contrast threshold measurement for a single grating (*left*) and a crowded grating (*right*). In each trial, the orientation of the adapting grating was either the same or different from the orientation of the test grating. Observers fixated on a point 25 degrees from the adapting and test gratings. **B:** Threshold contrast elevation after adaptation relative to baseline threshold contrast before adaptation. Data are averaged across four subjects. The difference between the same and different adapt-test orientations reflects the orientation-selective after effect due to the adapting grating. The data shows that this aftereffect is comparable for a crowded grating (whose orientation is not perceived) and for a single grating (whose orientation is readily perceived). Reproduced with permission (56).

gratings is almost unchanged—and disappears quickly.

He and colleagues projected a single patch of grating onto a computer screen (Fig. 2). It was clearly visible and their subjects showed the predictable orientation-selective adaptation effect. Adding one or more similar patches of gratings above or below the original grating—which remains exactly as before—removed it from visibility; it was masked. Subjectively, their subjects still saw "something" at the location of the original grating but were unable to make out its orientation (subjects were unable to reliably indicate grating orientation, even when given unlimited viewing time). Despite this inability to "see" the adapting stimulus, the aftereffect was as strong and as specific to the orientation of the "invisible" grating as when the grating was visible (Fig. 2). What this clearly proves, foreshadowed by earlier experiments (58), is that visual awareness must occur at a higher stage in the visual hierarchy than orientation-specific adaptation. This aftereffect is thought to be mediated by oriented neurons in V1 and beyond, implying that at least for this task, the neurons mediating visual awareness must be located past this stage.

These ideas are not disproven by positron emission tomography experiments showing that, at least in some people, V1 is activated during visual imagery tasks (59). Furthermore, severe damage to V1 is compatible with visual imagery in patients (60). There is no obvious reason why such top-down effects should not reach V1. Such V1 activity would not, by itself, prove that we are directly aware of it any more than the V1 activity produced there when our eyes are open proves this.

Our hypothesis, then, is a somewhat subtle one, although we believe that if it turns out to be true, it will eventually come to be regarded as completely obvious. We hope that further neuroanatomic work will make it plausible for humans and that further neurophysiologic studies will show it to be true for most primates. We have yet to track down the location and nature of the neuronal correlates of visual awareness. Our hypothesis provides a methodology to help locate the NCC and, if correct, would narrow the search to areas of the brain farther removed from the sensory periphery.

BISTABLE PERCEPTS

Before we close, let us discuss a promising experimental approach to locate the NCC. It involves the use of bistable percepts, that is, a constant visual stimulus that gives rise to two percepts, alternating in time, as in a Necker cube. The visual input, apart from minor eye movements, is constant; but the subject's percept can take one of two alternative forms. It was first suggested by Allman that a practical alternative to the Necker cube is to study the responses in the visual system during binocular rivalry (61). If the visual input into each eye is different, but overlapping, one usually sees the visual input as received by one eye alone, then by the other one, then by the first one, and so on. The input is constant, but the percept changes. Which neurons in the brain mainly follow the input, and which the percept? In one such case, a small image, say, of a horizontal grating, is presented to the left eye and another image, say, of a vertical grating, is presented to the corresponding location in the right eye. Despite the constant retinal stimulus, observers "see" the horizontal grating alternate every few seconds with the vertical one, a phenomenon known as binocular rivalry (62). The brain does not allow for the simultaneous perception of both images.

In a series of elegant, but difficult, experiments, Logothetis and colleagues (5,20,21; see also 63) trained macaque monkeys to report which of the two rivalrous inputs they saw. There is little doubt that monkeys and humans perceive the same basic phenomenon, given the similar distribution of switching times and the way in which changing the contrast in one eye affects these (Fig. 3). In early visual cortex, only a small fraction of cells modulated their response as a function of the percept of the monkey, whereas 20% to 30% of neurons

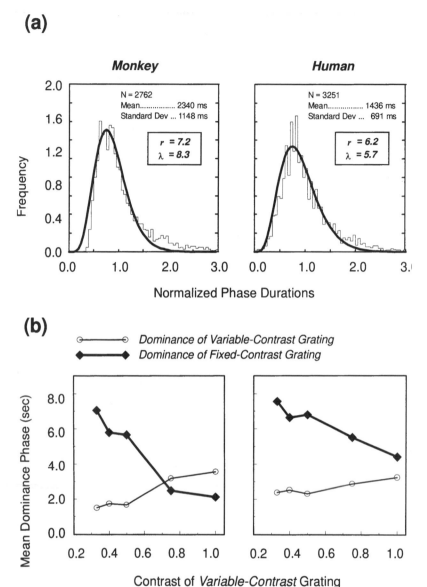

FIG. 3. Relationship between the perception of binocular rivalry for a macaque monkey and a human. The stimuli are two orthogonal gratings presented to the two eyes. **A:** Histogram of the times during which one or the other stimulus is perceived. These are normalized to the mean duration, which is on the order of a few seconds. These histograms, which can be approximed by a high-order gamma distribution, can be used to assess whether or not the monkey is "cheating." **B:** If the contrast of the grating in one eye is increased, the time for which this stimulus is perceptually suppressed is decreased. Here the fixed contrast of one grating was set to 1.0. This is true for humans as well as for monkeys. Reprinted with permission (20).

in MT and V4 cells did. That is, the majority of cells increased their firing rate in response to one or the other retinal stimulus with no regard to what the animal perceived at the time. In contrast, in a high-level cortical area, such as the inferior temporal cortex (IT), almost all neurons responded only to the perceptual dominant stimulus (in other words, a "face" cell only fired when the animal indi-

cated by its performance that it saw the face and not the sunburst pattern in the other eye; Fig. 4). This makes it likely that the NCC is located among (or beyond) IT neurons. These and other as yet unconceived experiments will tell us more about the nature of consciousness than the vast majority of philosophical speculations of the past several thousand years.

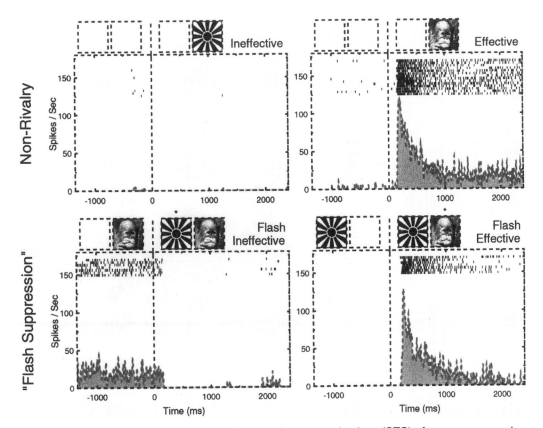

FIG. 4. The activity of a single neuron in the superior temporal sulcus (STS) of a macaque monkey in response to different stimuli presented to the two eyes. In the upper left panel a sunburst pattern is presented to the right eye without evoking any firing response ("ineffective" stimulus). The same cell will fire vigorously in response to its "effective" stimulus, here the image of a face (*upper right panel*). When the monkey is shown the face in one eye for a while and the sunburst pattern is flashed onto the monitor for the other eye, the monkey signals that it is "seeing" this new pattern and that the stimulus associated with the rivalrous eye is perceptually suppressed ("flash suppression," *lower left panel*). At the neuronal level, the cell shuts down in response to the ineffective yet perceptual dominant stimulus after stimulus onset (*dotted line*) even though the cell's optimal stimulus is still present. Conversely, if the monkey fixates the sunburst pattern for a while and the face is flashed on, the monkey reports that it perceives the face and the cell will now strongly fire (*lower right panel*). Neurons in V4, earlier in the cortical hierarchy, are largely unaffected by the perceptual changes during flash suppression. Reprinted with permission (21).

ACKNOWLEDGMENT

All of the ideas presented here were jointly developed with Dr. Francis Crick. The support of the Larry Hanson Foundation, the Office of Naval Research, and the National Science Foundation is gratefully acknowledged.

REFERENCES

1. Crick FCH, Koch C. Towards a neurobiological theory of consciousness. *Semin Neurosci* 1990;2:263–275.
2. Crick FCH, Koch C. Some reflections on visual awareness. *Cold Spring Harb Symp Quant Biol* 1990;55:953–962.
3. Crick FCH, Koch C. The problem of consciousness. *Sci Am* 1992;267:153–159.
4. Koch C, Crick FCH. Some further ideas regarding the neuronal basis of awareness. In: Koch C, Davis J, eds. *Large-scale neuronal theories of the brain.* Cambridge, MA: MIT Press, 1994:93–110.
5. Logothetis NK, Schall JD. Neuronal correlates of subjective visual perception. *Science* 1989;245:761–763.
6. Felleman DJ, Van Essen DC. Distributed hierarchical processing in the primate visual cortex. *Cereb Cortex* 1991;1:1–47.
7. Lee C, Rohrer W, Sparks DL. Population coding of saccadic eye movements by neurons in the superior colliculus. *Nature* 1988;332:357–360.
8. Efron R. Conservation of temporal information by perceptual systems. *Percept Psychophys* 1973;14:518–530.
9. Efron R. The relationship between the duration of a stimulus and the duration of a perception. *Neuropsychologia* 1970;8:37–55.
10. Efron R. The minimum duration of a perception. *Neuropsychologia* 1970;8:57–63.
11. Braddick OJ. Low-level and high-level processes in apparent motion. *Philos Trans R Soc [Biol]* 1980;290:137–151.
12. von der Heydt R, Peterhans E, Baumgartner G. Illusory contours and cortical neuron responses. *Science* 1984;224:1260–1262.
13. Fiorani M, Rosa MGP, Gattass R, Rocha-Miranda CE. Dynamic surrounds of receptive fields in primate striate cortex: a physiological basis for perceptual completion. *Proc Natl Acad Sci U S A* 1992;89:8547–8551.
14. Kihlstrom JF. The cognitive unconscious. *Science* 1987;237:1445–1452.
15. Tulving E, Schacter DL. Priming and human memory systems. *Science* 1990;247:301–306.
16. Berns GS, Cohen JD, Mintun MA. Brain regions responsive to novelty in the absence of awareness. *Science* 1997;276:1272–1275.
17. Weiskrantz L. *Consciousness lost and found.* Oxford, England: Oxford University Press, 1997.
18. Stoerig P, Cowey A. Wavelength sensitivity in blindsight. *Nature* 1991;342:916–918.
19. Wessinger CM, Fendrich R, Gazzaniga MS. Islands of residual vision in hemianopic patients. *J Cognitive Neurosci* 1997;9:203–211.
20. Leopold DA, Logothetis NK. Activity changes in early visual cortex reflect monkeys percepts during binocular rivalry. *Nature* 1996;379:549–553.
21. Sheinberg DL, Logothetis NK. The role of temporal cortical areas in perceptual organization. *Proc Natl Acad Sci U S A* 1997;94:3408–3413.
22. Fuster JM. Frontal lobes. *Curr Opin Neurobiol* 1993;3:160–165.
23. Crick FHC, Koch C. Are we aware of neural activity in primary visual cortex? *Nature* 1995;375:121–124.
24. Zeki S, Shipp S. The functional logic of cortical connections. *Nature* 1988;335:311–317.
25. Young MP. Objective analysis of the topological organization of the primate cortical visual system. *Nature* 1992;358:152–155.
26. Ungerleider LG, Desimone R, Galkin TW, Mishkin M. Subcortical projections of area MT in the macaque. *J Comp Neurol* 1984;223:368–386.
27. Maunsell JHR, Newsome WT. Visual processing in monkey extrastriate cortex. *Ann Rev Neurosci* 1987;10:363–401.
28. Greenfield SA. *Journey to the centers of the mind.* New York: WH Freeman, 1995.
29. Milner AD, Goodale MA. *The visual brain in action.* Oxford, England: Oxford University Press, 1995.
30. Rossetti Y. Implicit perception in action: short-lived motor representations of space evidence by brain-damaged and healthy subjects. In: Grossenbacher PG, ed. *Consciousness and brain circuitry: neurocognitive systems which mediate subjective experience.* Philadelphia: J Benjamins, 1997.
31. Bridgeman B, Lewis S, Heit G, Nagle M. Relation between cognitive and motor-oriented systems of visual position perception. *J Exp Psychol (Hum Percept)* 1970;5:692–700.
32. Fuster JM. *The prefrontal cortex,* 2nd ed. New York: Raven, 1989.
33. Barbas H. Architecture and cortical connections of the prefrontal cortex in the rhesus monkey. In: Chauvel P, Delgado-Escueta AV, Halgren E, Bancaud J. eds. *Advances in neurology.* Vol. 57. New York: Raven, 1992:91–115.
34. Gerfen CR. Relations between cortical and basal ganglia compartments. In: Thierry AM, Glowinski J, Goldman-Rakic PS, Christen Y, eds. *Motor and cognitive functions of the prefrontal cortex.* Berlin: Springer-Verlag, 1994:78–92.
35. Webster MJ, Bachevalier J, Ungerleider LG. Connections of inferior temporal areas TEO and TE with parietal and frontal cortex in macaque monkeys. *Cereb Cortex* 1994;5:470–483.
36. Birbaumer N, Elbert T, Canavan AGM, Rockstroh B. Slow potentials of the cerebral cortex and behavior. *Physiol Rev* 1990;70:1–41.
37. Saint-Cyr JA, Ungerleider LG, Desimone R. Organization of visual cortex inputs to the striatum and subsequent outputs to the pallidonigral complex in the monkey. *J Comp Neurol* 1990;298:129–156.
38. Sherk H. The claustrum and the cerebral cortex. In: Jones EG, Peters A, eds. *Cerebral cortex.* Vol. 5. New York: Plenum, 1986:467–499.
39. Fries W. Pontine projection from striate and prestriate visual cortex in the macque monkey: an anterograde study. *Visual Neurosci* 1990;4:205–216.
40. Bullier J, Girard P, Salin PA. The role of area 17 in the transfer of information to extrastriate visual cortex. In: Peters A, Rockland KS, eds. *Cerebral cortex.* Vol. 10. New York: Plenum, 1994:301–330.

41. Sparks DL. Translation of sensory signals into commands for control of saccadic eye movements: role of primate superior colliculus. *Physiol Rev* 1986;66: 1181–1172.

42. Robinson DL, Petersen SE. The pulvinar and visual salience. *Trends Neurosci* 1992;15:127–132.

43. Barbur JL, Watson JDG, Frackowiak RSJ, Zeki S. Conscious visual perception without V1. *Brain* 1993;116: 1293–1302.

44. Crick FHC, Jones E. The backwardness of human neuroanatomy. *Nature* 1993;361:109–110.

45. Land EH, McCann JJ. Lightness and retinex theory. *J Opt Soc Am* 1971;61:1–11.

46. Blackwell ST, Buchsbaum G. Quantitative studies of color constancy. *J Opt Soc Am [A]* 1988;5:1772–1780.

47. Zeki SM. Colour coding in the cerebral cortex: the reaction of cells in monkey visual cortex to wavelengths and colors. *Neuroscience* 1983;9:741–765.

48. Schein SJ, Desimone R. Spectral properties of V4 neurons in the macaque. *J Neurosci* 1990;10:3369–3389.

49. Gur M, Snodderly DM. A dissociation between brain activity and perception: chromatically opponent cortical neurons signal chromatic flicker that is not perceived. *Vis Res* 1997;37:377–382.

50. Engel S, Zhang X, Wandell B. Colour tuning in human visual cortex measured with functional magnetic resonance imaging. *Nature* 1997;388:68–70.

51. Pickersgill MJ. On knowing with which eye one is seeing. *Q J Exp Psychol* 1961;11:168–172.

52. Blake R, Cormack RH. On utrocular discrimination. *Percept Psychophysics* 1979;26:53–68.

53. Kolb FC, Braun J. Blindsight in normal observers. *Nature* 1995;377:336–339.

54. Morgan MJ, Mason AS, Solomon JA. Blindsight in normal subjects? *Nature* 1997;385:401–402.

55. He S, Smallman H, MacLeod D. Neural and cortical limits on visual resolution. *Invest Opthalmol Vis Sci* 1995;36:2010.

56. Koch C, Braun J. On the functional anatomy of visual awareness. *Cold Spring Harb Symp Quant Biol* 1996; 61:49–57.

57. He S, Cavanagh P, Intriligator J. Attentional resolution and the locus of visual awareness. *Nature* 1996;383: 334–337.

58. Blake R, Fox R. Adaptation to invisible gratings and the site of binocular rivalry suppression. *Nature* 1974;249: 488–490.

59. Kosslyn SM, Thompson WL, Kim IJ, Alpert NM. Topographical representations of mental images in primary visual cortex. *Nature* 1995;378:496–498.

60. Goldenberg G, Müllbacher W, Nowak A. Imagery without perception—a case study of anosognosia for cortical blindsight. *Neuropsychologia* 1995;33: 1373–1382.

61. Myerson J, Miezin F, Allman J. Binocular rivalry in macaque monkeys and humans: a comparative study in perception. *Behav Anal Lett* 1981;1:149–156.

62. Blake R. A neural theory of binocular rivalry. *Psychol Rev* 1989;96:145–167.

63. Bradley DC, Chang GC, Andersen RA. Activities of motion-sensitive neurons in primate visual area MT reflect the perception of depth. *Nature* 1998;392:714–717.

64. Block N. How can we find the neural correlate of consciousness. *Trends Neurosci* 1996;19:456–459.

65. Chalmers D. *The conscious mind: in search of a funda-*

mental theory. Oxford, England: Oxford University Press, 1995.

66. Distler C, Boussaoud D, Desimone R, Ungerleider LG. Cortical connections of inferior temporal area IEO in macaque monkeys. *J Comp Neurol* 1993;334:125–150.

DISCUSSION

Moderated by Benjamin Libet

Jeffrey A. Gray: Three comments. First, that was a splendid run through a very interesting approach to the problem. Second, I remember getting just as excited as you evidently are by the Kolb and Braun report (1) and giving a couple of lectures using the same description that you went through. But then Mike Morgan told me, and subsequently published a report to the effect, that he was quite unable after many tries to replicate that finding (2). I do not know whether you are aware of that, but if you are, you probably ought to be very cautious.

Christof Koch: Yes, I am aware of that report. Braun is now trying to use functional magnetic resonance imaging to develop an objective measure of what they have reported in the Kolb and Braun *Nature* publication.

Jeffrey A. Gray: The other comment is this: I do not know the anatomy well enough, but I have the suspicion that one could follow a similar logic to yours, but starting from the argument that the critical cells are the ones in the visual system which get feedback from the comparator system that I proposed in my paper earlier. I believe that this approach might even identify the same or similar cells to those identified by your approach. I think of this feedback as being a rather general "look out" signal; it is more of a modulatory signal, as you would expect from just switching on and off a major inhibitory route. But there is also a more specific route for feedback via the entorhinal cortex and on from there to various other cortical regions. Now, the entorhinal cortex is, of course, also a major target for the prefrontal cortex. So, if I followed your kind of logic from my kind of hypothesis, I would be saying that the critical cells for the neural correlate of consciousness are the ones that get feedback from the hippocampal system (via the subicular and entorhinal regions). And it would not surprise me if there were a great overlap between cells picked out this way and cells picked out by their forward projections to, and reciprocal projections from, the frontal cortex, because it is all part of the same overarching system. I would be interested to know what you think about that.

Christof Koch: Yes, your proposal is eminently sensible and eminently possible. The main reason we are cautious about involving the hippocampus too much in generating consciousness is the patient H.M. In him and in similar patients, the absence of the hippocampus proper, while severely affecting his ability to acquire new episodic or semantic memory, does not at all interfere with his sensory consciousness. There is little doubt that, *cum granulo salis,* H.M. sees the world as you or I do. Otherwise, I have no trouble with the notion that feedback from the subiculum or the hippocampus is involved—without being necessary—for some forms of consciousness.

Jeffrey A. Gray: Your hypothesis implies that prefrontal cortex is necessary for conscious vision. Do we not know of many prefrontal patients that can still see?

Christof Koch: I do not know of a single patient that had his or her entire prefrontal cortex, including Broca's area, on both sides taken out, not even Brickner's famous patient (3). We would like to study a patient in which all of the prefrontal cortex, including area 44 (Broca's area), is lesioned bilaterally. We believe that careful tests would reveal selective deficits in visual awareness in such a patient (which could be assayed using "subjective confidence" or similar measures) and that the patient might display some measure of blindsight.

Alan J. McComas: Like Dr. Gray, I was going to ask about the fact that one still has visual consciousness after prefrontal lesions. And in fact there are some patients, few patients, that have massive lesions of both frontal lobes. They are described by Freeman and Watts in a review many years ago. Of course there are many patients who had bilateral prefrontal leukotomies, including the orbital prefrontal fibers. That is one point. The second point is this: It goes back to your exclusion of V1 from consciousness. Surely a cell in V1 only knows which part of the visual field the object is in. It does not know which eye is presenting, unless there is information from some other point, the lateral geniculate nucleus, for example. What would happen if you would present a subject with a stimulus which the V1 cells are so uniquely able to respond to? In other words, a simple bar or edge or slit of light. Something that is not moving or does not have a more complex shape and so on.

Christof Koch: If I take a stimulus, say an oriented line, clearly cells in V1 will respond to that. The question is whether or not neurons that make this information accessible to consciousness are higher up in the cortical hierarchy or not. Crick and I would argue that they are located beyond V1. One way I can evaluate this hypothesis is by carefully matching receptive field

properties with what we are perceptually sensitive to on a trial-by-trial basis. As I pointed out in one of my slides, this becomes tricky if neurons in V1 and neurons in some higher cortical area correlate with the percept. Now, one could inactivate the higher visual areas and study whether the subject still retains visual consciousness with everything but V1—that included the neurons that do correlate with the particular percept—gone. There has been some anecdotal evidence (involving an orphaned child from Romania) in which everything but V1 was gone and in which V1 was still responding by evoked potential criteria. But it was not clear whether this child could still "see." So, we stand by our current hypothesis but point out, again, that it is a subtle one that will not be easy to completely test. The main thing to do is a careful matching between receptive field properties of cells at all different cortical processing levels and compare this with psychophysics.

As to the question regarding whether or not prefrontal patients are visually conscious, I can only repeat what I said in response to the previous question by Jeffrey. We do not know of a single patient in which all of the prefrontal cortex, on both sides, is lesioned. I would like to point out here that, unless one carefully evaluates such a patient, it might be difficult to detect such a subtle deficit. Let me remind you that the complete surgical section of the corpus callosum, an operation first performed in the 1930s, was argued by many of the neurosurgeons to cause no measurable symptoms or deficits (4). People did not find the very specific deficits we associate with split-brain patients today until Roger Sperry had carried out his seminal experiments on frogs, cats, and other animals, had predicted similar effects in patients, and Joe Bogen had tested for them. For me, it would be wonderful if we could have access to a patient whose prefrontal areas are lesioned on both sides. However—fortunately for such patients—this would be extremely unlikely today.

Pierre Caron: If you keep the setup from this one and you make the monkey aware of something else while this is continuing, will the neuron that was firing from what you thought was awareness of the phenomena become active from the new phenomena?

Christof Koch: Yes, an excellent idea. For example, what you could do in this case is to attract the visual attention of the monkey to some other, distracting stimulus (without getting the monkey to shift its eyes). In that case, you would expect the neuron that responded to the original stimulus to switch off. Also, you would really like to repeat the Logothetis experiments and record in prefrontal areas using single- or multiunit recordings. Can one find an area whose cellular response correlates perfectly with the behavior of the monkey? Ongoing experiments might yield an answer in a few years.

Discussion References

1. Kolb C, Braun J. Blindsight in normal observers. *Nature* 1995;377:336–339.

2. Morgan MJ, Mason AJS, Solomon JA. Blindsight in normal subjects? *Nature* 1997;385:401–402.

3. Damasio AR, Anderson SW. The frontal lobes. In: Heilman KM, Valenstein E, eds. *Clinical neuropsychology*, 3rd ed. Oxford, England: Oxford University Press, 1993:409–460.

4. Bogen JE. The callosal syndromes. In: Heilman KM, Valenstein E, eds. *Clinical neuropsychology*, 3rd ed. Oxford, England: Oxford University Press, 1993: 337–407.

Consciousness: At the Frontiers of Neuroscience,
Advances in Neurology, Vol. 77,
edited by H.H. Jasper, L. Descarries,
V.F. Castellucci, and S. Rossignol.
Lippincott–Raven Publishers, Philadelphia © 1998.

17

Consciousness and the Integration of Information in the Brain

Giulio Tononi and Gerald M. Edelman

The Neurosciences Institute, San Diego, California, 92121

Everyone knows what consciousness is: it is what abandons you every evening when you fall asleep and reappears the next morning when you wake up. This deceiving simplicity reminds us of what William James said of attention at the turn of the century: "Everyone knows what attention is. It is the taking possession by the mind, in clear and vivid form, of one out of what seem several simultaneously possible objects or trains of thought." More than 100 years later, many scientists think that we do not really understand the essence of either attention or consciousness. And yet, over the past 10 years, something has definitely changed in the scientific study of consciousness. Scientists seem less afraid of addressing the subject unabashedly, many books have appeared (1–3), new journals have been launched (*Consciousness and Cognition* and *Journal of Consciousness Studies*), and several studies have been conducted in which consciousness was treated as an experimental parameter (4,5).

This state of affairs has at least one advantage for our present purposes: much of the necessary background can be taken for granted. For a general introduction to the problem of consciousness and a discussion of its psychological and neurobiologic aspects, the reader can consult several recent monographs and reviews (3,7–17). A full neurobiologic account in which consciousness is ad-dressed from the perspective of a global theory of brain function, and which provides the foundation for the work reviewed here, can be found in a previous monograph (1). In this chapter, we will attempt to reexamine certain fundamental properties of consciousness and some of its key brain mechanisms in the light of recent experimental and theoretical developments. In particular, we will rely on the results of large-scale neural simulations and theoretical analyses that are part of a programmatic investigation of the properties and mechanisms of consciousness conducted at The Neurosciences Institute over the past several years (18–23).

A few initial statements should be sufficient to qualify our position with respect to some common philosophical arguments. As was pointed out some time ago (1), in order to develop testable hypotheses about consciousness, three assumptions are in order. The physics assumption states that only conventional physical processes are required for a satisfactory explanation. The evolutionary assumption states that consciousness is an evolved process. This implies that it is associated with certain biological structures and that it is likely to serve adaptive functions. The qualia assumption states that the subjective, qualitative aspects of consciousness, being private, cannot be communicated directly through a scientific theory, which by its nature is public and intersubjective. This does not mean that the necessary and sufficient conditions for consciousness cannot be described, only that describing them is not the same as generating them. Although we consider that the ontologic difference between being and describing is worth analyzing, for the moment it is better left to philosophers.

In analyzing consciousness, it is important to avoid addressing too many difficult problems at once. It is useful to distinguish, in particular, between primary consciousness and higher order consciousness (1). The former corresponds to the ability to build a multimodal "scene" that conjoins several different sources of information. Such a unified scene does not contain any self-referential aspect: it lives in the present, having no reference to the past, the future, or the self. Higher order consciousness emerges when these abilities become available, freeing the organism from the slavery of the here and now. This emergence appears to be tied to the emergence of language. By necessity, only individuals endowed with higher order consciousness can report and speak about consciousness. In what follows, we will concern ourselves mainly with primary consciousness; a discussion of higher order consciousness, including thought, language, and the notion of the self and self-reference, can be found in the text by Edelman (1). Accordingly, we will not address the nature or the mechanisms of memory, attention, and volition, although they are inextricably linked to the nature and mechanisms of consciousness.

Finally, when considering the necessary and sufficient conditions for consciousness to emerge, it is useful to distinguish between two levels of explanation: that of the general principles and properties that allow one to characterize consciousness, and that of the particular neural structures, mechanisms, and processes that instantiate these general principles and properties in the brain. We will address both of these aspects in turn.

OBSERVATIONS FROM PSYCHOLOGY: GENERAL PROPERTIES OF CONSCIOUS EXPERIENCE

At the beginning of Chapter IX of his magnum opus, considering the stream of thought, William James wrote: "Consciousness, from our natal day, is of a teeming multiplicity of objects and relations, and what we call simple sensations are results of discriminative attention, pushed often to a very high degree." A page later, he pointed out some of the essential properties of consciousness: it is individual (private); it is continuous and continually changing; it is about something (intentional); and it is selective (at any given time, certain aspects are inside consciousness, whereas others are out). Above all, James also insisted that consciousness is a process, rather than a thing.

Since the days of William James, and after the constraining parenthesis of behaviorism was relieved, a consensus seems to be emerging that such Jamesian properties are indeed at the heart of consciousness. Table 1 presents a list of key properties of primary consciousness that, in our opinion, must be accounted for by any theoretical approach to the problem. Following the insightful descriptions by James, several recent proposals have suggested that consciousness is like a scene in which much heterogeneous information can be combined into a coherent whole, and then used to influence a large number of brain processes. For instance, from the perspective of cognitive psychology, Baars (11,24) has elaborated on the metaphor of the scene, suggesting that consciousness is like a stage or a theater that can be used for accessing, distributing, and exchanging information, as well as for exercising global coordination and control—a kind of global workspace. Baars has reviewed much evidence, indicating that although such a global workspace has a great range of contents, great flexibility in relating such contents, and great internal consistency, it also appears to be slow, serial, error prone,

TABLE 1. *Key properties of primary consciousness*

Consciousness is a process, not a thing
It is integrated (unified, coherent, serial) and inherently subjective (private)
It is highly differentiated (an enormous number of different conscious states can be experienced)
The discrimination among integrated conscious states is highly informative and it occurs rapidly (fractions of a second)
Conscious experience is continuous, metastable over short intervals (fractions of a second), and constantly changing over longer intervals
It is selective (some information is in, some is out) and it has a center and a periphery
Information within consciousness is widely distributed, has wide access (it can lead to a large number of potential outputs), and is highly context dependent
Conjunctions within consciousness are dynamic and flexible, which is relevant for learning unanticipated associations
Consciousness is a product of evolution and serves an adaptive function

and subject to interference and to limited-capacity bottlenecks (11).

From a neurobiologic perspective, we have emphasized that consciousness concerns the rapid integration of signals from a great variety of modalities and submodalities to create a unified, coherent scene or idea (1). The number of possible conscious states is enormous, implying that conscious experience is highly differentiated or informative. The time scale of conscious integration is apparently around a few hundred milliseconds (25), although it can extend down to tens of milliseconds and up to a few seconds (26,27). Conscious integration in the brain implies vast distribution, wide access, and high context dependency of signals. Signals from subsets of specialized neuronal groups contributing to consciousness are distributed in parallel to many brain regions (wide distribution). Depending on the particular combination of signals, they can select among many different outputs (wide access), which may or may not involve behavior. Conversely, the activity of any subset of neurons contributing to a conscious scene can be influenced by that of many brain regions responding to different modalities and submodalities (context dependency). Such context dependency and flexibility of neural responses are of great adaptive significance. In particular, categorizations of causally unconnected parts of the world can be correlated and bound flexibly and dynamically together inside consciousness but not

outside it. Furthermore, present categorizations can be bound with past categorizations and with value-category memory, an ability that is needed to learn new and unexpected associations. Finally, we and others have emphasized the unity, coherency, and private nature of conscious states, as well as their ineluctable subjectivity (1).

OBSERVATIONS FROM NEUROLOGY AND NEUROPHYSIOLOGY: BRAIN MECHANISMS OF CONSCIOUS EXPERIENCE

The literature about brain structures, mechanisms, and processes that are involved in conscious experience is vast and heterogeneous (1). Here we offer a few observations that, taken together, provide important insights into the neural basis of conscious experience (Table 2). It is now established that some brain structures are more necessary than others for consciousness. First, it appears from studies of dreaming and imagery that, at least for short periods of time, consciousness can be generated within the thalamocortical system in relative autonomy from the rest of the brain, the body, or the world. There seems to be general agreement that the cerebral cortex is essential for determining the contents of consciousness. The results of lesion, stimulation, and recording studies indicate that the activity of specific cortical regions is closely tied to specific aspects of consciousness.

TABLE 2. *Neural mechanisms of primary consciousness*

Consciousness can be generated by the thalamocortical system in relative autonomy from the rest of the brain, body, or the world

The cerebral cortex is essential for determining the contents of consciousness

Different cortical areas and different groups of neurons within each area contribute specific aspects to conscious experience

No single cortical area is necessary or sufficient for conscious experience

Neurons whose activity correlates with consciousness are more easily found in "higher" cortical areas

Corticocortical loops are necessary for the conscious integration of signals from different modalities and submodalities

Thalamocortical loops that connect each cortical area to a specific thalamic nucleus sustain an ongoing activity that may be necessary for that area to contribute to consciousness

The reticular thalamic nucleus, which is interposed in all thalamocortical loops, may help in synchronizing thalamocortical activity or serve a gating function

The brain stem reticular activating system and the intralaminar thalamic nuclei are essential for maintaining the state of consciousness

Sheer number of neurons and connections are less important than their pattern and the resulting activity dynamics

Neural activity must be sufficiently long-lasting to contribute to consciousness directly

The intensity of specific neural activity is reflected in the intensity of specific aspects of conscious experience

Neural activity related to conscious experience is distributed more widely in the brain than neural activity that does not

Neural activity must possess sufficient variance to support conscious experience

Simultaneous activity without effective neural interactions is not sufficient for conscious integration

Synchronous neural activity, including synchronous oscillations in multiple frequency ranges, is indicative of globally effective long-range neural interactions

---

Within cortical areas, it is easier to find neurons whose activity correlates with consciousness in "higher" areas than in "lower" areas, at least for the well-studied visual system (4). Nevertheless, no single cortical area has been found that is necessary for supporting a conscious state (28). Instead, corticocortical connectivity seems to be essential for the conscious integration of signals from different modalities and submodalities.

Other brain structures, among which the brain stem reticular activating system and the intralaminar thalamic nuclei figure prominently, are essential for maintaining the state of consciousness (7,29,30). These structures may be important because they support or facilitate either the activity or the interactions among cortical regions, because they play a role in attentional modulation, or because they have some additional special function (31). In particular, thalamocortical loops that connect each cortical area to a specific thalamic nucleus sustain an ongoing activity that may be necessary for that area to contribute to consciousness (32). The reticular thalamic nucleus, which is interposed in all thalamocortical loops, may help in synchronizing thalamocortical activity or serve a gating function (9).

Neural activity in structures such as the cerebellum, which is comparable to the cerebral cortex in the number of neurons and of connections, does not seem to contribute to consciousness directly. This suggests that, rather than sheer numbers, what counts is the pattern of connections and the resulting dynamic activity. Moreover, some experimental evidence indicates that neural activity must be sufficiently long lasting and intense to contribute to consciousness directly. This is suggested, for example, by the experiments of Libet (33) and by studies of sensory masking (34). The occurrence of synchronous activity in certain frequency ranges in the thalamocortical system during conscious states (35–38) is an indicator of global neural interactions (19). In addition, synchronous oscillatory firing may facilitate the interactions among distant brain structures. In some cases, a correlation has been found between the intensity of neural firing in a specific cortical area and the attentional modulation of conscious experience (39–43). On the other hand, the evidence from split-brain cases (44) and, in all likelihood, from psychiatric dissociations (45,46) indicates that temporally simultaneous activity is not sufficient for integrating information within consciousness and that there is a need for causally effective neural interactions.

Finally, it seems that neural activity related to conscious experience is more widely or globally distributed in the brain than neural activity that is not associated with consciousness. For example, before habituation, neural activity related to sensory stimuli can be recorded in many brain regions. After habituation, when stimuli tend to fade from consciousness, they seem to evoke neural activity exclusively along their specific sensory pathways (47). When tasks are novel, as in learning to play a computer game, brain activation related to the task is widely distributed; when the task has become automatic, activation is highly localized (48). These examples also pertain to another issue that is not always emphasized enough in discussions of consciousness: neural activity must exhibit sufficient variance or change in time to support conscious perception. If images on the retina are stabilized, for example, perception fades rapidly, and a similar effect is seen in Ganzfeld stimulation. It is also clear that a sufficient degree of functional differentiation is needed to sustain consciousness. In states such as slow-wave sleep and generalized epilepsy, in which most groups of neurons in the cortex discharge synchronously, thereby obliterating any functional discrimination within the system, consciousness is diminished or lost. In our opinion, these neurologic and neurophysiologic observations (see Table 2) are severe constraints on any theory of the brain mechanisms of consciousness.

CONSCIOUSNESS AND THE FAST INTEGRATION OF INFORMATION: BEYOND METAPHORS AND STRUCTURES

Whether or not one agrees with this brief review of key properties of consciousness and its brain mechanisms, it is apparent that verbal summaries of psychological observations and neurologic data are necessary but not sufficient for a genuine scientific understanding of consciousness. The metaphor that consciousness is like a scene or stage in which information is integrated is a crucial one, but what exactly does one mean by integration of information? Where does the integration occur? And how would one measure it? It appears to us that, unless these notions are precisely specified, we cannot hope to gain a fundamental understanding of consciousness.

Likewise, in considering the brain mechanisms of consciousness, the emphasis is all too often on particular neural structures rather than on processes. Different investigators have their favorite structures. Some stress the importance of intralaminar thalamic nuclei (30), others of the reticular nucleus (49), others of the mesencephalic reticular formation (50), others of the tangential intracortical network of layers I and II (51), others of cortex and corticocortical connections (52), others of thalamocortical loops (31,32,37), still others in some combination of all the above (9,53), and, if these were not enough, it has been suggested that the hippocampus, the basal ganglia, or even the claustrum may have an important role to play (28). Furthermore, although there is a general agreement that the cerebral cortex is responsible for the contents of consciousness, there is controversy about which cortical areas may contribute to it. For instance, there are those who stress the importance of the primary visual areas for visual awareness and those who deny its role in conscious perception and prefer to look at higher areas, such as inferotemporal cortex (IT) (54). There are those who consider the occipitotemporal pathway more suited than the occipitoparietal pathway for mediating conscious experience (8), those who favor areas that have direct projections to prefrontal cortex (54), those who prefer infragranular layers of cortex and those who prefer supragranular layers (51,55), and those who like cortical neurons that burst (55) or oscillate at 40 Hz (15). Although each of these proposals can in some way be supported, we believe that it is crucial to concentrate on the processes, not just the areas, that support consciousness. We also believe that expecting that local, intrinsic properties of neurons or brain areas may explain why their activity correlates or not with conscious experience is a mistake; it is rather the way these neurons and areas participate in certain global interactions that should be examined. Finally, we believe that, due to the intricacy and the connectedness of thalamocortical circuits, large-scale modeling of integrative processes is necessary to develop a testable model of primary consciousness and conduct significant experimentation.

In a book published several years ago, *The Remembered Present* (1), one of us (G.M.E.) set forth to develop a testable, biologic theory of consciousness based on the then available evidence and on a general view of brain function. The book included the central notion of consciousness as a scene in which information from different modalities and submodalities is integrated; the notion of fast reentry among functionally specialized groups of neurons as the key process by which such integration is achieved; and a detailed analysis of the information that needs to be integrated for primary consciousness to emerge, namely current perceptual categorizations and past value-category memory. Since then, in a programmatic series of studies conducted at The Neurosciences Institute (18–23), we have attempted to clarify the notion of integration of information and to explore in detailed, large-scale models how such rapid integration of information can be achieved in the brain through the process of reentry. These studies have enabled us to be more specific about the general principles and the brain mechanisms involved in conscious experience. Three concise and specific proposals emerging from these studies will be stated at the outset. The first proposal deals with the fundamental nature of consciousness in terms of general principles. The second proposal concerns the specific brain mechanisms of consciousness, and the third concerns the nature of the information that is integrated in consciousness. Although these brief statements will inevitably sound obscure at this stage, the rest

of this chapter will illustrate each in some detail.

First proposal: In terms of general principles, a fundamental property of consciousness is the fast integration of a large amount of information within a dynamic core of strongly interacting elements.

Second proposal: In terms of specific mechanisms, the key process mediating the fast integration of information in the brain is reentry among specialized neuronal groups within the thalamocortical system.

Third proposal: For primary consciousness to emerge, ongoing perceptual categorization needs to be integrated with conceptual value-category memory.

In order to provide a concrete example, we begin by expanding on the second statement. We illustrate, by using large-scale computer simulations, how the fast integration of information can occur within the brain through the process of reentry and lead to a discriminative behavioral output. We then address the general properties of consciousness and offer a precise, theoretical formulation of the notion of integration of information within a dynamic core of strongly interacting elements. Finally, we consider the nature of the information that is integrated within consciousness, that is, the integration of current perceptual categorization with past value-category memory.

MODELING STUDIES: UNDERSTANDING THE MECHANISMS OF INFORMATION INTEGRATION IN THE BRAIN

Studying the mechanisms by which different signals are integrated in the central nervous system is a daunting task. Only over the past few years has it become experimentally feasible to record simultaneously from multiple neurons in awake, behaving animals. Neuroimaging techniques, such as positron emission tomography (PET) and functional magnetic resonance imaging (fMRI), can probe the activity of many brain areas at once, but their spatial and temporal resolution is insufficient to follow the fate of individual neural signals. For these reasons, we have embarked on a systematic effort to examine neuronal interactions by means of large-scale computer simulations of the thalamocortical system (18,19,21–23). These simulations have allowed us to follow the activity of individual neural units as well as to examine the spatiotemporal patterns of firing developing in intricately connected systems upon the presentation of, for example, certain visual stimuli. Moreover, these simulations offer the opportunity to perform various perturbations and manipulations in a way that would be experimentally difficult. Naturally, the results obtained from these detailed models are only as general and reliable as the anatomic and physiologic data that they embodied. Within these limits, such models have played an essential role in understanding the mechanisms by which information can rapidly be integrated in the brain and, inasmuch as the rapid integration of information is fundamental for consciousness to emerge, in understanding the neural mechanisms of conscious experience.

There is increasing evidence that a paramount mechanism for the rapid integration of information in the brain is reentry, a process of ongoing, parallel, and recursive signaling among groups of neurons that occurs along ordered anatomic connections (1,56,57). Anatomic studies have demonstrated the abundance and rich patterns of reciprocal connectivity linking neuronal populations both within and between brain areas. Neurophysiology has offered several examples, some of them linked to actual behavioral performance, of how reciprocal interconnectivity can give rise to temporal correlations or to local modifications in the response properties of neurons (58,59). By using large-scale computer simulations, we have explored how reentry can bring about the rapid integration, of information. Here we summarize some results obtained from two synthetic neural models that exemplify many of the issues discussed above. We first examine the role of corticocortical reentry in neural integration, and then consider the role of reentry along both corticocortical and thalamocortical loops in establishing coherent thalamocortical processes.

Solving the Binding Problem: Reentry and Corticocortical Interactions

The first model, a large-scale simulation of the visual system, provides a solution to the problem of integrating or "binding" the activity of functionally segregated brain areas (Fig. 1) (19). Given the complexity of the model, the reader is referred to the original publication for a description of how anatomic and physiologic properties of the visual system were simulated. In this model, reentry occurs among nine cortical areas, divided into three anatomic streams mediating responses to form, color, and motion, respectively. Consistent with functional segregation in the visual cortex, units within each separate area of the model respond to different properties of the stimuli, and the firing of each has different functional consequences within the network.

The model was tested with several tasks that required the integration of signals conveyed by the activity of multiple functionally segregated areas. For example, one task required the discrimination of a red cross from a red square, which were presented simultaneously in the visual field. A correct discriminatory response implied the conjunction of several properties of the stimuli, i.e., their color, their shape, and their position. After some training, the model achieved such discrimination with 95% accuracy. A still frame of the model after what would correspond to 200 milliseconds after the presentation of the stimuli indicates that short-term temporal correlations have emerged among the activities of neurons in segregated cortical areas (Fig. 2). These short-term correlations show a phase lag of close to 0 milliseconds for neurons responding to different attributes of the same object, whereas the activity of neurons responding to different objects is much less correlated at this time scale (their relative phase is indicated by color differences). On the other hand, at the time scale of the "be-

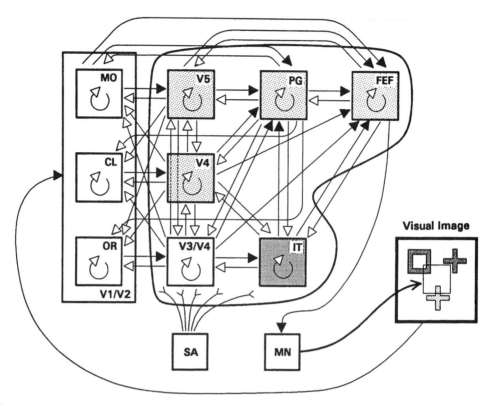

FIG. 1. Architecture of the visual cortex model. Segregated visual maps are indicated as boxes, and pathways (composed of many thousands of individual connections) are indicated as arrows. Filled arrows indicate voltage-independent pathways, and unfilled arrows indicate voltage-dependent pathways. Curved arrows within boxes indicate intraareal connections. The model comprises three parallel streams involved in the analysis of visual motion (*top row*), color (*middle row*), and form (*bottom row*). Areas are finely (*no shading*) or coarsely topographic (*light shading*), or nontopographic (*heavy shading*). The visual image (sampled using a color CCD camera) is indicated at the extreme right. The different areas in the figure are named after areas in the visual cortex that fulfill a similar functional role. For instance, units in V1/V2 OR respond to oriented line segments, units in V3/V4 to corners, and units in IT to entire objects such as crosses or squares in a position-invariant way. Units in V1/V2 CL respond to wavelength, whereas those in V4 display some degree of color constancy. Units in V1/V2 MO are responsive to local motion, and those in V5 to pattern motion. The model includes an output stage consisting of area FEF and a set of oculomotor neurons (MN) driving a simulated foveation response that can be used for operant conditioning. The box labeled SA refers to the diffusely projecting saliency system used in the behavioral paradigm; the general area of projection is outlined. The complete system contains a total of about 10,000 neuronal units and of about 1,000,000 connections. Reprinted with permission (19).

havioral" output, all activated neurons can be said to be firing together. The model was able to achieve unified, coherent responses to the visually presented scene as well as a differentiation among the different objects that led to a given discriminatory response.

What must be emphasized is that, in this model, the conjunction or integration of the correct object attributes to yield a specific output was not achieved in a particular simulated cortical area or in a particular group of neurons. The model contained no units that were directly selective for arbitrary conjunctions of object properties, such as "a red cross located in the upper left quadrant." Thus, integration was achieved not in any place, but in a coherent process. This process was the result of reentrant interactions among neuronal groups distributed over many areas, non-linearly amplified by fast, voltage-dependent synaptic changes. Furthermore, integration occurred rapidly, within 100 to 250 milliseconds from the presentation of the stimulus.

The short-term correlations with zero phase lag observed in the simulations were indicative of rapid, reciprocal interactions mediated by reentry. Their occurrence was strictly dependent on the presence of intact reciprocal intra- and interareal connections and on functioning voltage-dependent channels. Short-term correlations were observed not only in parallel, across different streams (occipitoparietal and occipitotemporal), but also hierarchically, between areas such as V1, that were topographically organized and responded to detailed features of the objects, and less topographically organized areas such as IT, that responded to invariant properties of the objects. Thus, integration did not occur just between different submodalities (position, movement, color, form), but also across different levels of stimulus generalization. In other words, reentry led to the emergence of a globally coherent process that included the activity of neuronal groups distributed over many cortical areas and levels.

Because an arbitrary conjunction of frequently encountered features can be detected dynamically through the process of reentry among specialized neuronal groups, this system can flexibly accommodate new combinations of features never encountered before without requiring the deployment of new committed units. It also can learn to respond preferentially to such combinations if they are paired repeatedly with some salient event, such as reward or punishment. In the model, this was achieved by enabling neural plasticity in the connections among distributed groups of neurons (indicated by the faint red lines in the figure) through the activation of neuromodulatory systems with diffuse projections that globally signal saliency (60,61).

In summary, simulations performed with this model of the visual system indicate that reentrant corticocortical interactions are sufficient to solve the binding problem dynamically, i.e., in a process and not in a place. They also show that a system capable of supporting dynamic integration can respond rapidly and flexibly to new, unexpected associations. Other simulations with this model provided evidence that the process of reentry was able rapidly to distribute signals from different neuronal groups to the rest of the system in a global way, to make the responses of any neuronal group in the model highly context dependent, and to provide global access to many different outputs. These aspects of the model performance are of particular importance in the present context because they are directly relevant to the explanation of some key properties of conscious experience as listed in Table 1. They also substantiate the suggestions about the brain mechanisms of consciousness that are expressed in our second proposal.

Layers and Loops: Neural Dynamics in a Model of the Thalamocortical System

It has been long recognized that, in addition to corticocortical interactions, thalamocortical interactions play a special role in the integration of distributed neural activity across wide cortical regions and in the generation of conscious experience (62). Even if there is general agreement, it is difficult to envision precisely how the interplay between corticocortical loops and thalamocortical loops might take place. For the same reason, it is difficult to imagine the dynamic consequences of the peculiar structural organization of the thalamocortical system in terms of realistic cellular and synaptic properties. To overcome this barrier, we have recently constructed a large-scale model that embodies the minimum features necessary for operation of the basic thalamocortical circuitry (23).

Figure 3 shows the overall architecture of the model. The model has more than 65,000 spiking neurons with over 5 million connections. Individual neurons, both excitatory and inhibitory, were modeled as single-compartment integrate-and-fire units using cellular

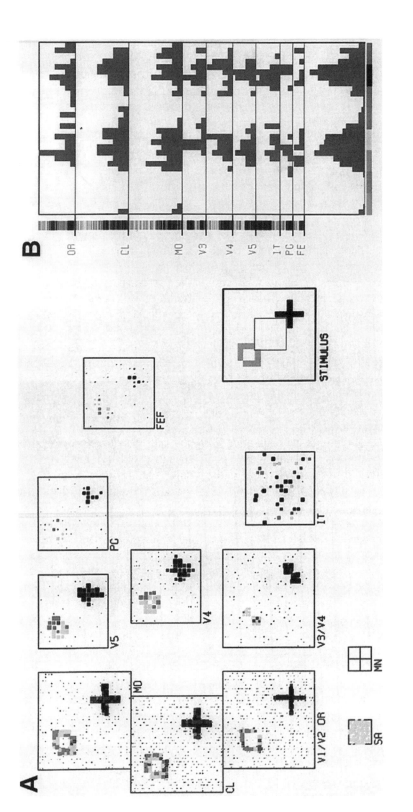

constants from regular-spiking and fast-spiking neurons, respectively. Synaptic interactions occurred through simulated channels that provided voltage-dependent (NMDA-like) and voltage-independent (AMPA-like) excitation, as well as fast (GABA$_A$-like) and slow (GABA$_B$-like) inhibition. All connections were endowed with conduction delays. In addition, through a balanced Poissonian excitation and inhibition, units were endowed with a background level of irregular, spontaneous activity.

The regions modeled consisted of in-register sectors in a primary and a secondary area of visual cortex (Vp and Vs), two corresponding regions of the dorsal thalamus (Tp and Ts), and two regions of the reticular thalamic nucleus (Rp and Rs). Vp represented a restricted portion of area 17 in the cat (about 1 cm^2), and it contained units with small receptive fields that were selective for oriented segments. Vs represented a corresponding part of an extrastriate area with coarser topography, containing units with larger receptive fields selective for oriented lines and for line crossings. Tp and Ts corresponded respectively to a portion of the lateral geniculate nucleus (LGN) and to a portion of the lateral posterior pulvinar complex (LP). A reticular nucleus (RT) was intercalated between the cortex and the thalamus.

A central feature of the model is the subdivision of the simulated cortex into three laminae with different patterns of afferent, efferent, and local connectivity. These laminae correspond to supragranular layers, infragranular layers, and layer IV, respectively. Another important feature of the model is the emphasis on the detailed simulation of various sets of connections that link cortical and thalamic areas, as well as of connections intrinsic to these regions. Among these, certain prominent "vertical loops" and "horizontal networks" stand out as key components of the thalamocortical circuitry: loops between cortical areas and their associated thalamic nuclei that incorporate the reticular thalamic complex; intracortical loops that link infragranular and supragranular layers; patchy networks of long-range excitatory connections that spread horizontally within each cortical area; and extensive reciprocal connectivity between cortical areas.

Emergence of a
Coherent Thalamocortical Process

In a standard experiment, the model was presented for 250 ms with a simulated stimulus consisting of two superimposed gratings, one vertical and one horizontal, moving in perpendicular directions at around two cycles per second. The membrane potential for all units in the model was recorded and is shown for a subset of cells (Fig. 4). Topographic displays of unit activity, averaged over a 250-millisecond

FIG. 2. Responses of the complete system to two objects at iteration 10 during a typical trial. **A:** Display of activity and correlation patterns during presentation of two objects, a red cross (*shown in black*) and a red square (*shown in gray*). Units responding to the same object are correlated both within and between (topographic or nontopographic) areas forming a cohort. The two cohorts corresponding to the two different objects are segregated by having different mean phases. Each small filled square represents one active unit, with the size of the square indicating the activation value and its gray level indicating the phase value (for gray scale see **B**). Binding occurs across three hierarchical levels, between topographically and non-topographically organized areas, and with little or no phase lag despite conduction delays. **B:** Histograms of phase distributions (for units with high activity values) at the same iteration displayed in **A**. There is one histogram for each area as well as a cumulative histogram for the complete system on the bottom. The column on the left represents the phase of the units in each area. Units within and between areas are strongly correlated, and there is little or no systematic phase shift from "lower" (*top*) to "higher" (*bottom*) areas, despite interareal delays of 10 phase bins. Note the segregation of units responding to different objects into two cohorts. A gray scale for the phase is given at the bottom. Reprinted with permission (19).

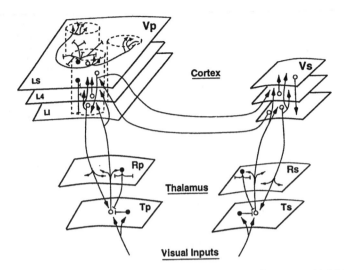

FIG. 3. Architecture of the thalamocortical model. In the figure, excitatory and inhibitory cells are depicted with the use of open and filled circles, respectively. The major connectivity loops incorporated in the model are as follows:

1. Thalamocortical loops. Thalamocortical pathways ascend in parallel from Tp to Vp and Ts to Vs, with terminations in the infragranular layer (LI) and layer IV (L4). En passant contacts from Tp and Ts are made in Rp and Rs. Thalamocortical pathways are reciprocated by corticothalamic projections originating in LI. En route, such fibers give collaterals to their associated RT sector.
2. RT networks. RT cells are embedded in a diffuse inhibitory synaptic network. Projections from RT to thalamocortical neurons are also diffuse.
3. Intracortical loops. Columnar projections are made from L4 to the supragranular layer (LS), from LS to LI, and from LI back to L4 and LS.
4. Networks of long-range horizontal connections within each cortical layer. Unlike inhibitory contacts, these excitatory projections are restricted to patches of cells with similar selectivities.
5. Interareal corticocortical loops. Forward projections ascend from LS of Vp to L4 of Vs; backward projections descend from LI of Vs to LS of Vp.

Reprinted with permission (22).

stimulation epoch, show the sharp orientation selectivity of the responses elicited in the primary visual area, Vp (Fig. 4A). Such orientation selectivity results from a weak geniculate (Tp) afferent bias amplified by mutual intracortical excitation of neurons with similar orientation specificity that receive nonspecific inhibition. Also visible in the displays is the coarser topographic mapping of cells in the secondary area, Vs. Note that part of the topographic spread is due to stimulus motion.

Membrane potential plots of the same units over the same epoch exhibit a clearcut spatiotemporal pattern of both subthreshold and action potentials (Fig. 4B). This is shown by the corresponding instantaneous population averages of membrane potentials and spike counts (Fig. 4C). These display a considerable degree of synchronous firing as well as oscillatory behavior. Synchronous oscillations occur at every level of the model, with sharp peaks in the power spectra of population activity at around 52 Hz. Note that model parameters underlying these synchronous oscillations were established a priori on the basis of experimental data and were not tuned to obtain any particular dynamic behavior. Thus, rapidly changing episodes showing the occurrence of coherent thalamocortical processes are an emergent feature of the anatomic connectivity of the model and of the physiologic properties of its units. The irregular occur-

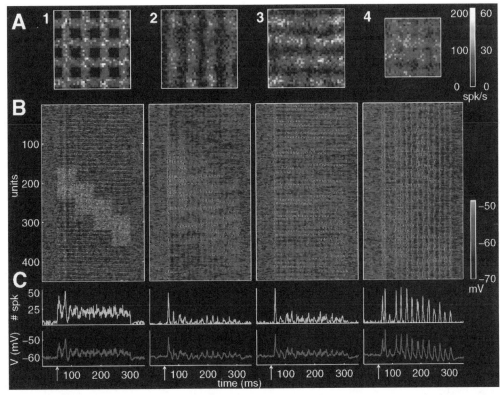

FIG. 4. Network response to a moving plaid in the thalamocortical model. **A:** Topographic displays of mean firing rates during a single stimulus epoch (250 milliseconds) in four thalamocortical structures: relay cells of Tp (column 1, 40 × 40 map), supragranular excitatory cells of Vp selective for vertical and horizontal orientations (columns 2 and 3, respectively; 40 × 40 map each), and supragranular cross-selective cells of Vs (column 4, 30 × 30 map). Firing rates are color coded according to separate scales for the relay cells (0–200 spk/s) and for the cortical cells (0–60 spikes/sec) (see colorplate 3). **B:** Membrane potential Vm of 450 cells in each of the corresponding maps over the same stimulation epoch, flanked on each side by an additional 50 milliseconds of spontaneous activity. Each horizontal line in each plot corresponds to the subthreshold voltage of a single cell, color coded in tones of blue. Spiking events are represented in yellow. **C:** Cumulated number of spikes per millisecond and mean voltage over the same time period and for each set of 450 cells shown in **B**. Arrows at the bottom of each column mark the stimulus onset. Reprinted with permission (23).

rence of these oscillatory episodes is reminiscent of the phenomenon of intermittency that has been described in a number of nonlinear systems (63).

Structural and Functional Determinants of Coherent Thalamocortical Processes

Simulations based on this model have been used to investigate in detail the influences on synchronous rhythms of physiologic parameters such as synaptic strength, time constant of inhibition, transmission delays, and structural parameters affecting horizontal or intralaminar, vertical or interlaminar, thalamocortical, and thalamoreticular macrocircuits. Here we will present some of the conclusions derived from such perturbation experiments that are pertinent in the present context. For a detailed analysis of the results of perturbing these various physiologic and structural parameters, the reader is referred to the original publications (22,23).

Intracortical and Thalamocortical Reentrant Loops

Experiments of one- or two-way lesioning of polysynaptic loops showed that the emergence of high-frequency synchronous firing in population-averaged activities depends critically on the dynamics of reentrant circuits (Fig. 5). An interlaminar cortical loop provided a high-gain amplification mechanism that drove the local cortical networks into an oscillatory regimen, even in the absence of thalamic rhythmicity. In addition to these circuits, a corticothalamocortical loop involving the reticular thalamic (RT) complex could induce synchronous oscillations at thalamic and cortical levels. Horizontal networks within each cortical layer as well as forward and backward interareal projections contributed to the spread of these coherent oscillations over extended cortical territories. Thus, reentry along specific polysynaptic loops both within cortex and between thalamus and cortex was crucial to the emergence of globally coherent states.

Opening of Voltage-Dependent Channels

Voltage-dependent channels with kinetic characteristics typical of NMDA receptors in the horizontal corticocortical connections of the model proved critical for the development of widespread coherency within and among cortical regions. The nonlinear opening of such channels provided a dramatic boost of long-range neural interactions while preventing an epileptic-like outburst of the entire model (Tononi et al., unpublished results). The simulated blockade of these receptors resulted not only in the reduction of the efficacy of individual synapses but also in the abolition of the global coherence that occurred in the intact model. These observations are of interest in view of the well-known action of certain so-called dissociative anesthetics, such as ketamine and phencyclidine. These anesthetics act as noncompetitive antagonists of the NMDA receptor, and their potency as anesthetics correlates with their affinity for the NMDA receptor (64). Although nonspecific anesthetics, such as halothane and isoflurane, tend to depress all cortical functions, these dissociative anesthetics induce a rather selective impairment of consciousness unaccompanied by generalized depression. The results of these simulations suggest that the role of NMDA voltage-dependent channels in supporting the emergence of globally coherent thalamocortical processes may be what is compromised by this class of anesthetics.

Neural Synchrony and Neural Activity

Synchrony of firing is a pervasive characteristic of highly reentrant networks (36,65). The issue of whether synchrony is merely a by-product of neural activity or whether it has causal consequences per se is as important as it is difficult to investigate in vivo. In an attempt to determine whether synchronous firing, in isolation from other parameters, plays a causal role in determining the dynamic behavior of the thalamocortical system, we used the model to perform an idealized perturbation experiment that would be beyond reach in experiments with the real thalamocortical system. The experiment consisted in jittering the timing of individual spikes by random amounts (a few milliseconds) while leaving everything else unchanged (22). Jittering the relative timing of spikes over the entire system by as little as 25% of the membrane time constants (equivalent to 4 milliseconds in excitatory cells and 2 milliseconds in inhibitory units) produced a firing level of less than 60% of the control rates of neurons in the supragranular layer of Vs (Fig. 6A). The results of spike jittering experiments in the thalamocortical model demonstrate that synchronous firing with a precision of a few milliseconds had a dramatic effect on the responses of the system to visual stimuli, in terms both of their magnitude and of their specificity.

In addition to global jittering applied to the thalamocortical model, we also performed selective jittering of corticocortical and corticothalamic reentrant loops and showed that their selective jittering considerably reduced

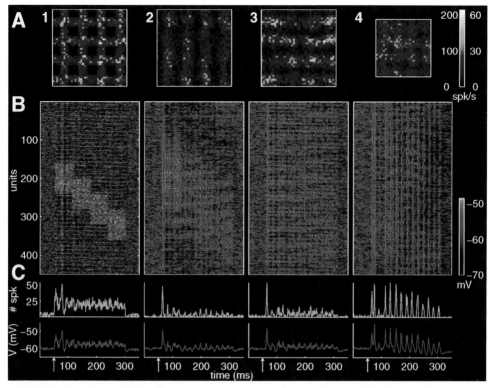

COLORPLATE 3. Network response to a moving plaid in the thalamocortical model. **A:** Topographic displays of mean firing rates during a single stimulus epoch (250 milliseconds) in four thalamocortical structures: relay cells of Tp (column 1, 40 × 40 map), supragranular excitatory cells of Vp selective for vertical and horizontal orientations (columns 2 and 3, respectively; 40 × 40 map each), and supragranular cross-selective cells of Vs (column 4, 30 × 30 map). Firing rates are color coded according to separate scales for the relay cells (0–200 spk/s) and for the cortical cells (0–60 spikes/sec). **B:** Membrane potential Vm of 450 cells in each of the corresponding maps over the same stimulation epoch, flanked on each side by an additional 50 milliseconds of spontaneous activity. Each horizontal line in each plot corresponds to the subthreshold voltage of a single cell, color coded in tones of blue. Spiking events are represented in yellow. **C:** Cumulated number of spikes per millisecond and mean voltage over the same time period and for each set of 450 cells shown in **B**. Arrows at the bottom of each column mark the stimulus onset. Reprinted with permission (23).

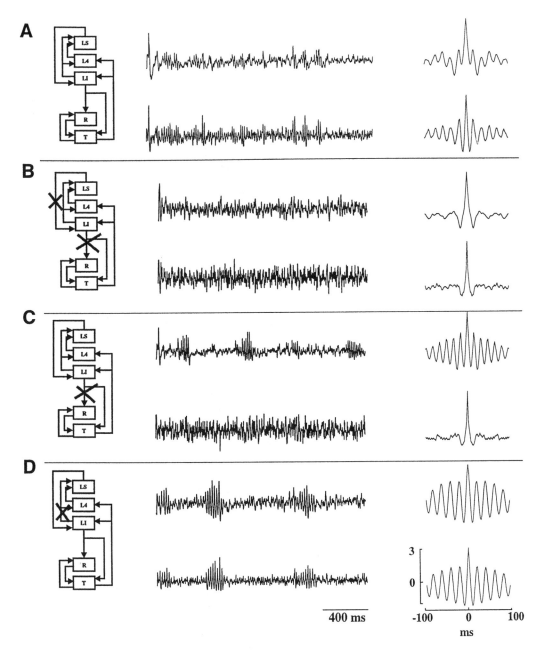

FIG. 5. Lesion experiments in a reduced thalamocortical model. Alterations of the connectivity are shown in the left column. The central column contains population-averaged voltage traces at a thalamic (T) and cortical level (layer IV). The corresponding autocorrelograms are shown on the far right. **A:** Unaltered thalamocortical model. **B:** Model in which backward intracortical and corticothalamic projections were removed. Notice the disappearance of fast activities. **C:** Restoring the interlaminar cortical loop alone leads to fast oscillations in the cortex in the 60-Hz frequency range. **D:** Thalamocortical loop alone. Sustained synchronous oscillations at 45-Hz span over the cortical depth and thalamus. Reprinted with permission (23).

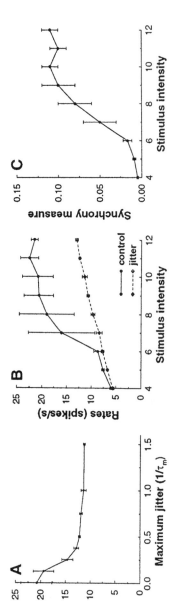

FIG. 6. Perturbations of synchronous firing in the thalamocortical model. **A:** Effects of jittering on the firing rate. The mean firing rate and SD over six successive 250-millisecond stimulus epochs of the supragranular excitatory cross-selective cells of Vs is plotted as a function of the maximum of the random jittering of spike timing introduced globally. This maximum is expressed as a function of the membrane time constant (τ_m). A value of 1 corresponds to 16 milliseconds for excitatory cells and to 8 milliseconds for inhibitory cells. **B:** Effects of synchrony on activity. The solid curve corresponds to the mean firing rate in the control (i.e., unjittered) runs, for increasing values of the stimulus intensity. The dashed curve gives the equivalent responses in a jittered system. Note the sudden increase of activity in the control system, which is reminiscent of a phase transition. This transition is not seen in the jittered system. **C:** Effects of activity on synchrony. The degree of synchrony among supragranular cross-selective cells of Vs is measured at each stimulus intensity in the control system. This measurement, which is based on the normalized temporal variance of the population-averaged membrane potential, demonstrates the simultaneous increase of both firing rates and synchrony of firing as the stimulus intensity is increased beyond a transition point. Reprinted with permission (22).

the firing rates of specific populations of units along these loops. That corticothalamic and corticocortical reciprocal connections form the structural substrate for functional loops is suggested by two further observations: highly correlated activity was observed among the neuronal populations connected in a loop (i.e., one expects that the elements of a loop will be highly correlated); jittering the spikes in the forward direction had similar consequences as jittering them backwards or both ways (i.e., one "cut" is sufficient to open a loop).

In another series of experiments, synchronous firing itself and its effectiveness were shown to depend in turn on mean activity levels. This was done by systematically increasing the intensity of the stimulus-evoked inputs to thalamic relay and interneurons while keeping every other aspect of visual stimulation identical. As a result of parametrically increasing the degree of activation in the thalamus, it was found that a critical amount of activity had to be reached in order to produce synchronous firing among neurons along thalamocortical and corticocortical reentrant loops. Below a critical value of sensory activation, cortical firing rates were low (Fig. 6B) and population activity was essentially asynchronous (Fig. 6C). At a well-defined transition point, firing rates, population synchrony, and the effectiveness of synchrony, as measured by the consequences of jittering, all increased steeply before saturating upon further increases of the stimulus intensity.

Nonlinearities and Phase Transitions

The sudden increase in the degree of synchrony and of the effectiveness of synchrony when the stimulus intensity reached a certain level was associated with a sudden increase of the mean level and variance of neural activity. This abrupt, nonlinear effect is characteristic of a nonequilibrium phase transition (63). Such phase transitions did not occur in the spike-jittered model; instead, a gradual and weaker increase of the firing rate was observed. Selective jittering of particular reen-

trant loops also prevented the occurrence of the phase transition. Thus, synchrony within the thalamocortical system showed a nonlinear dependence on activity levels, and activity showed a nonlinear dependence on synchrony. The "ignition" of corticothalamic and thalamocortical reentrant loops, in conjunction with the opening of voltage-dependent channels, seems to represent a necessary condition for the emergence of a globally coherent thalamocortical process. In other words, a globally coherent process, as indicated by a synchrony measure taken over all areas, layers, and units recorded in the model, only occurred when a well-defined nonlinear threshold was reached.

Spontaneous Activity

The thalamocortical model was designed to have significant levels of spontaneous firing even in the absence of any external stimulus activity, inasmuch as a Poissonian excitatory–inhibitory input was provided to each cell (the mean firing rate of excitatory cells was approximately 5 Hz). Although such spontaneous activity was not sufficient to generate a globally coherent dynamic process in these simulations, it played a major role in determining the speed of the global response to external stimulation. If the spontaneous activity was removed, external inputs needed a considerably longer interval of time to lead to globally coherent states, and the extent of long-range correlations was considerably reduced (Tononi, unpublished observations). These effects can be explained by considering that it is much easier and faster for an incoming stimulus to activate beyond the nonlinear ignition point a reentrant loop that is already active than one that is not. In this sense, intrinsic activity along reentrant loops can be said to be amplified, rather than triggered, by external inputs. It is an intriguing but still untested possibility that—with the addition of further cortical areas and corticocortical reentrant loops, of projections from a simulated intralaminar complex, and of neuromodulatory input from a diffuse ascending system—

the spontaneous activity in the model may become capable of generating a globally coherent process by itself.

In conclusion, this analysis of neural dynamics in a model of the thalamocortical system indicates that reentrant interactions within the cortex and between the cortex and thalamus, bolstered by voltage-dependent mechanisms and by spontaneous activity within the network, serve to establish a transient, globally coherent process involving widely distributed groups of neurons in both the cortex and thalamus. Such a globally coherent process, which is distinguished by strong and rapid interactions among the participating neuronal groups, emerges at a well-defined threshold with the characteristics of a phase transition. As we will discuss in a later section, the observation that a dynamic process characterized by the strength and speed of neural interactions can originate, in a nonlinear fashion, from the relatively continuous connectivity of the thalamocortical system, is of considerable significance for the understanding of certain key properties of conscious experience.

A THEORETICAL ANALYSIS: DEFINING AND MEASURING THE INTEGRATION OF INFORMATION WITHIN A SYSTEM

The large-scale simulations reviewed here, in conjunction with the experimental evidence upon which they rest, provide an effective demonstration of how the process of reentry can bring about the fast integration of information within the distributed thalamocortical system and lead to unified behavioral output. As mentioned above, however, in addition to an understanding of the mechanisms of integration of information in the brain, we need a full, theoretical understanding of the general principles of this integration. What does it mean that information is being integrated? Where does integration occur, and how can it be measured? To understand consciousness, a principled approach to these theoretical issues must be developed in order

to progress beyond the appealing but potentially misleading metaphors that describe consciousness as a theater or as a global workspace.

In attempting to define and measure the integration of information within a system, it is useful to rely on the statistical foundations of information theory (66,67). Applications of information theory in biology have been fraught with several problems and have had a notoriously controversial history. This is largely because at the heart of information theory, as originally formulated, lies the notion of an external, intelligent observer who encodes messages using an alphabet of symbols (66). "Information processing" views of the brain, in particular, have been severely criticized because they typically assume prior information (begging the question of what information is) and they often assume the existence of neural codes (57). However, the statistical foundations of information theory can be used profitably to characterize objective properties of any system, including the brain, without any reference to codes or to an external observer, as long as the currencies are multidimensional variance (measured by entropy) and statistical dependence (measured by mutual information) within the system. Such a purely statistical approach to information theory has been used successfully, for example, to address a growing number of fundamental issues in physics (68).

Effective Information

By using the statistical aspects of information theory, we have recently shown that it is possible to conceptualize and measure the integration of information from the point of view of a neural system without any reference to an external observer (20,21). For this purpose, it is essential initially to consider an isolated neural system composed of a number of elements (20). Imagine, for example, an isolated cortical area constituted by a number of neuronal groups. Imagine also that the activity of each neuronal group is subject to some independent source of change (variance) in the absence of external inputs. This situation is somewhat reminiscent of the spontaneous activity that is observed in the brain during rapid eye movement (REM) sleep (69). What information is there in such an isolated system? The standard approach of measuring information by the number and probability of states of the system that are discriminable from the point of view of an external observer will not do because in order to avoid the fallacy of the homunculus, we have assumed that the system is isolated. The only information present must be in those states of the system that are discriminable from within the system itself, that is, in those states that have differential effects on the system. We shall call the number and probability of states of the system that "make a difference" to the system itself "effective information." Effective information depends on the occurrence of causal physical interactions within the system, and it is completely independent of external observers, symbols, or codes (20).

To measure effective information, a simple approach is to consider an isolated system as "its own observer." This can be achieved by examining a system in isolation from its environment and by dividing it in two in all possible ways, i.e., by considering its bipartitions (20). Take, for example, a bipartition between an individual element of the system and its complement (the rest of the system, Fig. 7A). If the system is isolated, the effective information from the point of view of that element, i.e., the differences in the state of the rest of the system that make a difference to the state of that element (or vice versa), can be measured by their mutual information. Mutual information is a general measure of statistical dependence between two subsets of elements that can be easily calculated provided that certain conditions, such as stationarity, are satisfied (67). Note that, because mutual information is symmetrical, it measures the effects of the causal interactions across a bipartition of an isolated system without prejudice as to the direction in which they occur. Measuring effective information by assessing the mutual information across bipartitions of an isolated

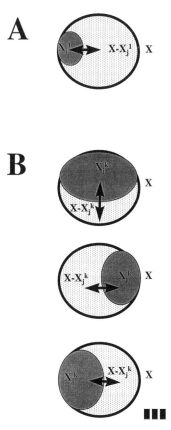

FIG. 7. Illustration of measures of effective information and complexity within an isolated system. **A:** The mutual information for a bipartition between one element X_j and the rest of system X (*double arrow*) measures their statistical dependence. In an isolated system, this corresponds to the effective information between them, i.e., to how much differences in the rest of the system make a difference to the state of that element, or vice versa. **B:** Mutual information is a multivariate measure and it can be measured between a subset of elements and their complement. The sum of mutual information values for all bipartitions of a system (averaged for subset size) corresponds to its neural complexity or total integrated information.

system fits well with the classical notion that information has to do with the reduction of uncertainty. It is specified, however, that the reduction of uncertainty must be in terms of the causal consequences for the system itself rather than from the point of view of an external observer.

Neural Complexity: A Measure of the Information Integrated within a System

If we consider the effective information between a single element and the rest of the system, it is easy to see that their mutual information measures the amount of information that is integrated by that element: the term "integration" is commonly used to refer to a single place or entity, for example, an individual neuron, or even an individual dendrite, that responds differentially to different combinations of inputs (70). But how can the effective information integrated by the entire system be measured? This is where the common use of the word "integration" collapses because, as just mentioned, we generally associate integration with a single, indivisible element or place. The theoretical considerations mentioned above permit us, however, to generalize the notion of integration of information to an entire system. Because mutual information is a multivariate measure of statistical dependence, it is theoretically equally valid to consider the mutual information between one element and another as it is between a subset of elements and the rest of the system. The value of mutual information will be a measure of how reliably the states of the entire subset discriminate between different combinations of input signals. On this basis, it is possible to proceed to a final generalization and to measure the total amount of information integrated within an isolated system by considering all possible subsets of elements within that system (Fig. 7B), as we will now show in a slightly more formal way (20,21).

Consider, in particular, a bipartition of an isolated neural system X into a jth subset X^k_j composed of k components (which can be taken to represent neuronal groups) and its complement $X - X^k_j$. The deviation from statistical independence between X^k_j and $X - X^k_j$ is measured by their mutual information, MI:

$$MI(X^k_j; X - X^k_j) = H(X^k_j) + H(X - X^k_j) - H(X)$$

where $H(X^k_j)$ and $H(X - X^k_j)$ are the entropies of X^k_j and $X - X^k_j$ considered independently,

and $H(X)$ is the entropy of the system considered as a whole. MI = 0 if X^k_j and $X - X^k_j$ are statistically independent and MI > 0 otherwise. The total amount of information integrated within the system is conveniently captured by a measure called neural complexity (C_N). This measure is the mutual information between each part of a neural system and the rest, summed over all possible bipartitions:

$$C_N(X) = \sum_{k=1}^{n/2} <MI(X^k_j; X - X^k_j)>$$

where we consider all subsets X^k composed of k-out-of-n elements of the system ($1 \leq k \leq n$) and the average mutual information between subsets of size k and their complement is denoted as $<MI(X^k_j; X - X^k_j)>$. The index j indicates that the average is taken over all $n!/(k!(n - k)!)$ combinations of k elements. Thus, complexity is higher the higher the average mutual information between each subset and the rest of the system. As we have discussed above, this occurs if, on average, subsets of the system can both have many different states and effectively communicate these differences to the rest of the system.

In a series of analytical examples and computer simulations (20), we have shown that systems such as the brain, which are composed of functionally specialized but highly interactive elements, will have high values of complexity. This means that these systems are able to integrate many different sources of information. By contrast, consistent with intuitive notions and with current attempts in physics and biology to conceptualize complex systems, systems in which the elements are either nonintegrated (e.g., a gas) or nonspecialized (e.g., a homogeneous crystal) will have minimal complexity. This measure of complexity has been validated recently on the basis of neurophysiologic data (71).

An Illustration

As an illustration, we calculated the integration of information, or complexity, associated with three examples of an isolated cortical area (20). The isolated cortical area was simulated on the basis of a detailed model of perceptual grouping and figure-ground segregation (18), although for the present purposes neuronal activity was triggered by uncorrelated Gaussian noise rather than by patterned external input. The first example (Fig. 8A) represents a cortical area in which the density of intraareal connections among (but not within) different groups of neurons had been dramatically decreased. In such a cortical area, individual groups of neurons are still active but, because of the loss of intraareal connections, they fire more or less independently. Such a system behaves essentially like a neural gas or, if examined on the computer monitor, like a television set when not properly tuned. The entropy of the system is high,

due to the large number of elements and to their high individual variance. Therefore, from the point of view of an external observer or homunculus who might assign a different meaning to each state of the system, this would indeed contain a large amount of information. But what about the effective information, the number of states that make a difference to the system? Because there is little interaction between a subset of elements and the rest of the system, whatever the state of that subset might be, it has little or no effect on the rest of the system or vice versa. The value of the mutual information is correspondingly low, and because this holds true for every possible subset, the complexity or information integrated within the entire sys-

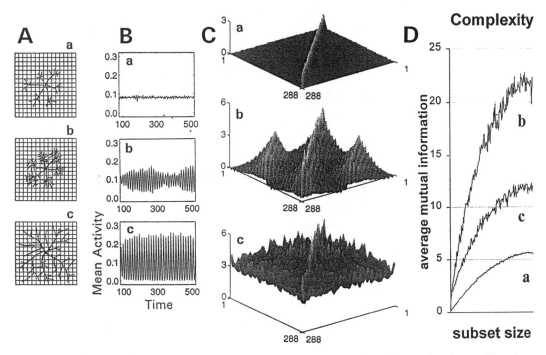

FIG. 8. Neural complexity. Complexity obtained from simulations of a primary visual area. The simulated cortical area contains 512 neuronal groups in two arrays (16 × 16) and modeled as collections of 40 excitatory and 20 inhibitory neurons that are mutually interconnected in a specific way (18,20). No external input is provided to the network; neuronal group activity is triggered by intrinsic Gaussian noise. The groups tend to discharge in an oscillatory fashion. To compute complexity, we sampled the mean activity traces of groups forming the central 12 × 12 portion of two arrays (one for each orientation preference) for 8,000 time steps and derived the covariance matrix. Complexity is computed and expressed as the sum of the average mutual information for increasing subset size and it corresponds to the area under the curve. Modified with permission (65).

tem is also low. In other words, although there are many differences within the system, they make no difference to it.

Consider now a second case in which every neuronal group is connected to all other neuronal groups in a uniform way (Fig. 8C). In the simulations, all groups of neurons soon started oscillating together coherently almost without exception. Because the system can take up only a limited number of states, its entropy is low. On the other hand, the average mutual information between individual elements and the rest of the system is much higher than in the previous case because there are strong interactions. Taking larger subsets into consideration, however, the mutual information does not increase significantly because the number of states that can be discriminated does not increase with the size of the subsets. The complexity or integration of information within the system is correspondingly low. In other words, because there are few differences within the system, the difference they make to the system is equally small.

Consider finally a third case (Fig. 8B). Here, subsets of neuronal groups are strongly connected to a small but specific subset of other neuronal groups. In the model, groups of neurons are connected to each other according to the following rules. Different neuronal groups are organized according to a topographic criterion and to an orientation-specificity criterion. They are connected so that the strength of the connections decreases with topographic distance and so that elements with similar orientation preference are preferentially connected to each other. Note that, as long as the system is isolated, it is the intrinsic connectivity among its elements that defines their functional specificity (here topography and orientation specificity) rather than vice versa. In this case, the dynamic behavior of the system is far more complex than in the previous two: groups of neurons show both an overall coherent behavior and yet they group and regroup themselves dynamically according to their specific functional interactions. For example, neighboring groups of similar orientation preference tend to fire synchronously

more often than functionally unrelated groups, but at times almost the entire cortical area may show short periods of coherent oscillations. The entropy of the system is high, although not as high as in the first case (although the system can have a very large number of states, some are more likely than others). The mutual information between individual elements and the rest of the system is on average high, reflecting their significant interactions, although it is not as high as in the second case. However, in contrast to the second case, the average mutual information increases considerably by considering subsets composed of a larger number of elements, and the overall complexity is high. This is because, in such a system, the larger the subset, the larger the number of different states that that subset can bring about in the rest of the system, or vice versa. In other words, there are many differences, and they make a lot of difference to the system.

Complexity Matching: The Role of External Stimuli

The previous analysis of the integration of information within an isolated neural system led to the conclusion that neural complexity strikes an optimal balance between segregation and integration of function. This is consistent with the view that a complex brain is like a collection of specialists that talk to each other. Several considerations justify our initial analysis of the integration of information within an isolated system. For instance, dreaming and imagery are striking phenomenologic demonstrations that the adult brain can spontaneously and intrinsically produce consciousness and meaning without any direct input from the periphery, at least for a short period of time. Physiologically, it is well known that the thalamocortical system is spontaneously active whether or not it receives exteroceptive inputs, and this is already so in utero. Finally, it is well established that, anatomically, most neurons in the thalamocortical system receive signals from other neurons rather than directly from sensory inputs. Notwithstanding this initial emphasis on the intrinsic integration of information within the brain, it is clear that the set of dynamic relationships among functionally specialized groups of neurons present in an isolated, adult brain must first be developed, selected, and refined in a long process of adaptation to the outside world. This process takes place during evolution, development, and experience through mechanisms of variation, selection, and differential amplification that accompany the continuous interactions between the body, the brain, and the environment (57). What must be determined theoretically and measured, then, is how the intrinsic dynamic relationships among specialized neuronal groups in an adult brain are adaptively related, over time, to the statistical structure of the environment. Moreover, given that the brain, at any given time, is integrating intrinsic information, it must be determined what is the moment-to-moment contribution of the extrinsic information that is provided by the environment.

A theoretical approach to these questions can be found in a recent paper that considers the fate of the signals transmitted from the sensory sheets during perception in information–theoretical terms (21). Although this study cannot be discussed here in any detail, its main conclusion is that extrinsic signals convey information not so much in themselves, but by virtue of how they modulate the intrinsic signals exchanged within a reentrantly connected neural system. In other words, a stimulus acts not so much by adding extrinsic information that needs to be processed, but by amplifying intrinsic information resulting from neural interactions selected through previous encounters with the environment. At every instant, according to this analysis, the brain goes far "beyond the information given" (72), and in conscious animals its response to an incoming stimulus is a "remembered present" (1). Furthermore, this corroborates the notion that, whatever memory is, it must be nonrepresentational (73).

These conclusions are supported by an information–theoretical analysis applied to simple, simulated systems. In particular, such analysis demonstrates that for a small value of

the extrinsic mutual information between a stimulus and a neural system there is a large change in the intrinsic mutual information among subsets of units within the neural system. This can be measured by a quantity, called complexity matching or C_M, which is the change in neural complexity as a result of the encounter with the stimulus (21). According to this approach, the distinction between transmission and storage of information in the brain vanishes completely. The analysis also shows that the extent to which this modulatory action of inputs is successful reflects the experience that the brain has of a set of related stimuli. In other words, high values of complexity matching indicate a high degree of "adjustment of inner to outer relations" (74).

In conclusion, the information–theoretical analysis summarized above aimed at defining precisely what it means to integrate information within a system, at evaluating such integration by a measure of neural complexity, and at assessing how such information is modulated by signals from the environment as measured by complexity matching. As indicated in our first proposal, such analysis represents a necessary step toward a theoretical definition of the fundamental nature of consciousness in terms of general principles.

WHERE DOES THE INTEGRATION OF INFORMATION OCCUR? THE DYNAMIC CORE HYPOTHESIS

Although in the previous sections we have suggested a way to define and measure the integration of information, it remains to be established where such integration takes place. What is the spatial extent of the neural system within which the integration of information relevant to conscious experience occurs? The entire brain? Or only a portion of it? How can the elements comprising such a neural system be identified? Based on their location in the brain? Based on some local, intrinsic property? Based on anatomic connectivity? Based on levels of neural activity? Or based on some global property, such as interactivity? And what is the appropriate time scale? Although these multiply related questions are rarely asked explicitly, they must be squarely addressed by any scientific account of consciousness.

After reviewing the scant physiologic literature of his age, William James concluded that there was as yet no evidence for restricting the neural correlates of consciousness to anything less than the entire brain (74). Since the days of James, we have discovered that only a certain portion of the neural activity in the brain either contributes to consciousness directly, as assessed by stimulation and lesion experiments, or is directly correlated with aspects of conscious experience, as assessed by recording studies. For instance, as reviewed briefly at the beginning of this chapter (see Table 2), we know that certain brain regions, such as the cerebral cortex and thalamus, are more important than others. Furthermore, we know that, even in the same cortical region, the activity of some neurons may at times be correlated with conscious experience whereas that of other neurons may not (41). The results of these experimental studies are invaluable in constraining our understanding of the neural basis of consciousness. Specifically, they prompt the question of what are the critical factors determining whether the activity of a neuron or group of neurons does or does not directly contribute to consciousness. The approach we have taken leads us to firmly reject the hypothesis, often entertained in recent discussions of the problem (15,54,55), that certain local properties of neurons, or mere geographic location in the brain, are endowed in some mysterious way with a privileged correlation with consciousness. Setting aside the logical and philosophical problems associated with such a hypothesis, the previous discussion indicates that, if the rapid integration of information is indeed a fundamental property of consciousness, the latter must be a global process, rather than a local property of certain neural systems. On these grounds, and on the grounds of evidence reviewed below, we suggest the following hypothesis:

The Dynamic Core Hypothesis *Whether the activity of a group of neurons contributes*

directly to conscious experience or not does not depend on its local, intrinsic properties. It depends instead on whether that group of neurons does or does not participate in a dynamic core of distributed thalamocortical elements identified by the strength of their mutual interactions over a period of hundreds of milliseconds.

Furthermore, this dynamic core must be sufficiently differentiated as indicated by high values of complexity.

According to this hypothesis, it should be possible to identify a set of brain regions that—above and beyond their location, their local properties, their anatomic connectivity, and their activity levels—are characterized on the basis of their strong interactivity at the time scale relevant for conscious experience. We propose to call a set of brain regions that are strongly interacting among themselves and have distinct functional borders with the rest of the brain at the time scale of fractions of a second a "dynamic core," to emphasize both its integration and its constantly changing composition. A dynamic core is therefore reflective of a process and is not a thing or a place. It is defined in terms of neural interactions rather than in terms of neural location, connectivity, or activity. Although a dynamic core will have a spatial extension, it will in general be spatially distributed and metastable and will not be localized to a single place in the brain. Based on the evidence reviewed above, the reentrant interactions leading to the formation of a dynamic core are likely to arise within the thalamocortical system and not elsewhere in the brain. Finally, the location as well as intrinsic properties of neurons are considered to be important not in themselves but only insofar as they can affect the emergence of such a dynamic process.

Although these predictions await direct experimental tests, several observations suggest that, within the thalamocortical system, a dynamic process may arise that is characterized by strong internal interactions and transient functional borders with the rest of the brain. At first sight, the sheer anatomic connectivity of the brain might hint that "everything interacts with everything else." If one were to wait long enough, or to consider sufficiently weak interactions, there is no doubt that the entire brain would have to be considered as a single system that integrates information. It would also become necessary to include the body and the surrounding environment in a single intricate network of interactions. However, within the time frame that is relevant to conscious experience, it seems more likely that the fast integration of information occurs within a reduced set of brain regions. For instance, many brain regions can be briefly stimulated or lesioned without any direct or immediate functional effect on other regions, despite the presence of anatomic pathways linking them. Likewise, the lesion or stimulation of these regions does not have direct consequences on conscious experience (75–77). This suggests that transient changes in the activity of such regions are functionally insulated, at least for short periods of time, from that of other parts of the brain.

As we have seen in considering the cortical and thalamocortical models, short-term temporal correlations in neural activity, at the time scales of fractions of a second that are characteristic of conscious experience, are the hallmark of effective reentrant interactions. Such short-term temporal correlations have been observed within individual cortical areas, between multiple cortical areas, and between cortical and thalamic regions (35,36). However, there are many brain regions in which such widespread short-term correlations have not been observed. Thus, at the time scale of consciousness, only certain brain regions, typically located within the thalamocortical system, show evidence of globally correlated activity (35,36). Modeling studies also indicate that although the organization of the anatomic connectivity within the thalamocortical system is particularly effective in generating coherent dynamic states through strong global interactions, that of other brain regions, for example the cerebellum, may not be equally effective (Tononi, unpublished observations). Thus, the mere presence of anatomic connections does not guarantee the presence of global functional interactions; only certain patterns of connectivity will do.

Within the thalamocortical system, it might be thought that simultaneous activity (increased mean firing rate of more than about 1 second) is all that is needed to guarantee interactivity. However, even within such a reentrantly connected system, a dissociation between activity and interactivity can be expected for several reasons. Structural factors can certainly produce functional borders between active populations of neurons. For instance, short-term correlation in the electrical activity of functionally related neurons in the two hemispheres is lost after sectioning the callosum and thereby impairing reentrant interactions (78). In split-brain patients, the absence of direct, fast interactions between the two hemispheres clearly impairs the conscious integration of information between them, even if they are comparably active. Modeling studies suggest that, despite the relative continuity of anatomic connectivity in the cortex, nonlinear interactions among neuronal groups, due for instance to voltage-dependent connections, may transiently increase the strength of the interactions among a subset of them, leading to the formation of distinct functional boundaries within the thalamocortical system (22,23). In some cases, equally active brain regions may, due to reciprocal inhibition or desynchronization, interact in such a way as to lead to the formation of two or more competing clusters (19). Some experimental evidence is available for the dynamic formation of functional borders in the visual cortex of the cat. For instance, orthogonal visual stimuli can result in the transient functional grouping and regrouping of the synchronous firing of multiple groups of neurons, which may be alternately correlated with or uncorrelated with each other (79). Psychiatric conditions, especially dissociative disorders such as multiple personalities, fugue states, depersonalization disorder, and conversion disorders (46), in which certain psychological processes seem to take place without access to the dominant conscious self, offer another important clue that certain brain processes, including cortical ones, may proceed in a local, encapsulated way without functional access to the main dynamic core of strongly interacting areas.

Finally, as mentioned above, over a sufficiently long time scale, all elements of the brain are bound to be functionally interactive to some degree. However, it is important to recognize that over a short period of time, only certain interactions are fast and strong enough to lead to global effects. As shown by large-scale simulations, reentrant interactions can result in the formation of a cluster of neuronal groups that are transiently but nonetheless distinctly differentiated from surrounding neurons. Most importantly, the defining feature of such clusters is that mutual interactions among their neuronal groups, if considered over a few hundred milliseconds, are stronger by an order of magnitude or more than those with the rest of the system. The simulations also show that such functional clusters arise as a result of a phase transition in the dynamic behavior of the system. As we have seen, only if certain conditions are satisfied—such as the activation of reentrant thalamocortical and corticocortical loops, the opening of NMDA channels, the synchronizing action of reticular and other thalamic nuclei, and a sufficient speed in transmission along thalamocortical loops—does a coherent thalamocortical process emerge. Below a well-defined transition threshold, such a dynamic process, collapses (22). Once a dynamic core has emerged at the time scale of hundreds of milliseconds, on the other hand, it is expected that its evolution at the time scale of seconds may be tied to the functioning of reentrant loops having longer time constants, such as those involving the basal ganglia and the hippocampus. These loops would support the conscious integration of information over longer periods of time (1,27).

DEFINING THE DYNAMIC CORE: MEASURES OF FUNCTIONAL CLUSTERING

Postulating the presence of a dynamic core endowed with specific properties within the thalamocortical system of a conscious subject may be important, but it remains to be shown how such a dynamic entity could be detected and measured directly. Specific experimental approaches clearly need to be developed, but to be operational, their design requires that the notion of a dynamic core of strongly interacting elements be clarified in theoretical terms. With this in mind, we have recently developed a measure of functional clustering among the elements of a neural system. This measure was designed to evaluate whether, within a given system, there are subsets of elements that are strongly interacting among themselves and much less with the rest of the system, irrespective of their activity level (80).

Although cluster analysis is a burgeoning branch of statistics, unfortunately no universally accepted definition of "cluster" exists in the statistical literature (81). Nevertheless, it is generally agreed that a cluster should be defined in terms of internal cohesion and external isolation. A general measure of functional clustering should therefore be based on a measure of the statistical dependence within a subset of elements (internal cohesion) versus the statistical dependence between that subset and its complement (external isolation). Clearly, simple pairwise measures of similarity of dissimilarity, such as correlation coefficients, are not sufficient for characterizing such multivariate statistical relationships, not to mention the fact that such measures are often not sensitive to nonlinear interactions.

To deal with the characterization of functional clustering, we developed a cluster index. We used mutual information and its derivatives as measures of similarity or dissimilarity for clustering because they have the advantages of being multivariate, of being directly related to functional interactions, and of being sensitive to nonlinear interactions. In particular, as we have seen, the statistical dependence between any subset of elements and the rest of the system can be measured conveniently in terms of mutual information. The total statistical dependence within a subset of elements can instead be measured by its integration, which is a generalization of the concept of mutual information (20). The integration $I(X)$ is defined as the difference between the sum of the entropies of all individual components $\{x_j\}$ considered independently and the entropy of the system X considered as a whole:

$$I(X) = \sum_{j=1}^{n} H(X_j) - H(X)$$

The relationship between integration and mutual information is as follows: the integration of a system X is equal to the sum of values of the mutual information between parts resulting from the recursive bipartition of X down to its elementary components. In particular, by eliminating one component at a time, $I(X) = \Sigma MI(\{x_j\};\{x_{j+1,...,n}\})$.

Because a functional cluster is intuitively defined as a set of elements that are much more strongly interactive among themselves than with the rest of the system (Fig. 9), a cluster index (CI) can be calculated for each subset i of the system according to:

$$CI(X_j^k) = I(X_j^k)/MI(X_j^k; X - X_j^k)$$

(The integration and mutual information are normalized in order to discount the effect of subset size.) Thus, a cluster index near 1 indicates a subset of elements that are as interactive among themselves as with the rest of the system. A cluster index much higher than 1 indicates instead a subset of elements that are strongly interactive among themselves but weakly interacting with the rest of the system, i.e., a set of elements that correspond to the notion of a functional cluster. In practice, when analyzing a given system, CI values for a representative fraction of the subsets of the system are first computed. The subsets are then ranked in descending order of their CI values (note that for systems containing more than a dozen or so elements, optimization procedures based

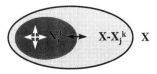

FIG. 9. Illustration of measures of functional clustering. A functional cluster corresponds to a subset of elements that are much more strongly interacting among themselves than with the rest of the system. In an isolated system X, the subset X_j has a high value of internal statistical dependence, as measured by its integration $I(X_j)$ (*white quadruple arrow*) but a low value of statistical dependence with the rest of the system $[MI(X_j, X - X_j)]$ (*black double arrow*). The ratio of integration over mutual information, appropriately normalized, corresponds to the cluster index value.

on the initial screening can be used to identify the subsets with the highest CI values). If such values are statistically higher than those expected for a homogeneously connected system, one can conclude that the corresponding subset(s) represent functional clusters within the test system. To validate this functional clustering procedure, we applied it both to simulated data sets and to a PET data set (80). The analysis of simulated data sets demonstrated that the procedure invariably identified whether functional clusters were present and defined their borders in a way that agreed with intuition as well as with how the simulated networks had been designed. The PET data set, obtained from subjects performing a simple cognitive task, had not been collected for the purpose of examining functional clustering, and it presented several limitations that made it far from ideal. Despite these limitations, its analysis allowed us to identify subsets of brain regions that were clearly part of a single functional cluster as defined here. In other cases, it was possible to find evidence of multiple clusters, with certain sets of brain regions belonging to one functional cluster and other sets to a different cluster, with a sharp border between the two. Finally, within an identified functional cluster, it was possible to rank the participating brain regions based on their mutual information with respect to the rest of the cluster. This provided a way to identify a center and a periphery within the cluster in terms of the strength of functional interactions.

However, a cogent assessment of functional clustering at the time scale of conscious experience will require several further developments. In particular, it will be essential to use imaging methodologies offering high temporal resolution, such as fMRI, topographic electroencephalography, and magnetoencephalography (MEG), to devise experimental protocols specifically aimed at probing the presence and extent of functional clustering and to develop analytical procedures capable of quantifying functional clustering over periods of time of hundreds of milliseconds to a few seconds. Such procedures should offer an opportunity to ask several relevant questions about brain dynamics. Is there, for any given task or group of subjects, a set of brain regions that interact much more strongly among themselves than with the rest of the brain over fractions of a second, i.e., is there a dynamic core? Does such a dynamic core correlate with the conscious state of the subject? Does its composition change depending on what cognitive activity the subject is engaged in? Are certain brain regions always included or always excluded from such a dynamic core? Can this core split, or can multiple dynamic cores coexist in a normal subject? And finally, are there pathologic conditions that are reflected in abnormalities of this core?

CONSCIOUSNESS AND INTEGRATION OF INFORMATION: A RECAPITULATION

The picture emerging from this discussion is that of a metastable neural process in the thalamocortical system, the dynamic core, within which any subset of functionally specialized neuronal groups rapidly and efficaciously interact with a very large number of other neuronal groups. The previous analysis suggests that the spatial borders of such a process can in principle be determined by comparing the strength of inside and outside interactions. The amount and diversity of these interactions, i.e., the amount of information integrated within the core, can be measured by evaluating its neural complexity. The fundamental mechanism by which such global and yet differentiated interactions are possible is provided by the process of reentry, aided by the nonlinear, voltage-dependent opening of activated loops.

This excursion into what integration of information within a system means, how it can be measured, and how a dynamic core can be identified should serve to substantiate our first proposal, that a key aspect of consciousness is the fast integration of information within a dynamic core of strongly interacting elements. The analysis through large-scale simulations of the major structural and functional determinants of the dynamic behavior of the thalamocortical system supports our second proposal, i.e., that reentry among neuronal groups within the thalamocortical system is the process by which the fast integration of information is achieved. Thus, in the light of the previous discussion, it may now be profitable to reconsider in more precise terms several of the properties associated with primary consciousness that were listed in Table 1.

Consciousness as a Process that Is Continuous, Metastable, but Constantly Changing, Selective, and Has a Center and a Periphery

The proposal that the rapid integration of information associated with conscious experience occurs in a dynamic core implies that, as James asserted, consciousness is a process, not a thing, and that it is both continuous and constantly changing. The definition of a dynamic core is a functional one because it is based on the strength of an ensemble of interactions rather than on a structure, a local property of some neurons, or on their location. It is implicit in the definition of the dynamic core that it can maintain its unity and metastability over time even if its composition may be constantly changing, which is the signature of a process as opposed to a thing. It is explicit in the definition of a dynamic core that, at any time, certain brain areas or groups of neurons are part of it while other areas or neuronal groups are not, even if they are equally active. This is the essence of the selective nature of consciousness discussed by James. Furthermore, not only is it possible to determine whether the activity of a certain group of neuron is inside or outside the functional borders of the dynamic core, but it is also possible to rank neuronal groups, based on the strength of their interactions with the rest of the core, as being at its center or at its periphery.

Serial Nature of Consciousness

The seemingly serial nature of conscious experience can be related to the dynamic evolution of the core: the core is by definition a highly integrated process, and its integration is maintained by moving from one global state to another. In other words, because the dynamic core is by definition a single system, its temporal evolution must follow a single trajectory, and what might appear as "decisions" or "choices" can only occur one at a time. This conclusion is consistent with the well-known difficulty of dual-task paradigms involving consciousness, as well as with the phenomenon of the psychological refractory period (81), according to which conscious choices or discriminations occur one at a time. The latter phenomenon also shows that the time required for such decisions is around 150 milliseconds, a figure remarkably close to the time typically needed for conscious integration. Although it is conceivable that at times it might be convenient to split one's consciousness into two or more components and allow each part to perform separate functions, the inevitable price to pay would be the lack of integration between such parallel processes. Everything considered, this may be a less adaptive solution. Consistent with this, the

substrate of neural integration, namely the complex pathways mediating reentry within the thalamocortical system, seems to almost force the system to behave in an integrated way. Any major functional split within this system seems to require either a large anatomic cut (as in a split brain or in various neurologic disconnection syndromes) or some major psychological trauma (as in psychiatric dissociation syndromes).

Unity and Inherent Subjectivity of Conscious Experience: Qualia as Subjective Discriminations

Both unity and inherent subjectivity are consistent with the notion of a dynamic core. A dynamic core has by definition a high value of integration (strong internal cohesion). Because in such a system any local change leads to global consequences, the system has unity. By definition, a dynamic core is also a system of elements that integrate information among themselves much more than they do with their environment. Changes occurring inside the core affect the rest of the core strongly and rapidly, whereas changes occurring outside the core affect it much less strongly or rapidly. Thus, there is a functional border between the environment and the informational states inside the core that makes these states effectively "subjective" or "private." Furthermore, in the present perspective, the subjective discrimination among different states that is associated with each conscious state, i.e., its "quale," is not a mysterious by-product of neural activity, nor is it a special informational state that an external observer associates, from the outside, with a neural state. It is simply one of the different internal states of the dynamic core that make a difference to the temporal evolution of the dynamic core itself. This is equivalent to saying that these states are discriminable by the system itself, i.e., from the inside or subjectively. Another consequence is that the higher the complexity of the dynamic core, the larger the number of states that have discriminable functional consequences on its temporal evolution.

Integration of a Large Amount of Information

The intuitive notion of integration of information within a system has been made explicit and theoretically well founded by the introduction of the concept of neural complexity. By considering a neural system in isolation, by considering only effective information, (i.e., the difference that changes in the state of one subset make to the rest of the system), and by considering simultaneously all subsets of the system, neural complexity avoids the ambiguities having to do with the introduction of symbols, codes, and external observers, as well as the ambiguities having to do with the idea that integration must occur in a single place. The notion of neural complexity is also helpful in conceptualizing neural states that are characterized by hypersynchronous global activity, such as slow-wave sleep and generalized epilepsy, which are associated with a loss of consciousness. Although clearly integrated, such states are associated with a dramatic loss of integrated information because functional specialization tends to vanish: in these high-integration but low-information states, neural complexity is expected to be low.

Coherence

The model of the visual system considered earlier shows how the integration of information can occur through the process of reentry among functionally segregated groups of neurons. Although it obviously cannot be said that such a model "experiences" a coherent, unified scene, the fact is that it is able to produce a unified behavioral output based on multiple sources of information. The model also illustrates that the coherence characteristic of a conscious scene is a natural consequence of global interactions: only those interactions that are mutually consistent and stable are favored by the dynamics of the system.

Speed of Integration

As we have seen, to be associated with consciousness, the integration of information must occur in a short period of time. The various models presented here indicate that reentry along corticocortical and thalamocortical connections is sufficient to ensure that the integration of information occurs within hundreds of milliseconds, i.e., at the time scale of conscious experience. At the theoretical level, however, it must be pointed out that a satisfactory measure of the integration of information over such short periods of time is presently not available. The estimation of neural complexity based on mutual information typically requires longer observation periods. Although neural complexity may be an acceptable indicator of the integration of information if the system is relatively stationary, it remains to be seen whether other measures, most likely derived from dynamic system theory, can deal with the integration of information over shorter periods of time.

Distribution of Information and Context Dependency

High complexity implies wide and efficient distribution of information among the elements of a system. A system in which the mutual information between any subset and the rest is maximized, i.e., a system that is complex, is by definition a system in which the consequences of a change in the activity of any (small) subset are maximally distributed to the rest of the system. The sensitivity to context is just the other side of the coin. In a system in which the mutual information between any subset and the rest is maximized, the activity of each (small) subset is very sensitive to whatever the different states of the rest of the system might be. Mechanistically, the wide distribution of information is guaranteed by thalamocortical and corticocortical reentry, which facilitates the interactions among distant brain regions. It should be noted that many attentional effects also could be conceptualized as contextual effects in the evolution of the dynamic core, although the emergence of conscious states should not be confounded with their attentional modulation.

Global Access

Considered from the perspective of the dynamic core within which information is integrated, the ability of "information that enters consciousness" to potentially access many different outputs has two separate connotations. One is the access to many different states of the same dynamic core, the other is the access by the dynamic core to many other brain processes. The existence of a large number of functionally discriminable states, i.e., states that make a difference to the functioning of the core, is by definition a property of a core that has high complexity. Which particular state will be accessed will in turn depend on which particular state the core was in previously, as well as on the triggering action of extrinsic stimuli. The fact that consciousness can access many different behavioral outputs or, more generally, many different brain processes, fits well with the notion that cooperative interactions among a large number of brain regions, leading to the emergence of a dynamic core, can greatly increase their effectiveness in accessing any other group of neurons in the brain. It is therefore not surprising that biofeedback training, which shows our ability to control, often in less than 1 hour, the activity of any chosen neuron in our brain, requires consciousness (83).

Flexibility and Ability to Respond to and Learn Unexpected Associations (Adaptive Value)

The ability of flexibly associating signals from different modalities and submodalities, or from the present and the past, is a consequence of the dynamic nature of integration, and of the nonlinear mechanisms that mediate it. Once the opportunity for interaction among neuronal groups is maximized, any subtle change in the activity of different brain regions can bring about new, dynamic associations, as illustrated in the model of the visual system. These new associations, which take the form of correlated firing among groups of neurons mediated by reentry, can be consolidated through distributed synaptic changes if they are accompanied by saliency signals mediated by diffuse ascending systems (19). Such an ability to learn unexpected associations among a large variety of apparently unconnected signals has obvious adaptive significance for animals facing a world open ended and full of novelty.

CONSCIOUSNESS AND THE REMEMBERED PRESENT: INTEGRATING CURRENT PERCEPTUAL CATEGORIZATIONS WITH PAST VALUE-CATEGORY MEMORY

The previous theoretical analysis of what integration of information is and where and how it takes place had little to say about the nature of the information that needs to be integrated in order for primary consciousness to emerge. In particular, the theoretical definition of a dynamic core had little to say about which brain regions are expected to be part of it. Even the large-scale models of the visual thalamocortical system by necessity dealt with just one sensory modality and did not include other brain areas that provide the highest degree of generalization, such as the ability to extract concepts or high-order invariants and to categorize present experience based on long-term adaptive values. Yet, all of these components are clearly present within a conscious scene. A full discussion of these points, which is not possible here, can be found in a previous monograph (1). Briefly, as stated in our third proposal, primary consciousness requires systems providing an ongoing perceptual categorization, as well as systems that have learned associations between perceptual categories and values, i.e., a conceptually based value-category memory. A summary of what elements such an extended model would require is outlined in Fig. 10. The neural basis for perceptual categorization of exteroceptive input—voluntary motor, proprioceptive, and polymodal sensory signals—is provided by the thalamus and cortical areas. The models discussed here have illustrated, albeit partially, how the integration of perceptual categories can be achieved within a single sensory modality. Perceptual categorization is generally driven by outer events, is fast, changes rapidly, and handles many signals in parallel. There is no doubt that its contribution to conscious experience is often overwhelming, although it is not exclusive, as will be mentioned shortly.

We will not discuss the neural basis for categorizing interoceptive inputs—autonomic, hypothalamic, and endocrine—except to say that limbic and brain stem circuits dealing with these inputs are evolutionarily earlier, are driven by inner events, and often show slow, phasic activity. It is likely that structures such as the septum, amygdala, and other centers in the limbic system respond to correla-

tions between events occurring in perceptual and interoceptive categorical systems. Finally, many regions of frontal, parietal, temporal, and cingulate cortex are probably involved in mediating the conceptual recategorization of such correlations. The conceptual recategorization implemented by these structures provides a value-dominated conceptual memory that far exceeds perceptual categorization in its generalizing power. Such a discussion highlights the need for large-scale models that extend beyond those attempted so far, to include prefrontal cortical areas and parts of the limbic system.

The final and key ingredient for the emergence of primary consciousness are reentrant circuits that allow present perceptual categorizations to interact with past value-category memories, as indicated by the thick double arrow in Fig. 10. Reentry along multiple corticocortical and thalamocortical loops should ensure that the integration of ongoing neural signals between the sets of structures mediating perceptual categorization and those

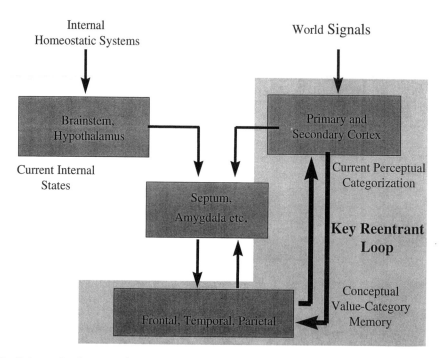

FIG. 10. Schematic diagram of structures and reentrant loops involved in primary consciousness. See text for explanation.

mediating value-category memory occurs within fractions of a second. This leads to the prediction that the neural structures outlined in the dotted box, but not those outside the box, will be part of a dominant dynamic core associated with conscious experience. A simplified translation of the respective role of these two sets of areas in the information theoretical framework discussed above would be that, within the dynamic core, the cortical areas mediating perceptual categorization provide a large number of different states to discriminate, whereas areas that mediate value-category memory provide a large capacity to discriminate among such states based on the highest levels of generalization and abstraction.

According to this picture, primary consciousness is accomplished by continual bootstrapping of current perceptual states into value-loaded memory states, and current perceptual events are always recategorized in terms of past value-category matches. This notion is fully consistent with the information-theoretical concept of complexity matching discussed above. Thus, a multimodal scene in the present acquires meaning in terms of what the organism had learned in the past about similar scenes and their saliency. This is why consciousness has been called the remembered present (1).

Because the discrimination of perceptual states based on value-category memories occurs in parallel across all perceptual modalities, it can alter the relative salience to the animal of particular events in the stimulus domain and help it choose goals and actions. In the absence of such mechanisms of primary consciousness, salience in a kaleidoscope of signals would be determined almost entirely by the dominance of one external event over another in each parallel sensory channel, rather than by the adaptive values of the animal. Previous matchings of those values to categories within a special memory system linked to separate perceptual channels by reentry allow an animal with primary consciousness to direct attention to particular events in a selective fashion that serves its own adaptive needs.

The necessary role that past history plays in the present state of consciousness implies that such a state can never be pure or removed from its biologic basis but is itself a product of selective processes. Even when the requirements for higher order consciousness are met by allowing the generative freedom of language, the conceptualization of the past and the future, and the reflection upon one's own consciousness, this heritage or anchoring point of primary consciousness in biologic processes is fundamental and cannot be dismissed.

ACKNOWLEDGMENT

The work performed at The Neurosciences Institute cited here was supported by the Neurosciences Research Foundation.

REFERENCES

1. Edelman GM. *The remembered present: a biological theory of consciousness.* New York: Basic Books, 1989.
2. Crick FHC. *The astonishing hypothesis: the scientific search for the soul.* New York: Charles Scribner's Sons, 1994.
3. Marcel AJ, Bisiach E. *Consciousness in contemporary science.* Oxford, England: Clarendon Press/Oxford University Press, 1988.
4. Leopold DA, Logothetis NK. Activity changes in early visual cortex reflect monkeys' percepts during binocular rivalry. *Nature* 1996;379:549–553.
5. He S, Cavanagh P, Intriligator J. Attentional resolution and the locus of visual awareness. *Nature* 1996;383:334–337.
6. Delacour J. An introduction to the biology of consciousness. *Neuropsychologia* 1995;33:1061–1074.
7. Kinney HC, Samuels MA. Neuropathology of the persistent vegetative state. A review. *J Neuropathol Exp Neurol* 1994;53:548–558.
8. Milner AD. Cerebral correlates of visual awareness. *Neuropsychologia* 1995;33:1117–1130.
9. Newman J. Thalamic contributions to attention and consciousness. *Consciousness Cognition* 1995;4:172–193.
10. Stoerig P, Cowey A. Visual perception and phenomenal consciousness. *Behav Brain Res* 1995;71:147–156.
11. Baars BJ. *A cognitive theory of consciousness.* Cambridge, MA: Cambridge University Press, 1988.
12. Anonymous. *Experimental and theoretical studies of consciousness.* London, 7–9 July 1992. *Ciba Found Symp* 1993;174:1–316.
13. Picton TW, Stuss DT. Neurobiology of conscious experience. *Curr Opin Neurobiol* 1994;4:256–265.
14. Koch C, Braun J. Towards the neuronal correlate of visual awareness. *Curr Opin Neurobiol* 1996;6:158–164.
15. Crick F, Koch C. Some reflections on visual awareness. *Cold Spring Harb Symp Quant Biol* 1990;55:953–962.

16. Porter RJ. Disorders of consciousness and associated complex behaviors. *Semin Neurol* 1991;11:110–117.

17. Velmans M. The science of consciousness: psychological, neuropsychological and clinical reviews. London, England: Routledge, 1996.

18. Sporns O, Tononi G, Edelman GM. Modeling perceptual grouping and figure-ground segregation by means of active reentrant connections. *Proc Natl Acad Sci USA* 1991;88:129–133.

19. Tononi G, Sporns O, Edelman GM. Reentry and the problem of integrating multiple cortical areas: simulation of dynamic integration in the visual system. *Cerebral Cortex* 1992;2:310–335.

20. Tononi G, Sporns O, Edelman GM. A measure for brain complexity: relating functional segregation and integration in the nervous system. *Proc Natl Acad Sci USA* 1994;91:5033–5037.

21. Tononi G, Sporns O, Edelman GM. A complexity measure for selective matching of signals by the brain. *Proc Natl Acad Sci USA* 1996;93:3422–3427.

22. Lumer ED, Edelman GM, Tononi G. Neural dynamics in a model of the thalamocortical system 2. The role of neural synchrony tested through perturbations of spike timing. *Cerebral Cortex* 1997;7:228–236.

23. Lumer ED, Edelman GM, Tononi G. Neural dynamics in a model of the thalamocortical system. 1. Layers, loops and the emergence of fast synchronous rhythms. *Cerebral Cortex* 1997;7:207–227.

24. Baars BJ. *Inside the theater of consciousness: the workspace of the mind.* New York: Oxford University Press, 1997.

25. Blumenthal AL. *The process of cognition.* Englewood Cliffs, NJ: Prentice-Hall, 1977.

26. Pöppel E. Temporal mechanisms in perception. *Int Rev Neurobiol* 1994;37:185–202.

27. Pöppel E, Artin T. Mindworks: time and conscious experience. Orlando, FL: Harcourt Brace Jovanovich, 1988.

28. Creutzfeldt OD. Neurophysiological mechanisms and consciousness. *Ciba Found Symp* 1979;69:217–233.

29. Moruzzi G, Magoun HW. Brain stem reticular formation and activation of the EEG. *Electroencephalogr Clin Neurophysiol* 1949;1:455–473.

30. Bogen JE. On the neurophysiology of consciousness. I. An overview. *Consciousness Cognition* 1995;4:52–62.

31. Llinás R, Ribary U, Joliot M, Wang XJ. Content and context in temporal thalamocortical binding. In: Buzsaki G, Llinás R, Singer W, eds. *Temporal coding in the brain.* Berlin: Springer-Verlag, 1994.

32. Harth E. The sketchpad model. A theory of consciousness, perception, and imagery. *Consciousness Cognition* 1995;4:346–368.

33. Libet B. The neural time factor in conscious and unconscious events. *Ciba Found Symp* 1993;174:123–146.

34. Baxt N. On the time necessary for a visual impression to come into consciousness. *Psychol Res* 1982;44:1–12.

35. Bressler SL. Large-scale cortical networks and cognition. *Brain Res* 1995;20:288–304.

36. Singer W, Gray CM. Visual feature integration and the temporal correlation hypothesis. *Annu Rev Neurosci* 1995;18:555–586.

37. Joliot M, Ribary U, Llinas R. Human oscillatory brain activity near 40 Hz coexists with cognitive temporal binding. *Proc Natl Acad Sci USA* 1994;91:11748–11751.

38. Gevins A, Smith ME, Le J, et al. High resolution evoked potential imaging of the cortical dynamics of human working memory. *Electroencephalogr Clin Neurophysiol* 1996;98:327–348.

39. Newsome WT. Visual attention: spotlights, highlights and visual awareness. *Curr Biol* 1996;6:357–360.

40. Treue S, Maunsell JH. Attentional modulation of visual motion processing in cortical areas MT and MST. *Nature* 1996;382:539–541.

41. Shenberg DL, Logothetis NK. The role of temporal cortical areas in perceptual organization. *Proc Natl Acad Sci USA* 1997;94:3408–3413.

42. Desimone R, Duncan J. Neural mechanisms of selective visual attention. *Annu Rev Neurosci* 1995;18:193–222.

43. Corbetta M, Miezin FM, Shulman GL, Petersen SE. A PET study of visuospatial attention, *J Neurosci* 1993;13:1202–1226.

44. LeDoux JE, Wilson DH, Gazzaniga MS. A divided mind: observations on the conscious properties of the separated hemispheres. *Ann Neurol* 1977;2:417–421.

45. Hilgard ER. The problem of divided consciousness: a neodissociation interpretation. *Ann NY Acad Sci* 1977;296:48–59.

46. Lynn SJ, Rhue JW. Dissociation: clinical and theoretical perspectives. New York: Guilford Press, 1994.

47. Morel JA, Vierck CJ Jr, Pribram KH, Spinelli DN, John ER, Ruchkin DS. Average evoked responses and learning. *Science* 1967;158:394–395.

48. Haier RJ, Siegel BV Jr, MacLachlan A, Soderling E, Lottenberg S, Buchsbaum MS. Regional glucose metabolic changes after learning a complex visuospatial/motor task: a positron emission tomographic study. *Brain Res* 1992;570:134–143.

49. Crick F. Function of the thalamic reticular complex: the searchlight hypothesis. *Proc Natl Acad Sci USA* 1984;81:4586–4590.

50. von Cramon D. Consciousness and disturbances of consciousness. *J Neurol* 1978;219:1–13.

51. Cauller L. Layer I of primary sensory neocortex: where top-down converges upon bottom-up. *Behav Brain Res* 1995;71:163–170.

52. Damasio AR. Time-locked multiregional retroactivation—a systems-level proposal for the neural substrates of recall and recognition. *Cognition* 1989;33:25–62.

53. Taylor JG. Breakthrough to awareness: a preliminary neural network model of conscious and unconscious perception in word processing. *Biol Cybernetics* 1996;75:59–72.

54. Crick F, Koch C. Are we aware of neural activity in primary visual cortex? *Nature* 1995;375:121–123.

55. Crick F, Koch C. The problem of consciousness. *Sci Am* 1992;267:152–159.

56. Edelman GM, Mountcastle VB. *The mindful brain: cortical organization and the group-selective theory of higher brain function.* Cambridge, MA: MIT Press, 1978.

57. Edelman GM. *Neural Darwinism: the theory of neuronal group selection.* New York: Basic Books, 1987.

58. Edelman GM. Neural Darwinism: selection and reentrant signaling in higher brain function. *Neuron* 1993;10:115–125.

59. Edelman GM, Tononi G. Selection and development: the brain as a complex system. In: Magnusson G, ed. *Lifespan development of individuals.* Cambridge, England: Cambridge University Press, 1996:179–204.

60. Rucci M, Tononi G, Edelman GM. Registration of neural maps through value-dependent learning: modeling the alignment of auditory and visual maps in the barn owl's optic tectum. *J Neurosci* 1997;17:334–352.
61. Friston KJ, Tononi G, Reeke GNJ, Sporns O, Edelman GM. Value-dependent selection in the brain: simulation in a synthetic neural model. *Neuroscience* 1994;59:229–243.
62. Adrian ED, Delafresnaye JF. *Brain mechanisms and consciousness: a symposium.* Boston: Blackwell Scientific, 1954.
63. Schuster HG. *Deterministic chaos: an introduction.* New York: Vch Publishers, 1988.
64. Flohr H. An information processing theory of anaesthesia. *Neuropsychologia* 1995;33:1169–1180.
65. Tononi G. Reentry and the problem of cortical integration. *Int Rev Neurobiol* 1994;37:127–152.
66. Shannon CE, Weaver W. *The mathematical theory of communication.* Urbana, IL: University of Illinois Press, 1963.
67. Papoulis A. Probability, random variables, and stochastic processes. New York: McGraw-Hill, 1991.
68. Zurek WH. Complexity, entropy, and the physics of information. In: *The proceedings of the 1988 Workshop on Complexity, Entropy, and the Physics of Information.* May–June 1989, Santa Fe, NM. Reading, MA: Addison-Wesley, 1990.
69. Llinás RR, Pare D. Of dreaming and wakefulness. *Neuroscience* 1991;44:521–535.
70. Sherrington CSS. *The integrative action of the nervous system.* New Haven, CT: Yale University Press, 1947.
71. Friston KJ, Tononi G, Sporns O, Edelman GM. Characterising the complexity of neuronal interactions. *Hum Brain Mapping* 1995;3:302–314.
72. Bruner JS. *Beyond the information given: studies in the psychology of knowing.* New York: Norton, 1973.
73. Edelman GM. *Bright air, brilliant fire: on the matter of the mind.* New York: Basic Books, 1992.
74. James W. *The principles of psychology.* New York: H Holt, 1890.
75. Penfield W. *The excitable cortex in conscious man.* Springfield, IL: Charles C Thomas, 1958.
76. Penfield W. *The mystery of the mind: a critical study of consciousness and the human brain.* Princeton, NJ: Princeton University Press, 1975.
77. Halgren E, Chauvel P. Experimental phenomena evoked by human brain electrical stimulation. *Adv Neurol* 1993;63:123–140.
78. Engel AK, Konig P, Kreiter AK, Singer W. Interhemispheric synchronization of oscillatory neuronal responses in cat visual cortex. *Science* 1991;252:1177–1179.
79. Engel AK, Konig P, Singer W. Direct physiological evidence for scene segmentation by temporal coding. *Proc Natl Acad Sci USA* 1991;88:9136–9140.
80. Tononi G, McIntosh AR, Russell PD, Edelman GM. Functional clustering: identifying strongly interactive brain regions in neuroimaging data. *Neuroimage* 1998 (in press).
81. Everitt B. *Cluster analysis.* Edward Arnold, New York: Halsted Press, 1993.
82. Pashler H. Dual-task interference in simple tasks: data and theory. *Psychol Bull* 1994;116:220–244.
83. Chase MH. The matriculating brain. *Psychol Today* 1973;7:82–87.

DISCUSSION

Moderated by Benjamin Libet

Christof Koch: I do not understand one point. In your model, oscillations in the 40-Hz range are a clear manifestation of the feedback. Yet, when we looked at data from single-unit recordings in cortical area MT in the behaving monkey (1), we failed to see any such oscillations. This has also been the experience of a number of other laboratories, that in the awake monkey such oscillations appear to be largely absent in high-order cortical areas (2). Do you have any explanations for this?

Giulio Tononi: Well, first of all this is a very precise model of area 17 and area 21 of the cat. We really built it from the bottom up, which means that we have put in all we knew about those areas. We switched it on and that is what we saw. Now in the cat, the situation seems to be reasonably close to what we showed here, not only from the older data of Gray and Singer, but especially from the more recent data of Steriade. In fact, the model makes rather specific predictions on the phase delays, for instance, between columns in cortex and in thalamus, which are consistent with experimental data. So, the only thing I can say is that as far as the cat thalamocortical system is concerned, the model fits very well with the data. About the absence of 40-Hz oscillations in the monkey, that is something I cannot comment upon. I do not have the answer.

Jeffrey A. Gray: If I understood the first part of the talk correctly, the rhythmicity is coming out straightforwardly from the modeled connections: you modeled the connections that are known to exist in anatomy, put in the channels and so on that are known to exist through physiology, and out comes the rhythmicity at around the gamma frequency range. And that seems also to be consistent with other things that we have heard at the meeting. I am struck by the difference between that and what happens in the septo-hippocampal system. Here you have a clear set of pacemaker cells in the septal area; you destroy those and the theta rhytmicity dissappears; and you have clear evidence for yet another input to the medial septal area, which provides the specific frequency, so you have a frequency signal coming into the medial septal area, and the medial septal area then takes that frequency and passes it on to the hipppocampus. You have an elaborate circuitry of inputs to the septohippocampal system which is saying: here is the theta frequency you should go after now. What are your feelings as to why there should be this total difference, assuming this model works correctly for the thalamic-type rhythmicity, why should this be so different?

Giulio Tononi: From what we have done in years of modeling, it is clear that even small changes in the anatomy or in the kind of channels that you have are going to make an enormous difference to the dynamic behaviour of the model. I showed you a few examples here. You cut one loop, you go to a completely different frequency of oscillation, and only in certain layers and not others. That means we cannot simplify the system too much because its real dynamics is what it is. If there is a message, that message has to be, although it has not been followed too much in modeling, that it is the anatomy that counts.

Laurent Descarries: I wish I knew more about your models, and particularly about the connectivity between the units. Does this strictly resemble classical synaptic connectivity, or is there anything to mimic modulation or a modulatory system?

Giulio Tononi: We had simulations of actual synapses as much as one can actually do that, and these were both of the AMPA type and NMDA type. So, if you want to consider the NMDA model neuromodulatory, maybe they are. They seem to have a different profile of the conductances over time. Also, I did not mention that a very important feature of the model was the presence of spontaneous activity. There was a constant background firing, around 4 to 5 Hz. Perhaps because this model involved two areas only it was not able by itself to generate a coherent thalamocortical process. You needed a stimulus in addition to that. But I do not know what will happen if, in addition to those two areas or, you actually had more areas or, since we are in the process of doing that, something like interlaminar nuclei (the matrix projection to the layer I of the cortex). But spontaneous activity is an important ingredient.

Bruno Vanasse: In your model do you only have transmission or also a learning rule to have correlation of activity throughout the model?

Giulio Tononi: In this case, the only thing that was plastic was the NMDA receptor on the short time scale of 200 milliseconds, but there was nothing else.

Discussion References

1. Bair W, Koch C, Newsome W, Britten K. Power spectrum analysis of bursting cells in area MT in the behaving monkey. *J Neurosci* 1994;14:2870–2892.
2. Young MP, Tanaka K, Yamane S. On oscillating neuronal responses in the visual cortex of the monkey. *J Neurophysiol* 1992;67:1464–1474.

Consciousness: At the Frontiers of Neuroscience,
Advances in Neurology, Vol. 77,
edited by H.H. Jasper, L. Descarries,
V.F. Castellucci, and S. Rossignol.
Lippincott–Raven Publishers, Philadelphia © 1998.

18

General Discussion

Moderated by Laurent Descarries, Edward G. Jones, Benjamin Libet, and Alan J. McComas

Laurent Descarries: My question is directed to David Chalmers. Valéry once wrote, "*Un problème bien posé est à moitié résolu.*" I think this is precisely what David Hubel told us a few moments ago. In your lecture, you described and discussed two types of conscious events: type I and type II. Although I am not convinced that type I events are as simple as you said, or as easy to understand from the neuroscientific point of view, they would represent the "easy problem." You analyzed them as the result of several operations, so to speak, each one of them being amenable to scientific elucidation. Then you spoke of type II events globally, under the expression "subjective experience." That left me puzzled. You assumed that this represents the "hard problem," and I believe we all agree that it does, as well illustrated by many of the lectures at this symposium. But you did not give us any analytical or operational description of what you actually meant by "subjective experience." I am sure this would be useful to many of us. What does the philosopher mean by subjectivity? How do you define it, or describe it in terms of components, perhaps amenable to some kind of experimental study. How do you define subjectivity?

David Chalmers: As I said in my talk, one thing you find out in philosophy is that making definitions is a mug's game. You come to definitions at the end of the day once you understand a phenomenon. To define a phenomenon at the beginning is to run the risk of changing and limiting the subject. For example, one might ask for an operational definition of subjective experience, perhaps in terms of verbal report. That may be useful for experimental work, but it is not really a definition: the verbal report is not the same as the subjective experience itself. One might have a subjective experience that one does not report, one might report something falsely, and animals might have all sorts of experiences without any language at all. Other operational "definitions" mis-

match the phenomenon in similar ways. So, what we really have are not definitions, but criteria. Of course, criteria are still useful for many purposes.

Rather than give a definition of consciousness, it is better just to point to the phenomena that one is interested in by giving various characterizations. One can say that consciousness is what it feels like to be a sentient being, for example, the internal aspect of experience. But even this is making the concept sound abstract. We are really just talking about what one sees and feels. That is a vivid and concrete thing. For example, look at Bill Newsome's work on monkeys. He stimulates them with certain patterns of moving dots, and their responses indicate that they detect certain sorts of motion. Newsome says, "I could come to know how all the neural areas are connected, how the monkey responds in different circumstances and different motor modalities, but the central thing I still want to know, once I know all that, is what does the monkey see." That is, he wants to know what the monkey experiences from the first-person point of view.

This is no definition, but I hope it is clarifying. Of course, to someone who has never had consciousness, no definition or description is ever going to tell what it is. One needs to have consciousness to understand consciousness. But I assume that you have consciousness, and that ultimately you do have some idea of what I am talking about.

Laurent Descarries: I hope so! May I thank you for this thoughtful answer to a difficult question. Does anyone wish to comment?

Vincent F. Castellucci: My question is about the bridges. You talked about type I and type II phenomena, and after that, you suggested to study type II phenomena in order to form a new approach to build bridges. But, if I understood you correctly, once the bridges are built, maybe all the type II will become type I phenomena?

David Chalmers: There will certainly be links between the phenomena, which will help us to understand the type II phenomena. I did not define the type I phenomena as those we understand and the type II phenomena as those we do not, though. It would be a mistake to define them this way. Rather, I define them in terms of the division between purely functional properties—reactions and responses—and experiences. Of course, there may be links between these properties: experiences may turn out to have functions, and certain functions may well yield experiences. But the conceptual distinction will still be there. Subjective experience will still be a type II phenomenon. So, rather than trying to turn type II phenomena into type I phenomena, the goal is to integrate both into a theory.

Christof Koch: Let me provide an example of what David means. There exist a small number of so-called complete achromats who are born without any cone receptors. Among other problems, they are unable to perceive any colors. One of them, a Norwegian called Knut Nordby, is actually a visual psychologist. Despite—or possibly because of—his severe visual deficit, he has concentrated on understanding the psychophysics of vision, including color and color perception. He has written articles on the subject (1); he has studied it in the laboratory; he uses a multitude of cues to identify the "color" of the clothes he wears; he has read about the neurophysiology of color and so on. Yet, fundamentally, for him color has no qualia, no sensory quality. Even though he knows about the neuroscientific and psychological basis of color, he does not "see" color.

David Chalmers: In principle, he has perfect access to all the type I phenomena. He knows about the reports, he knows about the responses, he knows about the words that people use for color, and so knows just what waveforms and wavelengths people respond to. But he still says, "I do not know the central fact about colour. That will remain an eternal mystery to me." So, the conceptual distinction remains, even once he has all the theory.

Herbert H. Jasper: If you do not have a way of understanding type II, in some way we know there is a type II. How do you know it?

David Chalmers: I know it the way I know it from knowing my own mind. I do not know it through looking at other people and observing their behavior. I infer and I presume in your case, but in my own case I know. I know my own mind perhaps more directly than I know anything in the world. So, one knows type II phenomena phenomenologically, from the first person. Remove first-person access, and one is just left with the observed phenomena of the external world, the type I phenomena. But then, there goes conscious experience. Denying it would be an extreme point of view.

Laurent Descarries: I would like to throw in another difficult one. It is well known from philosophy and psychology that, when conscious, we are always conscious of something. There is always something in consciousness. This is not to say that we know what it is. We do not even necessarily know that we are being conscious, but there is always something going on. Since William James, I think, this has been called intentionality. It is part of the philosophical definition of consciousness. It is also as if a projector were turned on and we were focusing on some aspects of the world, outer world or inner world, from time to time, and this scene was constantly being modified by ingoing and outgoing experience. Rodolfo Llinás very efficiently and almost poetically described neural events that give rise to synchrony and coincidences and which might help to solve the problem of binding. Or, at least, he offered these as a theory of binding. Now, what about the processes which allow for shifting attention? We have not heard much about attention at this meeting. Is the shifting of attention a totally probabilistic event, depending on the outside world or internal states, or is there a possibility to shift attention that might be, dare I say the word, voluntary? What do we know about the brain or neural processes through which we shift attention? Imaging studies must have been carried out on this process? Also, I wonder if the speakers who have discussed the disorders of consciousness might give us their view on whether some of these may represent a failure of this capacity to shift or switch attention, and then tell us something about what is then going wrong in the brain.

Jeffrey A. Gray: I can comment on the last point. I would have liked to use the word "attention" when I was discussing the problems that schizophrenics have with latent inhibition. It is in fact very common to talk about that phenomenon as a failure of selective attention. That is to say, when faced with two stimuli to learn about, the normal response is to focus on that which is novel rather than that which is familiar, because that is the one most likely to be correlated with whatever new event you have to learn about. That process of selective attention is very important in mobilizing resources so that they are used to the best effect. That is one of the things schizophrenics seem to lack. So, that was in fact an example of a disorder of selective attention. But, if you believe me, the dopamine systems have gone wrong in the way I have described.

Laurent Descarries: A question from Ted Jones?

Edward G. Jones: I am not sure that I have a question, or at least I have a question, but I am not sure how to formulate it. Let me throw it out as a general reflection or a general comment which relates to the field of consciousness and also to what, as I perceive, has gone on in the course of these few days. I think there is a prevailing view among laypersons and among many scientists, particularly if they have not thought about consciousness, that consciousness is some emergent property of whole-brain function, probably a relic of dualism. In the case of many scientists, I think they might localize it a little more to the forebrain, cerebral cortex, thalamus, and basal ganglia, perhaps influenced by brain stem mechanisms. But in general, it has been regarded as some sort of holistic property which emerges from the actions of brain parts working individually. I think one thing is very clear from what has emerged in the course of our last 2 days' discussions: it is that we have moved very close to a situation in which we feel that consciousness is a distributed function of the forebrain. Many of the speakers have touched on this and have skirted around it, but it perhaps reached its most explicit formulation in Christof Koch's presentation, where he has created an anatomical unicorn that related consciousness to the actions of individual cells. So, I guess my question now would be that we have heard about the how, the what, perhaps the when—a lot of work has been devoted to discussing timing. We may even have approached the idea of the why. But I want to know about the where. Where is consciousness localized? Is it localized? Some of the things we have heard about from say Mike Gazzaniga and Roch Lecours suggest that there are distributed layers of consciousness. Are these elements of consciousness which simply have a different content? Are they merged into one single framework or do they, as in the case of the right and left brain, remain largely separate? I am particularly impressed by dealings with schizophrenics, not ones who are overtly hallucinating, but those with whom one attempts to engage in a meaningful discussion. And I would suggest, Dr. Gray, that a difference in selective attention is not exactly what one gets out of these people. I would submit that it is an inability to switch between different frames of reference, and I think that in the course of our day-to-day conscious processing, we are actually switching between different frameworks. This must involve the switching between the activities of the different parts of the brain interacting together. And Christof, I would think that while vision may be all prevailing in your conscious experience, there are other aspects of consciousness as well. Now I know that this is not a question, but these are my thoughts on what has come to me

in listening to people skirt around this whole issue of what is consciousness. I think that we really are coming closer, as a result of what we have heard presented, to some understanding of consciousness as a distributed function of the brain rather than some vaguely defined holistic function.

Paul Cisek: I just have a comment that there is nothing wrong in saying that consciousness may be emergent in some sense. There are many phenomena which are perhaps not best understood when localized to specific brain regions. If, as Sherrington said, consciousness is a process, well, behavior is a process too. And behavior is really understood best when it is taken all into account, not just the things that happen in the brain, but some of the things that happen at the periphery, or even in the environment in which the behavior is involved. Therefore, we should not give ourselves the requirement that we can pin down an exact location where it all comes together, all makes sense. Instead we should look at the different regions of the brain and the world with which it interacts.

Serge Rossignol: I have a question for Dr. Jones. I would like to know if there is a hint in the fact that the intralaminar system you have described projects largely to layer I. Do we know anything on the physiology of layer I which would suggest that it may have a specific role in synchronizing cortical areas? To me, layer I has always been a mystery.

Edward G. Jones: Yes, but we should not regard the system as located only in layer I. Superficial layers are perhaps the best way to express it. It certainly gets down to layer II as well and possibly layer III. In terms of whether this is capable of synchronizing the activity of large groups of neurons, it has not been looked at from the modern perspective, as it were, which has focused upon mainly those neurons which are most immediately the recipients of the primary thalamocortical input in layer IV. So, one can only revert to the older literature which comes from, of course, Herbert Jasper, in which the activities of inputs to superficial layers are certainly capable of extending across large extents of cortex. Here, I am referring in particular to the recruiting response. But to my knowledge, no one in recent times has picked up on the possibility of the recruiting response being an element in the sort of synchronization that you are seeking.

Laurent Bouyer: My question relates more to the previous question than to this one. We have been talking a lot about behavior and subjective impressions and so on. One thing we haven not really discussed is that when you are dreaming, you are conscious of something, but there is no action. How can we put that into the model or should it be put aside? Or is this really part of the question?

Barbara E. Jones: Someone said that consciousness works much more slowly than other processes, and I am finding mine working terribly slowly at this moment! It should also be known that I do not study dreams. I have worked principally on animals and only recently on humans, looking at images of their brains and not questioning them about their dreams. I do know that when one dreams about running, one often also dreams that one cannot run. So, there is a level of perception that in fact the motor neurons are not working and the muscles are not working.

Laurent Bouyer: Still, you are quite aware of this fictive motion and you are conscious of it. So, in terms of mechanisms, what could that tell us?

Barbara E. Jones: Again, I would say that you are aware of two things in dreams. You are often aware that you cannot run, right? When you are dreaming that you can and are running, I would say that this perception is coming from a different level within the central nervous system. You are processing at a different level. But, when you wake up from a dream, you immediately know that you were not running or flying, as the case may be. So, there is ultimately a recognition of where the input was coming from. It was not coming from the skin receptors or the muscle receptors. There is a degree of consciousness that allows you to know where the information was originating.

André Achim: I want to react to previous statements that maybe consciousness is a function of the brain. I am not satisfied with that in the sense that vision is a function of the brain, and because it is a function we know what it accomplishes and we can work towards getting computers to accomplish the same function. Memory may be a function of the brain, I am not sure if it would be a function or a system to support functions, but we could approach the same objective, the same end effect by computers. It seems to me that, even if we produce everything the brain does, it is not clear that we would need a function of consciousness until we know what was the purpose of the function. So, I think it is like hand-waving that we would understand consciousness as if it were a function, and I do not think it is a productive approach. This brings back the original question that was asked: even if a prototypical human being could be completely explained on a scientific basis, the hard problem comes in that I do not feel it would explain myself because of this subjective experience I have. The hard problem is this in that I feel the others can be explained on a scientific basis that we share, but I myself could not be explained because I have this privileged

access to something which we have not identified how it comes on and what it is used for. So, I am not sure it is a function. It is just something that I can testify of, and when I do, other people seem to have a reference in their own head. The hard thing is that we could explain the others but it would not explain myself.

Laurent Descarries: A brief comment. I am sure that very few neuroscientists continue to believe that a machine will ever be produced to do what any one of us, as a subject, may be doing. We model functions to learn about their regularities, about the mechanisms or operations that the brain performs to realize them. It is not the purpose nor in the nature of science to account for individual experience, nor is it essential for it to do so to be useful. The type of understanding that we are trying to reach is a scientific and efficient one; hence, the types of answers that we are producing are different from those of philosophy or even clinical psychology.

David Chalmers: I agree with the questioner that the link between explaining functions and explaining consciousness is unclear, as is the question of the function of consciousness. A more tractable question, though, is to just look at the functions associated with consciousness. When one is conscious, one can perform certain functions that just cannot be performed unconsciously. Jeffrey Gray has stressed that gross functions such as perception and memory can be performed unconsciously. But there are more fine-grained functions that can only be performed at the conscious level. Implicit cognition research contrasts what we can do consciously versus unconsciously. It turns out that you can unconsciously perceive a single word, for example, but unconsciously perceiving and making sense of multiple words is very difficult if not impossible. We are gradually coming to a better understanding of this sort of association between consciousness and function, and it is clearly a promising empirical question.

Alan J. McComas: I am not sure that I could ask a particularly leading question, but perhaps I could make a few comments with particular reference to the session which I had the privilege of chairing. Just before that, though, Ted Jones raised the issue of the location of consciousness, and I think that we are already beginning to see some of the answers to that question. Michael Gazzaniga made it very clear that, on the basis of his unique studies of split brain patients, the left hemisphere is much more important than the right in terms of conscious-generating activities. We know from numerous neurological studies, including most recent ones by Oliver Sacks, that focal lesions of different sensory areas can produce very definite sharply defined defects in consciousness. For example, a lesion of part of the visual cortex may destroy color vision, such that one is no longer color conscious, and so on. On the other hand, the prefrontal areas to me appear to be unnecessarily large for the activities that they appear to perform. It is quite true that they are involved with planning, initiatives, emotional coloring, decisions, and so on. But I would not have thought that you needed billions of neurons to carry this out. After all, a monarch butterfly can manage to fly perfectly well from southwest Ontario to a relatively small forested area in the highlands of Mexico. This is a very considerable cognitive challenge which many of us would find difficult to solve even with a Rand McNally road atlas. Yet the monarch butterfly, with its very small population of neurons, performs this cognitive task beautifully. Of rather more interest for the location of consciousness, perhaps, are the posterior parietal areas. Someone mentioned earlier the extremely interesting clinical phenomenon of spatial hemiagnosia, in which someone with a lesion of the right hemisphere in the posterior parietal area is totally unaware not only of the left side of their body but of extracorporeal space, the surroundings of the body on the left side. If you imagine a similar lesion in the left hemisphere, that would presumably wipe out awareness of the right side. So, someone who had a lesion in both posterior parietal areas would, in theory, not be aware of anything having to do with their body or with extracorporeal space. I toss that out as sort of a mind experiment for you. Now, coming to my own session, I have asked Michael Gazzaniga whether subjects with congenital agenesis of the corpus callosum behave in the same way as adults who had the split-brain operation. He replied that they did not, and that many of the split brain phenomena could not be demonstrated. Thus, visual objects presented to the right hemisphere can be reported, and he thinks that this is mediated through the anterior commissure. Jeffrey Gray has been extremely articulate and has contributed to all of the discussions in a very positive way. I liked the boldness in his comparator hypothesis of consciousness. It was also very precise in that he brought together neuroanatomy, neurochemistry, and behavior, and made predictions. And that was very nice, since this hypothesis should be testable. Where I think some of us might challenge him is the implication that the conscious performance of a task is necessarily superior to the subconscious performance. Two examples which immediately came to my mind were playing the piano or indeed any musical instrument, since one seems to get very much better results if one relaxes and listens to the music as one is playing. The moment you start to pay attention to what your left

or your right hand is doing or what passage is coming up, the performance starts to fragment. Jeffrey also used the example of playing tennis at one point. It is well known since Steven Potter and his description of "gamesmanship" that the one way to win a game of tennis is to compliment your opponent on one of his strokes so that he immediately becomes aware of it and the performance disappears. So maybe he will want to comment there. But I would not like to forget the Zelazos. I think both father and son have made a very interesting contribution. Their approach to consciousness, through the study of infants, is obviously a very valid way of tackling the whole problem. So, let me finish by asking Jeffrey Gray this contrived question: What about the necessarily superior performance of conscious activities?

Jeffrey A. Gray: No, that is certainly not what I intended to say. What I meant was that if one adopts an evolutionary perspective, and I find it difficult to contemplate giving up the most successful theory that there is in biology, then one has to suppose that, on balance, consciousness provides a net survival gain. But there are other relevant examples from genetic conditions. For example, sickle cell anemia: the gene concerned gives rise to sickle cell anemia and does a great deal of harm to people in western civilization, but it is nonetheless of adaptive value, giving people resistance to malaria where malaria was prominent. In the same way, I suppose that on balance, consciousness must provide survival value but that does not mean that it cannot be harmful on particular occasions, and I fully endorse all of the examples that you gave, including the Steven Potter one. I think many of those cases are precisely ones where what you do that is harmful is to try consciously to concentrate on the details of your motor program, and that is hopeless because motor programming is precisely that which is done without conscious awareness of how it is done. Incidentally, a couple of people have suggested that in looking for brain systems that may mediate the neural correlate of consciousness it is an advantage that they have links to the basal ganglia. I would say that this is actually a disadvantage. The basal ganglia would seem precisely to be the best example of a large and complicated brain system which probably contributes very little indeed to what enters conscious awareness.

Benjamin Libet: I would like to add one short point in connection with the idea that the left hemisphere is perhaps the conscious one. I have seen videotapes of several adult patients who had their left hemisphere destroyed or removed, and they certainly looked like they were conscious. When asked a question, of course, they could hardly speak at all, but one of the chaps showed that he was very annoyed that he could not speak and articulate his answer. So, I would not dismiss the right hemisphere as lacking consciousness.

Alexander Chislenko: I have a remark on the connection between neurophysiology and computer science. I personally work on information theory and artificial intelligence, and work with people who are trying to build the machines that would have the perception of the environment, the optimization of behavior, and general problem-solving abilities. On one hand, the computer folks can look at neuroscientists with intense jealousy, because you have such a fabulous material for exploration, the brain, that already does all those things so well. But on the other hand, it is very difficult for you to research things, because the brain is an extremely complex system and the current research tools are just not sufficient for any detailed analysis of its functions. At the same time, the computer folks are building models of control system and problem solving tools that use memory, like error feedback, communications, knowledge representations, and many of the things that have been discussed in this symposium. These have been tested for which of them is useful for which functions. Practical systems have been implemented with them. So, I thought that it would be very useful for the people who build cognitive systems to talk to the people who try to analyze existing cognitive systems. Maybe you could invite information theorists for the next symposium, and see if they can tell you something useful from their point of view.

Giulio Tononi: That is exactly why we believe that the ability to rapidly integrate information is a crucial property of the conscious brain. It is equally crucial for any artificial or nonartificial system that faces the same problems. It is not surprising that those problems are difficult because integrating a lot of information in a short period of time is difficult. The conscious brain is the only object we know that does it well. And I strongly disagree with those who suggest that tasks that one performs consciously and tasks that one can perform unconsciously involve the integration of a similar amount of information.

Benoit Roux: Since there seems to be some conscious action and behavior in our brain while there are also a lot of subconscious actions taking place, I was wondering whether people believe in the power of introspection, or what would be the modern view of psychotherapy in general.

Bruno Rivard: My question is also for anybody who would like to answer it. Do you think that volition is intrinsic to consciousness or that, on the other hand, we are only conscious sensorimotor integrators that simply live with what happens to them?

Christof Koch: One of the thoughts on volition, which strikes me as perfectly sensible from a neurophysiological point of view, is that when "you" believe that you are acting in a free and indeterminate manner, that is with free will, some part of your brain, for instance the basal ganglia, makes a perfectly deterministic decision on the basis of the information available to it. If, however, the neurons in the basal ganglia do not form part of the neuronal correlate of consciousness (the NCC), then this information must be shipped to some other part of the brain that does have access to the NCC. To you, it appears that this idea or decision has suddenly entered your mind from nowhere, spontaneously. This would argue that volition is an illusion, brought about by the nonaccessibility of the decision-making neuronal structures to consciousness.

Jeffrey A. Gray: Can I just answer the point raised about psychotherapy? The evidence is very good that properly structured cognitive behavioral therapy programs can produce at least as good recovery from depression and most conditions involving anxiety as any drug treatment.

David Chalmers: Indeed there is actually some evidence from Jeffrey Schwartz at UCLA, who is working on cognitive-behavioral therapy for obsessive-compulsive disorder. It turns out that after 8 weeks of this therapy, without drugs, the same sort of changes turn up on a PET scan as turn up with drug therapy. He calls this "mind over matter." Of course, that description is controversial.

Herbert H. Jasper: I would like first to thank you all for your splendid and challenging contributions to this symposium on consciousness. You have given us a grand time, and I think everybody has been stimulated and has profited by your attempts to answer some very difficult questions.

I will be reading your manuscripts with great interest and pleasure. Together with the edited discussions, they will certainly make a significant contribution to this important subject, which is receiving much more attention by neuroscientists during recent years. I have recently reviewed a chapter entitled "Sleep and Arousal: Thalamocortical Mechanisms," by David McCormick and Thierry Bal, in the latest edition of *Annual Review of Neuroscience* (2). It gives a remarkable up-to-date account of this subject, including the work of many authors who have contributed to our symposium and conclusions with which I would generally agree.

I started out by trying to prove to you that there was a separate system of neurons in the brain that had quite different anatomical and electrophysiological properties than did the specific sensory and motor systems. The reticular systems of the brain stem and basal forebrain, which affect the activity of the entire brain by the liberation of neurochemical transmitter or modulator substances such as acetylcholine, the monoamines (serotonin, noradrenaline, and dopamine), and the excitatory or inhibitory amino acids, particularly glutamic and aspartic acids and GABA, have been shown to be modified in many ways during states of sleep and waking and arousal in experimental animals, which is no doubt important for establishing different states of consciousness throughout the brain. A number of peptides have also been shown to have significant effects as modulators of the specific sensory and motor systems, serving to fine-tune their state of reactivity throughout many regions of the brain.

Then there is the thalamic reticular system from which the recruiting response can be initiated by precise local electrical stimulation of the intralaminar and nonspecific nuclei of the thalamus, which is capable of controlling the electrical activity of the entire brain in a manner suggestive of a relationship to states of consciousness. Interactions between the recruiting system and specific sensory and motor systems have also been demonstrated.

Dr. E.G. Jones has elaborated on this system in his excellent presentation to this meeting, adding to his previous descriptions of the anatomy of the thalamic recruiting system. Using calbindin immunocytochemistry, he has shown that there are additional systems of neurons, adjacent to the specific thalamic sensory nuclei, which project to the upper layers of the cortex in a rather diffuse manner. We had already included some of these paranuclear thalamic regions in our initial outline of the thalamic reticular system which was not limited to the intralaminar nuclei.

May I also remind you that cortical responses to local electrical stimulation of the thalamic recruiting system are much slower, between 20 and 25 milliseconds, as compared to 1 or 2 milliseconds for cortical responses to stimulation of the specific projection systems. It seems to me that the diffusely bilaterally projecting thalamic recruiting system, originally described by Morrison and Dempsey, must have an integrative function of possible importance in the control of states of consciousness.

It is now well known that lesions within the thalamic reticular system or in the brain stem and rostral basal nuclei of the diencephalon have profound effects upon states of consciousness in human subjects as well as in experimental animals. Close relationships to states of consciousness have also been demonstrated in the reproduction of the transient loss of consciousness of petit mal (absence) epileptic seizures by stimulation of the pontine mesial brain stem and mesial thalamic reticular system with bilat-

eral spike-and-wave responses in cerebral cortices of experimental animals. Lesions within the specific sensory and motor systems affect mainly the content of consciousness and the ability to express our states of consciousness in speech or voluntary behavior.

The remarkable work of Steriade and his associates must also be mentioned here. In their intra- and extracellular microelectrode studies of the thalamus, in which they were able to reproduce the spike and wave of petit mal epilepsy, they made many other important observations, particularly with regard to the reticular nucleus and its relationships with the cortex and its inhibitory control of the thalamus.

I have been intrigued for years by the presence of rhythmic activity at 35 to 45 Hz in various parts of the brain and the proposal that synchronization of these rhythms contributes to the temporal binding of brain activity in attention and cognitive processes as first suggested by Galambos. I was particularly impressed with the work of Llinás and Ribary, who have been able to measure gamma band activity by magnetoencephalography in a 37-channel sensory array during wakefulness and sleep, and gamma band resetting and synchronization or resetting during different states of sleep and wakefulness. They concluded that "the time-coherent activity of the specific and nonspecific oscillatory inputs ... would enhance de facto 40 Hz cortical coherence by their multimodal character and in this way could provide one mechanism for global binding. The 'specific' system would thus provide the content that relates to the external world and the nonspecific system would give rise to the temporal conjunction, or the context, on the basis of a more interoceptive activity concerned with alertness that would together generate a single cognitive experience." I found this to be a most exciting proposal based upon remarkable experimental data.

It seems to me that brain mechanisms of attention have received rather inadequate consideration during our symposium. Attention has been considered as a process which focuses your consciousness on certain aspects of awareness. In this process, there must be a mechanism which blocks irrelevant or distracting stimuli. That this is a very effective block was demonstrated historically by the tragic death of Pierre Curie, when he was working with his wife Marie on radioactivity. I am sure he was in the middle of some intense thinking about how the radioactivity developed, when he walked across the street from his laboratory without noticing the truck that killed him coming down the street.

I agree with David Hubel that perhaps we are a little overwhelmed by the idea of consciousness being very mysterious. It is something we accept and get along with quite well in this world in spite of a lack of complete understanding. We have no major difficulties to communicate with each other in spite of the lack of direct contact with the content of each others' conscious minds. I am pleased to know that we still have some personal privacy without direct communication between each others' consciousness, though I begin to wonder sometimes when I see the remarkable images of the local activity of my brain during specific cognitive tasks.

If we understand what is being said to us, it is because it brings to our own mind experiences similar to those in our own, private consciousness. This is what makes science as a whole, physical sciences, possible. That is the world the physicist lives in, as well as the philosopher. There would be no physics if there was no communication between the minds of two physicists in discussing physical laws of this world. And we seem to get along quite well, even in quite different fields of physics, even when the hypotheses are almost contradictory as in quantum physics, for example. But that does not bother us. We adapt to these different ways of thinking about the world, and make it work with communication between people.

So, I do not think that there are any great unsolvable mysteries in this process. This is a result of brain function which we have accepted for hundreds of years and used profitably to develop many branches of science and recently including neuroscience. I think we will continue to profit by these interactions, and the information that we process in our brains will continue to be largely unconscious as it always has been. But it serves a very useful purpose. I am afraid I would not live long without the information supplied by the unconscious processes in my brain. However, we are more interested, of course, in what we are conscious of. That is our life, our conscious life, and we would like to know more about it and how it is produced, as so well expressed in the poetic preface written by one of us (under his *nom de plume*).

I hope that we do not forget that there is an anatomically and electrophysiologically separate neuronal system in the brain, which operates in conjunction with the specific fast sensory and motor systems and which is involved in regulating the activity of both hemispheres and its changes during sleep and waking, and which I am sure is involved in brain mechanisms of consciousness.

Dr. Barbara Jones has shown, in her studies of sleep and waking, that there are several neurochemical substances involved which are known to be of subcortical origin—acetylcholine, the monoamines, and the excitatory and inhibitory amino acids—all of which are distributed diffusely over both hemispheres and are capable of setting the reactive states of the entire cerebral cortex. There are of course many other neurochemically active substances, such as the peptides, which also have important functions related to states of consciousness and learning processes.

I think we have been given a good introduction to the progress that has been made in a number of ways. We can now approach this age-old problem with new techniques: neuroanatomical, neurochemical, even molecular biological, including the noninvasive measures of brain imaging such as positron emission tomography and magnetic resonance spectroscopy.

Finally, I would like to thank you all again for your many important contributions to the old problem of brain mechanisms of consciousness and their relationship to the control of behavior and conscious mental life. I am sure that our publication will be a lasting contribution to this forefront of neuroscience, which has gained so much interest during recent years.

I would like also to express much appreciation to our coorganizers and editors with whom I have had the pleasure of working over many years, Drs. Descarries and Castellucci, and especially Dr. Rossignol, Director of our Centre de Recherche en Sciences Neurologiques at the Université de Montréal, who has also organized the most delightful gala dinner and 91st birthday party, in collaboration with so many friends and colleagues and with his musical companion, Mme. Céline Dussault, who sang a beautiful soprano solo with piano accompaniment by Dr. Serge Rossignol.

I would like also to pay tribute to Mrs. Mary Lou Jasper, my good companion, who joins me in expressing our heartfelt thanks and appreciation to you all.

Discussion References

1. Hess RF, Nordby K. Spatial and temporal limits of vision in the achromat. *J Physiol* 1986;371:365–385.
2. McCormick DA, Bal T. Sleep and arousal: thalamocortical mechanisms. *Annu Rev Neurosci* 1997;20: 186–215.

Subject Index

Subject Index